Librarians of Congress

Librarians of Congress
1802–1974

LIBRARY OF CONGRESS   WASHINGTON   1977

Library of Congress Cataloging in Publication Data

Main entry under title:

Librarians of Congress, 1802–1974.

A collection of articles which first appeared in the
Quarterly journal of the Library of Congress.
Includes index.
1. Librarians—United States—Biography—Addresses,
essays, lectures. 2. United States. Library of Congress
—Biography—Addresses, essays, lectures. I. United
States. Library of Congress. II. United States. Li-
brary of Congress. Quarterly journal.
Z720.A4L52   020'.92'2[B]   77–608073
ISBN 0–8444–0238–9

For sale by the Superintendent of Documents, U.S. Government Printing Office
Washington, D.C. 20402

Stock No. 030–001–00080–0

Contents

Foreword

At its first session, the Sixth Congress of the United States passed "And Act to make further provision for the removal and accommodation of the Government of the United States . . . Approved, April 24, 1800." In effect, the fifth section of this act created the Library of Congress by providing for the acquisition of books for congressional use, a suitable place in the Capitol in which to house them, a joint committee to make rules for their selection, acquisition, and circulation, and an appropriation of $5,000 for this purpose.

In 1896, the Joint Committee on the Library held hearings on "the condition of the Library of Congress" in preparation for the forthcoming move into the new building. Among those who appeared before the committee was Herbert Putnam, librarian of the Boston Public Library at the time.

In reply to Representative Lemuel Ely Quigg's question, "What are the qualities that the chief administrative officer of this new Congressional Library ought to possess?" Mr. Putnam replied:

"This should be a library, the foremost library in the United States—a national library—that is to say, the largest library in the United States and a library which stands foremost as a model and example of assisting forward the work of scholarship in the United States. . . .

I should suppose that the man who is to have the final administration of that library must have above all things else administrative ability—the same kind of a man who is to manage the property or interest of any large corporation, is to handle large funds, is to manage a large force of employees; such a one should have administrative capacity. It is as much required in a library as anywhere else. When you have a department that has so many people there is need of an administrative officer who shall have superior executive ability and efficiency. I do not believe that your chief administrative officer, attending properly to the business problems of the library, need be a profound bibliographer or need to know the most of all the persons in the library, as to what the library contains. I should regard him as bearing a relation to the library something similar to that corresponding to, or borne by, the president of a university to the several departments of that university.

I take it that President Eliot would say that he does not know as much about Greek as the chief of that department, or of Latin, as the chief of that department, or about chemistry, as the chief of that department. I should doubt if President Low would say that he stood as a specialist with reference to any department of work undertaken by the University of Columbia. I presume that the modern college president considers that his chief function is to secure the best men for each department, and to administer on a large scale this business, and see that the business is conducted properly, and to secure great efficiency, and, more especially at the beginning, to consider and determine the scope of the work to be undertaken, to form plans on a large scale which might serve as recommendations to the committee—board of trustees—with reference to the larger service to be rendered. I don't say a knowledge of specialties, in addition to these capacities, would be inconsistent with them, but it seems to me that those capacities are undoubtedly necessary, and that the chief executive must have them preeminently."

A few days later, back in Copley Square, Putnam wrote to the chairman of the Joint Committee, Senator George Peabody Wetmore, outlining some of his views on the Library and supplementing his statement on the Librarian's qualifications. He wrote in part:

"If I recall rightly, my description of the capacities requisite to the chief executive of the Library was ill balanced. I laid stress upon the requisite that he should be predominantly the man of affairs of the Library rather than the man of books. In doing so I probably slighted the other requisite, equally indispensable, that he should know enough of the literary side of the Library, of bibliography, etc., to appreciate intelligently the needs of the several departments of specialized work."

To mark the 175th anniversary of the Library, the *Quarterly Journal of the Library of Congress* in April 1975 inaugurated a series of biographical articles on the eleven men who headed the institution from 1802 to 1974: John James Beckley, Patrick Magruder, George Watterston, John Silva Meehan, John G. Stephenson, Ainsworth Rand Spofford, John Russell Young, Herbert Putnam, Archibald MacLeish, Luther Harris Evans, and Lawrence Quincy Mumford. Collected in this volume, these articles form part of the historical record of the nation's library.

Preface

The Library of Congress has profited from the striking variety of backgrounds, interests, and talents of our past Librarians. Among them have been politicians, businessmen, newspapermen, authors, poets, lawyers, and even one professional librarian. This variety has been appropriate in a national library whose intimate relations to the Congress have given us a public and democratic direction unique among the national libraries of the world.

In the 177 years since our founding, there have been only twelve Librarians. Our Library, with so few breaks in leadership, has enjoyed a continuity of atmosphere and of policy that is rare in national institutions. Herbert Putnam served the Library for forty years, John Silva Meehan and Ainsworth Rand Spofford each served for more than thirty years, and most recently Lawrence Quincy Mumford served for more than twenty years. In our expanding, rapidly changing nation, these extensive terms have also challenged the ability of Librarians to meet changing needs.

The careers of these Librarians have spanned our growth from a nation of recently liberated seaboard colonies to a continent-nation of fifty states, from an age when knowledge was diffused almost exclusively by manuscript and the printed book, through the age of the democratized newspaper, of the power press, into the age of photography and cinematography, of recorded sound, of microfilm and microfiche, of radio and television and the computer. The responsibilities of the Library to Congress, our primary client, have grown beyond the imaginings even of Thomas Jefferson. Through a changing law of copyright our responsibilities to libraries, publishers, authors, composers, and performers have widened and multiplied. The growth of our nation's schools and universities and libraries has enlarged and transformed our opportunities to enrich the whole nation's resources of knowledge.

The lives of the Librarians, then, not only reveal to us the role that leadership can play in developing a great institution. They also show us some of the subtle needs, the nuances of vision, the traits of character and of personality required to make this institution truly collaborative. At a time when we give fresh attention to the Library's future, the careers of our Librarians will help us discover our traditions. We can discover, too, that our greatest tradition has been a tradition of change, of constant search for new ways to serve a changing, increasingly democratic nation.

DANIEL J. BOORSTIN
The Librarian of Congress

Librarians of Congress

John Beckley, 1802–1807

Patrick Magruder, 1807–1815

George Watterston, 1815–1829

John Silva Meehan, 1829–1861

John C. Stephenson, 1861–1864

Ainsworth Rand Spofford, 1864–1897

John Russell Young, 1897–1899

Herbert Putnam, 1899–1939

Archibald MacLeish, 1939–1944

Luther Harris Evans, 1945–1953

Lawrence Quincy Mumford, 1954–1974

In 1805 the House moved back into its old quarters temporarily while the permanent structure that would form the south wing of the Capitol was being built. The Library, in turn, had to move to an adjacent committee room, which proved to be woefully inadequate. Benjamin Latrobe's "Plan of the Principal Story of the Capitol, 1806" shows more spacious quarters for the Library on the west side of the north wing, which, according to the surveyor of public buildings, was in such a state of decay as to be dangerous. Prints and Photographs Division.

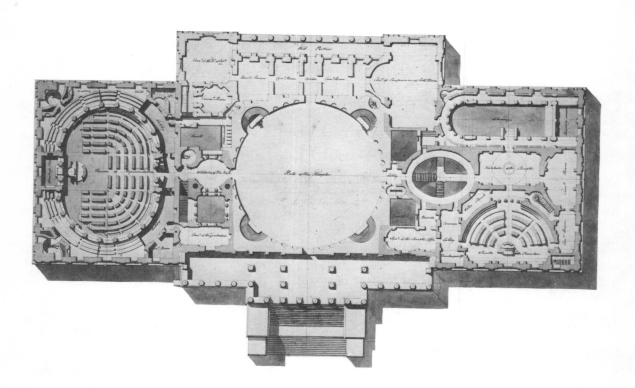

The First Librarian of Congress

John Beckley

by Edmund Berkeley and Dorothy Smith Berkeley

THE *National Intelligencer* of Washington for February 5, 1802, announced: "The President of the United States has appointed *John Beckley Librarian* of the two Houses of Congress." The name was a very familiar one at the time, requiring no identification. Since this is not the case today, some account of his career before 1802 may help to explain Jefferson's choice for the first Librarian. Beckley's librarianship came late in his life, and he is better known by historians as a political figure. His appointment as Librarian was, however, by no means a political appointment. He was undoubtedly the best qualified applicant for the position. Jefferson had a very real interest in and concern for the Library, and he was thoroughly familiar with Beckley's qualifications.

John James Beckley was born in England, August 4, 1757. Little is known of his family or of his early education. Accounts indicating he had attended Eton are not authenticated and are almost certainly erroneous. It is well established that he was sent to Virginia by the mercantile firm of John Norton & Son in response to a request for a scribe. The request had come from the elderly John Clayton, clerk of court for Gloucester County and a botanist well known in Eu-

ropean scientific circles. Beckley arrived in Virginia just before his 12th birthday and lived in Clayton's home as a member of his family for the next four years. Clayton was the grandson of one of the founding members of the Royal Society of London. His father had been attorney general of Virginia when the son became clerk of court in 1720. He had inherited his father's library and had added to it extensively. He was extremely well qualified to guide the continuing education of young Beckley and did so with enthusiasm.

John Clayton died in late December of 1773. Beckley, who had witnessed his will, proved it on January 6, 1774. Faced with a decision concerning his future, Beckley elected to remain in Virginia rather than return to London. In his close association with Clayton he had become acquainted with many of the more influential members of the colony, and intelligent, well-trained clerks were in short supply. He had no doubt that he could support himself. Soon after Clayton's death he was employed by Thomas Adams, clerk of Henrico County. In February 1775 he

Edmund Berkeley and Dorothy Smith Berkeley are the authors of *John Beckley: Zealous Partisan in a Nation Divided* (Philadelphia: The American Philosophical Society, 1973).

became clerk to the Henrico committee of safety. During this pre-Revolutionary period a remarkable number of committees were appointed in Virginia, and Beckley served as clerk to a surprising number of them. An ordinance establishing a committee of safety for the entire colony at Williamsburg was adopted August 24, 1775. Soon thereafter Beckley was assisting the clerk of that committee. On February 7, 1776, he was officially appointed assistant clerk, working with John Tazewell for Edmund Pendleton, president of the committee.

The functions of the committee of safety came to an end with the establishment of state government and the election of Patrick Henry as governor. Beckley was employed to complete the records and journals and to prepare a detailed ledger of the committee's accounts. The establishment of state government meant more committees, and Beckley was soon appointed clerk to the committee of trade and the committee of courts of justice and assistant clerk to the council of state. By November 1777 he had replaced John Pendleton as clerk of the Virginia senate. He was also finding time to study law, which he may well have begun in Clayton's library. It is very probable that he studied at Williamsburg with Edmund Randolph, attorney general of the new state, with whom he was closely associated throughout his life thereafter. Randolph was elected to the Continental Congress and resigned his post as clerk of the Virginia House of Delegates in June 1779. Beckley not only replaced him in this capacity, but also took over his law practice during his absence.

The Phi Beta Kappa Society had its beginning at the College of William and Mary on December 5, 1776, soon after Beckley came to Williamsburg. Since he was not a student at the college, Beckley was not eligible for membership. But on December 10, 1778, the constitution of the society was broadened to permit the election of nonstudents, and a few months later, on April 10, 1779, Beckley was elected. Within a month, as might have been predicted, he was chosen clerk, or secretary. He became a very active member in spite of his many other commitments. The group, at the time, was a remarkable one, including William Short, later minister to Spain, John Page, later governor of Virginia, and John Brown, later U.S. Senator from Kentucky. Brown and Page

remained close friends throughout Beckley's life. Beckley, Brown, and Short formed a committee of three to design a seal for the society. Beckley was also one of a committee of three who prepared resolutions to govern the expansion of the society to other areas, thus giving it its present national character. In his capacity as secretary, he drew up the charters for new chapters at both Harvard and Yale Universities. A few months after his election to Phi Beta Kappa, Beckley was elected to the Williamsburg Lodge of Freemasons. Among the members of the lodge were Edmund Randolph, James Madison, James Monroe, and Henry Tazewell. At about the same time, Beckley became clerk to the high court of chancery and also to the court of appeals.

The year 1779 was an eventful one for Beckley in several other respects. Thomas Jefferson was elected governor in June to succeed Patrick Henry. Beckley may have known him earlier, but certainly knew him well thereafter. In December the general assembly decided to move its meeting place from Williamsburg to Richmond for its next meeting in the spring of 1780. Also in that year his sister, Mary Anne, came to Virginia with Mr. and Mrs. John Baylor, who had recently married in London. Mary Anne later made her home with John in Richmond until she married one of his clerks, Nathaniel Gregory.

The move to Richmond began a new period in Beckley's life in many ways. He rented a house and acquired several slaves. He began to practice law on his own, and he involved himself in city affairs. He had not long been settled at Richmond when the arrival of Gen. Benedict Arnold with a fleet in Chesapeake Bay made it necessary for the general assembly to remove itself and its records briefly from the city. Soon after their return a threat developed from General Cornwallis, and the assembly removed first to Charlottesville and then to Staunton. During these dangerous times Beckley was impressed by the coolness and leadership shown by Governor Jefferson. He later gave strong testimony to this when political opponents accused Jefferson of cowardice.

Richmond was incorporated as a city in May 1782. In June of that year Beckley purchased a lot and thus became eligible to participate in the first city elections in July. Eight hundred freeholders of the city elected 12 councilmen for a term of three years, one of whom was the 25-

year-old Beckley. The councilmen then elected Dr. William Foushee as their mayor and Beckley as one of four aldermen. Another of the aldermen was Jacquelin Ambler, father-in-law of John Marshall. (Marshall later served with Beckley as a councilman. He was also a Mason and a member of Phi Beta Kappa, but in spite of all of these associations Beckley and Marshall were never on very cordial terms.) Beckley was soon very much involved in a multitude of problems of a new city government. He performed so effectively that he was elected as the second mayor of the city when he was but 26. He was continuously active in the city government during the nine years he lived in Richmond and three times served as mayor.

While the general assembly was in Staunton, Beckley was able to visit Warm Springs and adjacent areas of western Virginia after the assembly adjourned. He was tremendously impressed by the potential of this little-settled country and began to acquire land grants in the region. He became associated in land speculation with George Clendinen, a member of the assembly. Clendinen had established himself on the present site of Charleston, W. Va., and named the city for his father. Beckley's interest in land and in western Virginia and Kentucky increased, and he was continuously involved with both for the rest of his life though he never lived in that area.

Although Beckley's early life was spent in Virginia, he had his eye on the national scene on which so many of his Virginia friends were playing an active part. His first attempt to become personally involved seems to have been in April 1787, when he accompanied Gov. Edmund Randolph and James Madison to Philadelphia for the revision of the Articles of Confederation. If he hoped to become clerk of that convention, he was disappointed. He did make some useful acquaintances, and the experience whetted his appetite for national service. A year later he was very active in the state convention for ratification of the federal Constitution. When the elected delegates convened at Richmond in June, they chose Edmund Pendleton president and Beckley secretary. There followed the famous debates between those favoring ratification, led by James Madison, Edmund Randolph, and John Marshall, and the opponents led by George Mason, Patrick Henry, and William Grayson. It was Beckley who prepared the 15 copies of the ratification that were to be delivered to Congress and the various states.

Beckley's urge to participate in the federal government increased and by 1789 had become irresistible. He decided to make a determined effort to be elected first Clerk of the U.S. House of Representatives. With this in mind he obtained letters of recommendation from friends. Edmund Randolph wrote to Caleb Strong, of Massachusetts, and perhaps to others, in glowing terms of Beckley's ability as a clerk. James Madison also promised support. As an official cover for his trip to New York, and perhaps to help with expenses, he agreed to deliver the official report of Virginia's vote for the presidency. He went nearly a month before the vote for the clerkship would be held, hoping to campaign a bit for the office. He was joined in New York by various old friends, including Madison, John Brown, John Page, and Alexander White. It was well that he had support, for he had strong competition. The first vote for the clerkship resulted in a tie, but Beckley won on the second ballot.

Beckley had led an eventful life since coming to Virginia, but now an even more exciting period began. He was at first involved in all of the pomp and ceremony of Washington's inauguration and the absurd arguments over matters of titles and protocol. Following Washington's address to the Congress and his withdrawal from the Senate chamber, it was Beckley who read the manuscript of the address to the members with that clarity of enunciation for which he was to become famous. And then there was the activity of the Congress as soon as the initial formalities had been completed. Matters of critical importance had to be decided, and feelings were very strong about many of them. The most controversial of these were the financial questions involved in funding the new national government and settling the debts incurred during the Revolution, especially veterans' warrants. Unfortunately, the divergent views concerning the best solutions to these problems tended to be somewhat regional in character. What is more, the potential for quick profits attracted speculators in large numbers, and many members of the Congress were involved in speculation. Not surprisingly, feelings became very heated, and the

Congress soon became distinctly polarized on these issues. The story is much too long to be dealt with here, and it has been analyzed thoroughly by many writers. It did, however, directly involve Beckley and profoundly influenced the remainder of his life, so it must be discussed in general terms at least.

Alexander Hamilton, as secretary of the treasury, had the direct responsibility for proposing financial measures. Opposition to his proposals was led initially by James Madison. Beckley, having had considerable experience with accounts and financial matters, having served in the Virginia militia as well as the state government, and being closely acquainted with Madison, felt concerned. As Clerk of the House, perhaps he should have maintained a rigid neutrality regarding measures before the Congress, but he never did. His personal involvement was such that Senator Maclay, of Pennsylvania, noting in his diary that he wished to be associated with the southern group in Congress, indicated that the southern leaders were Madison and Beckley. Jefferson was not present during the early skirmishing. He had been in France and expected to return there when he came home in the fall of 1789, but Washington persuaded him to accept the post of secretary of state. Another Beckley friend was a member of the cabinet. Edmund Randolph had become attorney general.

Soon after Jefferson's arrival in New York he permitted Hamilton to persuade him to influence the Virginia group to soften its opposition to his proposed measures and break a deadlock on the funding and assumption bills. A compromise was reached—some said a "deal" was made—whereby Alexander White and Richard Bland Lee, of Virginia, would support Hamilton's measures in return for a promise to locate the permanent seat of government on the Potomac. This was one of the few times that Hamilton and Jefferson were able to reach agreement, and Jefferson had reason to regret it.

For many reasons, social and otherwise, Hamilton was rather closely associated with many of the individuals who were openly speculating in the government debts and who stood to make large sums if they were able to anticipate what measures Hamilton would propose and what would be passed by Congress. There can be no

doubt that some of these men were able to obtain information before it reached the general public. Their source, in many instances, was apparently William Duer, appointed assistant secretary by Hamilton. Related to Mrs. Hamilton, Duer had been a member of the old Board of Treasury. He was closely associated with many of the leading financial entrepreneurs, including Robert Morris, William Constable, Andrew Craigie, and Theodosius Fowler. The grave suspicions that many of Hamilton's political opponents had with regard to his office were greatly strengthened later by Duer's disgrace and imprisonment for debt. A distrust of the Treasury Department became widely held, and many, including Beckley, distrusted Hamilton personally. From such early beginnings there gradually evolved the Federalist and Republican Parties, and animosity between them became extremely bitter.

Beckley's intense absorption in political affairs was interrupted for a time when he fell in love. The young lady was Maria Prince, daughter of a retired New York ship captain formerly engaged in trade with Cayenne. After a brief courtship John and Maria were married just before Congress moved from New York to Philadelphia. They lived in Philadelphia from 1791 until 1801. Although Beckley had become acquainted with a number of New York political figures, he was not there long enough to take part in either city or state politics. At Philadelphia he played an active role in both and in national politics as well.

Soon after the move, Beckley quite unintentionally made a major contribution to the party split which was evolving. He had obtained from England the first part of Thomas Paine's *Rights of Man* and thought that it would, if republished, prove a good antidote to John Adams' *Discourses on Davila*. The latter series of essays seemed to advocate monarchy, nobility, and aristocracy and had produced a storm of protest. Beckley persuaded Jonathan Bayard Smith to republish the *Rights* but first lent it to Madison, who in turn lent it to Jefferson. At Beckley's request Jefferson sent it directly to Smith with an accompanying note expressing his pleasure that it would be reprinted. Smith included Jefferson's comments on the flyleaf of the reprint, and it sold rapidly, as Smith had correctly surmised it might. John

Adams and other Federalists were outraged by Jefferson's comments and a great commotion ensued. Jefferson had not intended to make a public attack on his friend John Adams, but all attempts to explain the incident proved futile.

Beckley was particularly delighted by an honor which came to him in this year (1791). He was elected to membership in the American Philosophical Society. He had long known of the society, since John Clayton had been one of the early members. Political prominence was no assurance of election. Although Jefferson, Randolph, and Hamilton were already members, John Adams was not elected until two years later. Meetings were held twice each month, at which papers were given. Since the society's building was close to the state house, Beckley was probably able to enjoy their fine library at other times. He presented to the society for its collections two specimens of printing. Calligraphy was one of his hobbies.

A new friendship developed for Beckley in 1791 when he joined Madison and Henry Lee in persuading Philip Freneau to come to Philadelphia and start publishing the *National Gazette.* The dominant Philadelphia paper at the time was John Fenno's *Gazette of the United States,* and Fenno's views were antagonistic to everything Beckley and his friends espoused. Freneau's paper gave them a much needed public voice for their views, and they supported it not only with their writing but also by obtaining subscriptions in Philadelphia and elsewhere. Beckley maintained a very close association with Freneau.

Soon after coming to Philadelphia Beckley became the close personal friend of Gen. William Irvine, of Carlisle. How the friendship began is not known but the two families became very intimate and exchanged long visits over a period of years, and the two men carried on an extensive correspondence when Irvine was not in Philadelphia. This was an important friendship for Beckley politically, since Irvine was a very active figure in Pennsylvania politics. He soon had Beckley equally involved. Another close personal friendship developed with Dr. Benjamin Rush. Their political views were congenial, and Rush was moderately active in political matters.

More old friends from Virginia arrived in Philadelphia, most importantly Senators James Monroe and Henry Tazewell. The Williamsburg Lodge of Freemasons was now represented at Philadelphia by at least five of its members: Beckley, Madison, Monroe, Randolph, and Tazewell. Monroe and Beckley had long been friends and became even closer. Tazewell made his home with the Beckleys while Congress was in session and died there in 1799. With so many close friends in the Congress and the Cabinet, Beckley would have found it extremely difficult to adopt a nonpartisan position had he been inclined to do so. He had no such inclination. He was ardently Republican in his views and became very active in promoting Republican causes at all levels. Since he maintained a home in Philadelphia while members of Congress were in the city only when Congress was in session, it was natural for him to keep in touch with many of them by correspondence in their absence. He thus became a sort of clearinghouse for information of concern to Republicans from all parts of the country and assumed the unofficial role of party chairman.

Beckley was also a voluminous writer. He became a frequent contributor to Freneau's *Gazette* under a variety of pseudonyms, including "Mercator," "The Calm Observer," and "Timon." As "Mercator" he challenged the Treasury Department's claim that it had reduced the public debt by almost two million dollars. He used his ability with figures and accounts to demonstrate that the debt had actually increased by almost the same amount. His attacks drew replies from Hamilton, writing as "Civis." Monroe and Beckley jointly published a pamphlet (long incorrectly attributed to John Taylor of Caroline) entitled *An Examination of the Late Proceedings in Congress Respecting the Official Conduct of the Secretary of the Treasury.* When Monroe replaced Gouverneur Morris as minister to France, Beckley wrote to him at length concerning political affairs at home. Monroe reciprocated with long letters to Beckley, copies of which went also to Jefferson, Burr, George Logan, and Robert R. Livingston. He suggested that Beckley and Logan publish these letters anonymously as an antidote to European news screened by the British before reaching the United States. These were published and had political repercussions.

Before Monroe's departure for France he became involved in an investigation of alleged speculation by Alexander Hamilton. The apparent evidence had been brought to the attention of Congressman F. A. C. Muhlenberg, who asked the assistance of Monroe and Congressman Abraham Venable. The three men conducted a quiet investigation and, finding the charges serious, sought an explanation from Hamilton. The evidence was all admitted to be true by Hamilton, but he explained the whole series of remarkable events by admitting he was being blackmailed by one James Reynolds with whose wife he had had an affair. The three investigators were reasonably convinced and, having had one of Beckley's more confidential clerks prepare copies of all papers involved, as requested by Hamilton, they asked Beckley to keep the findings secret. The details of the probe into the "Reynolds Affair" are confusing and lengthy and cannot be dealt with here. But more will be said about Beckley's connection with it later.

Beckley's antipathy for Federalists and Federalist causes was greatly intensified by their treatment of Edmund Randolph. Randolph, who had served briefly as an aide-de-camp to Washington during the Revolution and had played a very active part in the early planning of the new government, came to Washington's cabinet at considerable financial sacrifice. Intensely loyal to Washington, he was almost the only prominent Virginian in the government who maintained a genuine neutrality between Republican and Federalist commitment and thereby endeared himself to neither group. Republicans regarded him as something of a "trimmer," although none questions his integrity. The Federalists found him difficult to manipulate and did not like his influence on Washington. When he advised Washington against signing the Jay Treaty without further concessions by the British, the Federalists and their British friends determined to destroy his influence with Washington. They found a means of doing so when the British conveniently furnished Timothy Pickering with papers seeming to indicate that Randolph had accepted money from the French, or had expressed a willingness to do so. Pickering and Oliver Wolcott managed to convince the President of Randolph's guilt. Incredible as it may seem, Washington signed the treaty without even discussing with Randolph the charges against him and then demanded an explanation from Randolph in a full cabinet meeting. Guilty of nothing

other than devotion to Washington and to the best interests of his country, Randolph promptly resigned and set about trying to vindicate himself. It was very difficult to do, and historians have been all too slow to recognize that he was totally innocent of any wrongdoing.

In spite of divergent political views at times, Beckley and Randolph were devoted friends. He was infuriated when he learned of Randolph's treatment. He had known Washington a long time and had always referred to him in respectful terms. He was now completely disillusioned and convinced that Washington had become the head of a pro-British faction in this country. He had been strongly opposed to the Jay Treaty and had campaigned vigorously against its passage. Beckley retaliated by attacking Oliver Wolcott under the pseudonym of "The Calm Observer." He accused Wolcott of overpaying Washington's salary and drew Wolcott and Hamilton into a prolonged rebuttal of his charges. In spite of Wolcott's indignant denials, Beckley was able to demonstrate conclusively that Washington had repeatedly overdrawn his allowance by Congress. Many were shocked by such an attack on Washington but it had the effect of embarrassing the Federalists in a number of ways.

Beckley's disposition was not improved when he learned that the Federalists in the cabinet had persuaded Washington to recall Monroe from Paris in August 1796. It was evident that Republicans were to be ousted from any position of prominence which the Federalists could attack. He was inspired to assume a leadership role in the forthcoming national elections. Washington's Farewell Address was published in mid-September, and the campaigning to choose his successor began at once. This would be the first contested presidential election. The eventual candidates were John Adams and Thomas Pinckney for the Federalists and Jefferson and Aaron Burr for the Republicans. It was apparent that most of the votes of the northern states would go to Adams and that most southern votes would go to Jefferson. This made clear the importance of the middle states, especially New York and Pennsylvania. Beckley was convinced that the Pennsylvania vote could be won by the Republicans, and he dedicated himself to that end. He was a member of a five-man committee directing political strategy for the state, and he acquired a reputation as a vigorous campaign manager. So effective were his methods of organization at the grassroots level that the final vote was Jefferson 14, Burr 13, Pinckney 2, and Adams only 1. The national vote went to Adams by the narrow margin of 71 to Jefferson's 68. Pinckney received 59 and Burr 30. The delivery of the Pennsylvania vote assured Jefferson of the vice-presidency, and Beckley had played an important role in its delivery.

The Federalists were well aware of how narrowly they had averted the disaster of a Republican administration. The behind-the-scenes maneuvering which had destroyed the political influence of Randolph and Monroe had been successful and could now be directed to strengthening their control of government and the weakening of the Republican position wherever possible. Thus began the era of the Alien and Sedition Acts and all that went with them. Republicans were embarrassed and harassed in many ways, and British influence was strong. Even Vice President Jefferson was subjected to social ostracism. It is not surprising that Beckley was high on the list of politically active Republicans the Federalists would like to depose. Since he held elective office, he was clearly vulnerable. He was, obviously, aware of this, but since he had been consistently reelected by large margins, he had felt comparatively secure. He should have known better. Many of his most active supporters in Congress were prone to arrive at the last minute for the beginning of a session. This now provided a method for attacking Beckley. A Federalist caucus was called, and it was agreed to demand an early vote for the clerkship and to vote for a young law student named Jonathan Williams Condy. In spite of many protests in the House they were successful in demanding an immediate vote and Condy won by 41–40.

Republican outrage and Federalist glee were widely expressed in public and in private. Beckley's abilities as a clerk were generally recognized, and the purely political basis for his removal was beyond question. Beckley could derive small comfort from the indignation of his friends. His financial situation, which had been precarious, was suddenly critical. Many people were wholly or partially dependent upon him. His wife, her mother, and her younger brother were members of his household. His parents and an afflicted brother in England, his sister and her children in Virginia, another brother-in-law and his family all looked to him for help. He had invested all of his savings in land at various locations, primarily in western Virginia and Kentucky. His holdings were both extensive and potentially very valuable, but his efforts to sell any of the land had been frustrating. He had not developed a law practice in Philadelphia and to do so would be difficult. He had also been foolish enough to endorse notes for friends and relatives. The threat of debtors' prison was both real and frightening.

There followed for Beckley the most difficult period of his life. Desperate attempts to solve financial problems were just successful enough to avoid debtors' prison. He was humiliated at having to borrow money from friends, including Jefferson and Rush, not knowing when he could return it. His health had always been delicate, and his constant worry did nothing to improve it. None of this was alleviated by the arrogant jeers of the Federalist press and their almost complete dominance of the political scene. There seemed, for a time, no way in which he could strike back at his tormentors, but one means finally suggested itself. At the time of the Reynolds affair, Monroe had asked him to keep the records of the matter, but to keep them secret. He had made no commitment to do so but had honored the request. Now Beckley believed it was Hamilton who was directing the actions of Wolcott, Pickering, and others to bring about not only his, Randolph's, and Monroe's political destruction, but that of the whole Republican cause as well. Although Hamilton was no longer in the cabinet he was still the symbol of Federalism, and Beckley felt he was fully justified in letting the country know what manner of man was behind Federalist activity. Monroe was returning from France at the time and could not be consulted. Beckley alone made the decision to publish the full account of the Reynolds affair.

Beckley persuaded James Thomson Callender to edit the papers relating to the Reynolds affair as a supplement to his *History of the United States for 1796,* published by Snowden & McCorkle. It reached the public just as Monroe arrived from France in late June 1797 and had even more impact than Beckley could have anticipated. Hamilton refused to believe that Monroe was not involved in the release of the papers, an error of which many historians have been guilty ever since, and a duel was narrowly averted by the diplomacy of Aaron Burr. Monroe's conduct throughout the entire Reynolds affair was meticulously honorable, many historians to the contrary notwithstanding. Hamilton, to the consternation of his friends, published a defense. He left the public, as he had left Monroe, Muhlenberg, and Venable, with a choice of either accepting his account that he had repeatedly paid blackmail to a man because of threatened exposure of having carried on an affair with his wife or of suspecting that he had concocted the tale as a cover for having actually been guilty of speculations. Mrs. Reynolds steadfastly denied the story, contending that it had been fabricated by Hamilton and her husband. She promptly had Burr obtain a divorce for her.

Hamilton's friends condemned the publication of the Reynolds affair as mean and base, with little concern for the justification in doing so. They were, however, completely aghast when they read his published defense. Friend and foe alike were amazed that he had confirmed the authenticity of Callender's account by taking any notice of it. Many agreed that he had effectively put an end to his political ambitions, which were widely believed to include the Presidency. Beckley had indeed scored a direct hit on the Federalist leadership.

Federalist domination of the political scene continued for several years, and Beckley failed in his attempts to regain his clerkship. His financial affairs continued to be critical, and he gave serious thought to returning to Richmond or moving to Kentucky. Somehow he managed to survive in Philadelphia, and finally a break came in 1800. He worked hard for the election of Thomas McKean as governor and he was elected. Soon after his election he appointed Beckley clerk of the mayor's court for the city of Philadelphia and clerk of the orphans' court for the county. This was indeed just retribution. The man removed from office was Joseph Hopkinson, McKean's nephew (and, incidentally, author of the words to "Hail Columbia"), whose wife was Emily Mifflin, daughter of the former governor, and whose sister had married Jonathan Williams Condy, Beckley's replacement as Clerk of the House. The combined salaries of the two posts approximated Beckley's former salary as Clerk, of which McKean felt that he had been unjustly deprived.

From Beckley's point of view the tide was at last beginning to turn. Although he was seriously ill at the time, he must have been immeasurably cheered by the political news. John Adams had finally had more than enough of Hamilton's satellites in his cabinet and had disposed of both James McHenry and Timothy Pickering. There remained only Oliver Wolcott, and the opportunity for Beckley to help attack him again soon presented itself. Anthony Campbell, a clerk in the Auditor's Office of the Treasury Department, informed Israel Israel, sheriff of Philadelphia, that he had evidence of misuse of public monies on a large scale. He produced copies of the accounts of Pickering, Jonathan Dayton, Speaker of the House, and others, showing large sums due to the government. He insisted that these should be made public. Israel sought the advice of Beckley and William Duane, who had succeeded Benjamin Franklin Bache as editor of the *Aurora*. The men were intrigued but they were cautious. They wanted to see the actual records from which Campbell had obtained his information. They must be sure of the facts before giving the matter any publicity. Campbell then agreed to take the risk of "borrowing" the actual records on a Sunday morning for them to examine. He did so, and the group spent the day poring over them and recording the facts. They had Campbell return the books. Duane, with assistance from Beckley, then began a campaign of heckling Wolcott with pertinent questions about monies owed to the government, which Wolcott found very difficult to answer. This was continued throughout the summer. Wolcott soon realized that Duane had inside information and, as Campbell fully expected, he lost his job. So, too, did his friend William P. Gardner, who had aided him. In spite of Wolcott's defenses it was all too apparent that some rather dubious accounting practices had been followed in the Treasury Department and that considerable favoritism had been shown in the collection of monies due. Papers in other parts of the country naturally picked up this material from the *Aurora* and added their own commentary. Someone even suggested that a fire in the Treasury Department offices might be very convenient. Since the attacks had also involved Wolcott's predecessor in office, Hamilton considered suing Duane, but thought better of it. The attack achieved its objective when Wolcott submitted his resignation to take effect December 31.

This was, of course, an election year, and the Republicans were delighted by any ammunition they could use against the Federalists. Beckley, who was always inclined to take an optimistic view, began to see hope of a Republican victory in November and determined to do everything within his power to help bring it about. He dug out an essay he had written in 1795 dealing with Federalist attempts to establish a standing army and sent it to his friend Ephraim Kirby, in Connecticut, to be republished as a pamphlet. He worked closely with Mathew Carey, Tench Coxe, and others in giving wide distribution to Republican propaganda. He devoted many hours to writing a 32-page *Address to the Citizens of the United States,* signed "Americanus," in which he attacked the record of the Federalists and refuted each charge they had made against Jefferson. He included a seven-page biography of Jefferson, the first ever published. Mathew Carey printed 2,000 copies of the first edition, and there were later editions published elsewhere. In spite of the personal tragedy of the death of his small daughter, Mary, his only child, he undertook a series of essays in the *Aurora,* defending Jefferson from the attacks of the clergy.

Beckley's efforts toward party organization at the grassroots level were so effective that Federalists accused the Republicans of establishing presses in every town and county in the country. Beckley would have been happy were it true. In October he somehow managed to obtain a copy of a pamphlet written by Hamilton, viciously attacking Adams and promoting Pinckney. It had been intended for secret distribution to certain key Federalists. Even before many of them had received their copies, Duane was publishing choice excerpts in the *Aurora.* Adams and his many supporters were furious, and even Hamilton's friends were once more astonished. The effect was quite as sensational as Duane and Beckley had hoped. Once again Beckley had thwarted the political plans of Hamilton, to his intense satisfaction. He wrote to a friend that Hamilton's attempts to replace Washington had

failed permanently. Many a Federalist sadly agreed.

The long-planned move of the federal government from Philadelphia to Washington was occurring during the fall of 1800, with all of the confusion and problems which might have been expected. Records and papers were stored in temporary quarters at Washington, pending completion of permanent depositories. On November 12th a fire occurred in the quarters of the War Department. Duane and others of the Republican press immediately suggested that it conveniently prevented scrutiny of the records by the Republican administration which would be coming in. They were not really as optimistic as they attempted to sound. There were strong indications that the election would be close. Beckley and his friends had felt sure that they could deliver all 15 Pennsylvania votes for Jefferson, but they were outmaneuvered by the state senate and had to settle for eight. The national vote ended in a 73–73 tie between Burr and Jefferson, with 65 for Adams, 64 for Pinckney, and one for Jay. Republicans of Philadelphia were summoned by Beckley to a meeting on December 19th to plan a public festival. They held it on January 3d at the "Sign of the Green Tree."

The tie vote between Jefferson and Burr could not be resolved until Congress officially recorded the vote in February. On January 20th a second fire broke out, this time in the house rented by the Treasury Department. Any doubt which many Republicans had about the earlier fire at the War Department was fully erased by the second, and the Republican press loudly proclaimed that both fires had been set. A few of the more moderate Republicans were still prepared to give the Federalists the benefit of the doubt, but Beckley was not among them. The House of Representatives appointed a committee to investigate the fires. It reached no definite conclusions about either fire, but it received quite a bit of evidence suggesting that the second one had been set. The fact that Samuel Dexter, secretary of war, was temporarily in charge of the Treasury Department complicated matters. Wolcott's resignation had become effective, but he was present at the fire and was accused of trying to save only his own papers. Dexter was eventually sued by the owner of the house, who implied that Wolcott had set the fire. Wolcott returned to Washington from Albany for the trial and made a convincing defense against all charges.

Congress met on February 11 to decide the tie between Burr and Jefferson. Seven days later Jefferson won on the 36th ballot. It had been a tense and trying week, with talk of naming an interim President and threats of armed resistance to any attempt at usurpation. The reaction to the final decision was wild celebration by Republicans in all parts of the country. They had gone a long time without a major victory, and they had been subjected to every conceivable indignity by the Federalists during the Adams' administration. Few today realize that Republicans regarded this period when the Alien and Sedition Acts were in effect as a "reign of terror" and were genuinely afraid to make critical remarks in public or even in their private correspondence. It is not surprising that they celebrated. At Philadelphia one observer said that the bedlam was so continuous that he could not read a paper for three days. A grand "jubilee" was planned for March 4th, at which the "Ciceronian Beckley" would be the orator.

With the end of the hated Federalist domination, Republicans who had worked hard for their overthrow awaited Jefferson's appointments with interest. Few Republicans had held any public office under the earlier regimes. In fact, Adams had even made a number of last minute appointments before leaving office. Now at last the Republicans would have their turn. Few, if any, had worked harder than Beckley, and few had suffered more from loss of office. Surely he would be among the first to be rewarded. Jefferson was inundated with requests for appointment and letters of recommendation of friends. He was, however, reluctant to make appointments except where vacancies existed. He did remove from office those who had received "midnight appointments" from Adams. By July the outrage in the Republican press became so loud that he modified his stand and conceded that office holding should be equalized between the two parties. Slowly he removed from office any Federalist against whom any serious charges could be maintained. Many people sought Beckley's recommendation for appointment, and he wrote numerous letters for them. He was also consulted by cabinet members and others about the advisability of certain ap-

pointments. He made no written application on his own behalf. His friends began to be concerned. Monroe wrote to Jefferson about him. Governor McKean wrote on behalf of both Beckley and Tench Coxe, indicating he had done all he could for them. Jefferson replied that he shared McKean's concern but could see no immediate hope of a place for either of them. In October Jefferson wrote to Beckley that he assumed he would be reelected to his clerkship of the House and asked him to appoint one Samuel Hanson as an engrossing clerk. Beckley has left no written comment concerning Jefferson's treatment of him, but his son wrote many years later that Beckley had told his intimate friends that he thought Jefferson had failed him.[1]

Beckley was again called upon to deliver an oration at the Fourth of July celebration in Philadelphia. Soon afterward Samuel Otis heard a rumor that Beckley was seeking to replace him as Secretary of the Senate, which may or may not have been true. Beckley was busily involved in local Philadelphia politics at the time and with sundry legal matters, but he did visit Washington in November, and William Duane is said to have promised Otis to help him keep his post in return for receiving Senate printing. Be this as it may, Otis did retain his office, and Beckley was reelected Clerk of the House on December 7, 1801.

When the Beckleys first came to Washington to live, they boarded in the home of Louis André Pichon, French chargé d'affaires, but they soon leased a house on Capitol Hill, at Delaware Avenue, between B and C Streets. Life in the newly created city must have seemed a bit strange after New York and Philadelphia, but many old friends had also made the move. Their social activities were rather restricted at first, because John was on crutches, suffering from gout and leg ulcers, and Maria was pregnant. A son, Alfred, was born on May 26, 1802. They had lost several children and only Alfred survived.

On the same day Beckley was reelected as Clerk, the House acted on another matter of concern to him, namely, the question of a congressional library. This was by no means a new idea but had been considered off and on for 20 years. In 1782 the Continental Congress had appointed a committee to study the proposal. Its members included James Madison and Theodorick Bland, of Virginia, Dr. Hugh Williamson, of North Carolina, and Thomas Mifflin and James Wilson, of Pennsylvania. The committee prepared an impressive list of suggested books. It was a rather complete Americana for the period, with the exception of scientific works, including books by Cadwallader Colden, John Lawson, Robert Beverley, John Brickell, and others. In addition there were volumes on European, Chinese, and ancient history, geography, treaties, international law, and languages, as well as encyclopedias. A formal resolution that Congress establish its own library was presented by Bland, for the committee, but failed to pass. The probable reason for the failure was the availability of the facilities of the Library Company of Philadelphia, which had been founded in 1729 and owned something over 7,000 volumes.

Shortly after the first U.S. Congress convened in New York in 1789, the library question came up again. A committee made up of Elbridge Gerry, of Massachusetts, Alexander White, of Virginia, and Aedanus Burke, of South Carolina was appointed to investigate the subject. They drew up a list of books they considered necessary for the use of the Congress. Ten months later Gerry reported for the committee a recommendation that they make an initial investment of $1,000, to be followed by annual expenditures of $500, to purchase an extensive list of volumes on state laws, laws of European nations, treatises on diplomacy, parliamentary procedure, and other such subjects. Congress passed this resolution but did not implement it. Evidently the fine library of the New York Society proved adequate for their needs during the short time they remained in New York, and when they moved back to Philadelphia, again the Library Company of Philadelphia seems to have provided for them. They did, from time to time, add to their own limited holdings by the purchase of such treatises as Blackstone's *Commentaries* and Vattel's *The Law of Nature and Nations*. In a more frivolous mood they even acquired Burns' poems. Rush's dissertation on yellow fever was probably purchased in response to the frightful epidemic of that dread disease which took the lives of 4,000 citizens of Philadelphia in 1793. In 1802 Congress owned only 243 volumes, which were in the care of the Secretary of the Senate and the Clerk of the House. Beckley had had experience with this sort of library when he had been responsible for books and documents as clerk of the Virginia senate.

When the long-planned move to Washington became imminent, the Congress could no longer evade the issue of establishing its own library on a larger scale. The Capital City was new and afforded few amenities, and these did not include a library. On April 24, 1800, a bill was passed dealing with various problems connected with the removal from Philadelphia. One of its provisions dealt with the library question. Five thousand dollars was to be expended on books and furnishings to be purchased by the Secretary of the Senate and the Clerk of the House, as ordered by a joint committee. Senate members appointed to the committee were Samuel Dexter, of Massachusetts, William Bingham, of Pennsylvania, and Wilson Cary Nicholas, of Virginia. Qualifications of the House committee members were analyzed by Beckley's friend William Duane, no doubt to the delight of the readers of his *Aurora* (May 10, 1800): Robert Waln, of Pennsylvania, whose gift, said Duane, was the "study of bills of exchange, invoices and policies of insurance"; Virginia's Thomas Evans, "a heavy plodding attorney who has no doubt had great reading in *cases in point*"; and Leven Powell, who "has read Fisher's Arithmetic, Starke's Virginia Justice, and such other books as enabled him to fill with becoming dignity the important office of deputy sheriff, of the county of Loudon, in Virginia." In further lese majesty Duane suggested that the Library be decorated with numerous mirrors and paintings of royalty and that its books include 15 volumes by "Porcupine"; *"The Bloody Buoy* & *Cannibal Progress* for such members as are troubled with weak nerves"; Swift's "Art of political lying, and his tale of a tub—for the use of Mr. Pickering"; Machiavelli for Dexter "to be occasionally loaned to Liston"; and *"The Cuckold's Chronicle* for the use of General Hamilton." In spite of Duane's opinion of their abilities, the committee came up with a very respectable list of 152 works, totaling 740 volumes, at an estimated cost of just under £500. These were duly ordered from Cadell & Davies, of London, who had to supply many secondhand books for those out of print. They were shipped on December 9, 1800, and arrived in Baltimore in mid-April. They finally reached Georgetown in early May and were temporarily stored, unopened, in the office of the Secretary of the Senate.

The books had at last arrived, but no regulations had been established for the operation of the Library. It was the appointment of a joint committee to draw up regulations and make other provisions for the operation of the Library that occurred on December 7, 1801, the day of Beckley's reelection as Clerk. The report of the committee, written by John Randolph, was presented two weeks later. It recommended that the room first occupied by the House, but which they had vacated, be converted for the use of the Library. This was a large and airy room, 86 feet long by 35 feet wide, with a 36-foot ceiling, and well lighted with two rows of windows. The report went further into elaborate detail on every facet of Library procedure. It specified that books, carefully numbered and labeled, should be placed "in portable cases with handles to them for the purpose of easy removal, with wire netting doors, and locks." In view of the two recent Washington fires, this would seem to have been a wise precaution. The existing libraries of the House and Senate were to be combined with the newly purchased volumes. The Secretary and the Clerk should oversee all arrangements in placing these, hanging the maps, and in ordering the necessary furniture. They should also have printed catalogs prepared, showing the number of each book and map, and should order book withdrawal slips printed, whose form the report designated. No more than two books could be withdrawn by a member at one time. Folios were to be returned within eight days, octavos and duodecimos in six. The Library would be open daily, except Sunday, from 11 a.m. to 3 p.m. For the time being it would be presided over by the Secretary or the Clerk, or "some proper person for whose conduct they shall be responsible." At the beginning of each session of Congress they would give a report of the state of the library, including expenses and fines collected. In the meantime, the Secretary was directed to sell the hair trunks in which the books had been shipped from London and to render a statement of account.

While the above committee report provided for the Library to be presided over by either the Secretary or the Clerk for the time being, the act, when passed, provided for a permanent Librarian. He was to be paid not over two dollars for each day of attendance, and he would be required to post bond to ensure the safety of the Library furnishings. Randolph moved to strike out one provision of the bill which would have permitted use of the Library by heads of departments, members of the Supreme Court, and foreign ministers. This motion was approved and the bill passed. It was signed by Jefferson on January 26, 1802.

Although the salary specified for the Librarian of Congress was not exactly impressive, there were many applicants for the post. A number of them evidently believed they could use it to supplement income from some other source. On the day following the joint committee's first meeting, John McDonald, "late of Philadelphia," applied. On January 15 Augustus Woodward wrote to Jefferson recommending William O'Neal. On the following day Dr. Richard Dinsmore applied for the position and was recommended by Stevens Thomson Mason. Madison and Gallatin were named as references by Edward Nicholls, a Maryland lawyer serving as a clerk in the Treasury Department. A letter of application from Thomas Claxton makes mention of the large number of applicants. Among the many was a clerk in Beckley's office, Josias Wilson King. When the Federalists replaced Beckley with Condy as Clerk of the House, Condy appointed King as his principal clerk. Somewhat surprisingly, Beckley retained King but appointed his old friend William Lambert as chief clerk. This meant a smaller salary for King, which he hoped to augment with the pay as Librarian. When he had completed enrolling the Library bill on January 21, King wrote to Jefferson, seeking the appointment and stating that he had obtained Beckley's permission to apply. There is no way of knowing whether or not Beckley had also informed him that he had already approached his friend Judge Levi Lincoln, U.S. attorney general, about his own interest in the position. Lincoln had told him that he would speak to Madison about it, but after learning of King's application Beckley wrote to Madison directly.

When Jefferson appointed Beckley Librarian, he added measurably to an already heavy load of duties and responsibilities. It was rather generally recognized that the duties of the Clerk of the House were more burdensome than those of the Secretary of the Senate. This was the reason for the belief of many that Beckley coveted Otis's position. As early as the first session of Congress, Senator Maclay, of Pennsylvania, had noted in his diary that Beckley's goal was to be Secretary of the Senate. From time to time afterwards the word went around that Beckley would try to oust Otis. Many years earlier Beckley had replied to charges that he was overpaid as clerk of the Virginia house with a detailed description of those duties. They read like a very full-time job, indeed, and were certainly no less so in the U.S. House. As Librarian he would not be much concerned with the checking in and out of books, although he might do some. This part of the work would be done primarily by one of his many clerks. There would be a variety of time-consuming collateral duties, including lengthy meetings with congressional committees. One of the first such duties came when the committee asked him to determine how much of the original appropriation remained unspent, so that they might order additional books. When he investigated this, he discovered that there had been no statement of account rendered covering the books ordered from England.

Knowing Jefferson's deep interest in the Library, Senator Abraham Baldwin, a member of the joint congressional library committee, asked his advice concerning the purchase of additional books. On April 14, 1802, Jefferson replied:

I have prepared a catalogue for the Library of Congress in conformity with your ideas that books of entertainment are not within the scope of it, and that books in other languages, where there are not translations of them, are to be admitted freely. I have confined the catalogue to those branches of science which belong to the deliberations of the members as statesmen, and in these have omitted those desirable books, ancient and modern, which gentlemen generally have in their private libraries, but which cannot properly claim a place in a collection made merely for the purposes of reference.

In history I have confined the histories to the chronological works which give facts and dates with a minuteness not to be found in narrations composed for agreeable reading. Under the laws of nature and nations I have put down everything I know of worth possessing, because this is a branch of science often under the discussion of Congress, and the books written on it not to be found in private libraries. In law I set down only general treatises for the purpose of reference. The discussions under this head in Congress are rarely so minute as to require or admit that reports and special treatises should be introduced. The Parliamentary section I have imagined should be complete. It is only by having a law of proceeding, and by every member having the means of understanding it for himself and appealing to it, that he can be protected against caprice and despotism in the chair. The two great encyclopedias form a complete supplement for the sciences omitted in the general collection, should occasion happen to arise for recurring to them. I have added a set of dictionaries in the different languages, which may be often wanting. This catalogue, combined with what you may approve in those offered by others, will enable you to form your general plan and to select from it every year to the amount of the annual fund of those most wanting. . . .[2]

Early in July, Beckley was able to send a statement of the unexpended appropriation ($2,480.83) to Jefferson and to the committee. In his letter to Jefferson he suggested that the works of naturalists Georges Buffon and Mark Catesby be added to the Library. Surprisingly, he referred to Catesby as an American author. As Clayton's former scribe he should certainly have known that Catesby was English since Clayton had frequently sent specimens to Catesby in London. Beckley's servant, who brought the letter to Jefferson, also presented him with the House journals he had requested for Caesar Augustus Rodney. The latter, a Delaware Republican, was challenging James A. Bayard for his congressional seat. Beckley also wrote Jefferson that when Rodney came to the city he would make all of the newspaper files and printed documents available to him. On July 16th Jefferson notified Beckley that he had ordered 700 volumes approved by the committee for the Library. Six new presses, each four feet wide, would be needed to accommodate them.

Throughout the summer Beckley's ill health continued unabated. By late August he decided that only a cure at Virginia's sulfur springs could help him. Jefferson invited him to visit at Monticello for as long as he cared to stay, thinking he was going to the Augusta springs. He went instead to Berkeley Springs, near Martinsburg, a much easier trip. He spent September and October there during the congressional recess, returning home almost completely recovered. There he found that his old friend and family doctor, Benjamin Rush, had sent copies of six of his lectures. In thanking him he started what amounted to a new Library policy. He wrote that he hoped Rush would send him copies of all of his publications "that I may place them, where they so deservedly merit to be, on the first shelf appropriated, in our Congressional Library to works of Ethics and Philosophy."[3] From this time on he lost few opportunities to encourage authors to donate their writings to the Library. Some months later, on February 13, 1803, his friend Samuel Harrison Smith, editor of the *National Intelligencer,* noted that the Library "already embraces near fifteen hundred volumes of the most rare and valuable works in different languages. We observe with pleasure that authors and editors of books, maps, and charts begin to find that, by placing a copy of their works on the shelves of this institution, they do more to diffuse a knowledge of them than is generally accomplished by catalogues and advertisements."

Some years later Beckley evidently prompted Smith to repeat this advice for, on April 11, 1806, he again wrote in the *Intelligencer:*

It is worthy of the consideration of the authors and publishers of books in the United States, whether it would not be well worth their while to send copies to the keeper of the Congressional Library; By depositing their works in that collection, they will be seen and perused by gentlemen of distinction from all parts of the United States. The fame and emolument of the writers and proprietors of printed books can perhaps be promoted in no manner more effectually than by placing copies of them in this growing collection. It will be a publication of them to all the states and territories, in some respects more effectually than by advertisements in the newspapers, and by the distribution of catalogues. Gentlemen desirous of having their publications exhibited in this public and conspicuous place, may forward them, to Mr. Beckley the librarian, who will thankfully receive, and carefully preserve them, for the use of the Representative Bodies of the American nation.

One of the first Library matters to concern Beckley was the publication of a catalog of Library holdings as directed by the Congress. He prepared one and had it printed by William Duane in April 1802. It gave the number assigned to the work, the title, the number of volumes, the dollar value of the set "as near as can be estimated" and that of the individual book. There were 212 folios, 164 quartos, 581 octavos, and 7 duodecimos, making a total of 964 volumes. There were also nine maps and charts. A 2½-page supplement was published in October 1803, printed by James B. Westcott. A second catalog, 13½ pages long, appeared in 1804, with no printer's name mentioned. The "Record of Books Drawn—1800–1802," in manuscript, is still preserved in the Library.

Library accounts continued to pose a problem for some time. When Jefferson placed the second

CATALOGUE.

N°.	FOLIO's.	No. of Vols.	Value, as near as can be estimated.	
			WHOLE SET.	EACH BOOK.
			Dollars.	Dollars.
1	FATHERS PAUL's Council of Trent,	1	4	
2	Blair's Chronology, *(not to issue,)*	1	35	
3	Helvicus's Chronological Tables, -	1	3	
4	Booth's Diodorus Siculus, - - -	1	10	
5	Appian's History of the Civil Wars of the Romans, - - - - -	1	4	
6	Machiavel's Florentine History, -	1	3	
7	Duncan's Cæsar, - - - - - -	1	32	
8	Du Halede's History of China, -	2	24	12
10	De Soli's Conquest of Mexico, -	1	4	
11	Rapin's History of England, - -	5	50	10
16	Lord Herbert's Life of Henry VIII.	1	2	
17	Rushworth's Historical Collections,	8	24	3
25	Lord Clarendon's History of the Rebellion, - - - - - - -	4	24	6
29	Guthrie's Geography, - - - -	1	13	
30	Bayle's Dictionary, - - - -	5	30	6
35	Postlewayte's Dictionary of Commerce,	2	24	12
37	Beawes' Lex Mercatoria, - - -	1	12	
38	Domat's Civil Law, - - - -	2	12	6
40	Grotius, by Barbeyrac, - - - -	1	14	
41	Puffendorf, by ditto, - - - - -	1	24	
42	Sidney on Government, - - - -	1	10	
43	Bacon's Works, - - - - - -	5	55	11

Catalogue of Books, Maps, and Charts, Belonging to the Library of the Two Houses of Congress (Washington City: Printed by William Duane, 1802) is the first printed catalog of the holdings of the Library of Congress and was prepared by John Beckley. Volumes were not listed by alphabet but rather by size. According to rules set up a few years later, size also determined how long an item could be kept by a borrower, as well as the amount of fine imposed on an overdue book. Rare Book Division.

CATALOGUE. — Page 4

N°.	FOLIO's.	No. of Vols.	Value, as near as can be estimated. WHOLE SET. Dollars.	EACH BOOK. Dollars.
48	Biographia Britannica, - - - -	5	60	12
53	Coxe's Travels in Switzerland, - -	2	40	20
55	State Trials, - - - - - -	11	111	10
61	Atlas to Crutwell's Gazetteer, - -	1		
62	Atlas to Guthrie's System of Geography, - - - - - - - -	1		
63	American Atlas, - - - - - -	1		
64	Plates to Cook's third Voyage, - -	1		
65	Plates to Macartney's Embassy to China, - - - - - - - -	1		
66	Journals of the Lords and Commons, with the rolls and reports complete,	102	300	3

Additional from the respective Library of the Senate and House of Representatives.

168	Journals House Commons, - - -	18	54	3
186	State Trials, - - - - - - -	14	112	8
200	Coke upon Littleton, - - - -	1	10	
201	Mortimer's Dictionary, - - - -	1	10	
202	Chambers' Dictionary, - - - -	4	36	9
206	Index to Chambers' Dictionary, -	1	9	
207	Maritime Atlas, - - - - - -	5	35	7
212	Atlas to Guthrie's Geography, - -	1	10	

(Nos. 61–65 bracketed: "Not to issue.")

QUARTO's.

1	Smith's Thucydides, - - - - -	2	10	5
3	Hamptons' Polybius, - - - - -	2	14	7
5	Spellman's Dionysius, - - - - -	4	28	7
9	Murphey's Tacitus, - - - - -	4	30	7 50
13	Gibbon's Roman Empire, - - -	6	54	9
19	Davila's History of France by Farneworth, - - - - - - - - -	2	24	12
21	Roscoe's Lorenzo de Medici, - -	2	24	12
23	Clavingero's History of Mexico, - -	2	24	12
25	Robertson's Charles, - - - - -	3	18	6
28	Robertson's America, - - - - -	2	24	12

CATALOGUE. — Page 5

N°.	QUARTO's.	No. of Vols.	Value, as near as can be estimated. WHOLE SET. Dollars.	EACH BOOK. Dollars.
30	Robertson's Scotland, - - - - -	2	25	12 50
32	Hume's History of England, - - -	8	60	7 50
40	Leland's History of Ireland, - - -	3	18	6
43	Ludlow's Memoirs, - - - - -	1	7	
44	Belsham's History of George III. -	4	30	7 50
48	Edwards's History of the West Indies,	2	18	9
50	Harte's Life of Gustavus Adolphus,	2	10	5
52	Coxe's Walpole, - - - - -	3	27	9
55	Bouganville's Voyage, - - - -	1	6	
56	Stuart's View of Society in Europe,	1	6	
57	Keith's History of British Plantations,	1	4	
58	Hawkesworth's and Cooke's Voyages,	8	72	9
66	Coxe's Russian Discoveries, - - -	1	5	
67	Coxe's Travels in Poland, - - -	3	20	6 50
70	Bruce's Travels, - - - - - -	5	35	7
75	Staunton's Embassy to China, (plates,)	2	30	15
77	Morse's American Geography, - -	1	9	
78	Justinian's Institutes, - - - - -	1	7	
79	Jacob's Law Dictionary, - - - -	2	20	10
81	Hatsell's Precedents, - - - - -	4	22	5 50
85	Anderson's History of Commerce, -	4	32	8
89	Stuart's Political economy, - - -	2	16	8
91	Sinclair on the British Revenue, -	1	24	
92	Reid on the powers of Man, - - -	1	11	
93	Burke's Works, - - - - - -	3	21	7
96	Plates to Anacharsis' Travels, *(not to issue)* - - - - - - - -	1		

Additional from the respective Library of the Senate and House of Representatives.

97	Encyclopædia, - - - - - -	36	216	6
133	Statutes at large, - - - - -	21	126	6
154	Hazard's State Papers, - - - -	2	16	8
156	Precedents House of Commons, -	2	10	5
158	Hatsell's Precedents, - - - - -	3	15	5
161	Guthrie's Geography, - - - - -	3	18	6
164	Bibliotheca Americana, - - - -	1	6	

6   CATALOGUE.

N°.	OCTAVO's.	No. of Vols.	WHOLE SET. Dollars.	EACH BOOK. Dollars.
1	Universal History, Ancient and Modern	60	120	2
61	Rolin's Ancient History, - - -	8	20	2 50
69	Millot's Ancient and Modern History,	5	15	3
74	Gillie's History of Greece, - - -	4	8	2
78	Anacharsis's Travels, - - - -	7	18	2 50
85	Beloe's Herodotus, - - - -	4	8	2
89	Rooke's Arrian, - - - - - -	2	4	2
91	Spellman's Xenophon, - - - -	2	6	3
93	Leland's Life of Philip of Macedon,	2	4	2
95	Leland's Demosthenes, - - - -	3	6	2
98	Middleton's Cicero, - - - - -	3	8	2 50
101	Ferguson's Roman Republics, - -	5	10	2
106	Langhorne's Plutarch, - - - -	6	18	3
112	Russel's Ancient and Modern Europe,	7	18	2 50
119	Henry's History of Great Britain, -	12	28	2 33½
131	Guiciardini's History of Italy, - -	10	15	1 50
141	Littleton's Henry II. - - - - -	6	12	2
147	Bacon's Life of Henry VII. - - -	1	2 50	
148	Noble's Cromwell, - - - - -	2	5	2 50
150	Life of Monk, Duke of Albermale,	1	2	
151	Watson's Philip II. and III. - -	5	10	2
156	Voltaire's Lewis XIV. and XV. -	2	3	1 50
158	Voltaire's Charles XII. - - - -	1	1	
159	Memoir's of Philip de Comines, -	2	2	1
161	Sully's Memoirs, - - - - - -	5	10	2
166	De Witt's Maxims, - - - - -	1	1	
167	Temple's Works, - - - - - -	4	10	2 50
171	Constitution and Government of the Germanic Body, - - - - -	1	1 50	
172	Debrett's State Papers, - - - -	8	32	4
180	Rabaut's French Revolution, - -	1	2	
181	Hereras's History of America, - -	6	9	1 50
187	Raynal's Indies, - - - - - -	8	16	2
195	Wynne's British America, - - -	2	3	1 50
197	Neal's History of New England, -	2	3	1 50
199	Hutchinson's History of Massachusetts	1	1	
200	Stith's History of Virginia, - - -	1	1 50	
201	Jefferson's Notes on Virginia, - -	1	2 50	
202	Smith's History of New York, - -	1	2	

CATALOGUE.   7

N°.	OCTAVO's.	No. of Vols.	WHOLE SET. Dollars.	EACH BOOK. Dollars.
203	Smith's History of New Jersey, -	1	2	
204	Ramsay's History of South Carolina,	2	4	2
206	Colden's History of the Five Nations,	1	2	
207	Present state of Nova Scotia, - -	1	2	
208	Du Pratz's History of Louisiana, -	1	2	
209	Gordon's Hist. of the American War,	4	8	2
213	Ulloas's Voyage, - - - - -	2	4	2
215	Charlevoix's Journal, - - - -	2	3	1 50
217	Carver's Travels, - - - - - -	1	3	
218	Adanson's Voyage to Senegal, - -	1	3	
219	Crutwell's Gazetteer, - - - - -	3	15	5
222	Morse's American Gazetteer, - -	1	3	
223	Adams on the American Constitution,	3	6	2
226	Boswell's Journal, - - - - - -	1	2	
227	Rutherforth's Institutes of Nat. Law,	2	5	2 50
229	Montesquieu's Spirit of Laws, - -	1	2	
230	Vatel's Law of Nations, - - - -	1	4	
231	Burlemaqui on Natural Law, - -	2	4	2
233	Moloy de Jure Maritimo, - - -	2	4	2
235	Maxwell's Marine Law, - - - -	1	4	
236	Chalmers' Collection of Treaties, -	2	5	2 50
238	Jenkinson's Collection of Treaties, -	3	8	2 50
241	Coke's Institutes, - - - - - -	7	28	4
248	Viner's Abridgement, - - - -	24	100	4
272	Woodeson's Lectures, - - - -	3	18	6
275	Reeves on the Laws of England, -	4	8	2
279	Blackstone's Commentaries, - -	4	12	3
283	Forster's Crown Law, - - - -	1	3	
284	Beccaria on Crimes and Punishments,	1	3	
285	Cooke's Bankrupt Law, - - - -	2	5	2 50
287	Eden's Penal Law, - - - - -	1	2 50	
288	De Lolme on the Constitution, - -	1	2 50	
289	Lex Parliamentaria, - - - - -	1	2	
290	Atkyn's Power of Parliaments, -	1	2	
291	Parliamentary Debates, - - - -	104	312	3
395	Irish Debates, - - - - - - -	11	22	2
406	Petty's Political Arithmetic, - -	1	1 50	
407	Smith's Wealth of Nations, - - -	3	6	2
410	Steele's Book of Rates and Customs,	1	2	

Nº.	OCTAVO's.	No. of Vols.	Value, as near as can be estimated. WHOLE SET. Dollars.	EACH BOOK. Dollars.
411	Davenant on Trade, - - - - -	5	10	2
416	Price on Annuities, - - - - -	2	5	2 50
418	Reeves's Hist. of the Navigation Act,	1	3	
419	Sheffield on Commerce, - - - -	1	2	
420	Locke's Works, - - - - - -	9	27	3
429	Paley's Philosophy, - - - r -	2	4	2
431	Smith's Moral Sentiments, - - -	2	4	2
433	Burgh's Dignity of Human Nature, -	1	2 50	
434 452	Rambler, Spectator, Adventurer and Tatler, - - - - - - - -	18	45	2 50
	Blair's Lectures, - - - - - -	3	6	2
	Additional from the respective Library of the Senate and House of Representatives.			
455	Hume's History of England, - - -	14	56	4
473	Collection of Voyages, - - - -	4	16	4
477	New Annual Register, - - - -	12	48	4
489	Belknap's History, - - - - -	3	9	3
492	Belknap's American Biography, - -	2	6	3
494	Gazetteer of France, - - - - -	3	9	3
497	Paine's Geography, - - - - -	4	12	3
501	Morse's Geography, - - - - -	1	4	
502	Staunton's Embassy, - - - - -	1	5	
503	St. Mery's St. Domingo, - - - -	1	4	
504	Ramsey's South Carolina, - - -	2	8	4
506	Necker's Finances of France, - -	3	12	4
509	Anderson's Commerce, - - - -	6	18	3
515	Sheffield and Cox on American Commerce, - - - - - - - -	2	8	4
517	American Museum, - - - - -	3	9	3
520	American Senator, - - - - -	3	12	4
523	Congress Debates, - - - - -	3	12	4
526	Monthly Review, - - - - -	13	30	3
536	Paine's Miscellanies, - - - -	1	4	
537	Adams' Defence, - - - - -	2	8	4
539	Reeves's English Law, - - - -	4	12	3
543	Blackstone's Commentaries, - - -	4	16	4

Nº.	OCTAVO's.	No. of Vols.	Value, as near as can be estimated. WHOLE SET. Dollars.	EACH BOOK. Dollars.
547	Woodeson's Lectures, (*double set*) -	3	12	4
553	Robinson's Reports, - - - - -	1	4	
554	Cook's Bankrupt Laws, - - - -	1	4	
555	Millar on Insurance, - - - - -	1	4	
556	Williams's Digest, - - - - -	1	4	
557	Dallas's Reports, - - - - -	3	12	4
560	Swift's System of Laws of Connecticut,	2	8	4
562	Heywood on Elections, - - - -	1	3	
563	Luder on Elections, - - - - -	3	9	3
566	Frazer on Elections, - - - - -	1	3	
567	Hogan's State Trials, - - - - -	5	15	3
572	Chalmers' Collection of Treaties, -	2	8	4
574	Vattel's Law of Nations, - - - -	1	5	
575	Rush on Yellow Fever, - - - -	1	3	
576	Varlo's Husbandry, - - - - -	2	3	
578	Wenderborn, - - - - - - -	2	4	2
580	Burns's Poems, - - - - - -	1	2	
581	World Displayed, - - - - -	8	24	3

DUODECIMO's.

Nº.		No. of Vols.	WHOLE SET. Dollars.	EACH BOOK. Dollars.
1	Montesquieu's Roman Empire, - -	1	1	
2	Millot's History of France, - - -	3	3	1
5	Memoirs of Brandenburg, - - - -	2	2	1
7	Federalist, - - - - - - - -	2	2	1

B

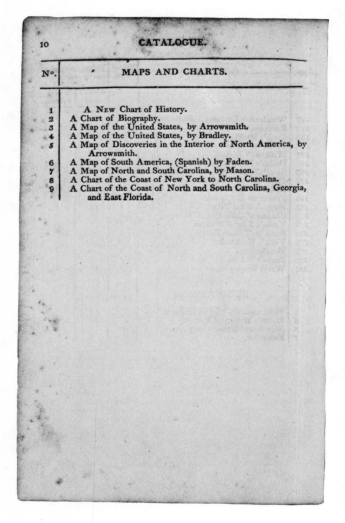

order for books, he requested George W. Erving, U.S. consul at London, to assist an agent of William Duane in purchasing the books. He did so because he thought that Cadell & Davies had been far too high on the first order. He advised Erving (July 16, 1802) to look for "neat bindings, not splendid ones," and smaller volumes rather than the expensive folios—"good editions, not pompous ones." Robert R. Livingston, U.S. minister to France, was asked to supervise the selection of books ordered from Pougers, Paris booksellers. Erving reported that the English books had cost £68 but no statement was received from Livingston. Jefferson decided to wait for his return to this country to inquire about the cost. When finally he was able to talk to Livingston, the minister could furnish no figures. He had supposed that the bankers involved had furnished him figures. On January 10, 1806, Jefferson wrote to Gallatin asking if the bankers had sent him an accounting. He suggested that if they had not done so, that he, Jefferson, and Beckley could work out an approximation.

By March Jefferson had solved the problem. He wrote Beckley that when he had written to Pougers placing the order for books, he had also ordered some volumes of an encyclopedia for himself. He had specifically warned Pougers not to confuse the two orders and to be careful to pack and address them separately. In spite of these instructions, Pougers had packed his books with those for the Library. Livingston had paid them $1,866 for the Library's books, and $535 for Jefferson's books. Packaging and shipping costs to Le Havre had been charged to the Library account. Matters were further complicated by the addition of two hampers of wine for Jefferson, who had paid transportation costs of everything from Le Havre to Georgetown. The confusion was ended by Jefferson's sending Beckley a check for $39.94, which he had decided he should pay. This, with Jefferson's explanatory letter, was presented by Beckley to the Vice President and the Speaker of the House for "their approbation, pursuant to law."

Among the Librarian's duties was that of acting as host to dignitaries visiting the Library. The new Capitol began to attract visitors, and the Library was becoming one of the sights. This was certainly one of Beckley's more pleasant duties. In June 1804, Charles Willson Peale, Dr.

25 John Smith   New York

1800
Novem 20. Adams's defence. 1 Vol: returned 1st March 1801
           Herty's digest. (packed up by General Van Cortland 27 Jul.)

1801.
Dec 10th. 17th Vol. Encyclopædia
      11th .... Herty's digest.—
1802.
Jany 2d .... American Senator 1st Vol.   } prt.

Part of a page from "Record of Books Drawn—1800–1802." This record book was used for other purposes as well; see page 103. Manuscript Division.

Library of Congress,
6th March 1806.

Dear Sir,

I have received your letter and statement of your account with the Committee of the Library, with a check enclosed for the ballance thereon of £39-94 cents. I shall lay the account before the Vice president and Speaker for their approbation, pursuant to law, and apply the check to your credit for the ballance agreeable to your statement. With unfeigned respect,

I am, dear Sir,
Your obedt. Servt.
John Beckley, Librarian.

Letter to Thomas Jefferson acknowledging receipt of his payment to the Library when Pougers, Paris booksellers, mistakenly packaged and shipped his personal order together with an order for books for the Library. Courtesy Massachusetts Historical Society.

Fothergill, of Bath, and other distinguished gentlemen accompanied the famous German naturalist Baron Alexander von Humboldt on a visit. They admired the Senate chamber, the view from the top of the Capitol, and Pennsylvania Avenue, with its four rows of trees. Peale recorded in his diary: "We first went to the Library, where Mr. Beckley received us with politeness, and also accompanied us through the other apartments. The Library is a spacious and handsome Room, and although lately organized, already contained a number of valuable books in the best taste of binding." [4]

There were personnel problems to worry Beckley. The most serious of these involved Josias King, the Federalist clerk whom he had inherited from Condy in the Clerk's office. Since King had sought the post of Librarian for himself, there was, naturally, resentment toward Beckley. Apparently it was to some degree suppressed for several years, but finally, in December 1805, Beckley fired him. King wasted little time in taking his case to the House. He prepared a memorial that made two major accusations against Beckley. The first was that Beckley had appointed him assistant librarian "to label, arrange and take charge of the books in the library" and had promised to divide the Librarian's salary with him but had failed to do so. For a number of reasons it seems most unlikely that Beckley had made such an agreement. In the first place he needed money desperately himself. Secondly, King was already fully employed in the Clerk's office and could easily have been assigned to library work instead. Furthermore, if Beckley had been making such an arrangement it would seem far more likely that he would have picked one of the clerks who had worked for him for years, such as Lambert. It also seems strange that King continued to work for several years without receiving the promised compensation. Evidently the committee of accounts, assigned by the House to investigate his charges, agreed, for they found no basis for this charge. The second charge involved a grant of additional compensation made by the House to certain employees for extra services rendered, March 27, 1804. This grant of $1,700 included $200 for King and was to be paid out of the contingency fund of the House. King did not receive his money at that time and borrowed it from a Washington bank

In "Record of Books Drawn—1800–1802" is what appears to be a fair copy of Josias Wilson King's petition to the House of Representatives outlining his grievances against Beckley.

In the first two paragraphs of his petition, presented by Joseph H. Nicholson, of Maryland, King charges that the salary of the Librarian of Congress was not divided equally with him as Beckley had promised. In the third paragraph he contends that Beckley withheld "reimbursement of interest on grants heretofore made by the House to the Memorialist." In the final paragraph he asks for redress for having been fired by Beckley in December 1805.

King then traces the course of his petition through committee, which concluded that "the memorialist has no claim upon the clerk of the House of Representatives, as prayed for by him, and that his memorial ought not to be granted." Manuscript Division.

Bailey Bartlett   New Hampshire
(Presented by Mr Nicholson (of Maryland.)

To the honorable the Speaker and Members of the House of Representatives of the United States of America, in Congress assembled.

The Memorial of Josias Wilson King, late a clerk in the office of the clerk, to the House;

Respectfully Sheweth

That at the first session of the Seventh Congress, immediately after the passage of the act "concerning the library for the use of both Houses of Congress," your memorialist was appointed assistant librarian, to label, arrange and take charge of the books of the said library; that the memorialist accordingly performed the said duty, and also executed the trust reposed in him as a clerk in the office of the clerk to the House, at the same time.

That the present clerk of your honorable body, who was appointed librarian by the President of the United States, agreed to divide equally the compensation with your memorialist allowed by the said act, during the time he continued to serve in the library; but the memorialist has not hitherto received the said compensation, as he had a right to expect, although repeated applications have in vain been made therefor, from the year 1802, to the present time.

Your Memorialist begs leave to call the attention of the House to another claim to which, he conceives he is justly entitled, that is a reimbursement of interest on grants heretofore made by the House to the Memorialist for extra services rendered by him in the office, which, in consequence of their being withheld by the clerk, he was compelled to pay to the branch bank of the United States at the City of Washington, to enable him to receive nearly the amount of the same; while it can be proved by incontestable evidence, that the present clerk to your honorable body allowed and paid interest on a certain demand on the same fund out of which your Memorialist, in his opinion, ought to have been punctually paid at the time the grants were made.

The Memorialist is likewise under the painful necessity of representing to the House, that after having constantly served as a Clerk in their office, from the Spring of the year 1797 to the 31 of December, 1805, he was, on that day, discharged by the present Clerk of the House, in the Winter Season—with a family to support, and no resources whatever to provide for them;—and (to heighten the cruelty and unfeeling inflexibility manifested in the proceeding) without any charge against him which could, in the smallest degree, impeach his diligence or fidelity in the execution of his public duty: He therefore prays, that you will be pleased to take the premises into consideration, and so far as may be consistent with equity and justice to afford that redress which has been denied to him, by one of the officers of your House.

And the Memorialist as in duty bound &c.

Josias Wilson King

---

18 February, 1806. Referred to the Committee of Accounts.

[Report made the 5th March, 1806, and referred to a committee of the whole House, on Monday next.]

The Committee of accounts, to whom was referred the memorial of Josias Wilson King, submit the following

Report:

That the only part of the memorial intitled to the consideration of the House, is a claim for interest on grants heretofore made, to the memorialist, from the contingent fund, and withheld from him by the Clerk.

The House of Representatives, on the 27th day of March,

1804, made a specific grant of additional compensation to their officers, amounting to $1700, payable out of the contingent fund of the House; in which was included a grant to the memorialist of 200 dollars. For want of funds in the hands of the clerk, these gratuities were not paid until the month of December, 1804; and that he had not funds for that object, appears by a balance due to him of $192_15, upon the settlement of his accounts with the Treasury, on the 19ᵗʰ day of October, in the same year; and by an appropriation made of $2,500, early in the session of Congress for that year; to supply the deficiency of the last appropriation for the contingent fund

    Your committee therefore report, that the memorialist has no claim upon the clerk of the House of Representatives, as prayed for by him, and that his memorial ought not to be granted

    [Not further acted upon]

and, of course, paid interest to the bank. He now asked that he be reimbursed for the interest paid. At the time the House made the grant, the contingency fund had already been overspent by $192.15, and Congress adjourned without replenishing the fund. It was not until the next session of the Congress that an appropriation was made to the contingency fund and King and others could be paid. It would appear that the committee was correct in concluding that the memorialist had no claim against Beckley.[5]

In view of his own sad experience, it seems most unlikely that Beckley would have fired a young man with a family to support at Christmas time without extreme provocation. He would have been well justified in firing King when he was reelected as Clerk but had kept him on for several years. In spite of the fact that the committee of accounts completely exonerated Beckley at the time, historians have tended to cite King's testimony in support of the thesis that Beckley neglected the Library. This cannot be justified.

The Library had other problems besides those of personnel. In 1805 the House took back the impressive room it had assigned to the Library and substituted a former committee room. This was situated in a wing of the building which was already in such bad repair that the floor was shaky and the roof leaked. In addition to these difficulties, the room was too small to accommodate the rapidly growing collections of books and maps. In spite of having moved the Library to inadequate quarters, Congress continued to provide for its growth. In December 1805, the Senate appointed a committee to "inquire into the expediency of purchasing maps and books for the library." The committee chairman, Samuel Latham Mitchill, was an excellent choice. At 28, he had been professor of chemistry, natural history, and agriculture at Columbia University. His erudition was not confined to these subjects, and he was known as the "Stalking Library" by his colleagues.

Mitchill reported to the Senate on January 20 that "Every week of the session causes additional regret that the volumes of literature and science within the reach of the National Legislature, are not more rich and ample." Not only did it lack "geographical illustrations" but it was deficient in works on historical and political subjects. He thought that an untutored government would be

Dr. Samuel Latham Mitchill (1764–1831). From an engraving in The National Portrait Gallery of Distinguished Americans, *vol. 1. Chairman of the committee to select books and later chairman of the Joint Committee on the Library of Congress, Mitchill, who served both as a Representative and as a Senator from New York, was known variously by his contemporaries as the "Nestor of American science," "the Congressional dictionary," "the Congressional Library," and "a chaos of knowledge," as well as the "stalking library."*

no danger provided that "steps be seasonably taken to furnish the library with such materials as will enable statesmen to be correct in their investigations, and, by a becoming display of erudition and reseach, give a higher dignity and a brighter lustre to truth." The Senate was impressed and his advice resulted in the act of 21 February 1806, which allocated $1,000 per annum for five years for the purchase of books and maps for the Library. It also officially, for the

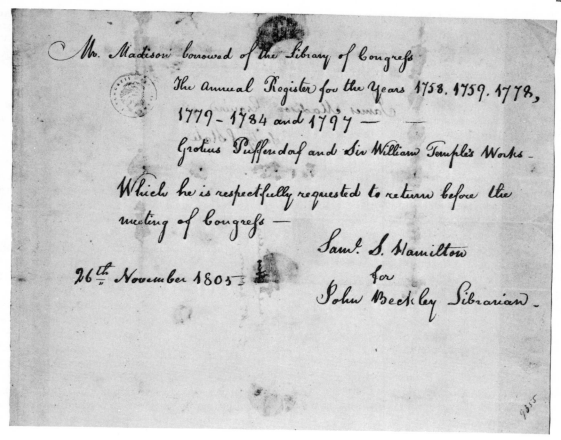

Mr. Madison borrowed of the Library of Congress

The Annual Register for the Years 1758. 1759. 1778,
1779 - 1784 and 1797 —

Grotius Puffendorf and Sir William Temple's Works —

Which he is respectfully requested to return before the
meeting of Congress —

26th November 1805

Saml. S. Hamilton
for
John Beckley Librarian —

The first Librarian's letter to James Madison, who was then secretary of state, requesting the return of material he had borrowed. At this time the privileges of the Library were limited to Members of Congress. James Madison Papers, Microfilm Series 1, reel 8. Manuscript Division.

first time, permitted the secretaries of state, war, navy and treasury, as well as the attorney general, to use the Library. There had already been times when these gentlemen had consulted works there and even withdrawn them. The previous November Samuel S. Hamilton, acting for "John Beckley Librarian," had sent a notice to the secretary of state: "Mr. Madison borrowed of the Library of Congress: The Annual Register for the Years 1758, 1759, 1778, 1779–1784 and 1797. Grotius Puffendorf and Sir William Temple's Works—Which he is respectfully requested to return before the meeting of Congress." Another new feature of the act was authorization for the

purchase of books published in the United States. Of the $1,000 appropriated for 1806, Mitchill, Joseph Clay, and John Quincy Adams were each allowed to spend $494 for books bought in New York, Philadelphia, and Boston. This idea may have been initiated by Col. William Tatham, who recommended purchasing Americana—perhaps exhibiting a personal interest since he offered to sell the Library his own collection.

The liveliest accounts of the Library come from the pen of Federalist Senator William Plumer, of New Hampshire. During Beckley's five years as Librarian, the two men continued a running feud. Plumer wrote in his *Memorandum of Pro-*

ceedings in the United States Senate, 1803–1807:
"It has been the practice of Congress to print the
journals of their proceedings, the messages of the
president, the reports of the heads of departments—of committees—board of commissioners
of the Sinking fund—&c &c &c. Of each of these
there has always been printed supernumerary
numbers, that is, more than one for the President,
Vice President, each senator & representative &
head of departments, who are regularly furnished
with them. These spare copies, & such copies as
the members leave in their drawers at the end of
the session, are in the recess carried up in the
large lumber room over the senate chamber.
When I came here in Dec. 1802, I was informed
that each member of Congress was entitled to
each document if he would take the trouble of
selecting them. I accordingly began—selected &
removed a considerable number when I received
a message indirectly from John Beckly [sic] clerk
of the House of Representatives, in whose custody the key of the chamber was, that those documents were the property of the United States
& that members of Congress had no right to
them. A few days after I found one of his favor-
ites: a member of the House selecting a number
of those papers. I then renewed my search &
in the course of the session procured a trunk
of them, which I sent home." [6]

Plumer continued his collections and four years
later possessed all copies of the *Congressional
Journal* from 1774 to 1806, as well as many
documents, the whole amounting to more than
70 volumes, although they did not constitute a
complete set. Finding that Otis would have the
journals bound and charge the cost to the government, Plumer had between 40 and 50 done
(the Clerk of the House maintained no such
practice). During December 1806 he spent two
hours daily, with the exception of Sundays, collecting. Towards the end of the month, Beckley
withheld the key from the librarian on duty.
Approached by Plumer, he was reluctant to give
it to him but finally consented to do so. Plumer
realized that his time was limited: "I was aware
that my spending so much time in this business
would induce other gentlemen to procure documents—& that the doors would soon be shut
against us all—I therefore pursued & closed my
search as soon as time would admit. I have procured a large box of these documents for the

*William Plumer's account of how he came to begin his
collection of congressional documents: "I found in
the large chamber over that of the Senate a great
body of them lying on the floor in promiscuous heaps."
From the William Plumer Papers, vol. 18, Autobiography. Manuscript Division. See also page 110.*

Massachusetts historical Society—& a large trunk
of them for my inquisitive friend Ichabod
Tucker, Esq. of Salem. . . . Neither of these two
collections of documents are half so large & extensive as mine. . . ." It was well that Plumer
made his collections, for many of these documents were housed in the lumber room for want
of any other place of storage. Here was kept the
glass for window replacements, which meant a
continual parade of workmen, unmindful of
where they stepped. The floor, where many of the
documents lay for want of shelves, was filthy with
plaster and rubbish and a leaking roof dripped
water over them.

By the end of 1806 Plumer reported approximately 2,000 volumes in the Library he considered a great boon to "this desert-city." Mr.
Kearney, the acting librarian appointed by Beckley, told Plumer that the Speaker of the House,
Nathaniel Macon, considered the Library "a useless expence" and would like to repeal the law
establishing it. Kearney said he had never known
Macon to borrow a book. Plumer noted that
Mitchill was one of those who had purchased
books with the 1806 appropriation, among which
was *The Secret History of the Court and Cabinet
of St. Cloud* (Philadelphia: John Watts, 1806),
an anonymous publication derogatory of Napoleon and his court. Plumer considered it a most
improper book for the Library, particularly since
Napoleon had complained to the British concerning a similar book. Bristling, Plumer immediately
approached Kearney and "asked him if that
book belonged to the library. He answered that
it did not. I told him I had seen it on the *written* additional catalogue. *He replied, it once
belonged to the library—but Dr. Mitchel had
withdrawn it.* I answered, I approve of that.
He said, *no book in the library was in so much
demand. It was constantly out—& in the Course
of a week it was several times read—The number
who took it for the week, read it, & lent it to
others.* Such a currency has scandal, especially
when its shafts are directed against a great man."
When Plumer questioned Mitchill, he was told

108. Aged 44. 1803

& reported an amendment, but when it was read in the senate I was so much embarrassed that I could not state the principles on which it was made. This circumstance surprised & mortified me, for I had long been in the habit of speaking freely in public.

Soon after my arrival at Washington I began to make a collection, for my own use, of the documents which had been printed by congress. I found in the large chamber over that of the senate a great body of them lying on the floor in promiscuous heaps. The practice of printing the documents commenced in 1789, & each member was furnished with a copy; & when a session terminated, several of the gentlemen not considering them of much value, or not having a convenient mode of carrying them home, left them & the door-keeper deposited them with the spare documents in a room appropriated to that purpose. After congress removed from Philadelphia these papers were transported in waggons to Washington & put into the place I mentioned. And at the end of each session the copies that remained were added to the heaps. To select from this vast mass a sett of the documents, was a laborious task, to which I devoted much of my leisure time. It is to the tedious days that I spent in that cold & damp chamber, that I am now indebted for a larger & more complete sett of those public papers than any other private individual in the nation possesses.

It to .... of New England could be maintained, it would

that the bookseller had mistakenly included it in the order. Acidly, Plumer noted in his memorandum, "How unwilling we are to own our errors, & how natural to charge them upon others." [7]

Beckley could not long suppress his love of city political affairs. He was soon involved in Washington city government, as he had been in Richmond and in Philadelphia. He was fourth in the number of votes received among nine men elected to the Second Chamber in June 1805, and he was soon acting as *President pro tem* of that body on numerous occasions. It is remarkable that he should have undertaken any of this, for he was entangled in serious legal problems concerning his land holdings in western Virginia, was desperately pressed financially, and was in extremely poor health. Although his health improved briefly from time to time, it

continued to deteriorate, and he died on April 8, 1807.

Like many great institutions, the Library of Congress began in a small way, beset by many problems. The first librarianship was a part-time appointment for an already very busy man. He held the office for only a few years and died before the Library was given much opportunity by Congress for rapid growth. There is, however, good reason to believe that Beckley took his duties seriously and that he foresaw future greatness for the Library. In his brief term as Librarian he established it as a well-organized and rapidly growing entity, enjoying the confidence of the Congress and the admiration of the public. On this firm foundation others have been able to build.

Postscript:

Beckley's death left his entire life savings tied up in a lawsuit which continued for the next 28 years. His wife, Maria, her mother, and his son, Alfred, were left without funds in a rather desperate situation. Even worse, there was the embarrassment of debts owed to Jefferson, Rush, and others who had rescued Beckley from the threat of debtors' prison during the "reign of terror," and whom he had never been able to completely repay. After various attempts to support herself, Maria found it necessary to make her home with Senator Brown's family and, later, the family of John Fowler in Kentucky. She died in Lexington in 1833. At the suggestion of Gen. William Henry Harrison, James Monroe appointed Alfred to West Point, from which he graduated in 1823. He had served at various military posts when the final settlement of his father's legal entanglement made him the sole heir to a very large and very valuable tract of unsettled land in what today is West Virginia. He resigned from the army and built the first house on what ultimately became the city of Beckley, which he named for his father.

NOTES

[1] "Autobiography" of Alfred Beckley, Paxton Davis Papers (made available by Prof. Paxton Davis, Washington and Lee University, who is a descendant of John Beckley).

[2] Andrew A. Lipscomb, ed., *The Writings of Thomas Jefferson,* 20 vols. (Washington: Thomas Jefferson Memorial Association of the United States, 1902), 19:128–29.

[3] Beckley to Benjamin Rush, 8 November, 1802, B1–2, pp. 96–97, Library Company of Philadelphia, Historical Society of Pennsylvania.

[4] Herman R. Friis, "Baron Alexander von Humboldt's Visit to Washington, D.C., June 1 through June 3, 1804," *Columbia Historical Society Records,* 1960–1962, p. 16.

[5] Joseph Gales, ed., *Debates and Proceedings in the Congress of the United States, 1789–1824,* 9th Congress, 1st Session, 19th February 1806 and 3 February 1806, p. 429.

[6] Everett Somerville Brown, ed., *William Plumer's Memorandum of Proceedings in the United States Senate 1803–1807* (New York: Macmillan Company, 1923), pp. 537–39.

[7] Ibid., p. 559.

ADDENDUM ON WILLIAM PLUMER

What follows is an excerpt from the William Plumer Papers, vol. 1, Diary, part 2, in the Manuscript Division, giving a full account of the New Hampshire Senator's "collecting activities."

William Plumer (1759–1850). From a reproduction of an engraving by St. Memins. Prints and Photographs Division.

576 *Dec 22. 1806.*

belong to Burr & his partizans—& to pre=
=vent them from descending the Ohio—
& to seize & arrest certain persons in
the western States.

Tuesday 23.

This day Robert Smith, the Secretary
of the Navy paid me a visit by leaving
his card at my lodging.

It has been the practice of Congress
to print the journals of their proceed=
=ings, the messages of the president,
the reports of the heads of departments— of
committees— board of commissioners of
the Sinking fund— &c &c &c. Of each of
these there has always been printed
supernumerary numbers, that is, more
than one for the President, Vice President,

Dec 23. 1806.   577

each senator & representative & head of departments, & who are regularly furnish= =ed with them. These spare copies, & such copies as the members leave in their drawers at the end of the session, are in the recess carried up in the large lumber room over the senate chamber.

~~when~~ I came here in Dec 1802, I was informed that each member of Congress was entitled to each document if he would take the trouble of selecting them. I accordingly began – selected & removed a considerable number, when I received a message, indirectly from John Beckly clerk of the House of Representatives, in whose custody the key of the chamber was,

578.   **Dec 23, 1806.**

that. those documents were the property
of the United States, & these members
of Congress had no right to them. A
few days after I found one of his favo=
=rites, a member of the House selecting
a number of those
papers. I then renewed my search
& in the course of the session procured
a trunk of them; which I sent home.
This session I have brot on a list of
those I obtained formerly, & have
now re examined the whole mass
that remained in the chamber. I
have obtained all the journals of
Congress from 1774 to this time, except
the journal of the Senate of their first session —

Dec 23 1806.   579

and a great many documents – more
than 70 volumes – but not a compleat
sett. Some of those I have are of
little value – but my object was to
get all ~~not having~~ time to discrimi=
=nate the useful & important from
the useless & trivial.

The key is now kept by Mr Kearney
the librarian, who owes his appointment
to Beckley. To the librarian I owe ma=
=ny thanks for his politeness & attention.
I have every day, sundays excepted,
this ~~morning~~ spent two hours in that
chamber. Near the close of it. the last
day, I discovered a disposition in
Beckley to withhold the key from
me. The librarian was deprived of
it. I went to Beckley requested, and

<u>580</u> <u>Dec 23, 1806</u>

he with great reluctance gave it to me. I was aware that my spending so much time in this busi= =ness would induce other gentlemen & that the doors would soon be shut against us all to procure documents. I therefore pursued & closed my search as soon as time would admit.

I have procured a large box of these documents for the Massachusetts historical Society. & a large trunk of them for my inquisitive friend Icha= =bod Tucker Esq of Salem. With this Society they will long be preserved & rendered useful. Mr Tucker contemplates a compilation of facts relative to this Country. in which these documents will aid him.

Dec 23, 1806.   581

Neither of these two collections of documents are half so large & extensive as mine— tho' as much so as I was able to make them.

The documents, principally, lay on the floor without any order—covered & mixed up with dirt, plaster and rubbish. They are much diminished since 1802. The water, on every rain, that falls, runs thro' the roof & wets these papers. They will soon be destroyed— They are trodden under foot by workmen —for in the same room are a great quan =tity of glass in baskets with straw— window sashes &c. The new edition of the Journals of the old Congress, which the United States have lately purchased are in the same situation. It is really a pity that documents, some of which are

582 <u>Dec 23, 1806.</u>

so valuable, should be suffered thus wan=
=tonly to be destroyed.

The quantity of water on the papers,
the dirt & filth in the chamber, has
rendered it unhealthy. and I greatly
rejoice that I have fulfilled the task
I imposed upon myself — & that I have
resened so many useful papers from
inevitable ruin.

At the session of 1803, I found it was
the practice of the Secretary of the Senate
to pay for the binding of the journals and
documents. Since that period I have had
about 40 ~~only 15 volumes~~ volumes bound at the
expence of the United States. This practice
has not been adopted by the Clerk of the House.

<u>Wednesday 24.th</u>
At the second election of President and,

Patrick Magruder

Citizen, Congressman, Librarian of Congress

by Martin K. Gordon

ONE of seven sons and four daughters of Revolutionary War Major Samuel Wade Magruder, Patrick Magruder was born in 1768 at "Locust Grove," the family estate in Montgomery County, Md. His father was one of the first justices of the county court when Montgomery County was separated from Frederick County in 1776. Prominent locally, he was also active in real estate speculation and operated a grist mill on his estate.[1]

Patrick attended Princeton College and returned home without graduating to become a lawyer. Apparently he had already suffered from the ill health that was to plague him throughout his life and that would force him to be out of Washington in 1814, when he was most needed there. In 1804 James McHenry, a Baltimorean and former secretary of war, wrote his nephew that he should not leave Princeton just because he worried about his health, holding up Magruder, who had been able to return to that school when his health improved, as an example.[2]

In the 1790's, the young attorney married Sallie Turner of Georgetown and had one daughter, Louisa, by this marriage. Becoming active in politics, he served in 1797 as a member of the Maryland House of Delegates from Montgomery County, his place being taken the following year by Robert P. Magruder, a relative of Patrick's.

By June 1799 at the latest, he had become a justice of the peace and was active in the area of the county near Georgetown. In 1802 he became an associate judge of the county circuit court.[3]

Magruder ran for the U.S. House of Representatives in 1801, losing to his Federalist neighbor Thomas Plater by 111 votes out of the 1,817 ballots cast in that election. In the spring of 1803, he endorsed a qualified Federalist who had other bipartisan support for the office of county surveyor. When the Democratic-controlled State Council appointed a lesser known Democrat as county surveyor, Magruder wrote what one paper called a "very insulting letter" to the council and resigned his commission as an associate judge of the circuit court. In the letter he suggested that someone in Annapolis, the state capital, knew Montgomery County well enough to make its recommendations better than its own residents could.[4]

Patrick Magruder, second Librarian of Congress.

Martin K. Gordon is a historian with the Reference Section, History and Museums Division, Headquarters, U.S. Marine Corps. He is also currently engaged in completing his doctoral dissertation in the joint LC–George Washington University doctoral program.

In August 1803 Magruder officially declared himself a Republican candidate for election to the Eighth Congress (1803–05). Partisan sniping had already begun the month before, however, when the local Republican newspaper accused the Federalists of trying to dictate from their Frederick County strongholds to the electors for the Congressional District made up of Montgomery County and part of Frederick County whom they should elect to the U.S. House of Representatives. Not only did Plater run for reelection but also his fellow Federalist Richard Wootton entered the contest along with Magruder. The Republicans accused the Federalists of trying to settle the problem of which candidate they would select behind the closed doors of a caucus without giving the people a chance to decide the question for themselves.

As the campaign heated up in August, the Federalists declared in mass meetings that their candidates were the better men, and the Republicans accused Plater of being a Tory and subservient to Frederick County interests. The Republicans also prided themselves on choosing their candidate by an open meeting rather than through a secretive caucus. Thus in 1803 three candidates, two Federalists and a Republican, ran for the seat in Congress to represent Montgomery County and part of Frederick County.[5]

Wootton, the second Federalist candidate, was accused of being a false candidate, not a true member of the party. His defenders replied that Magruder had carried Montgomery County in the last election and that only Frederick votes had kept Plater in office. Magruder, therefore, could only be defeated by another Montgomery resident, i.e., Wootton.

Magruder lost this election with 1,075 votes compared to Plater's 1,126 and Wootton's 43 votes in Frederick County alone. The local Republican newspaper published these results in tabular form for comparison with the previous election. The returns indicated, at least to the editor, that the new democratization of the electoral procedure—the dropping of the £30 property requirement for voters and the new written ballot—resulted in continued good prospects for the future of the Republican Party. This table analyzed Plater's declining victory margins to show that if a united Republican Party turned out in large numbers for the next election, it should carry both counties for its congressional candidate.[6]

A change in the election laws forced an election for the House of Representatives a year later. Trying again in 1804, Magruder once more faced his neighbor Plater. This fall campaign resulted in the usual tactics. When the Republicans heralded Magruder as distinguished, the Federalists asked "in what?" In turn, Republicans again accused the Frederick Federalists of attempting to control Montgomery County for their own ends. Through a combination of Federalist apathy, a disciplined Republican turnout, and a general move toward Republicanism in the state, Patrick Magruder, on his third try, was elected to the House of Representatives.

This election saw the Republicans gain two House seats for control of seven out of the nine allotted the state and also gain six General Assembly members for a majority of 52 to 28 in that body. Interestingly, Magruder owed his victory to his Frederick County constituency, which gave him a majority of 424 votes compared with Plater's 220-vote margin in Montgomery, where Republicans had complained the most about outside domination. Both candidates, after all, were from the same part of Montgomery County near Georgetown, D.C.[7]

Magruder's service in the Ninth Congress was rather ordinary. He did not make any major speeches. This attorney from the District of Columbia suburbs is mentioned principally for his service during both sessions on the committee analyzing the highly controversial proposal for a bridge linking the city of Washington with Alexandria. Although the committee reported out bills in favor of this aid to Washington-Alexandria commerce, Magruder voted with the minority against it, thus supporting Georgetown's claim to regional commercial supremacy as maintained by their control of the one bridge then spanning the Potomac and their open access from the ocean. This bill was later defeated in the Senate.[8]

The new Congressman was not able to hold his seat for the Republicans, however. After a bitter campaign, this was the only Maryland House of Representatives seat lost by the party in 1806. Philip Barton Key, the uncle of Francis Scott Key, had moved to Georgetown that year from Annapolis and purchased a summer estate in Montgomery County, which he then claimed as his place of residence and challenged Magruder for his place in Congress. In the months before the election, the Republicans accused Key of being in the pay of the British monarchy and thus a Tory. Furthermore, they claimed that his family had attempted to profiteer during the Revolution and that, anyway, he was a resident of the District of Columbia and not Maryland and thus ineligible to run in this election.[9]

The British ambassador, who was accused of secretly aiding Key's election efforts, caught the flavor of the campaign in his diary. Reporting on the orations given when both candidates appeared at the same barbecue, he observed:

Magruder, Key's opponent, talked of his blood being allied nearly to the whole District and insisted that he was therefore naturally the fittest Person to represent and maintain their Interests, but Key retorted that if the Question were about a Steed that argument might be good. It was not, however, in Discussion which of the two, he or this Rival, were of the best Breed, but which would make the best Member of Congress, when the Head was more worthy to be considered than the Blood, and he was accordingly preferred. . . .[10]

That October Magruder once again carried his Frederick County constituents with 964 votes which gave him a nine-vote margin over Key. His home jurisdiction deserted him, however, and gave Philip Barton Key 980 votes for a majority of 248 over Magruder in Montgomery County and an overall victory of 239 votes. In reporting these results, the local Federalist newspaper gloated, "rudeness and insolence will always meet with their proper reward, contempt and defeat." [11]

Magruder's term as a member of the Ninth Congress ended on March 3, 1807. John Beckley, Clerk of the House of Representatives and first Librarian of Congress, died a month later, on April 8, 1807.[12] When the 10th Congress convened on October 26, 1807, it found itself confronted with eight applicants for the vacant Clerkship of the House. The Representatives proceeded to elect a new Clerk as soon as they had organized and chosen a Speaker on the 26th. The tellers declared the first ballot for a new Clerk invalid when they discovered one of the Representatives had voted twice. Nicholas Van Zandt of Georgetown, Beckley's chief clerk in the last Congress, led the next ballot with 37 votes

compared with 26 for Magruder in second place and 16 votes for the third-place candidate, James Elliot. Josias W. King was in fourth place with 10 votes. Interestingly, Van Zandt, Elliot, and King were all on President Jefferson's May 30 list of candidates for the position of Librarian of Congress. A total of 59 votes was needed to win this position. On the third ballot, Van Zandt picked up 15 votes to fall only seven short of victory. Magruder gained two votes, one candidate dropped out, and the others all lost ground.

This routine was about to continue to another tally when John Randolph of Roanoke interrupted the procedure. No longer the power he once was in the House Chamber, he was still listened to when he implicated Van Zandt as one of the assistant clerks who in the previous Congress had not properly maintained the secrecy of a closed session of the House of Representatives. Thus accused of impropriety with confidential matters, Van Zandt, then acting as Clerk of the House, requested permission to speak in his own defense. The Speaker of the House turned down this request on the ground that it would set a new and unusual precedent. The Representatives then defeated motions to investigate the charge. They went directly to another ballot in which Magruder jumped to first place with 52 votes, James Elliot went to second place with 27 votes, and Van Zandt fell back to third with only 16 votes. Another vote was immediately taken, and Magruder finally won the trials with 72 votes. The tellers did not even bother to announce the tallies of the other candidates.[13]

Apparently Magruder was simply the accidental beneficiary of Randolph's real concern over Van Zandt's ability to meet the obligations of the Clerk of the House. The Representatives must have agreed with Randolph, or they would not have so quickly refused Van Zandt's plea for a hearing on the accusation. Later, when Van Zandt applied for a position with the Senate, John Quincy Adams argued that he was unfit for a position with that body.[14]

Also, still on the 26th, the day of Magruder's victory in the House, three Congressmen suggested his name to Jefferson as a likely choice for the position of Librarian of Congress. These Republicans, Willis Alston, Jr., and Thomas Kenan of North Carolina and John Smilie of Pennsylvania, wrote simply in the only known application of Magruder for this position, "Mr. Magruder having been appointed Clerk of the H. R. U. S. we recommend him to your notice as a proper person to be appointed librarian." [15]

His selection was not as automatic as it might seem, however. Jefferson, who had statutory responsibility for appointing the Librarian of Congress, was not convinced in his own mind that he wanted to give the post to whoever might be the Clerk of the House of Representatives. This doubt arose because of his friendship for one of Magruder's many competitors for the position. As of May 30 when Jefferson compiled his "Review of Appointments Wanting," there were 13 applicants listed for the vacancy of Librarian in Washington. Magruder's name was submitted on October 26. On December 12, 1808, long after Jefferson filled the vacancy, he received an application for it from J. Philip Reibelt, a French correspondent of his who was trapped in New Orleans by the embargo and needed a job. [16]

On April 9, 1807, the day after Beckley, the Clerk and Librarian, died, James Kearney of Washington applied for the Librarian's job. He stressed his professional education and his training as Beckley's deputy. Josias W. King, who had sought the position in 1802 and who also became a candidate for the Clerkship of the House, applied again for the Librarian's opening on April 10. In his application he reminded the President of the Congressmen who had endorsed his 1802 application and that, even though he had not received the appointment, he had still had care of the Library for some years as Beckley's assistant. The same day, Caesar A. Rodney, Jefferson's attorney general, wrote Jefferson among other matters that "Poor Beckley was buried today. Gov. Clinton requested me to mention to you Mr. Van Zandt as his [Beckley's] successor as librarian. The V. President [Clinton] seems anxious on the subject. . . ." [17] This part of Van Zandt's application took the same indirect form that Magruder's application for the position took six months later. Also, he was to be Magruder's closest opponent for the Clerkship when the House convened that October.

On April 11 William Mayne Duncanson, also of Washington, applied for the position. His application merely hinted that he was in great financial need. Finally, on May 8, after news of Beckley's death spread across the country, a

George Clark of Greencastle, Pa., wrote Albert Gallatin, Jefferson's secretary of the treasury and close associate, that his son-in-law, Dr. Patterson, lived in Washington and could use the job of Librarian of Congress. [18]

The Librarianship paid two dollars per day. James Kearney in his letter suggested that he had independent means and thus could devote the necessary time to the Library without the distractions which would preoccupy any other person applying for it. Patterson and King stressed their need for the income from the position. Duncanson not only needed the money but was also interested in using the collections, which meant to him that "the salary tho trifling, will be doubled to me by having the use of the Library." This was the application which nearly caused the President to break the precedent he had set when he had appointed Beckley, the Clerk of the House, to the additional post of Librarian. Jefferson had nearly appointed Duncanson marshal of the District of Columbia in 1801. He had been a loyal Republican Washingtonian from the days when the city was a Federalist stronghold and in the last few years had lost his independent means of wealth. Unfortunately for him, Jefferson was "a little puzzled . . . between doubt and inclination" over whether or not he should appoint Duncanson, who had been involved in Miranda's filibustering expedition to Venezuela in 1806 and may have had some knowledge of Aaron Burr's conspiracies, for which Burr was then standing trial in Richmond. Jefferson knew that Duncanson had been honest but was worried that his appointment would not be popular in Congress. [19]

Jefferson certainly had other problems on his mind as he commuted between Washington and Monticello. In addition to the Burr trial, that summer saw continuing British impressment of American seamen and, above all, the unprovoked attack of the British warship H.M.S. *Leopard* on the U.S. frigate *Chesapeake*. Apparently Jefferson decided not to risk Duncanson's appointment, and it was not until James Madison appointed George Watterston the third Librarian

City of Washington, April 10th 1807.

Sir,

The death of Mr John Beckley having vacated the office of Librarian to Congress, I beg leave Sir, to renew the application I had the honor to make at the time of the passing of the act establishing the Library.— Altho' I was disappointed in that application, yet the arrangement of the Library and duties of the appointment devolved on and were by me performed for a considerable time, being then a clerk in the office of the House of Representatives of the United States.

I deem it Sir, unnecessary to forward the recommendations for your perusal, which I had the honor to transmit you on my former application, but Sir, you will very much gratify and relieve a family, who at present seek assistance from the government of their native Country.

I have the Honor to be
With Great respect,
Sir, Your Obt Hle Servt
Josias Wilson King.

The President of the United States.

Sir   *Washington Nov. 6.07.*

I have this day directed a commission to be made out for you as Librarian to Congress. mr Van Zandt having been charged pro tem. with the care of the books since the death of mr Beckley, you will be pleased to receive that charge from him. I salute you with esteem & respect

mr. Magruder   *Th: Jefferson*

of Congress in March 1815 that the offices of Clerk and Librarian were separated.

Jefferson did not act until after Congress convened that October and elected its officials. On November 6, less than two weeks after Magruder's application for the position and about six months after the bulk of the other applications were submitted, he tersely wrote Magruder, "I have this day directed a commission to be made out for you as Librarian of Congress. Mr. Van Zandt having been charged pro tem with the care of the books since the death of Mr. Beckley, you will be pleased to receive that charge from him."

The same day, the President also wrote to Van Zandt, "Considering it as the surest course for the performance of my duty in appointing a keeper to the library of Congress, to follow their choice in the selection of their officers, I have conceived the election of Mr. Magruder as successor to Mr. Beckley as designating him also as his successor as Librarian." He then advised Van Zandt on the necessary paperwork for him to receive a salary for the interim period he had spent in charge of the Library.[20]

Beckley had largely delegated the day-to-day operations of the Library to one of his assistants,

Thomas Jefferson's letter of November 6, 1807, to Magruder informing him of his appointment as Librarian. Jefferson Papers, Manuscript Division.

On November 6, 1807, Jefferson also informed Nicholas Van Zandt, who had been acting as Librarian since Beckley's death, that Patrick Magruder was to take over as "keeper to the Library of Congress." Jefferson Papers, Manuscript Division.

as the two of Magruder's competitors who had been assistants pointed out in their letters of application for the job of Librarian. Magruder continued this tradition and was not much involved in the routine of the Library of Congress. This, of course, was based on the normal practice in libraries at the time. Librarians were regarded as custodial employees whose main tasks were to shelve and to circulate books; selection and procurement was left to a committee of the governing board of the institution involved. This same committee, as a rule, also handled the financial affairs of the library.[21] So by delegating some librarian's chores to one of his assistants, Magruder was not neglecting his major responsibilities.

For example, the Joint Committee on the Library of Congress published reports during two

Nov. 6. 07.

Sir

Considering it as the surest course for the performance of my duty in appointing a keeper to the library of Congress, to follow their choice in the selection of their officers, I have concurred the election of mr Magruder as successor to mr Beckley as designating him also as his successor as Librarian. I have therefore directed a commission as such to be made out for him. I do not know whether the rules of the Treasury will require a regular commission pro tem. to you for the time you have had it in charge. but that, or any other voucher which their forms require. for entitling you to the salary from mr Beckley's death to the meeting of Congress shall be furnished on being made known to me. I present you my salutations & respects.

Mr. Van Zandt.

Th: Jefferson

of the years that Magruder was Librarian, 1808 and 1809. These reports were in three parts: a letter of transmittal signed by Senator Samuel L. Mitchill, chairman of the committee; a list of donations received by the Library since the last list was published; and the report of the Treasury Department auditor on the account of Joseph Nourse, the committee's official agent for the purchase of books. James Kearney, who was apparently working as Magruder's assistant, not having received the post of Librarian himself, signed the list of gifts received in the 1808 report. The next report did not contain any names of Library personnel at all. The emphasis was on book selection and library finances, neither being the concern of the Librarian.[22]

A major preoccupation of the Joint Committee on the Library seems to have been the actual selection of books for the Library, as the members of the committee habitually drew the funds appropriated for that purpose directly from the Treasury. The committee decided on March 31, 1806, that the principal part of the purchase fund should be spent by three of its members, during a recess, in collecting books in Boston, New York, and Philadelphia. On February 28, 1807, the committee met without a majority present and still drew its annual appropriation out of the Treasury. They accomplished this by obtaining the signature of an absent member and then presenting the order at the Treasury. Again, the sum was divided three ways for book purchases.

At a meeting on November 20, 1807, they divided up the chores of writing the annual report,
preparing a new book catalog of the Library's
holdings, and calling on the President to discuss
the library facilities. There is no mention of the
Librarian of Congress attending any of these
meetings.[23]

The most important means of access to the
contents of a library before the development of
reference services and the card catalog was its
published book catalog. The first Library of Congress published book catalog came out in 1802,
with a supplement in 1803. The next catalog appeared in 1804, and then there was a hiatus until
the 40-page 1808 catalog appeared, tripling the
13-page size of its predecessor. It is questionable
to what extent Magruder involved himself in the
production of these catalogs. The 101-page 1812
catalog, listing slightly over 3,000 volumes and
maps, abandoned the earlier approach of organizing the books by size and instead divided them
into 16 subject and two form categories, making
the Library of Congress the sixth library in the
United States to publish this more helpful, broadly classed type of catalog. It was beginning to
be established in the first part of the 19th century that librarians, rather than supervising committees or boards, were responsible for compiling
the published catalogs. At a Library Committee
meeting of November 20, 1807, it was decided
that one of its members, Representative Samuel
W. Dana of Connecticut, would superintend "the
making and printing of a new list of the books." [24]
The rules of the Library of Congress required the
Librarian to "preserve due lists and catalogues"
of the books under his care, but given the customs
of the time and Magruder's sporadic ill health
as well as his delegation of operational control
of the Library, it is impossible to state what Magruder's role might have been in the production
of these catalogs other than his routine obligation
as Clerk of the House to oversee their printing
for the Joint Committee of Congress.[25]

There were several other changes in the Library during this period of Magruder's tenure.
The 1808 catalog promulgated a set of rules and
regulations for the governance of the Library
of Congress. These rules, revised in the 1812
catalog, spelled out the procedures for the routine operations of the Library. They held the
Librarian responsible for circulating, labeling,

*These 1808 rules and regulations specify the duties of
the Librarian and the stringent terms under which
Congressmen were allowed to borrow books. Manuscript Division.*

shelving, and listing the books as well as keeping a record of all expenses related to the Library
which were authorized by law. The Librarian
also had to issue to and receive from the Secretary of the Senate and the Clerk of the House
at the beginning and end of each session complete
sets of the laws and journals of the Congress
deposited in the Library for that specific purpose.
This clause indicates that it was not automatically assumed in these regulations that the Librarian of Congress would always be the Clerk of
the House. He also had to recover any books
charged out to any Congressman by the end of
the session in which they were charged out, as
well as to collect any overdue fines. His fine
money was to be turned over to the Joint Committee on the Library when they should request
it. Congress in these years continued its liberal
circulation policies and extended the privilege of
checking books out of the Library to the Agent
of the Joint Committee, Joseph Nourse, and to
the Justices of the United States Supreme Court.
Congress also renewed its annual $1,000 appro-
priation for the purchase of books.[26]

Although a Washingtonian and a congressional
employee, Magruder retained his interest in
Montgomery County and Georgetown politics.
On December 4, 1807, less than a month after
President Jefferson had appointed him Librarian
of Congress, he wrote Jefferson from his clerk's
office recommending Benjamin G. Orr for appointment to the vacant position of marshal of
the District of Columbia. He supported Orr as
"My fellow laborer in the cause of republicanism
in the County of Montgomery." Attached to this
letter was a petition supporting Magruder's
recommendation from 12 prominent Georgetown
residents, including Patrick's brother, George,
two former mayors of that city, and several ex-
militia officers. This practice of congressional or
other political support for an applicant for a
District of Columbia office was quite common.
Nevertheless, Washington Boyd, the previous
marshal's former deputy, was chosen for this
position.[27]

The following October, along with six prominent District residents, Magruder signed a peti-

RULES

AND

REGULATIONS

To be observed in the LIBRARY OF CONGRESS,

I. THE Library shall be opened every day during the session of Congress, and for one week preceding and subsequent thereto, Sundays excepted, from nine o'clock in the morning, to three o'clock in the afternoon, and from five o'clock to seven in the evening.

II. IN the recess of Congress, it shall be opened three days in every week, during the hours aforesaid, to wit : on Tuesday, Thursday and Saturday,

III. IT shall be the duty of the Librarian to label and number the Books, place them on the shelves, and preserve due lists and catalogues of the same. He shall also keep due account and register of all issues and returns of books as the same shall be made, together with regular accounts of all expences incident to the said Library, and which are authorized by law.

IV. BOOKS, to be issued by the Librarian pursuant to law, shall be returned as follows :

> *A Folio, within three*
> *A Quarto, within two* } WEEK,
> *An Octavo or Duodecimo, within one*

And no member shall receive more than one folio, one quarto, or two octavo's or duodecimo's, within the terms aforesaid, unless where so connected as to be otherwise useless.

V. FOR all books issued, a receipt or note shall be given, of double the value thereof, as near as can be estimated, conditioned to return the same, undefaced within the term above mentioned, or to forfeit the amount of such note ; at the expiration of which, unless application has been made by another person for the same book, and the Librarian requested to take a memorandum thereof, the said Librarian, upon the books being produced to him, may renew the issue of the same for the time and on the conditions aforesaid : *Provided,* That every receipt or note shall contain a further forfeiture or penalty for every day's detention of a book beyond the specified term, that is to say : for

> *A Folio—three dollars per day.*
> *A Quarto—two dollars per day.*
> *An Octavo—one dollar per day——*Which forfeiture or penalty may, for good cause, be remitted by the President of the Senate and Speaker of the House of Representatives for the time being, in whole or in part, as the case may require.

VI. WHEN a member shall prefer to take a book for the limited time, without removing it from the Library, he shall be allowed to do so without giving a receipt or note for the same, and to preserve his priority for the use of such book for the time limited, in like manner as if he had withdrawn the book from the Library, and given a receipt or note therefor. And the Librarian shall keep due account and entry of all such cases.

VII. BOOKS returned shall be delivered to the Librarian, to be examined whether damaged or not.

VIII. IF a book be returned damaged, the party returning it shall not be entitled to receive another until the damage for the first shall be satisfied.

IX. NO book shall be issued within one week of the termination of any session of Congress.

X. ALL books shall be returned three days before the close of a session, whether the time allowed for the use thereof be expired or not.

tion which asked Jefferson to find an appointment for James H. Blake, of Georgetown, a long-time Republican who had become poor through investing in District of Columbia real estate at the wrong times. The result of this petition is not known, but Dr. Blake did recover sufficiently from his losses to join some of the most socially acceptable Washingtonians in planning President Madison's inaugural ball the following March.[28]

On May 22, 1809, the 11th Congress convened, and Magruder automatically came up for reelection as Clerk of the House. He handily won his position on the first ballot with 63 votes to 38 for his nearest competitor, Daniel C. Brent, a friend of Jefferson's and the man who had vacated the position of marshal of the District in the winter of 1807 to become the chief clerk of the State Department. Nicholas B. Van Zandt, Magruder's principal rival in 1807 at the time of the 10th Congress, came in third with 14 votes, and there were two other minor candidates. On November 4, 1811, at the start of the 12th "War Hawk" Congress, Magruder won reelection without any recorded opposition at all. Patrick Magruder came up for his fourth election bid as Clerk of the House on May 24, 1813. The 13th Congress then reelected him Clerk with 111 votes, and just as had happened two years earlier, stenographers in the House did not even bother to record his opposition.[29]

On May 30, 1811, Patrick married Martha Goodwyn, the eldest daughter of Col. Peterson Goodwyn, a Democrat who had been in the House of Representatives when Magruder was a member and who continued to serve in that body until his death on February 21, 1818. The marriage ceremony was conducted at his father-in-law's plantation "Sweden," near Petersburg, Va., and it was there that Patrick Magruder and his wife settled after he resigned his congressional posts in 1815. They had two children, Adelina Virginia and Napoleon Bonaparte. Both before and after his marriage, Magruder was occasionally seen at presidential parties, and after their marriage, Martha accompanied him to these functions.[30]

The Clerk/Librarian was active in local Masonic affairs. He belong to the old Federal Lodge No. 15 of the Maryland Grand Lodge and was a delegate to the meeting of the Georgetown and Washington Lodges which established the independent Grand Lodge of the District of Columbia. When Lodge No. 15 was reconstituted as Federal Lodge No. 1 of the District of Columbia in February 1811, Magruder served as its first junior warden. In addition, the Magruders had an informal but active social life because of their proximity to the Library of Congress, which also served as a Capitol Hill social facility.[31]

In December 1813 Magruder's ill health returned, and on the ninth, three days after the opening of the second session of the 13th Congress, the House of Representatives voted approval of George Magruder, his brother and his chief clerk in the Office of the Clerk, as acting Clerk of the House.[32]

On August 24, 1814, Patrick Magruder was on sick leave at the Springs of Virginia, having left Washington toward the end of July. On the evening of that August date, the British army captured the city of Washingon and burned the United States Capitol and with it the Library of Congress. President James Madison immediately called Congress into session, convening it on September 19, 1814. Magruder, back in Washington by then, wrote the Speaker of the House the next day. He reported the destruction of not only the Library but also the vouchers which proved that he had properly spent the government funds entrusted to his office. He asked for a congressional investigation into both the conduct of his office before the fire and his accounts and the handling of the funds for which he was responsible. The Speaker promptly appointed a select committee, chaired by Joseph Pearson of North Carolina, to investigate the circumstances discussed in Magruder's letter.[33]

Magruder had appended to his letter a statement which he had received on September 15 from J. T. Frost, who had charge of the Library of Congress for Magruder, and one of his clerks, Samuel Burch. This letter set forth the basic facts about the destruction of the office records and the books of the Library.

Washington had appeared peaceful and safe when Magruder left the city, they claimed. But on August 19, the entire militia had been called up for service, and all the clerks, except the overage Frost, responded. Two days later, in the field, Col. George Magruder, Patrick's chief clerk, arranged to have Burch furloughed to return to the

An artist's conception of the British using Library books to kindle the fire in the Capitol, published more than 50 years after the event. From Harper's New Monthly Magazine *46 (December 1872): 44.*

Capitol to assist Frost if it became necessary to evacuate the records. George Magruder ordered them not to begin packing their records until the clerks at the War Department began to evacuate their files. On noon of the 22d, Burch and Frost discovered that the War Department staff had already been evacuating their files for a day. Frost immediately began packing the records, while Burch went in search of transportation. Having started after the army and the government agencies had cornered most of the available wagons in the city and when private citizens were fleeing in those that were left, all Burch could acquire was the use of a cart and four oxen from a man who lived six miles from the city. They set to work and were able to evacuate most of their valuable items nine miles into the country. Finally, on the morning of the Battle of Bladensburg, they were forced to stop work. After the battle, Frost was able to move some of the remaining records into a nearby house just to get them out of the Capitol. Unfortunately, the British also set fire to this house.

Especially unfortunate for Patrick Magruder was their neglect of his fiscal records, although they saved almost all the other papers. As they reported,

We regret very much the loss of your private accounts and vouchers, amongst which . . . were the receipts and accounts of the expenditure of the con-

tingent moneys of the House of Representatives; they were in the private drawer of Mr. George Magruder, which being locked, and the key not in our possession, we delayed to break it open until the last extremity, after which it escaped our recollection.

This loss included all of Congress' financial records relating to the Library of Congress. The loss of the Library of Congress financial records was not a concern of Magruder's, however, because the Joint Committee which controlled the purchase fund had always dealt directly with an agent at the Treasury Department, and they simply asked him to reconstruct these records as best he could from the preserved Treasury files.[34]

Through the fall and winter, as this select committee deliberated, the executive departments reported their losses to Congress, as requested, noting that all of their useful current records had been preserved in every case. Apparently of all the government agencies, Magruder's office was

the most impaired by the British destruction. The committee reported on December 12, 1814. It had divided its investigation into three subjects.

The first was the availability of transportation for the removal of the records of the House for safekeeping. It secured reports from the Treasury, War, and Navy Departments on how they had managed to save their records. It then concluded on this point that the clerks of the House had not even begun to make any effort to save their records until the afternoon of August 22, about the time that the other agencies were completing their evacuations started two and one-half days earlier.

The committee did not go into the nature of Magruder's indisposition which required him to leave Washington at that serious time, but for its second conclusion it observed, "due precaution and diligence were not exercised to prevent

"A View of the Capitol of the United States after the Conflagration of 24th August 1814," by W. Strickland after G. Munger. Construction of the Capitol was not complete—the two wings had not been permanently joined—when the fire destroyed much of the interior. Prints and Photographs Division.

the destruction and loss which has been sustained."

The Congressmen devoted most of their attention to Magruder's financial records, inasmuch as these were the only important files not saved from the British. They accepted the reports of the destruction of the records as true but were greatly annoyed at Magruder's resistance to their reconstruction of his accounts. He disclaimed any knowledge of the financial affairs of his office and referred the committee to George Magruder, his chief clerk, who in turn refused to identify his specific accounts and the expenditures made in each one. George Magruder admitted receiving $50,863.16 from the Treasury and claimed, in a three-line statement, routine expenditures of $45,000 and congressional newspaper subscriptions of roughly $3,000, leaving an unaccounted sum of $2,863.16.

Patrick and George Magruder had other financial problems at this time. Patrick was sued by Buller Cocke, a local politician and innkeeper, for $593.44 that November. George had borrowed that sum from Patrick and given him a promissory note for it. Patrick in turn had endorsed the note over to Cocke, who, in due course, presented it for payment at the appropriate time. George Magruder refused payment, and following the procedure of the era, Cocke sued Patrick Magruder and in the winter of 1816 won a $1,000 judgment against him.[35]

Against this background, the committee felt that George Magruder's report was "great and unprecedented" in terms of its expenditures and unsatisfactory in terms of specific details. The committeemen then examined the books of the Magruders' checking accounts and the records of their principal suppliers, interviewed other House staff members, and compared these figures with the amount Patrick Magruder had satisfactorily accounted for when he had last settled his accounts at the Treasury in January 1814. This tabulation revealed, among other things, that Mr. Frost had been paid $20 at periodic intervals for his work in the Library of Congress,

which was considered additional to his duties as a clerk in the House. Also, Roger Weightman, who held most of the House's printing contracts in this period, noted on a duplicate receipt that he gave the committee that once when he had needed money to pay a subcontractor, Patrick had paid him out of George's checking account at the Bank of Washington.

In its analysis, the committee confirmed the sum of $50,863.16 as the amount to be accounted for. It then computed $30,988.57½ as the total which Patrick Magruder might properly have spent in the period for which the vouchers were destroyed and asked that the House of Representatives, by resolution, credit him for that amount. He still had to account for the remaining $19,874.58½. The House ordered this report printed but took no other action at that time.[36]

Patrick Magruder lost no time replying to this report. Five days after its release, on December 17, 1814, he answered its charges. He first defended his absence both in terms of his health, because his physicians advised him to leave Washington for the Springs, and in terms of the calmness of the city. No one at that time had expected a British assault on the Capital. Magruder next answered the charge of lack of planning. He furnished documentation that all of his staff, with the exception of old Mr. Frost, had been called up for active service, with his chief assistant George Magruder actually serving as a regimental commander. Thus, they could not have moved his files to safety until one of them, Burch, was released for that purpose. The executive department heads, he continued, could start evacuating earlier because they were better informed than his office clerks. Furthermore, most of their clerks were over 45 years old and thus had remained in their offices and could spend their time packing rather than in military service. The embattled Clerk devoted most of his attention to his financial arrangements. He defended his ignorance of the handling of money in his office as being standard procedure in all the departments wherein the principal clerk handled the records although the head of the office signed for the authenticity of the expenditures. Furthermore, he claimed that the House Committee on Accounts had approved all of his expenses. He reiterated that if only the vouchers had not been destroyed, he could prove all of his expenditures. Neither he nor George

Magruder could remember all their payments, but they hoped that an advertisement in the local paper asking their contractors to submit duplicate receipts might clear up this matter to Congress' satisfaction.

The House took Magruder's reply under consideration, and Congressman Pearson's select committee formally answered it on January 16, 1815. The committee clarified its criticisms of Magruder. It emphasized that in regard to the absence of the clerks, the problem was in the failure to provide the means of transportation for removing the records. This was a task which Mr. Frost either could have done himself or could have hired someone from outside the staff to do. By referring to the report of the select committee inquiring into the causes of the invasion of the city, the members emphatically disagreed with the Magruders' contention that the city was in no danger that summer.

Again devoting the bulk of the report to Magruder's fiscal records, the committee commented that Magruder's letter did not provide any new information but consisted of "inferences derived, in most respects, from incorrect premises, and from information given by his chief clerk, and not from any information of his own." It seemed that the Committee of Accounts had approved Magruder's drawing advances from the Treasury so that he could make advances on his contracts and in general meet his bills in advance of settlement and audit when necessary. Thus they hadn't always approved his expenses as he had claimed. Furthermore, there were errors in what specifications Magruder did present to the committee, e.g., at least one messenger was paid for one month longer than the session for which he had been hired. More importantly, several thousands of dollars worth of bills which the Magruders claimed had been paid with the missing vouchers had been paid the previous year when George Magruder had last had his account audited and settled at the Treasury Department. The committee went on to note that Magruder had paid many of his 1813 bills at the last minute so that at the time of his January 1814 audit and settlement, he could properly report the expenditure of his funds. Even then, he was still holding $6,000 for which he could not provide the proper receipts. The Magruders had even been unable to tell the committee which bank this

balance was in. This was information the committee had had to determine by investigation. Furthermore, George Magruder was unable to describe any one bill he had paid between January 15, 1814, when with the $6,000 balance still outstanding he drew another $10,000, and March 12, when he drew another $9,288.29 allegedly for the payment of outstanding accounts. This was a total of almost $26,000 he had held in a period when he could not prove or even describe any payments made against this fund. In fact, the committee believed that more than $4,000 of this sum had been "applied to private uses." At the end of this analysis the committee again recommended that Magruder be credited for $30,668.78 at the Treasury Department, a sum slightly less than they had previously recommended, and that this report be filed in the auditor's office at the Treasury.[37]

On January 19, three days after this report was filed, the House of Representatives accepted it, after a long but unrecorded debate, and agreed not only to credit Magruder with the $30,668.78 of the funds he had drawn from the Treasury but also to allow him credit for any of the balance of $20,194.78 still outstanding which at any time he could prove that he had properly paid out. Two days later, on Saturday, January 21, 1815, Representative James Clark of Kentucky introduced a resolution which simply stated that Patrick Magruder should be removed from office and a new Clerk elected on Monday. The House tabled this resolution until Monday. Several Congressmen spoke on both sides of this resolution to remove Magruder from his Clerkship. Unfortunately this debate was not recorded, only summarized. Magruder's opponents charged him with neglect in confiding his contingent fund to his deputies and being ignorant of their actions. His defenders simply based their arguments on his "unimpeachable character and general good conduct." Congressman Goodwyn of Virginia, his father-in-law who had once been accused and later acquitted of similar misconduct when sheriff of Dinwiddie County, was not recorded as speaking out on either side of the issue. He was at that time boarding with his son-in-law. The House voted 71 to 71 on postponement of this resolution for a week, and the Speaker of the House, Langdon Cheves of South Carolina, cast the deciding vote in favor of delay.[38]

This resolution was not debated again, however, because on January 28, 1815, Patrick Magruder resigned the office of Clerk of the House and by inference also the office of Librarian of Congress. He stated that he could defend himself against the report and that there were errors in its financial statements, but he did not feel that at his age he should have to explain his conduct. He had been tried without opportunity to defend himself and did not expect to benefit by an appeal to "those who have already pronounced judgment against him." Magruder had been in public life from the age of 18 and had not expected this end to what he felt had been an honorable career.[39]

The House read and tabled Magruder's resignation the same day he presented it. On January 30, without further official action on Magruder's resignation, they elected Thomas Dougherty Clerk of the House of Representatives and then began considering legislation to require the Clerk to give bond for the performance of his duties.[40] In March President Madison separated the offices when he appointed as the third Librarian of Congress George Watterston, whose wife Maria Shanley was a cousin of Patrick Magruder's.

Thus, it was not the destruction of the Library of Congress and Congress' resultant indignation that caused Magruder, the second Librarian of Congress, to lose his position, as at least one historian has maintained.[41] Rather, it was the question of impropriety in the use of his contingent fund which forced his indignant resignation. Magruder, perhaps realizing something was wrong when he returned to Washington, had raised this question himself when it was discovered that his records had been accidentally left behind for the British to destroy. Congress, already in a questioning mood after the American defeat at Bladensburg, had simply, perhaps to Magruder's surprise, followed through on his request for an investigation.

On December 29, 1815, several months after Patrick Magruder left Washington to settle on his wife's family plantation "Sweden," the auditor of the Treasury closed his books on Magruder's account with the entry that Magruder owed the United States $18,167.09 in funds that he had withdrawn from the Treasury but had not accounted for. In February 1816, the federal government filed suit against Magruder for this sum. There is no record of this case ever coming to trial, however.[42] Martha G. Magruder died on March 31, 1816. Less than four years later, on December 24, 1819, Patrick Magruder died and was buried at "Sweden" with his second wife.[43]

NOTES

[1] Biographical information is contained in two of the famous *Sunday Star* (Washington, D.C.) columns of the Rambler: "Locust Grove, Old Home of the Magruders," June 3, 1917, and "The Rambler writes of Famous Men," March 12, 1922. Fragments of these articles and related clippings are also in the Magruder and Related Families Scrapbook, MS 961, Maryland Historical Society. Further information on both Patrick Magruder and his father-in-law Col. Peterson Goodwyn can be found in the *Biographical Directory of the American Congress* (Washington: U.S. Govt. Print. Off., 1949). "Locust Grove" is still standing and is now being preserved as a historic site. *Washington Post,* February 3, 1973.

[2] James McHenry to Daniel W. McHenry, June 10, 1804, James McHenry Papers, MS 647, Maryland Historical Society.

[3] John Thomas Scharf, *History of Western Maryland,* 2 vols. (Philadelphia: L. H. Everts, 1882), 1:664, 666. Indenture of June 2, 1799, in the Magruder Papers, MS 546, Maryland Historical Society.

[4] Certificates of Election for Frederick and Montgomery Counties for April 6, 1801, Maryland Hall of Records; *Frederick-Town Herald,* May 21, 1803.

[5] *Fredericktown Republican Advocate,* July 1, August 5, 19, 1803.

[6] *The Hornet,* September 20, October 11, 1803; *Fredericktown Republican Advocate,* October 7, 1803.

[7] Maryland, *Laws of 1802, Ch. 66; Frederick-Town Herald,* September 22, 1804; *Fredericktown Republican Advocate,* October 5, 26, 1804.

[8] *Annals of Congress,* 15:263; 16:47, 114–15, and 167.

[9] L. Marx Renzulli, *Maryland: The Federalist Years* (Rutherford: Fairleigh Dickinson University Press, 1973), p. 234; Edward S. Delaplaine, *Francis Scott Key, Life and Times* (Brooklyn, N.Y.: Biography Press, 1937), pp. 48–50; *Biographical Directory of the Amer-*

ican Congress (1949 ed.), p. 1409 for P. B. Key. Key was absolved of these charges during a congressional investigation into them after his election. The charge of being in the pay of the British throne was true because for a short time he had received a pension for his Revolutionary War services as a British officer. The investigation was concluded on March 18, 1808 (*Annals of Congress,* 18: 1848–49).

[10] "Sir Augustus J. Foster in Maryland," ed. Margaret K. Latimer, *Maryland Historical Magazine* 47 (1952): 286. A copy of the manuscript upon which this excerpt is based is in the Library of Congress.

[11] Certificates of Election for Frederick and Montgomery Counties for October 6, 1806, Maryland Hall of Records; *Frederick-Town Herald,* October 11, 1806.

[12] *National Intelligencer,* April 10, 1807.

[13] *Annals of Congress,* 17: 783–87; photostats of Josias Wilson King papers are in the Manuscript Division (MMC), LC; "Review of Appointments Wanting," May 30, 1807, Thomas Jefferson Papers, Manuscript Division, LC.

[14] William C. Bruce, *John Randolph of Roanoke,* 2 vols. (New York: G. P. Putnam's Sons, 1922), 1: 308–09; John Quincy Adams, *Memoirs,* 12 vols. (Philadelphia: J. B. Lippincott & Co., 1874), 1: 487–88.

[15] Willis Alston, Jr., et al., to Thomas Jefferson, October 26, 1807, Letters of Application and Recommendation during the Administration of Thomas Jefferson, 1801–1809, Record Group 59, National Archives Microfilm Publication M 418, roll 8, frames 190–91. Hereafter cited as RG59M418.

[16] The President's authority is in 2 Stat. 128. The list is in the Jefferson Papers, LC. J. Philip Reibelt to Thomas Jefferson, December 12, 1808, Jefferson Papers, LC.

[17] James Kearney to Thomas Jefferson, April 9, 1807, RG59M418, roll 6, frame 275; Josias W. King to Thomas Jefferson, April 10, 1807, RG59M418. Caesar A. Rodney to Thomas Jefferson, April 10, 1807, Jefferson Papers, LC.

[18] William M. Duncanson to Thomas Jefferson, April 11, 1807, roll 3, frame 417; George Clark to Albert Gallatin, May 8, 1807, roll 9, frames 311–12, both from RG59M418.

[19] 2 Stat. 128. The Kearney, King, Clark, and Duncanson letters are cited in footnotes 17 and 18. Thomas Jefferson to Henry Dearborn, April 21, 1807, Jefferson Papers, LC; also William M. Duncanson to Thomas Jefferson, December 5, 1807, RG59M418, roll 3, frame 418.

[20] Thomas Jefferson to Patrick Magruder and to Nicholas B. Van Zandt, November 6, 1807, Jefferson Papers, LC.

[21] Jim Ranz, *The Printed Book Catalogue in American Libraries, 1723–1900* (Chicago: American Library Association, 1964), p. 16, makes this point about the purely clerical function of the librarian in this period as a generality, and Stuart C. Sherman, "The Library Company of Baltimore, 1795–1854," *Maryland Historical Magazine* 39 (1944): 6–24 makes this same point in his study of a particular library organization close to Washington. William D. Johnston, *History of the Library of Congress, 1800–1864* (Washington: Govt. Print. Off. 1904), p. 44–45, confirms the existence of this practice at LC itself in this period.

[22] U.S. Congress, Joint Committee on the Library, *Annual Report of the Library Committee of the Two Houses of Congress.* April 11, 1808, and January 27, 1809. Copies of these are in the Rare Book Division, LC, under Z733U575 and the date. The relationship of Congress to LC in this period is fully developed in Johnston, p. 44–48, and David C. Mearns, *The Story Up to Now* (Washington: Library of Congress, 1947), p. 13–16.

[23] Adams, 1: 424, 463–65, 478.

[24] Ranz, p. 12–13, 16, 21–22, 25, 104n30; U.S. Library of Congress, *Annual Report of the Librarian of Congress . . . 1901* (Washington, 1901), p. 362; Adams, p. 478.

[25] U.S. Library of Congress, *Catalogue of Books, Maps . . . for the two Houses of Congress* (Washington, 1812), p. 13. Magruder's ill health has been discussed earlier and will be discussed again later in this essay. A set of these early catalogs is in the Rare Book Division, LC.

[26] U.S. Library of Congress, *Catalogue of Books, Maps . . . Congress* (Washington, 1808 and 1812). These rules are reprinted in full in Johnston, p. 58–61. Congressional legislation is contained in the 1812 edition, p. 6–8.

[27] Patrick Magruder to Thomas Jefferson, December 4, 1807, RG59M418, roll 9, frames 195–97. For Boyd's selection see Wilhelmus B. Bryan, *A History of the National Capital,* 2 vols. (New York: The Macmillan Co., 1914), 1: 572n2.

[28] Patrick Magruder et al. to Thomas Jefferson, October 15, 1808, Jefferson Papers, LC. *National Intelligencer,* March 1, 1809.

[29] *Annals of Congress,* 20: 56; 23: 331; 26: 107.

[30] *National Intelligencer,* June 1, 1811. American Clan Gregor Society, *Year Book, 1920–1925* (1931), p. 26.

[31] Kenton N. Harper, *History of the Grand Lodge and of Freemasonry in the District of Columbia* (Washington: R. Beresford, printer, 1911), p. 34–38; Johnston, p. 49.

[32] *Annals of Congress,* 26: 787.

[33] *American State Papers: Miscellaneous Series,* 2: 245. Hereafter cited as *ASP:MS; Annals of Congress,* 28:305.

[34] *ASP:MS,* 2: 245–46; Robert H. Goldsborough, Joint Committee on the Library, to Joseph Nourse, Treasury Dept., October 3, 1814, LC Archives, "Miscellany."

[35] *ASP:MS,* 2: 248–57; Records of the District Courts of the U.S., National Archives Record Group 21, Circuit Court, D.C., Case File 226 and 92.

[36] Ibid.; Account No. 31,215, Miscellaneous Treasury Accounts of the First Auditor of the Treasury Department. Record Group 217, National Archives Microfilm Publication M235, roll 134, frame 1069, hereafter cited as RG217M235. *Annals of Congress,* 28:872.

[37] *ASP:MS,* 2: 258–66; Account No. 31,215, RG217M235, roll 134, frame 937.

[38] *Annals of Congress,* 28: 1084–1085, 1100–1101; Writers' Program of Virginia, *Dinwiddie County* (Richmond: Whittet & Shepperson, printers, 1942), p. 91.

[39] *ASP:MS,* 2: 267–68.

[40] *Annals of Congress,* 28: 1107, 1113–14, 1116.

[41] Johnston, p. 68.

[42] "Statement of the Account of Patrick Magruder," RG217M235, roll 134, frame 941 and frame 936 for the suit. The Records of the District Courts of the U.S., National Archives Record Group 21, Circuit Court, D.C., do not contain a case file for this case.

[43] American Clan Gregor Society, p. 26.

Sir,   Washington ⟨ March 25th 1815.

I have had the happiness to receive the commission
of Librarian with which you were so good as to honor me
I accept it with pleasure & tender you my thanks for
the favour conferred. Unwilling to intrude on your
moments of leisure & relaxation, I nevertheless deem it
my duty to apprise you that, according to an act of last
session, you are directed to cause an appartment to be
immediately selected & prepared for a library room &c. In
the 3rd story of the present Capitol, a room sufficiently com
modious & convenient might, at a small expence be
prepared & this could immediately be done, by authori-
sing the Commissioners of the public buildings, or the
Superintendent of the City, to have it prepared without
delay— I would suggest the propriety of having the books
conveyed by water to this City as more safe & less expensive—

I have the honor to be,
with great respect & esteem,
Your obt servt.
Geo. Watterston

His Excell. Js. Madison
President of the U. S.

George Watterston

Advocate of the National Library

by William Matheson

Steady employment was not a conspicuous feature of the careers of the earliest Librarians of Congress. Patrick Magruder resigned his office on January 28, 1815, in the face of charges that he had neglected his duty.[1] His successor, George Watterston, served from March 21, 1815, until his partisan involvement in politics brought his term to an abrupt end on May 28, 1829. Unlike his predecessors, Watterston did not have to contend with dual duties as Clerk of the House and Librarian of Congress. The first holder of the office to be able to devote full time to his duties, he is sometimes called the first Librarian of Congress.

George Watterston was controversial throughout his tenure—critical (even of the Congressmen he served), thin-skinned, outspoken, and strongly partisan. His wide interests frequently took time away from his library duties and left him open to criticism. Though the records surviving from this early period in the Library's history are fragmentary, the tone of the man is consistent throughout these fragments. He was a man of contradictions—unlovable in many ways, but with close family ties; venomous to his enemies (of which he had an imposing number), but loyal to his friends; possessing the predisposition of a dilettante but capable of significant accomplishment. The Library of Congress in the years he spent in office had an equally contradictory history. Although Watterston served without even one budgeted assistant for 13 of his 15 years in the Library, he faced many of the problems which, in enormously magnified form, continue to be central concerns to this day.

The basic source of information on Watterston's career, and indeed on all aspects of the Library's early history, is William Dawson Johnston's 1904 *History of the Library of Congress*.[2] In writing his book Johnston leaned heavily on the Watterston papers, which were presented to the Library by David Watterston in 1901. The papers, which consist of three bound volumes of letters and memoranda and two small manuscript volumes, are central to any consideration of Watterston's life and career but frustratingly incomplete. Since the publication of Johnston's *History,* a few additional pieces of information have come to light. They seem to indicate that Watterston's hold on his position was at all times more tenuous than Johnston's account suggests

William Matheson is chief of the Rare Book and Special Collections Division.

and his personality more abrasive. Anne Royall's description of Watterston in her *Sketches* presents him as a more serene and gentle man than other evidence supports:

Mr. W. is a man of good size, neither spare nor robust; he is a fine figure, and possessed of some personal beauty; his complexion fair, his countenance striking, shows genius and deep penetration, marked with gravity, though manly and commanding. A sweet serenity diffuses itself over his countenance, which no accident can ruffle; and under the veil of retiring modesty, discovers his blushing honors thick upon him.[3]

This is quite a tribute from a woman known better for a sharp tongue than for flattering descriptions. Her saying a few sentences before that "he does not appear to be over twenty-five at this time" (he was, in fact, 41) leads me to doubt her powers of observation.

In *The Story Up to Now* David Mearns provides the following characterization of Watterston:

[He] was not a person graciously to receive guidance nor was he thick-skinned enough to accept rebuke without deep and vituperative resentment. It may be that his was the most treacherous of attributes: a sense of superiority.[4]

There are many evidences of Watterston's sense of superiority and resulting bitterness. In *Wanderer in Washington* he puts feelings, which are surely his, in the mouth of a character:

Because I am but a scribe, and a scribe makes a very small figure in the estimation of a member of congress or his lady. We of the quill are apt to be considered as animals of a different race, as belonging to the class *vermes*, that crawl in obscurity, and are only fit to be trampled on.[5]

By the end of his life Watterston was one of the few inhabitants of Washington who had known the city in its earliest days. In his "Reminiscences of the Metropolis" in the *National Intelligencer,* December 13, 1852, he gives the reader "these reminiscences, supposing that they may be interesting . . ., as the recollections of one now, I believe, with two others, the only inhabitants of Washington in 1793." [6]

He was born on October 23, 1783, on a ship in New York Harbor, the son of a Scotch immigrant, David Watterston, by profession a master builder. His father moved to Washington in 1791, attracted by the building opportunities in the developing federal city. Watterston later remembered witnessing the laying of the corner-stone of the Capitol by Washington on September 18, 1793. He was sent to Charlotte Hall School, in St. Marys County, Md., and spoke of the school in laudatory terms in a reminiscence, "Twenty Years After," in the *National Intelligencer* for August 17, 1825. Unfortunately there is little that is personal in the piece, which is more of a puff for the seminary than an account of his school days. He began to practice law in Hagerstown, Md., but was not destined for a legal career. His experiences as a lawyer left a bitter taste in his mouth and from his first book, *The Lawyer; or, Man As He Ought Not to Be,*[7] published anonymously, he "never missed an opportunity in any of his books to make a derogatory remark about the law and lawyers. . . ." [8] An inheritance from a rich uncle gave him an opportunity to get away for a time, and he visited Jamaica where he kept a journal (in the Watterston papers) and wrote the separately published poem, *The Wanderer in Jamaica.* Following his return he briefly became a law partner of John Law in Washington, married Maria Shanley, and established his residence on Capitol Hill where he remained until his death.[9]

As a young man he also published the novel *Glencarn; or, The Disappointments of Youth* (1810); a play, *The Child of Feeling* (1809); and another poem, *The Scenes of Youth* (1813).[10]

James Madison appointed George Watterston Librarian of Congress on March 21, 1815. There have been various reasons advanced for the appointment, none of them certain. Watterston had dedicated his poem, *The Wanderer in Jamaica,* to Dolley Madison in 1810 in the following terms: "Madam, I have presumed to address this poetical effusion to you, from the reputation you have acquired of being desirous to promote the cause of general literature." [11] Some commentators have surmised that this dedication to his wife may have led Madison to favor Watterston.

Although Watterston in 1826 told W. C. Bradley that Madison "voluntarily offered" the position to him,[12] Watterston had written to the President about at least one other position, "collector of this District," in 1813.[13] Probably Madison's recognition of Watterston's literary accomplishments was the deciding factor. In 1815 his novels, play, and poems had established

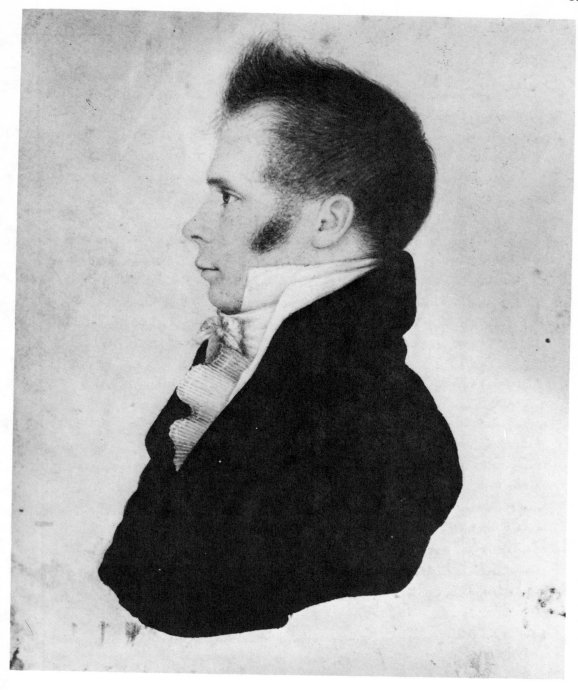

*Watercolor portrait of George Watterston, attributed
to Thomas Birch of Philadelphia, 1811. Rare Book
and Special Collections Division.*

(4)

Sir   Monticello May 7. 15.

I have duly recieved your favor of Apr. 26. in which you are pleased to ask my opinion on the subject of the arrangement of libraries. I shall communicate with pleasure what occurs to me on it. two methods offer themselves, the one Alphabetical, the other according to the subject of the book. the former is very unsatisfactory, because of the medley it presents to the mind, the difficulty sometimes of recollecting an author's name, and the greater difficulty, where the name is not given of selecting the word in the title which shall determine it's Alpha- betical place. the arrangement according to subject is far preferable, altho' sometimes presenting difficulty also. for it is often doubtful to what particular subject a book should be ascribed. this is re- markably the case with books of travels, which often blend together the geography, natural history, civil history, agriculture, manufactures, commerce, arts, occupations, manners &c. of a country, so as to render it difficult to say to which they chiefly relate. others again are poly- graphical in their nature, as Encyclopedias, Magazines &c. yet on the whole I have preferred arrangement according to subject; because of the peculiar satisfaction, when we wish to consider a particular one, of seeing at a glance the books which have been written on it, and selecting those from which we expect most readily the information we seek. on this principle the arrangement of my library was formed, and I took the basis of it's distribution from Ld. Bacon's table of science, mo- difying it to the changes in scientific pursuits which have taken place since his time, and to the greater or less extent of reading in the several sciences which I proposed to myself. thus the law having been my profession, and politics the occupation to which the circumstances of the times in which I have lived called my particular attention, my provision of books in these lines, and in those most nearly connected
36275
Mr. Watterston

him as Washington's leading (and for all practical purposes, only) literary figure. Knowing what we do of his subsequent career, we can guess that he was already involved in the political activities which became such a prominent part of his life. An awareness of his usefulness to the Whig party is a feature of an 1818 contretemps which will be discussed later. Two years before his appointment as Librarian, Watterston had become editor of the *Washington City Gazette,* which had been established by William Elliot to support the Republican party.

The imminent arrival of the 6,000-plus volumes in the library of Thomas Jefferson was the specific occasion for Madison's "recess appointment" of a new Librarian. On hearing that the fledgling Library of Congress (approximately 3,000 volumes in size) had been destroyed by the British when they burned the Capitol on August 24, 1814, Jefferson offered his considerably larger collection to the Joint Committee on the Library on September 21, 1814.[14] The details of the purchase of the Jefferson collection are better documented than any other aspect of the Library's early history. Though the negotiations are of great interest, they precede Watterston's appointment by some months and are fully reported in Johnston's *History*. The purchase had major implications for the future growth of the Library. Undoubtedly the importance of the collection and Magruder's unfortunate experience suggested to Madison the wisdom of having the appointee serve only in a single capacity. This idea had been advanced as early as September 24, 1814, by the bookseller Joseph Milligan in a letter to Thomas Jefferson in which he noted that the "place of Librarian would be well to be a distinct office from the Clerk of the House of Representatives."[15]

One of Watterston's first jobs was to oversee the installation of the Jefferson library in the attic of Blodget's Hotel, located at the corner of 7th and E Streets NW., a considerable distance from the burned Capitol. Though the building had never served as a hotel, this was one of the few functions it failed to be used for in this period: in 1815 it housed both Houses of Congress, the congressional committees, the Library of Congress, the General and City Post Offices, and the Patent Office. Although Watterston later took credit for moving the collection three

times during his term in office, his actual physical involvement in this first move is left up in the air by Joseph Milligan's July 31, 1815, letter to Jefferson: "The Library . . . was safely laid into the passages of the General Post office of Congress Hall [Blodget's Hotel]. About three weeks ago I commenced unpacking it, and accomplished it last Monday."[16] Whoever unpacked the books had his job greatly simplified by Jefferson's sending his collection in the pine fixtures used to house them at Monticello and in the classified arrangement he had devised.

As one of his early actions, Watterston wrote to Jefferson on April 26, 1815, asking for his opinion, "as a gentleman of literary taste," on the best way to arrange the books.[17] "Your long acquaintance with books & your literary habits have, doubtless, led you to the adoption of some plan of arrangement with respect to libraries, which I should be happy, if you would communicate." Jefferson obliged on May 7, 1815, with an explanation of his classification, which was based on Francis Bacon's table of science, broken down into 44 "chapters" of knowledge.

To Watterston fell the job of creating a printed catalog of the Jefferson collection. His resulting effort, *Catalogue of the Library of the United States,*[18] the work of several months and based on Jefferson's manuscript catalog, was received a little reservedly by Jefferson, who thought the arrangement less scientific than his own, and very coldly by the Joint Committee on the Library, which found it too scientific and had nothing good to say about it. When asked how he liked the arrangement within the chapters, Jefferson replied, "Of course, you know, not so well as my own," but then went on to see some possible advantages to readers.[19] Watterston had alphabetized the books within chapters, rather than using the subdivisions "sometimes analytical, sometimes chronological, & sometimes a combination of both" which Jefferson had devised.

The printed Joint Library Committee report of January 26, 1816, can hardly have raised Watterston's spirits. He was taken to task for the arrangement:

This form of catalogue is much less useful in the present state of our library, consisting chiefly of miscellanies, not always to be classed correctly under any particular head, than a plain catalogue in the form which had been adopted for the formation of the catalogue of the old library. . . .

The committee's principal objection was the cost, $1,356.50, "one third more than the annual appropriation made heretofore by Congress for the additional increase of the library, and more than one twentieth of the actual cost of our whole library." Elsewhere in the report the committee considered additional compensation for the Librarian for services already performed but concluded that many of the duties had been performed by people Watterston hired (and paid out of his own pocket), and made the following assessment of his expertise:

The manner in which the scientific part of the duties, devolving upon the librarian, has been fulfilled, do not, in the opinion of your committee, warrant the allowing of an additional compensation, which your committee suppose must be interpreted as conveying on the part of Congress, something like an approbation of past conduct. The only evidence of the literary services of the librarian, within the knowledge of your committee, is the publication of the catalogue which we were presented at the time of the beginning of the session; and the merit of his work is altogether due to Mr. Jefferson, and not to the librarian of Congress.

Despite the cool tone of the remarks, the committee recommended an increase in the Librarian's salary for future services to $1,000 per year. The arrangement which Watterston adopted, a modification of Jefferson's classification, was also used in the first substantial supplement to the *Catalogue,* published in 1827, and continued to be used by the Library of Congress for the rest of the century.

In telling Jefferson about the committee's reaction to the *Catalogue* on January 29, 1816, Watterston gave little sign of being chastened by their strictures. Instead the letter has the superior tone which we hear again and again throughout his life: "The Library Committee are dissatisfied with me for having the catalogue printed, without having waited to consult their *superior judgment* [his italics]. . . ." [20]

From our perspective Watterston's attempts during his first two years in office to establish the Library as the national library, comprehensive in its collections rather than limited to the needs of Congress, are admirable, though at the time they were controversial. On July 31, 1815, shortly after Watterston's appointment, the *National Intelligencer* carried an article on national libraries in other countries and observed that the example should be instituted and "the Congressional or National library of the United States become the great repository of the literature of the world. . . ." Watterston's influence is almost certainly there. On September 15, 1815, he inserted a notice in the *National Intelligencer* in which reference again is made to the "great national repository of literature and science" and in which he calls for "American Authors, Engravers, and Painters . . . [to] transmit to the Library . . . such work as they may design for the public eye. . . ." In addition, Watterston's title for the 1815 *Catalogue,* referring ambitiously to the "Library of the United States," also emphasized a national rather than strictly congressional responsibility.

On January 9, 1817, the Senate passed a bill which embodied the idea Watterston had advanced in the *National Intelligencer* on the deposit of books, engravings, etc. The bill read:

That the Joint Library Committee . . . be authorized to make, from time to time, a selection of such books as they may deem proper to have deposited in the Congressional Library, out of the books which by the existing laws are to be deposited by the authors or publishers in the office of the Secretary of State, and are now lodged in the Patent Office.

This forward-looking idea, later embodied in the copyright deposit regulations, failed to become a law. Johnston speculates that the only reason Congress failed to pass the bill (and another bill increasing the appropriation for the purchase of books from $1,000 to $1,500 per year) was that the committee had on hand an unexpended balance of $1,526.61 for the purchase of books.

On February 18, 1817, Eligius Fromentin of the Joint Library Committee reported a resolution calling for a separate building for the Library. Watterston lamented the defeat of this proposition in an article in the March 25, 1817, *National Intelligencer,* noting that "in all other countries, this is an object of national pride. . . ." Knowing what we do of the attic quarters the Library was then occupying in Blodget's Hotel, we may smile at his suggesting as the standard for the United States the "elegant and splendid design for a national library at Paris," with "an immense gallery of 266 feet long by 47 breadth, and 6 vast halls. . . ." Still, there is no denying that he took positive steps to put his points across and that he spoke up on numerous occasions in behalf of his ideas.

While Johnston accepts the importance of Watterston's efforts to promote the Library, David Mearns makes rather light of their impact. Refuting the assumption that the title of the 1815 *Catalogue* signaled official acceptance of the national library concept, he points out that the catalog was prepared and issued during the absence of Congress from Washington, the Joint Committee on the Library was not consulted, the committee disavowed the makeup of the catalog, and the title of the catalog has not since been used.[21] However, even if we acknowledge that Watterston was not supported by the Joint Committee in his concept of the Library, this takes nothing away from him. Though he was unable to effect the changes he sought (as was the Joint Committee in most of the areas in which it made proposals), Watterston kept to the idea of a larger function for the Library, was a pioneer in that respect, and deserves full credit for his efforts. In a two-year span, 1815–17, ideas were advanced which could have changed the history of the institution, had they been adopted.

Despite his labors, by 1818 Watterston was in serious trouble with the Joint Committee. In a December 29, 1818, letter to President Monroe, Senator Jonathan Roberts says, "I have learned today with equal surprize and regret that exertions are [urged] at this moment among the members of Congress to recommend Mr. Walsh to you for librarian to the removal of Mr. Waterston [sic]." He continues a few lines later: "In the first session after his appointment I had to oppose the most villainous combination form'd in the joint committee against him." After picturing the "small but comfortable house" Watterston had recently purchased on credit and the "wife & several small children" dependent upon him he speaks of his "diligence & obliging assiduity." Next he characterizes Watterston as a scholar and man of taste, with "good moral character and uniformly Republican principles." The clinching argument is the point about Republican principles: "I know his pen has been efficiently employed in the Republican cause while Mr. Walsh was understood to have been assailing it with much violence." He returns to the same theme in a P.S.: "I may add on the subject of the librarian that I believe Mr. W-n could two signatures in Congress & ten among the citizens for one Mr. Walsh could."[22]

Roberts' pleas, or other factors of which we have no evidence, were successful, for Watterston remained in office for 11 more, occasionally shaky, years. In the same month (December 1818) the Library moved to another attic, this time in the north wing of the Capitol, in rooms on the west side, on the same elevation as the upper gallery of the Senate Chamber.

After the promising beginnings, the six years the Library occupied the attic of the partially rebuilt Capitol can only be called an anticlimax. Johnston calls this the Garret Period in the Library's history. Frances Wright D'Arusmont, one of many travelers who visited Washington in this period, comments on "the national library, which a native of England now feels awkward at finding bestowed in a few small apartments; at present it comprises little more than the collection supplied by Mr. Jefferson. . . ."[23] Watterston in his *L. . . . Family at Washington* has one of his characters visit the Library, which "consists of a suit of rooms, where I met a man that I thought looked devilish sour at me: this was the librarian."[24] In truth Watterston had little to look happy about. The Joint Library Committee's printed report (December 19, 1820) reveals that no considerable purchases had been made because the Librarian has informed them that "no preparations were making, or expected to be made, before the meeting of Congress, for putting up additional shelves in the library rooms, and that a large portion of the books purchased during the last year were still lying upon the tables. . . ." These arrearages understandably discouraged the committee and expenditures for the Library remained low. However, the $2,000 set up for the purchase of books on April 11, 1820, represented the first separate annual appropriation for this purpose.

Watterston met Jefferson for the first and apparently only time in July 1820. An apologetic letter from Jefferson to Watterston dated July 27, 1820, tells the Librarian that he failed, because of his bad hearing, to catch his name when they were introduced and as a consequence had not "pressed for a longer continuation of the favor of [his] visit" as he would have had he known to whom he was talking.[25] Watterston's reply of August 4, 1820, is tactful and the exchange shows both men in a favorable light. Watterston says

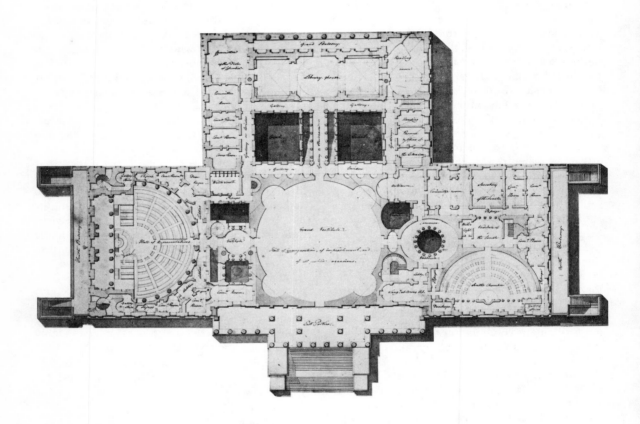

"Plan of the Principal Floor of the Capitol," drawn by Benjamin H. Latrobe in 1817. The spacious library in the center of the west front was not ready, however, until 1824. Prints and Photographs Division.

to Jefferson of his visit, "Both Dr. Hamilton & myself were more gratified, by the reception you gave us as *strangers,* than we should have been, had we had the honor of your acquaintance." [26]

Watterston apparently talked of resigning in 1823. Taking into account the tenacity with which he attempted to regain the position once it was taken from him in 1829, the resignation episode can only be judged one of the mysterious incidents in Watterston's tenure. Jefferson wrote to President Monroe on December 19, 1823: "Mr. Girardin, president of the college of Baltimore understanding that the office of Librarian of Congress is expected to become vacant by resign.$^{\underline{n}}$, and desirous of being placed in it, has requested me to state to you what I know of his qualif$^{\underline{us}}$." [27]

It is possible that the talk of resignation was the result of another Joint Library Committee effort to remove Watterston and that the man on whose behalf Jefferson was writing either believed Watterston was resigning or misled Jefferson in saying this was so.

From a very early period the Library was a center of social activity in Washington. Describing the character of the Library in the earliest period, Johnston notes that "because there were no other sources of amusement" before 1814 and indeed later, the Library "was much resorted to as a place of relaxation." [28] This continued to be true in the Garret Period as Watterston's description in his 1822 novel, *The L. . . . Family at Washington,* makes clear.

In August 1824 the Library moved into spacious new quarters in the center of the Capitol and became a showplace of the city. Readying this space for the Library had taken the architects several years, and at one point, on March 21, 1822, the Library's right to the space was threatened by a resolution proposed by Congressman Mark Hill "to inquire into the practicability of preparing, for the accommodation of the House of Representatives, the room in the center building designed for the Library." Though the resolution to take this highly desirable space for the House came to nothing, there was a direct modern parallel in 1974, when newspapers carried reports that the House was gathering signatures for a possible takeover of the Madison Building, under construction as the third building of the Library of Congress.

The *National Intelligencer* for January 1, 1825, describes the new Library accommodations in detail, complimenting their "style of great beauty and elegance" and going on to call the apartment "the most beautiful . . . in the building." This was a widely shared opinion. The *National Journal* went further in describing the room as "decidedly the most beautiful, and in the best taste of any in this country." [29] Frances Trollope, another traveler of the period, calls it a "very handsome room . . . elegantly furnished; rich Brussels carpet; library tables, with portfolios of engravings; abundance of sofas, and so on. The view from it is glorious, and it looks like the abode of luxury and taste." [30]

This glory threatened to be short-lived, for a fire broke out in the Library quarters on December 22, 1825. The subsequent investigation revealed that the fire was started by a candle in one of the galleries. There are conflicting newspaper reports about the length of time it took to put the fire out, but apparently the Library, and indeed the Capitol itself, had a close call. Since the gallery in which the fire took place housed largely duplicate sets of public documents, the loss was not particularly heavy. The book collection emerged unharmed. The House issued a resolution calling for an inquiry into the cause of the fire. Watterston wrote to Edward Everett, a member of the Joint Committee, on January 2, 1826, in response to an inquiry on the topic, "Enclosed are my answers to your second interrogatories. . . . I feel a little hurt that the committee should think, I would deliberately *state any thing* on an occasion like this, that I would not feel myself justified in *swearing to.*" [31] Watterston followed up with another letter on the same topic the following day: "My answers have been as full & ample as they could be made consistantly [sic] with a strict regard to truth & I regret that it is not in my power to designate the individual from whose inattention I conceive the fire to have originated on the night of 22d ult." [32]

On January 4 the Joint Committee reported that it did not feel prepared to express an opinion on the question of whether any person in the employ of the government was chargeable with negligence, and the report was ordered to lie on the table. Various ways to fireproof the Library were subsequently considered. The physical nature of the rooms made some of the recommended alterations either too expensive or impossible to accomplish. There were debates about replacing the wood walls with metal and stone, and fears that excessive moisture would accumulate. The final conclusion, February 6, read that "as the Library can, in the judgment of the committee, be made sufficiently safe by proper care of the lights and fires, the committee do not deem it expedient that the House should adopt any measure in the premises." Unfortunately, it was only after the disastrous fire of 1851 that significant measures were taken to improve the situation.

The fragmentary surviving evidence indicates that the fire exposed Watterston to threatening attacks on his position, as the burning of the Capitol had left Patrick Magruder vulnerable in 1814. In the Watterston papers there is a letter of considerable interest from Watterston to W. C. Bradley, July 8, 1826 (a 1953 addition to the collection and thus not available to Johnston and other earlier historians of the Library). After striking hydra-headed federalism several sharp blows and summarizing his "laborious" situation (which in his account sounds convincing; the duties of running such a large operation by himself must frequently have been onerous), he turns to a theme which recurs in letters written after his dismissal:

... I believe, until last winter, no murmur of complaint was ever heard. But there are so many greedy & hungry expectants of office who flock to the seat of govt. during the sessⁿ or who, at a distance, pester & harass the members for situations, that, upon the occurrence of the slightest accident, & indeed where no cause exists, they rush forward open mouthed & in full cry to fill the vacant space by any means whether just or unjust or whether fitted for it or not.

To anyone familiar with Watterston's style, that account has a touch of the gothic excess to which he was prone. He continues:

I was sure that neither you nor any of my friends & acquaintances in Congress, would for a moment countenance any attempt which might be made to do me an act of the grossest injustice. . . . I should like to know the name of the man who was laboring to undermine me last sessⁿ. that I might mark him & be put upon my guard in future.

In the journalistic war which followed Watterston's dismissal in 1829, Watterston's opponent in the *Telegraph* cautioned him that his situation was not one to "ensure perfect complacency" and urges him to "recal [sic] the affair of the burning of the Library. . . ." [33] Obviously the fire opened Watterston to attack from his enemies. With no more evidence than is available, we can only assume that enough friends came to his rescue in 1826 to keep the situation under control.

From the standpoint of the Library's history Watterston's extensive correspondence with Edward Everett, member of the Joint Library Committee from December 6, 1825, to beyond Watterston's term in office, is of the greatest interest. At first reading Everett's letters to Watterston seem to reveal a thorough dislike of him, suggesting that Everett might have made some of the difficulties Watterston reported to Bradley in the letter quoted above. A check of Everett's diary, which contains many entries on his activities as a member of the Joint Committee on the Library (unfortunately mostly of a very pedestrian nature), fails to bear this out. It is likely that the two men were not fond of one another, but the coolness in the letters may have been typical of Everett's dealings with an underling. It is certainly true that Everett made no public expression of regret about Watterston's dismissal and it is quite possible that he was happy at the turn of events. The letters from Watterston's successor, John Silva Meehan, are much more obliging and tactful, and Meehan continued to write to Everett for years after the Congressman had left the Joint Committee and the House.

There is evidence that Watterston ran into still another difficulty with Congress, in this instance with the Ways and Means Committee, in 1828. On July 12 of that year he wrote to Everett, "You will, perhaps, be as much surprised as I was to know that, by a most singular oversight, the Chairman of the Commee of Ways & Means, has omitted altogether both the Liby & Librarian & has made no provision, in the general appropriation bill, for the salary of the one or the expenses of the other." [34] Everett responded in a typically unemotional manner: "I wonder that the Committee of W. & M. in deliberately omitting it from their bill (as I presume they did, for they could not well draft a new bill without having the old one before them) should not have notified the library committee if they wished us to attend to it." He concludes with a more sanguine observation than Watterston may have felt appropriate in the circumstances: "The omission can be rectified early next winter. Meantime you will enjoy the comfort of being a man in good credit." [35]

In 1827 Watterston began writing regularly for the *National Journal,* earning an additional $500 a year for his contributions, which were largely devoted to furthering the Whig cause. His interest in politics was, of course, not new. In his novel *Wanderer in Washington,* published in 1827, his commentator speaks very favorably of Henry Clay and "a warm partizan of General Jackson" exhausts "the fountain of his panegyric on Gen. Jackson, and of vituperation against Messrs. Adams and Clay. . . ." [36] His partiality for Henry Clay was of long standing and Clay, in a letter of July 21, 1829, two months after Watterston's dismissal says, "In your particular case, as in some others, I have been inexpressibly grieved by the reflection that friendship for me may have been one of the causes which led to this exercise of vengeance upon you and upon them." [37] Given what today strikes us as Watterston's incredible recklessness in identifying himself so closely with politics, it is hard to understand how he could have been surprised, as he apparently was, by Jackson's action. When Watterston learned on May 28, 1829, of Meehan's appointment to his position he was furious, and on leaving office he took with him his record books and the manuscript catalog of Jefferson's library. [38]

His connections with the *National Journal* enabled him to launch a journalistic war on all his opponents. In the exchange which appeared in the newspapers following Watterston's dismissal, the *Telegraph* for June 12, 1829, carried the following description of the ex-Librarian:

It is notorious that the manners of the ex-librarian were of a peculiar disgusting order; his conduct to those who had occasion to visit the library, as well to those who had a right, was of the most rude and supercilious description; so much so, that many of our members of Congress and citizens, rather than encounter the *obliging* Mr. Watterston, sought elsewhere the information they might have obtained more readily in the library.

The exchange between Watterston and the *Telegraph* is markedly abusive and slanted and these remarks certainly cannot be taken at face value, although there is undoubtedly more than a grain of truth in the description. Responding to this article in the June 16, 1829, *National Journal,* Watterston fell into a trap of sorts (which the *Telegraph* picked up with glee):

If my manners were at any time "supercilious," it was found necessary to assume them to get rid of such impertinent and vulgar intruders as he and his satellites, and to save the books from being *purloined.*

Watterston was a man used to handling the pen and occasionally he resorted to hyperbole and excess in putting down his opponents. At the height of the exchange the *Telegraph* accused him of foaming at the mouth.

Some of his best invective was poured out on his successor, John Silva Meehan, whom he characterized in the most unflattering terms. The *National Intelligencer* of June 16, 1829, in a piece speaking favorably of Watterston's "assiduous and praiseworthy" official conduct, quotes a letter from the ex-Librarian. To the charge that the Library was in a state of derangement and confusion during his tenure he replies that if books cannot be found he is "not answerable for the ignorance or stupidity of those who have been put into a situation for which they may be wholly unfit." This was but a warm-up for the next round. In a February 1830 letter to Asher Robbins, chairman of the Joint Library Committee, he replies to the charge that books are missing:

What must be the feelings of the man who can thus trump up a statement which he *knows* to be *erroneous* and which he has, no doubt made from an impression that it would never reach my ears. He may have been misled by the practice which has lately prevailed in a higher sphere, of shooting the poisoned arrows in the dark and leaving the victim to suffer without his knowledge by whom it was discharged. It would seem that he had mistaken his men. . . . This must be ascribed either to malignity or ignorance or may possibly originate from a *requisition* to justify an act of usurpation, by misrepresentation and falshood [sic]. [39]

Watterston came early to his sharp tongue, for there is evidence that he had a tongue as dangerous to himself as to others as far back as his days as a young lawyer. In *Greenleaf and Law in the Federal City* Allen C. Clark tells that Watterston was on opposite sides of a case with John Law after they had dissolved their association. Law won the judgment and Watterston exclaimed in front of the judge before whom the case was being tried, James S. Morsell: "There is not a *morsel* of *law* in the case." Clark adds, "The judge did not appreciate the humor of the double-barreled pun; he did remark concerning contempt of court." [40]

Unsuccessful in regaining office in 1829, he pinned his hopes on electing a Whig President, who in gratitude would set things right. For whatever reasons his position was not restored to him when the Whigs next took office in 1841. Watterston was still hopeful in 1849 when the Whigs once again triumphed. Though he petitioned President Taylor, the President showed to him "a manner and recep[tio]n . . . such as lead me to believe that there was no in[ten]tion on his part to make a removal & to do me the act of simple justice." [41] Watterston had still one more chance when Taylor died and Vice President Fillmore succeeded him. When his appeals to the new President brought him no more satisfaction than all his previous petitions, Watterston lost all patience with the Whig party. In October 1850 his daughter Sara wrote to her sister Eliza: "Father has seen Mr. F. and he says he does not like to remove the present librarian. . . . The result is that father is disgusted and very much hurt, and has left the Whig party!" [42]

In a prescient observation Frances Wright D'Arusmont characterized the Jefferson collection in the following manner in 1821: "These volumes, . . . marked with the name of America's president and philosopher, will always constitute the most interesting portion of the national library." [43] Although the Library of Congress today reveres the 2,400 survivors from the original 6,700-volume purchase and accords them a place of honor in the Rare Book Division, their purchase was hotly debated in 1814 and the legislation authorizing their acquisition barely squeaked past. The debate, marked by party interests, narrow prejudices, and parsimony, makes sad and frequently embarrassing reading today. Johnston summarized the objections to the purchase as generally

its cost, its extent, the nature of the selection, and the number of the works in foreign languages, particularly French, many of them the writings of Voltaire, Rousseau, and other literary apostles of the French Revolution; nor did English works of progress and speculative freedom, such as Locke's, escape animadversion. Other works were said to be of too

philosophical a character, and some, as Callender's *Prospect* before us, were otherwise objectionable.[44]

In the debate there was talk of returning volumes inappropriate for the Library's collection to Jefferson. In the end the collection was purchased in toto and all the books were retained. Despite the size and variety to which the opposition had taken exception, the Joint Library Committee report of January 26, 1816, written by Eligius Fromentin, found the collection inadequate.

It is enough to cast a rapid glance over the catalogue of the library of Congress to become immediately sensible of the immense *hiatus* which some of the departments of arts or sciences exhibit. Some of the branches of the arts or sciences are swelled to a prodigious size, which at the same time that it is by no means a certain proof of a greater degree of health in these parasite branches, manifests every symptom of threatening decay of the tree itself. This was observable likewise in the old library of Congress, although in a less degree.

Fromentin goes on to observe that this last-named state of affairs was hardly surprising considering the limited sums which had been available for taking advantage of the many opportunities to purchase books from Europe. These opportunities had not all passed and he calls for an appropriation of $10,000 to "place within the reach of every member of Congress all the most valuable books in every department of arts and sciences, of which there is now such a lamentable deficiency." Though Fromentin's proposal was not successful, his report demonstrates that the 1816 library committee took a broad view of the Library's responsibility to Congress. In the 1810's the Library had an opportunity to acquire the "invaluable collection of American topography made by Col. William Tatham." [45] Johnston devotes several pages to the collection but has no explanation of the Library's failure to acquire the "valuable stock of maps, plates, charts, and explanatory manuscripts" which filled six rooms of Tatham's house at the time of his suicide in 1819.[46] Perhaps the lack of space in the "garret" and the arrearages already stacked on tables were determining factors.

The January 6, 1817, report of the Joint Committee takes a more strictly practical view of the development of the collection. The principal recent thrust of the collection building effort had been in serials, which were consuming a sizable part of the annual appropriation. The categories specifically mentioned in the report are periodical publications, both literary and political (which should be acquired from their beginning to the present day); transactions and papers; and general catalogs from foreign countries. The committee invited the chairmen of the various congressional committees to provide lists of maps and books needed to conduct their business. They arranged to have a box placed in the Library to receive recommendations for book purchases from members of both houses. They proposed, but were not given, an appropriation of $3,000 to strengthen the law collections.

If the Joint Committee wavered between a comprehensive collection and a collection focused on day-to-day practical needs, one man consistently took a broad view of the Library's responsibilities—Thomas Jefferson. While he was President, he submitted desiderata lists which were used to form the collection that the British destroyed. In his September 21, 1814, letter offering his library to the Joint Committee he observed, "I do not know that it contains any branch of science which Congress would wish to exclude from their collection. There is in fact no subject to which a member of Congress may not have occasion to refer." [47] He gave another expression of his philosophy of collection building in a September 1, 1820, letter to Watterston:

Having lately met with a very full catalogue of books relating to America, I have supposed it could not be better placed than in your hands for the use of the library committee with which I presume it is a primary object to obtain every thing of that description. [48]

An article under the heading "The National Library" in the August 28, 1823, *National Intelligencer,* commented on the opportunities the room in the center of the Capitol, shortly to be opened, would provide for the growth of the collection:

It is obvious, that a certain frivolous class of books may, and ought to be excluded; but there should be no work of high character and unquestionable utility, published in any part of the world, which ought not, in time, to find its way into the National Library of the United States.

On February 24, 1824, the Committee of Ways and Means (at the instigation of Joel Poinsett from the Joint Committee) made a report underlining the Library's deficiencies:

The committee have discovered the Library of Congress, in its present state, to be defective in all the principal branches of literature; and they deem it of the first necessity, that this deficiency should be speedily supplied, at least, in the important branches of *Law, Politics, Commerce, History* and *Geography,* as most useful to the Members of Congress.

To implement this statement—which is considerably more limited in its implications than the Jefferson point of view or the *National Intelligencer* recommendations of the previous year—the report proposes $5,000 to supply the defects in the Library's collections. A bill making an appropriation in that amount was passed, May 26, 1824, the largest such appropriation to that point.

The responsibility for selecting materials for the Library's collections belonged to the Joint Committee, not the Librarian of Congress, and Watterston necessarily played a limited role in the development of the collection. Mahlon Dickerson of New Jersey was appointed chairman of the Joint Committee on December 1, 1817, and remained in the position for the next 10 years. Though Johnston says that Dickerson was "famed for his love of books" [49] and Watterston called him a "biblical cormorant" in the *L. . . . Family at Washington,* [50] the Library's growth in the period 1817 to 1824 was very slow. However, with the new quarters in the Capitol matters looked more hopeful, and the $5,000 appropriation of 1824 was followed by $5,000 in 1826, $3,000 in 1827, and $5,000 in 1828.

Perhaps the most important event in this period was the appointment of Edward Everett to the Joint Committee on December 6, 1825. He quickly became the most active member and set out to do something about the deficiencies in the Library. In the months of October and November 1826 Everett took a particularly keen interest in the Library's collection. His diary entries and letters from that period show him compiling want lists, seeking information from Watterston on the Library's holdings, visiting bookstores, attending auctions, examining duplicates in libraries, etc. In his search for information he asks Watterston for reports by return mail, and it is not hard to imagine Watterston, trying to run the Library by himself, exclaiming furiously when still another letter arrived. On October 31, 1826, Everett wrote to Watterston: " . . . I think American works (tho' not excellent) ought to be in the Library to furnish, I trust, to after times the means of proving the ratio of advancement." [51] In the same letter he calls upon Watterston to "prepare & keep on hand a Catalogue of books most wanted in Every department, to which New books c'd be added as they appear." To one of his suggestions Watterston replied on December 13, 1826, with something of the asperity typical of his personality, "Perhaps it may not be improper to suggest that it may be leaving too much to the taste & discretion of the Librarian to select such books as he may deem imperfect or defective from any cause, for the purpose of excluding them from the Liby." [52]

In the category of lost opportunities, of which there were many in this early period, falls one possible purchase advanced by Everett: a collection of manuscripts and books relating to America in the possession of Obadiah Rich. Rich (1783–1850), consul of the United States in Valencia, Spain, at the time and an important bookseller specializing in manuscripts and printed books relating to America, served American collectors and libraries well. In the 1820's he had unbelievable opportunities to acquire remarkable material, at prices which today make a collector weep. Everett submitted the list of one collection offered by Rich to the House, which had it printed December 27, 1827. This 24-page list leads off with 9 pages of manuscripts and follows with printed books in a chronological arrangement from 1506 ("Americus Vespuccius' Voyage, in German . . . Leipsick, 1506") through 1825 ("Navarrette Viages de Colon"). The list concludes with a note:

A very large collection of Tracts relating to America, both in English and in Spanish; and a great many English and French books, which, not being at hand, are omitted in the foregoing list. [53]

Here was an opportunity indeed, and one which Everett had hopes would come to something at least as late as May 17, 1828. A diary entry on that date notes that the "joint committee on the library met; & agreed to sanction the demand for $5000 with a view to the purchase of Rich's books." [54] To gain a perspective on the list and on the opportunity it offered, I consulted the list of major desiderata which the Library of Congress published in 1926. [55] One of the first sections of the list is "Letters of Vespucci" (these letters, of course, being our central first-hand

source of information on the voyages of Americus Vespuccius (1451–1512), the man after whom America is named). The Leipzig 1506 edition of Vespucci's "Letters," the first printed item on Rich's list, is a Library of Congress desideratum, still lacking from the collection. The second item on Rich's list, Fracanzano da Montalboddo's *Itinerarium Portugalensium,* Milan, 1508 (the Latin edition of *Paesi novamente retrovati,* the first printed collection of voyages and travels), is on the Library's 1926 desiderata list but has since been acquired. The third item, the Milan 1508 edition of *Paesi novamente retrovati,* is still a Library of Congress desideratum. These first three titles give a pretty clear indication of the quality of Rich's collection, which contained between 300 and 400 titles. There is nothing in the printed record, in the Watterston papers, or in Everett's diary to indicate why the purchase fell through. Inertia perhaps, or eventual resistance of the other members of the Joint Committee. The Rich collection was eventually acquired by the great American collector, James Lenox, whose library in turn became the foundation stone of the New York Public Library rare book collection.

Though Everett remained a member of the Joint Committee through Watterston's term in office and beyond, his later diary entries show no other burst of energy equivalent to the period in late 1826. In general his comments in his diary on the committee's meeting are factual and brief. Apparently he was irritated, as well he might have been, by the meeting of January 4, 1827, for his diary notes:

At a meeting of the Library Committee I proposed the purchase of Humboldt's large work on America. No one gentleman cordially seconded me. Most opposed me, & the most I c'd get from them to consent to was to buy it, if on consulting several members they would approve it. [56]

Perhaps his interest faltered in the face of this kind of discouraging reception to his recommendations.

However, there were some good days. The *National Journal* on January 31, 1829, reprinted an account from the *New York Evening Post* on one of Everett's successful purchases:

We learn that Professor Everett, acting officially as one of the Library Committee of Congress, has purchased about five hundred dollars worth of the rarest and most valuable books in Signor Duponte's collection. . . . We hardly know which deserves the most praise, the good taste which selected these inestimable books for the Library of the Capital, or the interesting enthusiasm which prompted this venerable *savant* to risk, with extremely limited means, the importation of a collection which we reluctantly confess New York has not been able to appreciate.

The article describes several of the books purchased from the Duponte collection in a very general fashion, providing no information on the place of printing, printer, or date. The Duponte copy of one of the works almost certainly survives in the Rare Book Division today: "the extremely rare Voyages of Marco Polo and other celebrated navigators, by Ramusio. . . ." The first volume of the Library's copy of the second edition of Ramusio's *Delle navigationi et viaggi* (Venetia: nella Stamperia de Giunti, 1554) contains an 1830 date-stamp on the title page.

Johnston points out that the Library's manuscript collection was of little consequence when Watterston's administration ended. The *Washington City Chronicle* in the summer of 1829 described in some detail "a Catholic missal or breviary, in Latin and French, and though admirably executed with the pen, rather difficult to read. . . ." [57] The *Chronicle* piece gives the rather unlikely information that the manuscript is dated 1591 (could this have been an owner's note?) and compliments the illumination, though noting that "some illustrations . . . are . . . badly drawn and executed. . . ." Though it would be highly instructive to see the manuscript and judge its quality, I have not been able to locate it in the Library's collections.

Various individuals commented on the collection in the decade of the 1820's. Jared Sparks wrote on May 18, 1826: "On American History the library is exceedingly meagre, containing nothing but a few of the commonest books; but on American politics it is full, particularly to the year 1808, when Mr. Jefferson left the government." [58] The poet Henry Cogswell Knight felt that the collection had an undue proportion of antiquated editions and of foreign-language works, which he thought would be of little use to Congress. [59] Anne Royall criticized Watterston for letting the books of the Sunday School Union into the Library, saying, "These Sunday school books are lying useless in the library, as I would suppose no member of Con-

gress reads them. Let Mr. W. sell them and give the amount to the suffering poor—if he is so pious. . . ." [60] Johnston notes that these criticisms are "not altogether fair" indications of the character of the collection. Of the comments on the Library he felt that Mrs. Trollope's was perhaps "as fair as any." She said that the Library was "very like that of a private English gentleman, but with less Latin, Greek, and Italian." [61]

Because of congressional control of materials selection, Watterston had little influence over the development of the Library's collections, and, though Johnston called him a "bookman," he was using the term with a meaning different from one others would be likely to employ:

He was a journalist, and therefore interested in live questions, public questions; an author of several books, and therefore understood books as only an author can; and above all he was a bookman—it is necessary only to quote from his commonplace books to indicate this. [62]

Watterston was an author, but was he a man broadly familiar with the book trade, with book values, with bibliography, rare books, etc.? Probably not. His first letter to Jefferson makes clear that he was not familiar with the former President's library, for he describes the collection as "considerably larger, & I presume much more select & valuable." [63] He says of himself in an undated draft communication in the Watterston papers: "His knowledge of books & the extent of his reading & attainments were such that it was thought by those who visited the Liby, he was acquainted with the contents of every vol. in it." [64] There is no indication in any of the surviving records that he pushed for acquiring any significant collections for the Library. Everett had to ask him to prepare want lists and on May 23, 1828, reminded him that the Joint Committee wished him to complete the collection of the laws and law reports of each state. [65] If his role in the development of the collections was small, it is hardly to be wondered. Had he contented himself with his library duties, he would have had more than enough to do without seeking responsibilities that were not really his. He also had broad and time-consuming literary and journalistic interests outside the Library.

In a postscript to a letter of May 23, 1828, Everett nudges Watterston, "Would it not be well to make a little interest with the Senators for our appropriation bill." Though later Librarians would work closely with the Congress on such matters, there is no evidence that Watterston interested himsef in this activity. He had a superior attitude toward the Congressmen he served and on more than one occasion got in some jabs at their expense, some after his removal from office and some before. As editor of the *Washington City Chronicle,* he commented on November 7, 1829:

The Reports of the British Parliament . . . are not so "well thumbed" . . . as they ought to be by the American legislator. These volumes of Reports contain an immense mass of political information. . . . We are sorry to say . . . that there are but few who have as yet discovered their value.

In his *Wanderer in Washington* he has a character say of the Library, "It is undoubtedly an invaluable privilege, and he must, indeed, be happy who can retire from the agitating scenes of political strife, to lounge in the splendid repository of wisdom and learning, and repose in this Attic temple of the Muses.—But I fear it is not so often resorted to as might be expected, by those who have free admission into its recesses." [66]

There is at least some question about Watterston's success in keeping the Library in respectable shape. The *Telegraph* on December 19, 1828, described the enormous collection of public documents in the western gallery as "that awful pile . . . 25 feet high and 100 long. . . ." Watterston's successor, Meehan, wrote to Edward Everett on July 16, 1830:

We are getting on pretty well with our labors; cleaning the books, destroying worms, and washing the shelves. The evil you pointed out last winter, will not exist in the Library when we again have the pleasure of seeing you. The shelves shall be altered, where it is necessary, so that the books may be placed erect. Some of them have been injured by standing awry on the shelves for several years. [67]

A British traveler, Frederick Marryat, called the Library the "best lounge at Washington" but added "the books are certainly not very well treated. I saw a copy of Audubon's Ornithology, and many other valuable works, in a very dilapidated state. . . ." [68] Marryat balanced his criticism by adding that this state of affairs is "much better than locking it up, for only the bindings to be looked at." The librarian's problem of preserving his collections and at the same time making them available to users is an old one indeed.

Julia Kennedy, in her study of Watterston's literary career, takes account of everything good that can be said of him as a writer, but leaves the conviction that his talent was minor. Her bibliography is extensive and suggests a wider interest in Watterston's writings than actually exists. Many of her references contain no mention of Watterston but are rather studies of his time, genres in which he wrote, people who influenced him, etc. With some justice, she takes issue with Johnston's statement that "after his appointment [Watterston] became an interpreter of the literature in his custody and ceased to make any notable contribution to literature itself." [69] In making this remark Johnston was defining "literature" very literally. *The L . . . . Family at Washington* (1822) and *Wanderer in Washington* (1827) have considerably more life than his other literary efforts and are likely to retain their interest longer. These books—they are hard to characterize but closer to novels than anything else—comment on actual Congressmen, cabinet members, and local institutions and events, and have definite historical interest.

In a recent book, *The Early American Novel,* Henri Petter accords little space to Watterston. In discussing *The Lawyer* and *Glencarn* he speaks of the "wildness and incoherence" that often make the two novels "pretentious and ridiculous." [70] In another passage he calls *Glencarn* "a preposterous book." [71] Ridiculous or not, *The Lawyer* is now a book of some rarity, as a recent price of $250 in a dealer's catalog for a copy with some imperfections indicates. The book is described in that catalog as the first novel printed west of the Alleghenies (in Pittsburgh) and as the first American novel with a lawyer as subject. To the tally of "firsts" Kennedy adds two more: "He was the first to use the National Capitol as a setting for fiction, and the first to realize the potentialities of Washington society as good humorous material." [72]

Watterston's literary and journalistic efforts were diverse. A secretary of the Washington Botanical Society for years, he wrote on tobacco, landscape gardening, and assorted horticultural topics. After his removal from office as Librarian he launched even more ambitiously into publishing guidebooks, statistical compendiums, biographical sketches, textbooks, and lectures and well earned the title which Kennedy accords him—"the metropolitan author."

Among his nonliterary activities he is remembered locally for his close identification with the Washington National Monument Society. He served as the society's secretary from its beginnings until the end of his life, and before his death had the satisfaction of seeing the shaft reach a height of 150 feet. The obituary notice which appeared in the *National Intelligencer,* February 6, 1854, two days after his death, did not even mention his years as Librarian of Congress but instead spent much of the space discussing his contribution to "the great enterprise of erecting in this city the Monument to the memory of the Father of his Country. . . ."

Watterston's sharp tongue, which amuses us today in the frequent outrageousness of its excess, is, of course, only one side of the man. Despite the inadequate financial support which Watterston and the Joint Committee lamented, the Library grew under his stewardship. When he left office in 1829, the Library of Congress had the fourth largest collection in the country. Jefferson's classification, an innovation in the book world, had been adopted and would continue to be used throughout the century. The Library was established in handsome quarters, not yet inadequate as they were to become later in the century. Issues had been raised which would remain both central and hotly debated to this day—the role of the Library (should it be a library of record for the American experience or an authoritative collection for the entire world?); the Library's proper clientele; the concept of a national library; the most appropriate use of book funds (should the emphasis be on current books at the expense of important books not previously acquired?); the qualifications desirable in the Librarian of Congress. And finally, though it would be no salve to Watterston, his career served, as an unfortunate example, to remind his successors of the desirability of keeping the Library of Congress out of politics.

NOTES

[1] Martin Gordon, "Patrick Magruder: Citizen, Congressman, Librarian of Congress," *Quarterly Journal of the Library of Congress* 32 (July 1975):154–171.

[2] William Dawson Johnston, *History of the Library of Congress, 1800–1864,* vol. 1 (Washington: Government Printing Office, 1904).

[3] [Anne Newport Royall], *Sketches of History, Life, and Manners, in the United States* (New-Haven: Printed for the author, 1826), p. 151.

[4] David C. Mearns, *The Story Up to Now* (Washington: Library of Congress, 1947), p. 30.

[5] [George Watterston], *Wanderer in Washington* (Washington: Jonathan Elliot, Jr., 1827), p. 137.

[6] *Daily National Intelligencer* (Washington), December 13, 1852.

[7] [George Watterston], *The Lawyer; or, Man As He Ought Not to Be* (Pittsburgh: Zadok Cramer, 1808).

[8] Julia Elizabeth Kennedy, *George Watterston, Novelist, "Metropolitan Author," and Critic* (Washington: The Catholic University of America, 1933), p. 5.

[9] Johnston's *History,* p. 109, and other sources indicate that Watterston was a partner of Thomas Law. However, Allen Culling Clark, in *Greenleaf and Law in the Federal City* (Washington: W. F. Roberts, 1901), makes no mention of any connection with Thomas, who in the years in question was a prominent Washingtonian. Clark says on p. 306 that Watterston was associated with John Law (1784–1822), Thomas Law's son.

[10] *Glencarn; or, The Disappointments of Youth* (Alexandria: Cottom & Stewart, 1810); *The Child of Feeling. A Comedy, in Five Acts* (George Town: Joseph Milligan, 1809); *The Scenes of Youth. A Poem* (Washington: Printed by Rapine and Elliot, 1813).

[11] George Watterston, *The Wanderer in Jamaica. A Poem* (Washington: W. Cooper, printer, 1810), p. 3.

[12] Watterston to W. C. Bradley, July 8, 1826, Watterston papers, Manuscript Division, Library of Congress.

[13] Watterston to James Madison, October 28, 1813, Madison papers, Manuscript Division, Library of Congress.

[14] Jefferson to Samuel Harrison Smith, September 21, 1814, Jefferson papers, Manuscript Division, Library of Congress.

[15] Jefferson papers.

[16] Ibid.

[17] Ibid.

[18] *Catalogue of the Library of the United States* (Washington: Library of Congress, 1815).

[19] Jefferson to Watterston, March 2, 1816, Watterston papers.

[20] Jefferson papers.

[21] Mearns, *The Story Up to Now*, p. 28.

[22] Monroe papers, Manuscript Division, Library of Congress.

[23] Frances Wright D'Arusmont, *Views of Society and Manners in America* (New York: E. Bliss and E. White, 1821), p. 378.

[24] [George Watterston], *The L. . . . Family at Washington; or, A Winter in the Metropolis* (Washington: Davis and Force, 1822), p. 37.

[25] Jefferson papers.

[26] Ibid. Watterston described his visit in "Monticello and Montpelier," *National Intelligencer,* August 15, 1820.

[27] Jefferson papers.

[28] Johnston, *History,* p. 49.

[29] *National Journal* (Washington), April 12, 1827.

[30] Frances Milton Trollope, *Domestic Manners of the Americans,* 2 vols. (London: Printed for Whittaker, Treacher, & Co., 1832), 1:326.

[31] Watterston papers.

[32] Ibid.

[33] *United States' Telegraph* (Washington), June 16, 1829.

[34] Watterston papers.

[35] July 19, 1828, letterbook copy in Edward Everett, *The Microfilm Edition of the Edward Everett Papers,* ed. Frederick S. Allis, Jr. (Boston: Massachusetts Historical Society, 1972).

[36] Watterston, *Wanderer in Washington,* p. 11.

[37] Watterston papers.

[38] For information on the Jefferson "fair copy of the Catalogue of my library," see the preface in *Catalogue of the Library of Thomas Jefferson,* comp. E. Millicent Sowerby, 5 vols. (Washington: Library of Congress, 1952).

[39] Draft of letter in the Watterston papers.

[40] Clark, *Greenleaf and Law,* p. 306.

[41] Watterston to [J. M. Clayton?], October 15, 1849, draft in the Watterston papers.

[42] October [27?], 1850, Watterston papers.

[43] D'Arusmont, *Views,* p. 378.

[44] Johnston, *History,* p. 74.

[45] Ibid., p. 50.

[46] Richmond *Enquirer,* February 25, 1819.

[47] Jefferson to Samuel Harrison Smith, Jefferson papers.

[48] Jefferson papers.

[49] Johnston, *History,* p. 158.

[50] Watterston, *L. . . . Family,* p. 77.

[51] Letterbook, Everett, *Microfilm Edition.*

[52] Watterston papers.

[53] Obadiah Rich, *Manuscripts and Printed Books in*

Possession of Obadiah Rich, Esq. (Washington, 1827), p. 24.

[54] Everett, *Microfilm Edition.*

[55] *The Library of Congress. Some Notable Items That It Has; Some Examples of Many Others That It Needs* (Washington: Library of Congress, 1926).

[56] Everett, *Microfilm Edition.*

[57] *Washington City Chronicle,* August 22, 1829.

[58] Herbert Baxter Adams, *The Life and Writings of Jared Sparks,* 2 vols. (Boston and New York: Houghton, Mifflin, 1893), 1:461–62.

[59] [Henry Cogswell Knight], *Letters From the South and West,* by Arthur Singleton [pseud.] (Boston: Richardson and Lord, 1824), p. 54.

[60] Anne Newport Royall, *The Black Book,* 3 vols. (Washington: Printed for the author, 1828–29), 3:210–11.

[61] Trollope, *Domestic Manners,* 1:326.

[62] Johnston, *History,* p. 108.

[63] April 26, 1815, Jefferson papers.

[64] This draft, which Johnston transcribes in part on pp. 201–2 of his *History,* can be dated after March 3, 1841, on the basis of internal evidence. On that day the son of John Silva Meehan, Watterston's successor, was appointed second assistant librarian. In the draft Watterston compares the "outrageous" expenses of running the Library with the economy of his own day and loudly protests the "throw[ing] away" of $1,150 on the young Meehan.

[65] Watterston papers.

[66] Watterston, *Wanderer in Washington,* p. 220.

[67] Everett, *Microfilm Edition.*

[68] Frederick Marryat, *A Diary in America,* 3 vols. (London: Longman, Orme, Brown, Green, & Longmans, 1839), 2:7–8.

[69] Johnston, *History,* p. 111.

[70] Henri Petter, *The Early American Novel* (Columbus: Ohio State University Press, 1971), pp. 326–27.

[71] Ibid., p. 322.

[72] Kennedy, *George Watterston,* p. 8.

John Silva Meehan

A Gentleman of Amiable Manners

by John McDonough

John Silva Meehan (February 6, 1790–April 24, 1863), fourth Librarian of Congress, served from May 28, 1829, to May 24, 1861. In terms of length of service he ranks behind only Herbert Putnam and Ainsworth Rand Spofford.

Early records relating to Meehan are few and unreliable. He was born in New York City,[1] where he received his education and became a printer. In 1811 or 1812 he went to Burlington, N.J., to take part in the printing of Richard S. Coxe's *New Critical Pronouncing Dictionary of the English Language*; however, in January 1815 he was back in New York City, where he was warranted as a midshipman in the United States Navy. He was assigned to serve aboard the brig *Firefly* and remained with it until the following April. The *Firefly* had been purchased by Captain David Porter and fitted out as the flagship of a squadron of five small ships designed to cruise in the West Indies and prey upon enemy commerce.[2] Looking back many years later upon his naval career in the War of 1812, Meehan remarked that the "dashing expedition" that had been planned against the British was thwarted by the restoration of peace. The squadron's young adventurers, having anticipated a "plentiful harvest of laurels," were sadly disappointed. Yet they were spared hardships and "perhaps many wounds" as a result.[3] In 1856 Meehan was to receive a bounty land warrant for 160 acres, based on his limited naval service.[4]

After the war Meehan was offered a commission in the Marine Corps. However, with the responsibilities assumed by marriage to Margaret Jones Monington of Burlington in 1814 and the birth of a daughter, Susan M., in April 1815, he elected to take up printing again and moved to Philadelphia. There, with Robert Anderson in 1818, he began publishing the *Latter Day Luminary*, a religious journal issued five times a year, sponsored by a committee of the board of managers of the Baptist General Convention. Early in 1822 the firm of Anderson and Meehan moved to Washington and started publishing the *Luminary* monthly;[5] by 1824 Meehan was publishing it alone.

Another, more ambitious venture which they

John Silva Meehan (1790–1863), fourth Librarian of Congress, held the office for 32 years, serving under nine Presidents. LC–USZ62–55859

John McDonough is a manuscript historian in the Manuscript Division.

initiated after relocating in Washington was the publication of the *Columbian Star,* a highly derivative weekly newspaper also associated with the Baptist denomination. The *Star,* with Rev. James D. Knowles as its editor, proclaimed in its first issue that its main design was to be an "authentick repository of Missionary and other religious intelligence." Yet not to be neglected were "passing tidings of the times," and readers were assured of receiving information on "the progress of the sciences, and all those liberal and useful arts which embellish society, and meliorate the condition and economy of life." Withal, the *Star* also hoped to be able "to throw an occasional beam upon the path of classical and elegant literature." There would be no concern with "politicks," for the pages of the *Star* would willingly leave to others the "unprofitable conflicts of partisan animosity." [6] In such a controlled climate John Silva Meehan prospered for more than four years. Early in 1823 Anderson's name was dropped from the paper's masthead and Meehan alone appeared as the publisher. Special items, such as *Mr. Webster's Speech on the Greek Revolution,* were also published by Meehan at the *Star* office and were offered to the public.[7] On July 9, 1825, the *Star* contained an announcement of the relinquishment by Reverend Knowles of the editorship and, although there was no formal indication that Meehan was his successor, no name other than his appeared on the front page. Readers were assured on July 16 that the objects for which the paper had been established would be promoted, and that no "unfriendliness or illiberality" would be manifested.[8]

In January 1826, Meehan abruptly relinquished control over the *Columbian Star.* Baron Stow, a bright ministerial light from Columbian College (later to become George Washington University), took charge. On January 28 it was reported that Meehan had "determined to commence the publication of a political journal" in Washington and therefore had "deemed it judicious" to separate himself from all connections with the *Star.* Stow acknowledged the "able, faithful, and assiduous manner" in which Meehan had discharged his numerous duties and noted that he had given "high satisfaction" to the paper's patrons and friends. The discontinuance of the *Latter Day Luminary* was announced at the same time.[9]

John Silva Meehan had reached a turning point in his life. He was in his midthirties, his family included six children, and he was abandoning a placid career as publisher of a religious weekly to take up the publication of a partisan political newspaper designed to be in the forefront of the controversy resulting from the election of John Quincy Adams. The extent to which Meehan's own ambition was involved in this dramatic change of careers cannot be assessed, particularly since Senator John Henry Eaton of Tennessee may have been the instrumentality through which the change was made. Eaton, who had already written a life of Andrew Jackson, who was to become his secretary of war in 1829, and who, more memorably, was to take Peggy O'Neale as his bride, was the focus of the forces in Washington that intended to see to it that the Jacksonian point of view would be vigorously expressed in the national capital. The *Washington Gazette,* of which Jonathan Elliot had long been the proprietor, was the chosen medium, and Meehan became the nominal purchaser thereof. It was said that Eaton was responsible for the purchase, and the notes were endorsed by John P. Van Ness, a wealthy and distinguished resident of Washington who later became its mayor.[10]

The tone of Meehan's newspaper, which had its name changed to the *United States' Telegraph,* was set in its first issue on February 6, 1826. The paper's motto proclaimed that "Power is always stealing from the many to the few," and this view was supported editorially by a declaration that "in common with a decided majority of the American people," the *Telegraph* was "not satisfied with the recent course of political events in our country." The election of President Adams, as well as his selection of Henry Clay as secretary of state, had been brought about only by the open condemnation and violation of "the most sacred principles of the Constitution." [11] Recognition of this view was quick in coming. The Boston *Courier* of February 13 noticed that "Mr. Meehan very frankly avows his principles, and the course he intends to pursue." [12] This course was immediately controversial, and that it would meet with the approval of the distant but watchful Andrew Jackson seemed likely. Upon reading the prospectus of the *Telegraph,* Jackson remarked:

There has been a new paper established at the city called the *United States Telegraph;* from its prospectus I would Judge, it is intended to sustain the amendment proposed to the constitution [for direct election of President and Vice President], and to oppose the principles by which Mr. Adams got into the Presidency; and to unite the republicans into one solid colum against Mr. Adams second election. . . .[13]

Almost from its inception there was discussion concerning the actual control of the *Telegraph.* It must have been clear that John Meehan was not the man to mount the type of attack that was beginning to be carried on against the Adams administration. The Richmond *Whig* commented that the *Telegraph* was "edited by nobody knows whom, supported, nobody knows how," and was, furthermore, "faithless in its principles, scurrilous in its language, insincere in its opinions, in 'bad odour at home,' and worse repute abroad." [14] Much of this was standard, clamorous fare in the press of the times, but the *Telegraph*'s rebuttal of the charges of anonymity was weak in claiming that the name of the editor was "not a secret" in Washington, while failing to name him. It was at this juncture that Meehan, or those who had sponsored him, decided that it was time for a change. He may or may not have been inept in his role as spokesman for the *Telegraph,* but a more dynamic and forceful personality had appeared on the scene and the time had come for Meehan to step aside.

Duff Green was all that Meehan was not—a "man of versatile interests, wide information, shrewd insight into human nature, with a penchant for political intrigue, and an unflagging industry." [15] He could be depended upon to assail the Adams administration in the manner expected. Green's takeover, however, had to be gradual, probably because of the need to work out financial arrangements. Green's own account, written in 1866, states that Jackson unsuccessfully urged him, as early as 1825, to take charge of a Washington paper in his behalf. The following year, while visiting Washington, Green submitted several items for publication in Meehan's *Telegraph* and the resulting abuse in the pages of the opposition press led him to march into Meehan's office, negotiate a price for the sale of the paper, and draw a check for the amount.[16] Actually the takeover was more prolonged and depended once again upon the financial maneuvering of John Eaton, who with 11 other subscribers—10 of whom were Members of Congress—signed a note on May 20 for $3,000, thus enabling Green to assume control.[17]

On April 26, 1826, Green formally announced in a signed column in the *Telegraph* that the control of the editorial department of the paper would henceforth be his. Meehan, he declared, had been responsible for the establishment of the paper, had been its sole proprietor, and therefore had been free to act and to do "as his judgment advised." [18] With this gesture made, Green proceeded to take command. On June 5 an agreement was concluded between Green and Meehan,[19] and on October 17 Meehan's name appeared in the *Telegraph* as publisher for the last time. No further indication of the change in affairs at the *Telegraph* was made and there was no appreciative farewell to Meehan, such as that which had been extended by Baron Stow when Meehan left the *Columbian Star* some months before. Meehan himself has left no record of his feelings upon giving up the *Telegraph,* but judging from his life before and after this brief interval, it is likely that he had been discomfited by the role of aggressive editor.

In the summer of 1826, as Meehan's tenure as editor and publisher was drawing to a close, a personal tragedy overtook him. His wife of 12 years died just after the birth of her seventh child, on July 17, and the child did not live out the day.[20] With six children at home, Meehan remained a widower for little more than a year, marrying Rachel T. Monington, his wife's sister, on October 27, 1827. Two children were born of this second marriage. Rachel was to survive her husband for many years, dying on Capitol Hill in 1882, but only three of Meehan's nine children are known to have outlived him.

Some time after leaving the *Telegraph* Meehan found himself serving the Baptist cause once again, this time as secretary of the board of trustees of Columbian College. During this period he is also said to have supported the election of Andrew Jackson in 1828.[21] He had certainly been an early advocate of Jackson, and his services in 1826, whether availing or not, had demonstrated his loyalty. In 1829 loyalty and perseverance were about to be rewarded, just as the upholders of "bargain, intrigue, and corruption" were to be punished.

One who was destined to be removed from office was George Watterston (1783–1854), who from 1815 had served as Librarian of Congress. Watterston was a literary man, and otherwise a man of parts, who has been described as "not a person graciously to receive guidance nor . . . thick skinned enough to accept a rebuke without deep and vituperative resentment." [22] As early as 1826 he had expressed to William Czar Bradley, a Vermont Congressman, his uneasiness over the "greedy & hungry expectants of office" who flocked to Washington, and he asked Bradley for the identity of a man who had been laboring to undermine him, in order that he might "mark him & be put upon my guard in future." [23] By the spring of 1829 there was nothing that Watterston could do to save himself. Even while serving as Librarian of Congress he had been in the pay of Peter Force's *National Journal,*[24] and some of his connections, powerful in their day, could only serve him ill in the aftermath of Jackson's election. Not the least of these associations was that with Henry Clay, the man to whom Jackson attributed his loss of the Presidency in 1825. Jackson saw removal as "reform" and, although the duty was disagreeable, likened it to the cleansing of "the augean stables." [25] The metaphor was congenial to the Jacksonians, for Sam Houston rejoiced that the "stalls of Washington" had been cleaned. He went on to urge Jackson: "Get rid of all the *wolves* and the barking of Puppies, can never destroy the *fold.*" [26] Whether Watterston was considered a wolf or a puppy cannot be determined; that his outcry upon removal was loud and long cannot be denied.

Watterston first presented his case in the press, principally in the pages of the *National Journal,*[27] and then prepared a printed statement for distribution to members of Congress. Watterston's complaint was threefold: his removal was an act of injustice, it was illegal, and his replacement was incompetent.[28] Henry Clay was indignant and seized upon a shopworn analogy in comparing Watterston's removal to "that act by which the famous Alexandrian Library was reduced to ashes." But Clay admitted that it was not in his power to do anything more than assure Watterston of his "high esteem and regard." [29] Finding himself unable to reverse the situation, Watter-

Meehan's diary entry for June 29, 1852, commenting on the death of Henry Clay. Although Clay had been indignant over the removal of George Watterston as Librarian of Congress in 1829, looking upon it as a step "in keeping with the despotism" that ruled in Washington, Meehan was characteristically magnanimous in his estimate of Clay. LCMS–93898–1

ston nonetheless never abandoned his ambition to be restored as Librarian of Congress. He used cajolery, threats, and flattery, particularly when the Whigs came to power, but in vain. William Henry Harrison was elected, but died almost at once and "gave no sign"; John Tyler, who succeeded him, "proved a traitor from whom no Whig could expect favor"; Zachary Taylor "paid no attention"; [30] and Millard Fillmore, in a personal interview, refused "the simple act of justice" Watterston desired.[31] If it has been said that "the injury to the Library became incalculable" as a result of Watterston's removal, it has also been said the he had been "Librarian on one side of the aisle rather than Librarian of Congress." This was not to be a mistake made by his successor.[32]

John Silva Meehan replaced Watterston on May 28, 1829. It is said he was not Jackson's first choice, that honor having been accorded Charles P. Tutt, who preferred an appointment as U.S. Navy Agent at Pensacola.[33] Meehan, however, was eminently acceptable on the score of past loyalty, and the commission he received designating him as Librarian of Congress noted that the President reposed "special Trust and Confidence in the Intergrity, Diligence and Discretion of John S. Meehan." [34]

Meehan was 39 years old when he became Librarian. He was of medium height (5 feet, 7 inches) and had brown hair, brown eyes, and a complexion tending toward the florid.[35] The only known surviving daguerreotype provides the likeness of a much older man, but in the opinion of an admirer it reveals a man "remarkably handsome, possessed of regular features, a well molded chin, thin lips, hair worn long upon the temples, a straight nose, bushy brows, and fine eyes behind the crow's feet which betrayed his self-possession and good humor." [36] The Library that Meehan took over occupied the greater part of the central portion of the western front of the Capitol. There were about 16,000 volumes in his

516

June, 1852.

Tues. 29. It rained a little, very early this morning; and continued to rain with little in-
termission, until about 5 o'clock, p. m.; the
wind very fresh, from the S. E. — A part
of the time, this morning, and some time
before it ceased, this afternoon, it rained
very hard, deluging our streets, &c. &c.....
We have not had a more copious rain, for
some time. — It cleared off, beautifully, about
six o'clock, p. m., and remained clear, except
down in the S. S. E., all the evening; the wind
very light, from the S. E.; the atmosphere
very humid; and rather cool, outdoors. —
Owing to the stormy state of the weather,
to-day, we have neither visited nor been
visited. — The Hon. Henry Clay, of Kentucky,
U. S. Senator, who has been lingering on a
bed of sickness, at the National Hotel, in
this city, since last December, died this
morning, about 11 o'clock, in the 77th year of
his age.....Mr. Clay passed more than half
of his life in the political arena, most of
the time as a leading gladiator, and was
at length deserted by his political associates,
who crooked the pregnant knee to him as
long as they found that thrift would follow
fawning.......Alas! that such should be
the end of all greatness! — Both Houses
of Congress adjourned, to-day, without entering on legislative business......His remains
will receive the highest funereal honours! —
— His remains! — Ah! Why did not his
friends expend half the zeal and means

Death of H. Clay

custody there and they were arranged on the shelves in the Library's alcoves in accordance with the various chapters constituting the classification scheme inherited from Thomas Jefferson. Once, when asked for his opinions on shelving books, Meehan insisted on the virtues of *"immoveable"* as opposed to *"moveable"* shelves. He believed that "any deviations in the line of shelves would offend the taste of a precise man," and he was a precise man, as he thought all librarians should be. On these immovable shelves the books were "first classified as to their *subjects*," and then according to *"size, or form,"* with spaces between shelves adjusted so that all the duodecimo or smaller books were on the upper shelves, followed by shelves for octavos and quartos, with folios and super-royal volumes occupying the bottom shelf. The little space that might be gained by movable shelves would be "a very inadequate compensation for marring the beauty of our present lines...." [37]

The arrangement of the books in the Library even had a bearing on the almost unceasing cataloging activities that Meehan and his assistants had to perform. In making out their catalogs they would "first arrange the books in their proper classes, as 'Ancient History,' 'Modern History,' 'Politics,' 'Religion,' etc., and then, under each classification, place the works in alphabetical order." This methodology, he remarked to Charles James Faulkner, chairman of the Virginia State Library Committee, tasked the Librarian "rather severely in arranging the books to their proper position." [38] In his time Meehan prepared the general catalogs of 1830 (258 pages), 1839 (747 pages), 1849 (1,022 pages), and 1861 (1,398 pages). These catalogs were bewildering enough with their multiple alphabets within chapters, but when the books that had been received in the years between the general catalogs were accounted for in annual supplements the result was stultifying as a compendium and stupefying to use. For example, anyone consulting the Library's published catalogs in 1848 would have had to pore over not only the general catalog of 1839 but also eight individual supplements, totaling 210 pages, again with the alphabet dispersed throughout the many chapters. A wholesale reformation of the system of cataloging was badly needed. One attempt was made in the 1850's but it did not originate with Meehan and

was not carried through to completion.

When Meehan first came to the Library he had one assistant. He soon added a messenger and eventually had two other assistants, one of whom was his son, Charles Henry Wharton Meehan. Edward B. Stelle, who had worked briefly with Watterston and was removed with him, returned to the Library in 1830 and remained as Meehan's faithful assistant thereafter. [39] The Librarian's salary, set at $1,500, stayed at that level for 25 years, whereupon it was increased to $1,800, and finally, in the fiscal year 1855, to $2,160. The total appropriation for the Library of Congress in 1830 was $7,750, which included $5,000 for books and $450 for contingent expenses. The $5,000 appropriation for books, except for a few notable years, remained steady at that amount throughout the long period of Meehan's service. After 1831 an annual appropriation of $1,000, later increased to $2,000, was made for the purchase of lawbooks. During Meehan's last year in the Library the total appropriation was $17,000. [40]

On July 14, 1832, Congress approved an act designed to increase and improve the law department of the Library of Congress. A nearby room, north of the main Library room, was fitted out accordingly and the Library's 2,011 lawbooks, of which 693 had been in Jefferson's library, were moved. The site was shifted two more times before Meehan's retirement—once in 1843 to a room in the basement of the west side of the north wing, and again in 1860 to the room in the basement floor formerly occupied by the Supreme Court. As a result of the legislation of 1832, the members of the Court were to have free access to the Law Library and were to make its rules and regulations; the chief justice was to have the decisive role in selecting books for the collection. Although it remained a part of the Library of Congress, the direction of the Law Library then came effectively under the control of the justices of the Supreme Court. [41]

C. H. Wharton Meehan, who had been previously employed in various positions in the Library, eventually emerged as the custodian of the Law Library. As the only survivor of the changes made during the first days of the Lincoln administration, he remained at his post until his death on July 5, 1872. The *Catalogue of the Law Department of the Library of Congress* (Washington: Lemuel Towers, Printer, 1860) bears his name as compiler. In the preface to this 225-page catalog, Meehan noted that his department now numbered "15,939 volumes of works exclusively treating of law." Like his father, Wharton was known for his cheerful disposition and obliging manner. Perhaps an indication of this relaxed approach to life can be detected in a slim volume by "a Professor," the authorship of which has been attributed to C. H. W. Meehan. On page 32 of *The Law and Practice of the Game of Euchre* (Philadelphia: T. B. Peterson & brothers, 1862), the "Professor" declared: "Of all sedentary amusements—except a fourth class clerkship in the Treasury Department—*we* most 'affectionate' Euchre." Meehan was, however, greatly esteemed, and one of his eulogists asserted that he had "made the Law Library of Congress . . . probably the best law library in the world." [42]

The Congress had two opportunities, in 1836 and 1844, which, if they had been acted upon successfully, would have done away with the notion that the Library of Congress was meant to be solely a legislative library and would have gone far toward setting it upon its course once and for all as the first library in the land. Meehan appears to have been only a spectator on both occasions, but since that in itself tells something of the role of the Librarian in those times, and because the results affected the Library that he was charged with administering, a mention of these lost opportunities should be made.

The first involved an offer to purchase the library, famed throughout Europe, of Count Dimitriî Petrovich Buturlin. While living in Florence, the count had assembled a magnificent, scholarly, multilingual collection of 25,000 volumes and a number of valuable manuscripts. The price for this unique collection was known to be in the range of $50,000 to $60,000—far below its true value. Support was forthcoming from withing the Library Committee, including that of Daniel Webster, and the committee recommended a resolution looking to the negotiation of a contract for the purchase of the collection. When the resolution came up on the floor of the Senate, however, it was rejected by a vote of 17 to 16, Henry Clay voting with the majority. Buturlin's library was sold piecemeal in Paris a few years later. The loss of the Buturlin library served as a precedent for the rejection of the

library of the Durazzo family in Italy also. Although not of the same order of significance as the Buturlin library, the Durazzo library of more than 10,000 volumes was considered to be one of the choicest private libraries in Europe. Offered at $30,000, it was rejected in June 1844 as consisting preponderantly of literature in languages other than English. The rejection of these two collections, particularly the Buturlin, had the effect of giving notice that the essential character of the Library of Congress was to remain unchanged and that proponents of a national library would have to look elsewhere. [43]

Meehan always kept in mind that he was a creature of the Congress and took pains to see to it that the bidding of its Members was carried out. His opportunities to be of service were never ending. Some substantiation of this can be seen in the elaborate receipt books, or borrower's ledgers, that he carefully maintained. These occupy 10 large volumes in which are preserved fascinating records of the reading—or at least borrowing—habits of the Representatives and Senators of three decades. Each interested Member was apparently asked to place his signature on a partly printed page that was reserved for him in the receipt book. Items borrowed were entered, almost always in Meehan's hand, and duly checked off upon return, providing an indication of the frequency and extent of his dealings with these individual Members. On many pages the signatures have been cut out, not by autograph seekers it is believed, but by the Member himself as an added precaution that his liability for the books recorded on that page had terminated. [44]

The Librarian's most significant encounters, of course, were with the members of the Joint Committee on the Library, and particularly with its chairman. This relationship, in all its ramifications, is very clearly developed beginning in the fall of 1843, from which time forward there are Librarian's Letterbooks containing fair copies and letterpress copies of Meehan's outgoing correspondence. Earlier evidence of the posture taken before the committee is scarce, but from the little information that is available there can be no question of the deferential nature of the relationship. As early as June 1830, even with Jacksonianism in the saddle, Meehan was handling Edward Everett, a National-Republican of

A page from one of the Receipt Books maintained by Librarian Meehan, in which he kept track of books in circulation to Members of Congress. This page reflects the reading habits of "the pathfinder," John C. Frémont, and perhaps of his wife, the incomparable Jessie Benton Frémont. LCMS–93898–2

Massachusetts, with great circumspection, seeking his opinion, keeping him fully informed, and closing a letter with an expression of "sincere gratitude for the many kind offices I have received at your hands." In July Everett was assured that an "evil" he had pointed out last winter would "not exist in the Library when we again have the pleasure of seeing you." A copy of a letter to Obadiah Rich, recently appointed London agent of the Library, was enclosed to Everett "for a friendly correction" in case he noticed "any omissions or improprieties in it."

Late in 1831, Meehan made "considerable inquiry" and exerted himself in other ways in attempting to serve Everett in seeking "accommodation in our city," and did succeed in finding a house that he thought would be "agreeable" to him. And finally, in 1832, after a visit to the "principal Libraries in the cities North and East" of Washington, a visit that Everett had once urged upon him, Meehan reported that he was considerably improved by what he had seen and heard and was now "much more than *half a yankee.*" [45]

It was in 1845, however, the year that Senator James Alfred Pearce of Maryland came to the committee, that an era of extraordinarily close collaboration between the committee—in the person of its chairman—and the Librarian really began. In the same year William Q. Force, in *Force's Picture of the City of Washington and Its Vicinity for 1845,* characterized the Library in the following charming manner:

Within the Capitol is a Library of about forty thousand volumes, in a large and elegant room, and disposed in order by an excellent librarian. The Library is open to visiters daily during the session, and every other day in the week during the recess. The librarian is a gentleman of amiable manners and takes pleasure in exhibiting the books under his charge.

This was what Pearce had inherited and what he wished to preserve and build upon.

Pearce is a figure of much interest. He was born in Alexandria, Va., in 1805, and attended Princeton College, graduating with first honors at age 17. After studying law and gaining admission to the Maryland bar, he spent three years as a planter in Louisiana. Returning to Maryland he resumed the practice of law and also commenced farming in Chestertown. He was soon called into public life, serving first in the Maryland legislature and then in the U.S. House of Representatives. In 1843 he was elected to the Senate and remained there continuously until his death in 1862.[46] He has been described as "a type of the gentleman of the old school," and in appearance was "tall, with a commanding figure, expressive features, blue eyes, and light hair."[47] John J. Crittenden, a Senate colleague, considered him "a noble fellow—a man of first rate talents, & a gentleman of the highest order." He was possessed of "a high spirit & quick temper," but great allowances nonetheless had to be made for "friends of so much truth & worth."[48] William Pitt Fessenden, who served with him in later years on the Joint Committee on the Library, testified to Pearce's distinction as a scholar, and saw him as a man "thoroughly imbued with a love of letters and of science." His mind was "disciplined to logical exactness," but he was fond of the beautiful "in all its forms and quick to discern it." He was held to be a master of the language, to whom an "awkward phrase was . . . an annoyance, and vulgarity

James Alfred Pearce, Senator from Maryland and for many years chairman of the Joint Committee on the Library. Complete understanding existed between Meehan and Pearce. Librarian John Stephenson said of Pearce: "The elegant courtesy of his manners, and the kindness of his feeling, made his presence in the Library always a pleasure to every one employed there."

almost a crime."[49] A man of culture, therefore, and of conservative views, the objects of his "fostering care" were the Library of Congress, the Botanic Garden, the Smithsonian Institution, and the Coast Survey Department. During the Fillmore administration he was nominated and confirmed as secretary of the interior but declined, preferring his position in the Senate to any other.[50]

About the time Pearce came to the chairmanship of the Library Committee and the working arrangement with Librarian Meehan was beginning, a plan that had much promise for the future of the Library of Congress was reaching its final stages. The matter was complicated, because it involved the creation of the Smithsonian Institution and the direction that institution was to take, the establishment of a national library, and the use of federal copyright law to enrich library collections. James Smithson's bequest of half a million dollars to the United States in 1838 was the starting point of a sequence which by August 10, 1846, resulted in the act establishing the Smithsonian Institution. The debate leading up to this legislation had been long and wide ranging. Some of the more eloquent participants, such as Rufus Choate and George P. Marsh, as well as James A. Pearce, were members of the Library Committee and at various times had been advocates of the idea of a national library, with its seat at the Smithsonian Institution. None of these men saw the Library of Congress as eventually filling this role. In the Smithsonian Act of 1846, however, there was a copyright provision directing that one copy of each book, map, chart, muscial composition, print, cut, or engraving produced in the United States should be placed in the Library of Congress as well as in the Smithsonian library. At last the concept of utilizing copyright deposits for the building of national library resources had been enunciated, even though the implementation of the idea was beset with practical difficulties and differences of opinion. For one thing, the legislation had no teeth, since neither institution could compel deposits and the actual validity of a copyright did not appear to depend upon a deposit. Furthermore, those responsible for the development of the collections of the Library of Congress seemed to be indifferent, if not hostile, to the processing of copyright deposits. Charles C. Jewett, the Smithsonian's librarian, fully recognized the significance of these deposits and yearned to see his library become the national library. But he lost the confidence of Joseph Henry, secretary of the Smithsonian, and left Washington. Without him on the scene copyright deposits dwindled even more, and the law requiring that items be forwarded to the Smithsonian and the Library of Congress was repealed on February 5, 1859. Single copies of items were then to be sent to the Patent Office, for legal evidence of copyright only, not for use.[51]

Meehan had undoubtedly found the task of attending to copyright matters burdensome. Even though Edward Stelle was responsible for the major part of this work, there were few enough hands available to carry on the routine business of the Library, while attending to the unpredictable wants of the Congress and coping with a steady stream of visitors. Meehan himself, because of his reputation as a careful and precise businessman, had in addition to his regular duties the responsibility of keeping the books for a bewildering variety of special funds and conducting the correspondence relating to them. Among these were the Wilkes Fund for publishing the results of Charles Wilkes' United States Exploring Expedition; a fund of $22,500 for purchasing the published works of John Adams; the Botanic Garden Fund, which sometimes included actual supervision of workers, as well as the diplomatic handling of Congressmen seeking botanical specimens for their own gardens; a $20,000 fund for acquiring works of art for the Capitol; a fund to print the Library of Congress catalog on the Smithsonian plan; a $6,000 fund for printing the papers and manuscripts of Alexander Hamilton; a $5,000 fund for portraits by G. P. A. Healy of the Presidents; and funds totaling $12,000 for printing the papers of Thomas Jefferson and James Madison.[52]

As the year 1851 approached its close, Librarian Meehan was about to undergo the most dramatic and searing experience of his long incumbency. On the whole, his days and years had been tranquil enough, and his domestic and public careers had proceeded along largely unremarkable lines. His diary, which over hundreds of pages underscores this view, offers a sharply contrasting picture of the events of December 24, 1851. Writing on Christmas Eve, he dutifully recorded the changes in the day's weather, as was his unchanging custom. It had been "Very cold, cloudy, disagreeable weather, all this day; the wind fresh, from the S.E. Clear cold, beautiful; the wind very light, from the S.E." With these somewhat contradictory essentials out the way, he turned to the events of the day: "Before 8 o'clock this morning I was informed that the Library of Congress was on fire, and went over to the Capitol immediately." When he arrived there Meehan found "the principal room of the Library on fire throughout, the flames having spread with great rapidity." Little could be saved from that room, but large numbers of books in nearby rooms were moved to places of greater safety. The loss, however, was "very severe." Many of the books had been very rare and it would "be difficult if not impossible to replace them." As he concluded this diary entry he heard the "perpetual jingle of numerous sleigh bells" and the firing of guns by merrymakers in the streets. He wrote, "I feel sad!" [53]

Benjamin Brown French, a longtime resident of Capitol Hill, a friend of Meehan's, and an indefatigable diarist, had also observed the fire close at hand. The night had been "the coldest that has been known here for many years (the thermometer 4 below zero)," and French was just finishing his breakfast when his son announced that the Capitol was on fire. As a former Clerk of the House—and soon to become commissioner of public buildings—his concern was genuine and he hurried to the Capitol, ran up the eastern steps, and "found the Congressional Library in flames." Some 20 people were near at hand and soon a line was formed for passing water up from a fountain near the western steps. Fire apparatus arrived from several points, but the unusually low temperatures caused some difficulty with freezing hoses. French continued to work on, "sometimes in one place, sometimes in another," until the fire was "completely subdued" at approximately 11 o'clock. [54]

The fire, the third in the Library's history, was a disaster. Meehan reported at once to Senator Pearce, who was at his home in Chestertown, Maryland. It was his "melancholy duty" to inform him that "nearly everything in the room was destroyed." A few buckets of water if at hand at the outset would have been enough to extinguish the flames, but the rapid and extensive spread of the fire soon carried the situation beyond all control until "the late beautiful room, with its invaluable contents" was left "a smouldering mass of ruins." Meehan was concerned about the origins of the fire, probably feeling that he might be charged with negligence. He reminded Pearce that "no fire or lights [had] been used in any rooms of the Library for several years," and repeated the conjecture of some that "the fire was communicated to the wood work adjacent to the flue used for warming the room." Others suspected that the fire was "the work of an incendiary," and Meehan for a time shared in that opinion. [55]

On Christmas day, Meehan addressed letters to the Speaker of the House and the President of the Senate in which he performed "the painful duty" of communicating to the Congress the news of the destruction of much of its library. Again he was careful to give assurance that no fires had been used in the Library for a long time and that "no candles, lamps, or other lights have ever been used in it during the time that it has been under my charge." It had not been possible to ascertain precisely the number of books destroyed, but it was estimated to be 35,000. Of the 20,000 volumes remaining, many, according to Meehan, "belonged to the Library of the late President Jefferson." [56]

On the 26th of December a joint resolution was passed calling for an inquiry into the origin of the fire. Official negligence, defective construction, and the possibility of incendiarism were all to be considered. [57] The same day Meehan answered questions put to him by William Easby, commissioner of public buildings, giving assurance that fires and lights were strictly and routinely excluded from the Library and that on the day preceding the fire the room had been closed "about 4 o'clock, p.m. everything in it appearing to be perfectly safe as usual." Meehan was also careful to point out that the Library rooms were warmed by "flues from furnaces not in my charge." [58] Thomas Ustick Walter, Architect of the Capitol, also responded to a request for information from Easby. On the basis of a "careful examination" of the subject he concluded that the fire "was caused by the timbers which formed the alcoves of the Library having been inserted in the chimney flues." One of these timbers extending into the chimney had taken fire, and by this means the fire was finally communicated to the Library. The evidence was too conclusive to admit of doubt and was "sufficient to remove all censure from those who have charge of the building." [59] Walter's authoritative explanation seems to have been generally accepted and no further legislative action was taken with regard to the origin of the fire. [60]

Senator Pearce had been following events as well as he could from Maryland's Eastern Shore. In a letter to Meehan dated December 31, 1851, he wrote feelingly of the calamity that had occurred and which had affected the two of them more than any others.

> I heard with absolute grief and dismay of the loss of our Library. . . . The destruction of so noble a collection any where would be a subject of much regret; but to lose our own valuable and admirable Library,

WASHINGTON.
"Liberty and Union, now and forever, one and inseparable."

THURSDAY, DECEMBER 25, 1851.

THE NATIONAL LIBRARY DESTROYED BY FIRE!

THE FIRES which occurred yesterday morning in our city will long be remembered with a distinctness of recollection far beyond ordinary conflagrations.

The first in point of time broke out a little past one o'clock in the Franklin Hotel, at the northeast corner of D and Eighth streets, kept by Mr. Thomas Adams. It was communicated, as we learn, from the bedroom of a lodger in the upper story, and had got so great a hold of the building before the engines could be brought to bear upon it, that by its efforts could the house be saved, though the chief part of the furniture was happily rescued from the devouring element. The building was owned by Mr. Patrick Kavanagh, and was insured.

SOUTH CAROLINA.

The LEGISLATURE of this State finally adjourned late on the night of the 16th.

INTERESTING FROM MEXICO.

We are in possession of papers from the city of Mexico to the 25th ultimo, inclusive, and from Vera Cruz we have dates up to the 6th instant.

THE STEAMER PAMPERO CONDEMNED.

FROM THE JACKSONVILLE REPUBLICAN of December 18.

This case has at last been finally investigated and decided. On Monday, the 1st instant, the United States Court convened at St. Augustine; McQUEEN McINTOSH, Esq. appeared on behalf of the claimant, Mr. Sigur; G. W. CALL, Esq., United States Attorney

THE AMERICAN PRISONERS IN SPAIN.

The Charleston Courier contains a letter from the Hon. DANIEL M. BARRINGER, our Minister at Madrid, in which he promises to use every endeavor to secure the pardon of the American prisoners in Spain.

M. KOSSUTH arrived at Philadelphia yesterday morning, and was publicly received.

THE SMITHSONIAN INSTITUTION.

Notwithstanding the severity of the weather of late, we witness no relaxation in the business of improving and adorning the public grounds around the Smithsonian Edifice.

TO THE EDITORS.

WASHINGTON, DECEMBER 23, 1851.

MESSRS. EDITORS: The correspondent of the Baltimore Sun of this morning [is in a quite error in charging in the nature of] &c.

NEW BOOKS.

We have received from our neighbor, Mr. GRAY, Bookseller, on Seventh street, copies of a variety of books adapted to the amusement and instruction of youth, and suitable for Christmas presents.

CHRISTMAS PRESENTS.

MARRIAGES.

DEATH.

SUPREME COURT OF THE UNITED STATES.

WEDNESDAY, DECEMBER 24, 1851.

BENTON D. FREEMAN, Esq., of Mississippi, and CHARLES EATON, Esq., of Wisconsin, were admitted as attorneys and counsellors of this Court.

THE DEBT OF TEXAS.

The last Austin Gazette contains the report of the Auditor and Comptroller on the public debt of Texas, giving a clear and intelligible description and classification of the character and amount of the liabilities of the Republic.

EDITORS' CORRESPONDENCE.

BALTIMORE, DECEMBER 24—4 P. M.

THE FIRST FUGITIVE CASE IN CONNECTICUT.

FROM THE NEW HAVEN REGISTER OF FRIDAY.

A novel case—at least in practice—under the fugitive from service act, came off in this city yesterday, before CHARLES R. INGERSOLL, Esq., United States Commissioner.

NATIONAL THEATRE.

MR. E. A. MARSHALL .... Sole Lessee
W. M. FLEMING .... Stage Manager

Fourth night of the engagement of the celebrated SEGUIN OPERA TROUPE.

CHRISTMAS NIGHT,
THIS EVENING, December 25,
LA SOMNAMBULA

FRIDAY EVENING, DECEMBER 26,
BETSY BAKER

F. MORRIS & CO., Managers

The National Intelligencer *for December 25, 1851, in reporting the fire that destroyed the Library of Congress, notes that the heat was so intense that it caused the paint and stone of the pillars in the west front of the Capitol to scale off to a depth of a quarter of an inch in places.*

of which you and I have thought so much, which has been so long our pride, and has yielded us so much pleasure. . . . which is so necessary to Congress, and to me was more attractive than any political honors, is really a deep affliction. I thought of you, and knew how distressing it would be. I rejoice that the mode of its origin is so well ascertained. . . . Had that remained in mystery, there are many who would, however unreasonably, have censured you.[61]

Meehan was deeply moved by these thoughtful words and confided to his diary: "It is truly grateful and reviving, to receive so kind a letter, in my deep affliction, from so eminent a gentleman, and so discriminating a friend, as Mr. Pearce. . . . May the Lord bless him, and prosper him!"[62]

The days and months following the fire were unusually busy ones. Senator Pearce arrived in Washington on January 4, sent for Meehan, and the two had a long conversation about the fire and the best means of renewing the Library.[63] Congress, in a cooperative mood, appropriated $5,000 on January 13 for the removal of the rubble that remained at the site, for cleaning and preserving what had survived, and for the building of a temporary roof over the Library Room. An additional $10,000 was earmarked for the purchase of books. On January 23 the sum of $1,200 was appropriated for the preparation of temporary quarters for the Library. In this same period Thomas U. Walter was at work on plans and drawings for the reconstruction of the Library Room, and on March 19 Congress appropriated $72,500 to carry them out. Eventually, an additional $20,500 had to be authorized for completion of the repairs. Replacement of the lost books was underwritten on August 31, 1852, by an appropriation of $75,000.[64]

Two courses of action, therefore, were to be carried on simultaneously—the reconstruction of the Library Room and the acquisition of the books and other library materials that were to stock it. Meehan, although he had no responsibility for the former, took great interest in it and

grew impatient over inevitable delays. Temporary facilities for the Library were ready by March, and Members of Congress and other visitors were "much pleased with the room." The workmen then turned their attention to the main room, and Walter told Meehan that it would be completed in three months and would be much more beautiful than before. But spring ended and summer wore on and Meehan exclaimed, "O! slow, indifferent mechanics!!" In September, in the company of Walter, he looked at "the beautiful iron work" and then went on top of the roof to examine the progress made there. He regarded all that he had seen as "beautiful enough, and to spare," but everything proceeded so tardily he despaired, correctly as it turned out, of getting into the Library before the next meeting of Congress.[65]

Finally, in the spring of 1853, a year and a half after the fire, Walter's assignment was nearly completed. Meehan was impressed and wrote to Senator Pearce, telling him that the work had been done "in the most elegant manner." The ceiling was finished and the scaffolding had been taken down. The walls were paneled "in fresco" and harmonized perfectly with the "richness and splendor of the massive ornaments in the ceiling." Three coats of cream-colored paint were to be placed on "all the work in the upper gallery, and upon all the pillars and pilasters, and in all the alcoves on the two lower floors." The "ornamental portions of the work" would then be gilded. Meehan thought that the room would be "rather gorgeous." Completion was expected by July 1, and Meehan asked Pearce, "Cannot you stroll over to Washington about that time, and take a view of the premises?"[66]

On July 6, 1853, Meehan took formal possession of the room. Walter was delighted with it and Meehan agreed that it was "truly beautiful." President Franklin Pierce had visited the room a few days earlier with the British geologist, Sir Charles Lyell, and a workman had reported that Sir Charles had "pronounced it the most beautiful room in the world." It was then necessary to close the Library for a month "to get the books in it, and to lay the carpets, and bring up the documents for exchanges from the room or cellar under the crypt, where they were placed after the fire."[67]

The prompt appropriation of $10,000 for the

purchase of books had demonstrated that the Congress was anxious to see the shelves of its Library filled once again. This form of restoration, however, was to involve far greater difficulties than had the physical restoration of the Library Room. Meehan set about the task almost at once, writing to the Library's London agent, Rich Brothers. He told them of the destructive effect of the fire and gave them to understand that it was the intention of the Library Committee "to commence operations without delay, for restoring the Library to its great usefulness, and for extending it in every department of literature." A want list was enclosed for immediate action. Competition from American booksellers would be great but Meehan wrote Rich Brothers that he expected they would "maintain in our approaching dealings, the superiority your house has maintained for promptness, accuracy, cheapness, and fidelity." [68]

Rich Brothers had already learned of the fire and had written to Meehan as early as January 6. They assured him that since in the past they had had the honor of supplying so considerable a part of the Library of Congress they would again "be most happy to be entrusted with the commission of making such purchases as might be required." In apparent anticipation of the strictures laid down by Meehan the firm offered, in the event that the purchases were considerable, to undertake them on "the lowest possible terms, say 5 per cent on the cost price of the books." They would also be happy to give their almost "exclusive attention" to this work for a considerable time. Meehan, who had dealt with this firm for years, was touched. "How very different," he entered in his diary, "is all this from the hyenas that are now striving to prey on us in our own country! 'Hail! Columbia!!' " [69]

Meehan's industry and concern were not all that was required at this crucial juncture in the Library's history. Critics have pointed out that he was not a collection-builder, that he had very limited bibliographical experience, and that he lacked imagination.[70] An anonymous contemporary—probably Charles C. Jewett—raised a number of important points in a two-part article in the *National Intelligencer,* April 8 and 14, 1852. The auction season in Europe, the article said, was almost over and a number of important private libraries had already been sold off. An

agent of the Library, if he had been appointed promptly and sent abroad, would have had an opportunity to acquire some of these. Also lacking was a carefully prepared list, with as many as 100,000 titles, of the books that the Library of Congress should have. The $10,000 appropriated for the purchase of books on January 13 was clearly not enough; more should be made available at once. Essentially, in the view of this critic, the new Library of Congress "should be a systematic collection of books chosen with competent bibliographical learning for a specified and well defined purpose." By following the proper program the Library of Congress might become a truly national library, like the British Museum and the Bibliothèque nationale.[71]

Those in authority, however, did not do as they were bid. In fact, in a letter to Senator Pearce, Meehan appeared to be responding directly to the articles in the *Intelligencer*:

I am sorry to see that the project of an agent to *select* and *purchase* books for us is again revived. It will not meet with favor in Congress, I think. I have heard the remark made by a number that the Library used to be considered very excellent, and they presumed it could be renewed in the same manner in which it was first formed. They have no idea of placing Congress in a position which admits that they cannot select the books they need.[72]

This was the expedient philosophy under which Meehan operated. He knew the situation firsthand and could judge the temper of Congress. When faced with criticism from the outside he relied upon his sense of knowing what the Congress wanted. It was not in his makeup to lead elsewhere, even if he had the capacity to do so. Meehan proceeded on his own way, therefore, the way that met with the approval of Senator Pearce.

Want lists were prepared, largely on the basis of earlier catalogs. They filled hundreds of pages and gave testimony to Meehan's diligence and habits of business.[73] The preparation of these lists represented a departure from former practices in a sense, because the bibliographical direction of the Library, formerly the province of the Library Committee, had been placed in the hands of the Librarian. This, at least, seemed to be the burden of a resolution that came out of the Library Committee on March 3, 1853.[74] That Meehan was not thirsting for this power is

evident in a letter written to Pearce in which the Librarian remarked that the resolution did not offer "a single advantage over the mode we were pursuing to restore the Library . . . and to improve it." Meehan, stepping back gingerly from any notion that his role in the acquisition of books was to be expanded, assured Pearce that since the resolution did not specify that the Librarian was to exercise judgment in determining which proposals and offers should actually be

Interior of the Library Room in the Capitol, restored "in the most elegant manner" following the disastrous fire of December 24, 1851. LC–USZ62–1818

accepted, then "the power to make that decision rests, as it did before the resolution was adopted, with the Chairman of the Committee." [75]

Another interesting feature of this resolution related to the matter of making the want lists generally available in order to stimulate competition. Meehan was quick to alert Rich Brothers and suggested that, in his view, the resolution was provoked by "many of our booksellers, who complain that the patronage is sent abroad without giving them an opportunity for competition." In closing, Meehan confided, "The Chairman told me to say to you that the resolution will be rescinded next winter." [76]

By the autumn of 1853 Meehan was able to tell Pearce, whose ill health frequently kept him away from Washington, that during the upcoming session of Congress many of the Library's shelves would be bare, but before the close of that session they would "present a very different appearance." He went so far as to predict that "the Library will be much richer than it was the day before the fire." [77] Pearce was pleased with this news and used the occasion for a bit of self-congratulation. He had, he told Meehan, "taken a good deal of responsibility in authorizing so many purchases," but trusted that he should "not only be sustained but commended for filling the shelves without being restrained by the absurd resolution of the Cmee." [78]

The Pearce-Meehan relationship, although formal because both men were aware of the line of authority between them, was nevertheless often as cordial as it was effective. In a long and otherwise uncharacteristic letter written in November 1853, at a time when the Library was standing in readiness for inspection by the legislators arriving for the first session of the 33d Congress, Meehan expressed the hope that Pearce would consent to remain as chairman of the Library Committee until the Library was fully replenished and other projects completed. Meehan believed that "no man in Congress could so well discharge those duties" as Pearce. He had the "entire confidence of Congress" and even though the labors performed by the chairman were sometimes "oppressive and vexatious" they were "rendered tolerable" by the gratification he conferred on everybody in discharging them.[79] Whether influenced by Meehan or not, Pearce continued as chairman of the Library Committee

A view of the west front of the Capitol from Pennsylvania Avenue, about 1857. The Library of Congress occupied the space behind the pillars, at the center of the west front. LC–USA7–5044

until the day he died.

As a result of the special appropriations of 1852, totaling $85,000, and annual appropriations of $5,000 thereafter, the Library continued its rapid growth in the years after the fire. Separate annual appropriations of $2,000 contributed to the steady growth of the Law Library. Life in the Library at this time was sketched by Meehan in response to a letter from a Canadian

librarian. The Library of Congress, he wrote, had a staff of five employed the year round. The Library was open every day when Congress was in session, and three days a week during recesses. It was a circulating library for the President, Vice-President, Senators and Representatives, heads of executive departments, judges of the Supreme Court, the resident diplomatic corps, and some few officers of the government to whom special use had been granted. According to Meehan the duties of the persons employed in the Library were "so various and frequently contingent" that it would have been almost impossible to designate them. "It may suffice to say," he added, "that they are never unemployed." [80] Dr. Joseph G. Cogswell, librarian of the Astor Library, New York City, who visited the Library of Congress in October 1855, was very much pleased with it and pronounced it "the first, in quality, in the United States." He also considered it "the foundation of the greatest Library in the world." [81]

By early 1856 Rich Brothers was told that the shelves in the new Library were already overflowing and that orders would be more limited in the future, although as liberal as they had been before the fire.[82] In April Meehan announced to Senator Pearce that the losses had been entirely made good, in many instances with better editions, and in every case "with more elegant and better bindings." At least 36,000 volumes had been purchased and at a cost "very far below the prices given for the lost books." [83] Within the limits that those responsible had set for themselves, the Library had been restored. The Library Committee, meeting on July 26, expressed its gratitude for the exertions of Rich Brothers and in a generous mood decided that the firm's old commission of 10 percent should be allowed on all future purchases. The firm's "patriotic and prompt offer" to reduce its compensation after the fire and the "assiduous and masterly" attention given to the Library's orders had not been forgotten.[84]

If Alexandre Vattemare (1796–1864) had been able to win the confidence of Librarian Meehan, as well as that of various chairmen of the Joint Committee, to the degree that the Library's agents in London had, the collections of the Library of Congress might have been of a much different character. Vattemare, a French citizen of noble lineage, a medical man, mimic, ventriloquist, and bibliophile, had, in spite of all these interests, an idée fixe. It was to bring about the establishment of a system of international exchange whereby duplicate library materials in one nation would be made available to libraries in others. He had achieved a measure of success in Europe and, with the encouragement and backing of a number of prominent Americans, had traveled to Washington in 1839. He found Congress in a receptive mood and on July 20, 1840, a joint resolution had been approved authorizing Librarian Meehan to "exchange such duplicates as may be in the Library for other books or works." Authorization was also given for the exchange of documents and provision made for the printing of 50 additional copies of those printed by order of either House for ex-

change purposes in foreign countries.[85] Membership of the Library Committee, however, underwent frequent changes during the next few years, and Meehan was not one to step forward and lead. It is also likely that Meehan had developed an early dislike for Vattemare. Little was done to implement the resolution of 1840. Vattemare returned to the United States in 1848 and memorialized Congress, proposing a more ambitious scheme involving the establishment of a central agency in Paris with subordinate agencies elsewhere in Europe and the United States. He also called for the forwarding of 50 copies of congressional documents to Paris and urged that the Librarian be "directed" rather than "authorized" to carry out the purposes of congressional resolutions bearing on exchange matters. Legislative acts and committee resolutions of 1848 implemented much of Vattemare's plan and over the next few years the program of international exchange began to show some results.

Vattemare, the French man of the world, and Meehan, the provincial American, were separated by more than miles. Meehan, however, had the advantage of being much closer to the Library Committee. In the autumn of 1848, after Vattemare's return to France, Meehan complained to Chairman Pearce that he was being pressed for the duplicates in the Library. Yet the Library had "very few duplicates . . . so considered," and Vattemare did not seem to understand that books could not be delivered to him without an order from the Library Committee. The requirement that the Library house the books and documents ordered for exchange was also onerous. In Meehan's view all the room available in the Library "was required for books entered in its Catalogue." [86] In 1850 he complained to Pearce about the quality and completeness of the materials sent by Vattemare from France. In the case of printed documents, it would cost more to have them bound in the United States than if they had been both purchased and bound in France.[87] Charles C. Jewett of the Smithsonian Library and other bookmen and scholars were also becoming disenchanted. Whatever the reasons, Vattemare's grand plans for international exchange were not working and on June 15, 1853, the law providing for these exchanges was repealed.[88]

Meehan, who was called upon to inform

Vattemare that the law under which he had been appointed agent of the Library Committee had been rescinded, undoubtedly found his assignment congenial. He pointed out that the committee had been "greatly disappointed" in not receiving complete copies of official documents of the French government, or from any other government, through Vattemare's agency. Those which had been sent were imperfect as collections, "done up in pamphlet style merely," and seemed to have been selected by Vattemare himself, rather than to have been intended by the government of France as a continuation of the carefully prepared volumes that had formerly come to the Library through Mr. Pageot, minister plenipotentiary of France. Meehan added that, under the circumstances, France might consider it "undignified" to hold "national intercourse except through recognized officers of the Government." [89]

Failing to comprehend that he had been cut loose, or choosing to ignore the fact, Vattemare continued to forward books to the Library from time to time, thereby bringing further criticism upon himself. Meehan found that the latest boxes from France contained "a number of worn out old books . . . evidently the refuse of a French library." Furthermore, he had learned that French library officials considered Vattemare "a charlatan, and could not allow him to be their agent." [90] Redoubtable and audacious as ever, Vattemare sent a final case of books to the Library in 1858. Meehan curtly reminded him that his services had been terminated "so far back as the year 1852." The case would remain unopened and he would be expected to reclaim it and pay all expenses.[91] Thus ended, inelegantly and ignobly, the first organized attempt at international exchange. Distribution of public documents was transferred to the Department of Interior in 1857 and the exchange of public documents with foreign countries to the Department of State.

Cataloging activities before the fire, as has been seen, were limited in scope and the catalogs cumbersome to use. Beginning in March 1853 an effort was made to change this when Congress appropriated $3,000 in support of a plan designed and widely publicized by Charles C. Jewett, librarian of the Smithsonian Institution. Jewett, who has been characterized as being as full of energy as one of Joseph Henry's electromagnets, had published an address on "A Plan for Stereotyping Catalogues by Separate Titles. . . ." The plan, although emanating from the Smithsonian, was to be applied to books in the Library of Congress. The catalog would be compiled and printed under the superintendence of Professor Jewett, and the stereotype blocks prepared for titles would be preserved at the Smithsonian for future use. Once the initial cataloging effort was completed it was envisioned that annual additions could be readily accounted for and a complete annual catalog issued, rather than mere supplements. The beginning of cooperative cataloging—in effect, central, uniform cataloging—was also understood to be involved in this plan, for it was meant to take account eventually of the catalogs of other libraries in the United States. Meehan was not intimately concerned in the plan and its implementation. It had been recognized from the outset that the small staff of the Library was not sufficient even for the regular work that it was expected to perform.[92] Meehan did, however, handle some of the contractual matters that had to be arranged between Joseph Henry and the Library Committee and played a role in hiring assistants for Jewett.[93]

Work began in the summer of 1853 and by the end of the year 6,000 volumes had been cataloged. Some 4,000 of these were from chapter I of Thomas Jefferson's classification system and these were stereotyped and printed at the Smithsonian in 1854. The greater part of the original appropriation having been used up, Congress, on May 31, made an additional $5,000 available. But Jewett and his plan now entered upon hard times. Joseph Henry, with whom he had not seen eye-to-eye for some time, especially with regard to the real mission of the Smithsonian Institution, dismissed him in July 1854. The program for stereotyping continued for a time under other direction, but eventually faltered and came to a close. Without Jewett on hand to defend it, critics came forward and spoke out against his catalog. Meehan must be classed among them for he sent on to Senator Pearce, with a favorable introduction, a report on Jewett's cataloging system that described it as a scheme "without a single really valuable end to be accomplished even if it were practicable." The plan was "altogether visionary" and considerations and obstacles not apparent when taking a general view arose "at every step of investigation." Moreover, Jewett's plan "would be useless as a Catalogue in the Library of Congress." [94]

Not long thereafter work on it ceased altogether, and Meehan chose to return to the old ways of cataloging that he and his associates had followed in producing the general catalogs of 1831, 1839, and 1849. The resulting printed catalog of 1861 covered the accessions of the Library into 1859. As an inventory of the collections it was adequate, but as a means of extending intellectual control over them it was a failure. Ainsworth Spofford, in illustrating the defects of this catalog, and the ancient system of classification upon which it was based, called attention to the fact that in the 1,400-page volume the titles were distributed "through a series of 179 distinct alphabets, arranged in an arbitrary sequence, and without an index." Few readers would have the leisure, he wrote, and "fewer still the inclination," to study and master the intricacies of such a system. [95]

Meehan, who had survived the denunciations of former Librarian Watterston and had successfully seen Whig administrations come and go, did have his position threatened, or so it seemed, at the outset of the Democratic administration of Franklin Pierce. On May 20, 1853, Meehan wrote to his ally Senator Pearce to tell him he had seen a newspaper account stating that Samuel E. Coues of Portsmouth, N.H., had been appointed Librarian by President Pierce. Unable to determine whether this announcement was "founded on fact, or a mere rumor," Meehan thought it proper to bring the matter to the chairman's notice. [96] Pearce advised him to seek the support of Jefferson Davis, who had been a member of the Library Committee from 1847 to 1851 and was now secretary of war in President Pierce's cabinet. Davis let it be known that there was no truth in the report, as far as he knew, and he believed that there was no intention to make any change in the Library. [97]

When Buchanan replaced Pierce in 1853, Meehan must have felt threatened once more, for he wrote to various members of the Library Committee about his appointment. Among the favorable replies he received was that from Lewis Cass, one of the most omniverous readers in Congress, who expressed himself as having every rea-

son to be satisfied with the manner in which Meehan executed his duties. Cass had never heard a single complaint against his "official course" and trusted that the Library would not lose the benefit of his services. [98] And for the time being it did not.

The lives of Senator James Alfred Pearce and John Silva Meehan had been linked for years through their association with the Library of Congress. Their origins and stations in life were far different, but their like-mindedness with respect to the Library made it easy for them to work together harmoniously and, by their lights, to good effect. With the election of Abraham Lincoln in November of 1860, and the onset of the secession crisis, their quiet, untroubled world began to break up. Pearce had been a Whig through most of his political career, but in 1856, with that party on the point of dissolution in Maryland, he became a member of the National Democratic party, believing it to be the "only conservative National Party in the country," and favored the election of James Buchanan. The election of 1860 now put Pearce, and Maryland, in a difficult position. The state was generally pro-Southern, and secession was not entirely out of the question. Yet, because of their geographical position, most Marylanders hoped that the Union would persist and that armed conflict could be avoided. Pearce was a spokesman for this point of view; [99] yet, as his biographer has indicated, he could not give a "bold, clear summons to support the Union." [100] As far as the Library of Congress was concerned this meant, inevitably, a diminution of the chairman's influence. As far as John Meehan was concerned, it meant the end of his long career.

In addition to his being so closely identified with Pearce, Meehan may also have lost favor as a result of rumors of pro-Southern sympathies. [101] He had been cautiously nonpolitical throughout his public life and had his record of survival to prove it. A few of his letters to Pearce, particularly at the time of John Brown's raid on Harpers Ferry, do reveal a decided lack of sympathy toward the insurrectionists. But he was not alone in feeling that John Brown and his followers were "traitors" or "abolition myrmidons," nor in believing that the excitement caused by the raid and trials would not subside "until the malefactors [had] been executed." [102] What might have been more to the point, if it had been brought out in the inflammatory atmosphere of the times, was the fact that there was a Confederate at the very bosom of the Meehan family; but there is no indication that this was known. The Librarian's first-born child, Susan, had married Sidney Taylor, who eventually became a colonel in the Confederate army. In the Meehan Papers there is a letter from Taylor to a brother in Washington, written on April 23, 1861, a week after Lincoln's call for troops, telling of his arrival in Virginia from Pennsylvania: "I don't suppose you ever knew of, read of, or heard of so delighted an individual as I was when I found myself, and my dear little family, on a soil upon which we could express our sentiments, and feel that we were among friends." [103] This, however, is slight evidence of any wrongheadedness on Meehan's part, for divisions in border state families were commonplace. The decline in Meehan's fortunes may, in fact, have been owing to nothing more than that he was "a very ancient fossil," in the inelegant words of 35-year-old Ainsworth Spofford, who added: "It was this, more than party reasons, which induced the President to make the change." [104]

Senator Pearce had realized from the outset that his old friend was in danger of being removed and wrote to President Lincoln on March 8:

I venture to address you in regard to the appointment of Librarian to Congress whose appointment the Law has vested in you, and as I shall address you only on this subject I trust that I shall not be considered obtrusive. I have been chairman of the Library Comee. on the part of the Senate for fifteen years and have had therefore a good opportunity to judge of the competency, fitness and merits generally of the Librarian and of his assistants. The latter are appointed by the Librarian. During all this time no change has been made in these appointments, the President having always deferred to the wishes of congress and neither House having desired any change. The present officers understand and perform all their duties with singular care fidelity and ability. They *know* the Library which now contains nearly 70,000 volumes, can refer directly to any desired book and understand the character of the collection as no one could do who had not been long engaged in their duties—any *new* Librarian or assistant would require a considerable time to learn what these officers already know and during that period congress would find a new appointment the reverse of a reform. They are not politicians but men of books, devoted to this specialty and singularly well qualified in their duties, uniting to knowledge, great suavity of

manners and accuracy of habits. I trust that they may still be as they have heretofore been, unaffected by political charges, & safe from the influence of political partisanship which has heretofore had no influence in the republic of letters. With the expression of this wish I beg to subscribe myself

with great respect.
Yr. OSt. Jas. Alfred Pearce [105]

There was little else that could be said. Pearce did, however, get the support of the other two senatorial members of the Library Committee and might have been encouraged by the fact that one was from Maine and the other from Vermont. William Pitt Fessenden noted his full endorsement and approval of what Pearce had written, and the taciturn Vermonter Jacob Collamer simply wrote "I concur in." There is no record of any reply having been made to this appeal.[106]

In the meantime Meehan remained at his post, advising a New York bookseller on May 3 that business was being conducted as usual and confidently assuring him that the "Government of the United States is as firm now as it ever was, and it will remain so throughout the present difficulties." [107] A few days later John G. Stephenson, an Indiana physician, sat down to urge his claim to the office of Librarian of Congress upon the President. There should be no unnecessary delay in making this appointment, he cautioned, in order that the new incumbent might so "familiarize himself with his position before the meeting of Congress, that by the order and energy of his administration of its affairs, he [might] bring credit to himself and the power that appoints him,—and convince protesting Senators that they erred in their protest against a change in that office." [108] Lincoln, with a myriad of distractions before him, reacted by asking Secretary of State William H. Seward on May 23 to send him a commission for Stephenson and on May 24 Stephenson wrote his letter of acceptance.[109] Of this purely political appointment it has been said, "Mr. Lincoln with his remarkable genius for understanding men was not infrequently a miserable failure in his judgment of a man." [110]

Meehan took his dismissal calmly and without rancor. He advised Edward Allen, a London bookseller, that his duties as Librarian would terminate on the last day of May and that there could not be the least doubt that Allen's official relations with Stephenson would be as "satisfactory and happy" as they had been with him.[111] If anything, he was even more nonchalant with Pearce, to whom he wrote: "Mr. John G. Stevenson [sic], of Indiana, who has been appointed by the President, Librarian of Congress, will enter upon the duties of the office on the first day of June next." The rest of the letter dealt only with routine business matters.[112] There is no indication that Meehan discussed the matter with Pearce again, although a year later the chairman did intercede in his behalf with Salmon P. Chase when Meehan, who was "constrained by the augusta res domi to seek employment," had hopes of getting a clerkship in the Treasury Department.[113]

Meehan's retirement was not entirely untroubled. His successor discovered much in the Library with which he readily found fault and under the date of December 16, 1861, prepared an elaborate "Report of the Librarian of Congress to the Joint Committee on the Library." The manuscript draft of this report is not in Stephenson's hand, is not signed by him, and was probably the work of an assistant, perhaps Spofford. The report indicated that the Library had to be thoroughly cleaned and almost entirely rearranged, found that in many instances books were "hidden amid rubbish and in dark out-of-the-way corners," and noted that, except for the law chapters (which were in a "commendable state of cleanliness and order"), the entire collection of 70,000 volumes "was in a condition of dirt and disorder which appeared . . . equally unnecessary and disgraceful." Serious gaps existed in the collections and titles on 1,000 books had been discovered to be either "grossly mis-spelled, or so defective as to furnish no clue whatever to the true contents of the work." The system of classification which had been employed in the Library, and upon which the catalog was based, was also defective and the "deficiences and embarrassments" of this system were "developed more & more by daily use in the Library." A change was called for in the method of ordering books, since the commissions paid to agents were excessive, and several removals were justified because of the incapacity of those assistants for their posts.[114]

Pearce had learned of some of this criticism beforehand, but he was in very poor health, preoccupied by the events of the war, uneasy over the administration's course in Maryland, and shaken by recent personal financial losses. He could do little more than notify his fellow committeeman, Senator Fessenden, that the new Librarian was complaining of "disorder and neglect" in the Library, which Pearce thought was only fancied. If there was anything wrong with the Library, it was the inability of its officers to compel members to return all the books they had taken out. In Pearce's opinion too much authority was being assumed by the Librarian in purchasing books and, furthermore, he had taken it upon himself to purge the Library of some *"trash,"* which he had no more right to do than remove "the best book in the collection." Pearce admitted that there was nothing he could do about the assistants that had been released, and felt that Fessenden was equally powerless.[115]

Beyond the criticism leveled at Meehan immediately upon the conclusion of his long administration of the Library, there is that which followed him throughout the years and persists to this day. It is based on the broad grounds that Meehan and others who had influence and authority in Library matters were willing to settle for too little. The history of the Library over the period 1829–61 appears to be a chronicle of lost opportunities, opportunities for the enhancement of the Library collections through international and domestic exchanges, through the vigorous observance of copyright provisions, through timely special purchases, and by many other means as well. Vision, imagination, and vigor seemed to be lacking, particularly in matters that would have placed the Library on the road to becoming a true national library. And it cannot be said that this forward-looking concept of the Library did not have its supporters at the time, for again and again the notion was articulated and urged.

Yet, given the reality of the situation, it is not so surprising that the Library remained essentially a legislative library, that is to say, the kind of library that Congress wanted. The apathy of Congress where Library affairs, especially appropriations, were concerned and its frequent manifestations of provincialism and sectionalism worked against the growth of a national institution. The conservative outlook of Senator Pearce, chairman of the Joint Committee on the Library, and the measured manner in which he controlled Library affairs also inhibited expansion. If a Charles Coffin Jewett had come into the Library during these years much might have been achieved. But not the least of his problems would have been the relationship that such a man would have had to maintain with a Library Committee whose overall membership seemed to change almost kaleidoscopically and whose dominant figure in the later years was the proud, formal, and patrician James Alfred Pearce. The tempestuous politics of the period presented obstacles enough to survival alone and would surely have rendered difficult the task of anyone determined on shaping a national library. Many tragedies grew out of those times, and the fact that the Library did not become all that it might have is due in part to its amiable Librarian, but only in part.[116]

Pearce and Meehan died within a few months of each other. Pearce died at his home in Chester-town, December 20, 1862. He could have held positions of much greater power, but he was a self-effacing man who left his mark, in the words of Librarian Stephenson, "ineffaceably" upon the Library. He had also been its "friend and guardian." [117] Meehan died suddenly, of apoplexy, at his residence on South B Street, Capitol Hill, at 4 p.m., April 24, 1863. An obituary mentioned his years of service in the Library, and its composer must have known Meehan well, for he wrote:

> He was remarkably punctual and assiduous in his duties, unobtrusive, moral, and domestic in his habits, and of sterling integrity as a man. He died suddenly, but not without preparation; and he leaves to his family that best inheritance, an unsullied name.[118]

Benjamin Brown French, in his diary, bade his friend of many years farewell in these words, "If ever a pure hearted, honest, upright, honorable man lived, it was John S. Meehan. He lived a cheerful, happy life, and died without apparent pain. . . ." [119]

NOTES

[1] William Dawson Johnston, *History of the Library of Congress, 1800–1864,* vol. 1 (Washington: Government Printing Office, 1904), p. 213; David C. Mearns, *The Story up to Now; The Library of Congress, 1800–1946* (Washington: Government Printing Office, 1947), p. 36. Johnston was indebted to one of Meehan's daughters for early biographical data, some of which is undoubtedly inaccurate. Meehan himself was uncertain of the exact year of his birth and indicated on August 21, 1855, on an application for bounty land that he was "about 57." Bounty land application, RG 15, National Archives and Records Service (NARS). Johnston and Mearns have written the most extensive and authoritative histories of the Library of Congress and the usefulness of their works throughout the preparation of this sketch is hereby acknowledged. John Y. Cole, Jr., in his doctoral dissertation, "Ainsworth Spofford and the 'National Library,'" George Washington University, 1971, includes a considerable amount of material pertinent to the Meehan period.

[2] *Dictionary of American Naval Fighting Ships* (Washington: Government Printing Office, 1959–), s.v. *Firefly.*

[3] Diary of John S. Meehan, February 11, 1852, John Silva Meehan Papers, Library of Congress.

[4] Bounty Land Papers, RG 15, NARS. In 1878 Meehan's widow began receiving a pension of $8 per month as a result of this service.

[5] "Supplement" to the *Columbian Star,* n.d., but ca. October 1824. The *Luminary* expired in 1825.

[6] *Columbian Star,* Washington, D.C., February 2, 1822. When Congress was in session the paper did give a nonpartisan summary of the activities of both Houses.

[7] Advertisement in the *Columbian Star* for January 3, 1824.

[8] Ibid., July 9 and 16, 1825.

[9] Ibid., January 28, 1826.

[10] John Quincy Adams, *Memoirs of John Quincy Adams,* ed. Charles Francis Adams, 12 vols. (Philadelphia: J. B. Lippincott & Co., 1876), 8:217. Recounted is a conversation of April 9, 1830, between Adams and Elliot in which Elliot claimed that Eaton stood behind the purchase of the *Gazette.*

[11] *United States' Telegraph,* February 6, 1826. The editor said he expected to give the paper "a new and improved dress, and to render it, as to its mechanical execution, equal to the best printed journals in the country."

[12] Reprinted in the *Telegraph, February* 18, 1826.

[13] Jackson to R. K. Call, March 9, 1826, Andrew Jackson Papers, LC. John Quincy Adams thought he recognized in the prospectus "a sample of bad English peculiar to Calhoun." Quoted in Charles M. Wiltse, *John C. Calhoun, Nationalist, 1782–1828* (New York and Indianapolis: Bobbs-Merrill, 1944), p. 328.

[14] Reprinted in the *Telegraph,* April 25, 1826.

[15] Fletcher M. Green, "Duff Green, Militant Journalist of the Old School," *American Historical Review* 52, no. 2 (January 1947): 247.

[16] Duff Green, *Facts and Suggestions* (New York: Richardson & Co., 1866), p. 27.

[17] Memorandum, May 20, 1826, James K. Polk Papers, LC. Polk subscribed for $100. See also Charles G. Sellers, *James K. Polk, Jacksonian, 1795–1843,* (Princeton: Princeton University Press, 1957   ), p. 129.

[18] *Telegraph,* April 26, 1826.

[19] Sellers, *James K. Polk,* p. 129n.

[20] *Columbian Star,* copied into scrapbook, Meehan Papers.

[21] Johnston, *Library of Congress, 1800–1864,* p. 214, and Mearns, *The Story,* p. 37.

[22] Mearns, *The Story,* p. 30.

[23] Watterston to Bradley, July 8, 1826, George Watterston Papers, LC.

[24] A journal entry in the Watterston Papers reveals: "Commenced writing for Natl. Journal at 500 dolls. pr ann: the 13th of March 1827."

[25] Jackson to John Coffee, May 30, 1829. In Andrew Jackson, *Correspondence of Andrew Jackson* ed. John Spencer Bassett, 7 vols. (Washington: Carnegie Institution of Washington, 1926–35), 4:39.

[26] Houston to Jackson, September 19, 1829. Ibid., 4:75.

[27] Johnston, *Library of Congress, 1800–1864,* pp. 189–98.

[28] Watterston Papers, December 8, 1829.

[29] Clay to Watterston, July 21, 1829, Watterston Papers.

[30] Watterston to Clay, July 17, 1850, draft, Watterston Papers.

[31] Watterston to [Fillmore], October 16, 1850, copy, Watterston Papers.

[32] Johnston, *Library of Congress, 1800–1864,* p. 199; Mearns, *The Story,* p. 36.

[33] Johnston, *Library of Congress, 1800–1864,* p. 213n.

[34] Commission, May 28, 1829, LC Archives. Meehan never wrote his middle name in full.

[35] This information was given on his widow's claim for a service pension. Pension Records, RG 15, NARS.

[36] Mearns, *The Story,* p. 37.

[37] Meehan to Robert C. Winthrop, April 7, 1856, Librarian's Letterbooks, LC Archives. Winthrop was for many years the president of the Massachusetts Historical Society. The Library Room is described in great detail in Johnston, *Library of Congress, 1800–1864,* pp. 215–22.

[38] Meehan to Faulkner, February 20, 1849, Librarian's Letterbooks.

[39] Meehan's diary includes frequent references to Stelle, e.g., on October 29, 1852, Mr. Stelle was "off, a-fishing, to-day, and did not come up to the Library, at all. Happy man!" The Stelles were well known in Washington. See Maud Burr Morris, "The Life and Times of Pontius D. Stelle," in *Records of the Columbia Historical Society,* vol. 7 (Washington, 1904), pp. 49–65.

[40] Johnston, *Library of Congress, 1800–1864,* pp. 515–16.

[41] Johnston, *Library of Congress, 1800–1864* p, 308, 249–50, prints the act of July 14, 1832; Mearns, *The Story,* pp. 39–40, discusses the background of the act and comments on its significance.

[42] Obituary (unidentified newsclipping), Meehan Papers.

[43] Mearns, *The Story,* pp. 44–49; Johnston, *Library of Congress, 1800–1864,* pp. 229–45; Cole, "Ainsworth Spofford," p. 9.

[44] Receipt Books, LC Archives. There is a gap for the period 1846–49.

[45] Meehan to Everett, June 14 and July 16, 1830; November 7, 1831; November 7, 1832; Watterston Papers.

[46] Bernard C. Steiner, *Men of Mark in Maryland,* 4 vols. (Washington: B. F. Johnson, 1907–12), 1:281–83. Steiner also published a series of biographical articles on Pearce in the *Maryland Historical Magazine,* commencing in the issue for December 1921 and terminating in that of June 1924.

[47] Benjamin Perley Poore, *Reminiscences of Sixty Years in the National Metropolis,* 2 vols. (Philadelphia: Hubbard Brothers, 1886), 1:176–77.

[48] Crittenden to John M. Clayton, July 23, 1849, John J. Crittenden Papers, LC.

[49] Quoted by Steiner in "James Alfred Pearce," *Maryland Historical Magazine* 19, no. 4 (December 1921): 324.

[50] Steiner, *Men of Mark,* p. 282.

[51] The account here is based on the work of John Y. Cole, who has written the most recent studies elaborating on the connection between copyright deposits for Library use and the development of a national library. See "Ainsworth Spofford," pp. iii, 9–11, 29; and "Of Copyright, Men and a National Library," in the *Quarterly Journal of the Library of Congress* 28, no. 2 (April 1971): 114–36. Johnston devotes a long chapter to "The Smithsonian Institution and Plans for a National Library," *Library of Congress, 1800–1864,* pp. 403–506.

[52] In the LC Archives there is an account book that was used in keeping track of these funds in summary form. Each fund generated a considerable amount of correspondence; copies of Meehan's outgoing letters pertaining to them are contained in the Librarian's Letterbooks.

[53] Diary of J. S. Meehan, December 24, 1851, Meehan Papers.

[54] Diary of Benjamin Brown French, December 25, 1851, B. B. French Papers, LC. French often wrote up events on the following day.

[55] Meehan to Pearce, December 24, 1851, Librarian's Letterbooks.

[56] Meehan to William R. King, December 25, 1851, Librarian's Letterbooks. Only one-third of Jefferson's library survived the fire of 1851. E. Millicent Sowerby, comp., *Catalogue of the Library of Thomas Jefferson,* 5 vols. (Washington: Library of Congress, 1952–59), 1:vii. When Meehan was informed that a flaw discovered in a chimney flue passing by the wall of the Library was the apparent cause of the fire, he wrote "Laus Deo!" in his diary. Diary of J. S. Meehan, December 25, 1851, Meehan Papers.

[57] Johnston, *Library of Congress, 1800–1864,* pp. 278–79.

[58] Meehan to William Easby, December 26, 1851, Librarian's Letterbooks.

[59] Walter to Easby, December 26, 1851, in Johnston, *Library of Congress, 1800–1864,* pp. 280–81.

[60] Some exceptions to Walter's explanation are recorded in Johnston, *Library of Congress, 1800–1864,* pp. 281–84, and in Mearns, *The Story,* p. 62.

[61] This letter was copied by Meehan into his diary, January 2, 1852, Meehan Papers. The ellipses are Meehan's but he commonly used these marks in his diary without intending to indicate omissions.

[62] *Ibid.* Meehan also wrote a long letter to Pearce detailing and categorizing the losses of the Library. Meehan to Pearce, January 7, 1852, Librarian's Letterbooks.

[63] Dairy of J. S. Meehan, January 4, 1852, Meehan Papers.

[64] Johnston, *Library of Congress, 1800–1864,* pp. 285–87, 291–92, and 309, comments on these appropriations and prints some of the pertinent acts.

[65] Diary of J. S. Meehan, March 3, April 7, August 7, and September 28, 1852, Meehan Papers.

[66] Meehan to Pearce, May 30, 1853, Librarian's Letterbooks. A formal description of the work on the Library Room is contained in a letter from Walter to William Easby, January 27, 1852, in Johnston, *Library of Congress, 1800–1864,* pp. 288–91.

[67] Meehan to Pearce, July 6, 1853, Librarian's Letterbooks.

[68] Quoted in Mearns, *The Story,* p. 65.

[69] Dairy of J. S. Meehan, January 24, 1852, Meehan Papers. Meehan had also copied the letter from Rich Brothers into his diary under this date.

[70] Cole, "Ainsworth Spofford," p. 27; Johnston, *Library of Congress, 1800–1864,* p. 309; and Mearns, *The Story,* p. 66.

[71] Quoted in Johnston, *Library of Congress, 1800–1864,* pp. 302–6.

[72] Meehan to Pearce, April 9, 1852, Librarian's Letterbooks.

[73] Want List Letterbook, 1853, LC Archives.

[74] Johnston, *Library of Congress, 1800–1864,* p. 308, prints the resolution and comments upon it.

[75] Meehan to Pearce, May 4, 1853, Librarian's Letterbooks.

[76] Meehan to Rich Brothers, March 31, 1853, Want List Letterbook, 1853. Meehan had always been partial to Rich Brothers. On March 24, 1852, he wrote in his diary upon the receipt of four large boxes of books from them: "We had before received large supplies from Franck Taylor, bookseller, our Agent in this city, and from Little & Brown, booksellers, of Boston; but the supplies from London are very greatly superior."

[77] Meehan to Pearce, October 3, 1853, Librarian's Letterbooks.

[78] Pearce to Meehan, October 29, 1853, Letters Addressed to the Library of Congress, LC Archives.

[79] Meehan to Pearce, November 2, 1853, Librarian's Letterbooks.

[80] Meehan to W. A. Adamson, December 18, 1852, Librarian's Letterbooks.

[81] Cogswell's visit is described in a letter from Meehan to Pearce, November 2, 1855, Librarian's Letterbooks.

[82] Meehan to Rich Brothers, February 28, 1856, Librarian's Letterbooks.

[83] Meehan to Pearce, April 18, 1856, Librarian's Letterbooks.

[84] Meehan to Rich Brothers, July 25, 1856, Librarian's Letterbooks. In 1857, poor health made it necessary for the proprietor to leave London and suspend business. In expressing his regret, Meehan spoke of "the friendly bonds that have so long united your house to the Committee on the Library of Congress." Meehan to Rich Brothers, March 16, 1857, ibid.

[85] Johnston, *Library of Congress, 1800–1864,* pp. 256–57, prints the resolution. Mearns, *The Story,* pp. 49–56, and Cole, "Ainsworth Spofford," pp. 110–13, discuss Vattemare and international exchange.

[86] Meehan to Pearce, September 25, 1848, Librarian's Letterbooks. The more traditional ways of acquiring books appealed to Meehan. In his diary for January 27, 1846, he discusses, for example, a proposition made by the booksellers of Leipzig "to establish a large bookstore in New York, through which societies and individuals in this country may be supplied with the choicest German literature, on the most favorable terms."

[87] Meehan to Pearce, November 18, 1850, Librarian's Letterbooks.

[88] Cole, "Ainsworth Spofford," p. 113, and Johnston, *Library of Congress, 1800–1864,* p. 264. Vattemare, in a letter to Pearce, January 25, 1853, Miscellaneous Accessions, LC Archives, complained that he had received "not a single letter, nor one book" from the

Library of Congress in over a year. All his efforts to communicate had been "without result," and all his letters "without reply."

[89] Meehan to Vattemare, June 16, 1853, Librarian's Letterbooks.

[90] Meehan to Pearce, September 6, 1854, Librarian's Letterbooks.

[91] Meehan to Vattemare, October 8, 1858, Librarian's Letterbooks.

[92] The Jewett plan is described in Johnston, *Library of Congress, 1800–1864,* pp. 358–64. Mearns, *The Story,* p. 101, contains an assessment of Jewett.

[93] Meehan to Henry, May 6, 1853; Meehan to Jewett, May 18, 1853; and Meehan to Pearce, September 14 and 21, 1853. All from Librarian's Letterbooks.

[94] Meehan to Pearce, April 2, 1855, Librarian's Letterbooks. Meehan was transmitting a report made by Charles M. Hinman, who had been hired by Meehan to work on the stereotyping of the catalog.

[95] Quoted in Johnston, *Library of Congress, 1800–1864,* p. 364.

[96] Meehan to Pearce, May 20, 1853. The letterpress copy is in a volume of LC Want Lists for 1853, LC Archives. There is not a copy in the Librarian's Letterbooks.

[97] Meehan to Pearce, May 30, 1853, Want Lists Letterbooks, 1853.

[98] Lewis Cass to Meehan, June 11, 1857, Meehan Papers, Meehan to [Pearce], June 16, 1857, Librarian's Letterbooks.

[99] William J. Evitts, *A Matter of Allegiances, Maryland From 1850 to 1861* (Baltimore: Johns Hopkins University Press, 1974), pp. 154–55, 164, 168. Bernard C. Steiner, "James Alfred Pearce," *Maryland Historical Magazine* 17 (March 1922):44.

[100] Steiner, "James Alfred Pearce," *Maryland Historical Magazine* 19 (March 1924):28.

[101] Johnston, *Library of Congress, 1800–1864,* p. 215; and Mearns, *The Story,* p. 70, who disputes the charge.

[102] Meehan to Pearce, October 17, 20, and 27, 1859, Librarian's Letterbooks.

[103] Sidney [Taylor] to Charlie [Taylor], April 23, 1861, Meehan Papers.

[104] A. R. Spofford to [Sarah Spofford], August 5, 1861, Ainsworth Rand Spofford Papers, LC.

[105] Pearce to Lincoln, March 8, 1861, Abraham Lincoln Papers, LC.

[106] In 1864, Collamer told Charles Lanman, who was seeking a position in the Library, "In 1861 I joined with Senators Pearce and Fessenden . . . in

recommending to the President the retention of Mr. Meehan as Librarian. This recommendation was not regarded by the President & I have therefore no reason to believe my recommendation would be now regarded." Collamer to Lanman, November 17, 1864, Charles Lanman Papers, LC. Lincoln had written to Pearce in 1851 in behalf of a Mr. Constable, a native of Maryland, but then resident in Illinois, who wished to receive a judgeship in Oregon. Constable did not receive the appointment. In his letter to Pearce, Lincoln had felt obliged to say, "You will probably not remember me; and therefore, as an appology for addressing you, I have to say that I had an introduction to you while I was a member of the H. R. of the 30th. Congress." Abraham Lincoln, *The Collected Works of Abraham Lincoln,* ed. Roy P. Basler, 9 vols. (New Brunswick, N.J.: Rutgers University Press, 1953), 2:97.

[107] Meehan ot Paul Bossange, May 3, 1861, Librarian's Letterbooks.

[108] Stephenson to Lincoln, May 7, 1861, Lincoln Papers.

[109] Abraham Lincoln, *The Collected Works of Abraham Lincoln, Supplement, 1832–1865,* ed. Roy P. Basler (Westport, Conn.: Greenwood Press, 1974), p. 71.

[110] Mearns, *The Story,* p. 70.

[111] Meehan to Allen, May 28, 1861, Librarian's Letterbooks.

[112] Meehan to Pearce, May 28, 1861, Librarian's Letterbooks.

[113] Pearce and William Pitt Fessenden to Chase, May 24, 1862, Salmon P. Chase Papers, LC.

[114] Manuscript report of the Librarian, December 16, 1861, Miscellaneous Accessions, LC Archives. Mearns, *The Story,* pp. 71–73, discusses this report.

[115] Pearce to Fessenden, September 25, 1861, William Pitt Fessenden Papers, LC.

[116] One commentator, describing the Library as it was in 1864, wrote: "The wonder is, not that the Library of Congress was so small, but that it was so large. . . ." Frederick Ashley, "Three Eras in the Library of Congress," in *Essays Offered to Herbert Putnam,* ed. William W. Bishop and Andrew Keogh (New Haven: Yale University Press, 1929), p. 60.

[117] Manuscript report of the Librarian, January 7, 1863, Miscellaneous Accessions, LC Archives.

[118] Obituary from unidentified newspaper, Meehan Papers.

[119] Diary of B. B. French, April 26, 1863, B. B. French Papers, LC.

John Gould Stephenson

Largely Known and Much Liked

by Constance Carter

The November 12, 1883, front-page obituary in the *Washington Post* for John Gould Stephenson, fifth Librarian of Congress, is headlined, "A Well Known Figure Passes Suddenly Away." [1] The notice states that Dr. Stephenson, a medical examiner in the Pension Office, was born in Illinois about 1825 and had had a splendid army record, being one of three men especially recognized for bravery at the Battle of Gettysburg. Mention is also made of his appointment to the post of Librarian of Congress by President Lincoln and of the fact that he was "very largely known and much liked." The *Evening Star* for the same date reports the sudden death at the age of 58 of medical examiner Dr. J. G. Stephenson at the home of Capt. Albert Grant and gives Stephenson's place of birth as Illinois. [2]

In actuality, John Gould Stephenson was born in Lancaster, N.H., on March 1, 1828, the fourth son of Reuben Stephenson and Mary King Baker. Unpublished records in the Lancaster Historical Society (compiled by Henry O. Kent, editor of the *Coös Republican* and transcribed by Faith Kent for volume 2 of the *History of Lancaster, New Hampshire*) and *Early Settlers of Lancaster, New Hampshire* (compiled by Mrs. J. Wendell Kimball

in 1947 and available in the collections of the New Hampshire Historical Society) list eight children, five boys and three girls, as being born to Reuben and Mary Stephenson.

John Gould Stephenson's great-great-grandparents emigrated from England and settled in Cohasset, Mass. His great-grandfather Capt. Reuben Stephenson was born in Cohasset in 1727. [3] Reuben's son Bryant married Deborah Turner in Scituate, Mass., February 1, 1784. [4] Reuben, the second of their seven children, was the father of John Gould Stephenson, Librarian of Congress, 1861–64.

The Bryant Stephenson family left Massachusetts in the 1790's and, after settling briefly in Lyme, N.H., established residence in Lancaster in 1799.

Dr. John G. Stephenson, fifth Librarian of Congress. Photographic portrait by L. C. Handy Studios. Prints and Photographs Division. LC–USZ62–57283

Constance Carter is head of the Reference Section, Science and Technology Division.

The Stephenson family was active in Lancaster town and county affairs. John G. Stephenson's grandfather was town moderator in 1803 and served as town clerk from 1808 to 1809. His father, a merchant, served three terms as county coroner, four terms as selectman, and four terms as deputy sheriff and officiated as high sheriff from 1849 to 1855. His civic responsibilities also included the offices of constable and fire warden. John's younger brother Oliver and his uncle Benjamin Stephenson also served as county coroners and as fire wardens. His uncle Turner Stephenson served as town clerk in 1828 and as judge of probate court from 1855 to 1865.[5] An early map depicting Lancaster Village in 1828 in Somers' *History of Lancaster, New Hampshire* (Concord, N.H.: Rumford Press, 1899) shows the location of Reuben Stephenson's store. John's brother Bryant made trips to Boston and Portland once or twice a year to buy goods for their father's dry goods and variety store.[6]

James Brackett, in his *Historical Sketch of Lancaster, New Hampshire,* noted that the town's merchants had always been among its leading citizens.[7] Reuben Stephenson was one of the nine incorporators of Lancaster Academy, chartered by a special act of the legislature, December 24, 1828. The academy opened its first term in "the old flat-roofed court house on the corner of Bridge and Main Streets, with a recent graduate of Dartmouth College as preceptor."[8] Most of its early record books were burned, but a program reprinted in Somers' *History* lists both John and Oliver Stephenson as principals in a program held at the academy on Tuesday evening, November 26, 1844. John played the part of Fontrailles in *Richelieu* and the part of Frank Webber in *College Life*.[9]

J. G. Stephenson continued his education at Dartmouth Medical School[10] and at Castleton Medical College. Frederick C. Waite's *The First Medical College in Vermont, Castleton, 1818–1862,* lists a Joseph G. Stevenson as a member of its fall 1849 graduating class.[11] In a letter dated September 29, 1881, addressed to S. J. Kirkwood, secretary of the interior, Stephenson verifies the fact that he attended Lancaster Academy as well as the Medical Department of Dartmouth College and was awarded his doctorate in medicine on November 23, 1849, from Castleton Medical College.[12] Turner Stephenson, John's uncle, attended Dartmouth College, as did John's older brother Reuben Henry, who graduated with the class of 1845.[13]

Nine members of the Stephenson family are noted in the 1850 census of Lancaster. John G., at age 22, is listed as a physician; however, it is not known whether he actually practiced medicine in Lancaster. According to Brackett, Lancaster had three physicians in 1850. Yet, Somers does not mention Stephenson in the chapter reviewing the practice of medicine in Lancaster in the 1850's.

In 1858 John G. Stephenson is listed in the first published city directory for Terre Haute, Ind. (p. 94). It is highly probable that Stephenson resided in that city during the decade before the Civil War. Stephenson himself, in 1861, referred to Vigo County as the place "where I have lived and ... practiced physic & surgery for ten years."[14] The 1860 census for Indiana, taken July 2, 1860, cites J. G. Stephenson, 32, physician, born in New Hampshire, as an inhabitant of ward 1 in Terre Haute.

Stephenson's younger brother Oliver, listed in Lancaster, N.H., in the 1850 census as a farmer, appears as a surveyor in Marshall, Ill., in the 1860 census. The Clark Hotel, in which Stephenson lived during the 10 years he was in Terre Haute, provided daily four-horse hack service to Marshall.[15]

Because of its location on the Wabash River and the Erie Canal, Terre Haute in the 1850's and 1860's was a thriving center of commerce and in need of lawyers, physicians, and other professionals. We have no documentation to account for either John G. Stephenson's migration westward or his choice of Terre Haute as the community in which to practice medicine. We do know that his brothers Charles, Bryant, Reuben, and Oliver also left New Hampshire and sought their fortunes in Arkansas, Iowa, Ohio, and Illinois, respectively.[16]

Stephenson became interested in the Republican party in its beginnings and in 1858 was an "efficient speaker" in Lincoln's behalf during the contest with Douglas.[17] He was one of Lincoln's earliest supporters for the presidential nomination at the Chicago convention,[18] exerting influence upon the Kentucky delegation.[19]

A note in the February 15, 1860, *Wabash Express* indicated that Dr. Stephenson was to address the Opposition Club at its next meeting on February 20. A notice entitled "Let the Record Be Changed" in the February 22, 1860, issue of the same paper called attention to the fact that "Dr. J. G. Stephenson did not say that all men were created *free* and *equal*. He held just what the writers and signers of the Declaration of Independence held—namely, 'that all men are created equal.' " [20]

An article in the June 6, 1860, *Wabash Express* reported the organization of the Lincoln Club for the purpose of advancing the interests of the Republican party, "promoting the election of the Hon. Abraham Lincoln and Hannibal Hamlin to the offices of President and Vice-President of the United States, and [declaring] the Chicago Platform as our political principles." Dr. J. G. Stephenson was appointed one of five to solicit signers to the constitution of the club in ward 1 of Terre Haute.

John G. Stephenson of Indiana and Gustave Koerner of Illinois are mentioned by Allen Nevins in *The Emergence of Lincoln* as well-informed politicians reporting grassroots feelings about the election of 1860 and on Lincoln's chances of winning it.[21] In a letter dated March 25, 1860, at Terre Haute, Ind., and addressed to the Hon. Lyman Trumbull, Stephenson writes:

Sir—At the risk of trespassing upon your patience, I write again, for the purpose of inquiring how great is the danger Mr. Seward will receive the nomination of the Chicago Convention—If my intrusion needs excuse, please to remember that Mr. Davis misrepresents this district in the House and that Indiana is not represented in the Senate and there be some of us who were engaged in the contest in Illinois two years ago, whose interest has now diminished in that direction—we feel the importance of putting a man like Henry S. Lane in the place of Fitch and of your own return to the Senate (if the people should not now bid you "go up higher") yet we feel that the nomination of Seward would render that almost impossible. Much as we respect Seward, we find that fear of his nomination and the impossibility of his carrying Indiana is paralyzing all our efforts—men who have the means refuse to subscribe the money necessary to carry on the canvass, alledging it to be useless in view of the probability of Mr. Seward's nomination, to expend money in Indiana until, after the convention—and in the meantime, friends of . . . Douglas are gaining strength a part of which they will be able to transfer to the Charlestown nominee if it should not be Douglas. With Lincoln or almost any other western Republican (except Chase) for our Presidential Candidate, *we can elect our State ticket and secure a Republican Senator from this State—with Seward this is impossible*—and it is much to be feared that the same condition exists in Illinois—

Is there any way in which we can get rid, in any degree,

of the fear of his nomination, that now rests like a incubus upon us? The valuable time between this and the sitting of the Convention, our opponents are able to improve to better advantage than we can do for reasons above stated.

[Galusa Aaron] Grows speech and the vote in the House on the "Homestead Bill" strengthens us—Germany is with us for any Republican outside of Massachusetts (except Bates) and Ireland will help a little.

If your time will permit and you will give me an early reply you will greatly oblige. Your obt. servt.

John G. Stephenson

P.S. Letter lately received from Dr. Payne and others, from Illinois, all concur in the opinion that "we will have a hard road to travel if Chase or Seward is nominated"— I expect to be in Illinois for some time during this canvass.

JGS

If the combination attempted by a part of the Ohio delegates, succeeds in nominating Judge McLean, 'twill help us much in this section, but not so much as would the nomination of Lincoln.[22]

In another letter to Trumbull, dated June 2, 1860, Terre Haute, Ind., Stephenson asks for "a copy of the Report of the Secr'y of the Treasury made Jan. 7–10th 1860, on expense collection revenue—a copy of Trumbull's speech at Chicago, Aug. 7th 1858 with the political record of S. A. Douglass [*sic*] and a copy of the last Appropriations bill." He goes on to say that "we are confident that we can carry Indiana for Lincoln, but we expect a hard fight. I have spent some weeks in Illinois this summer (in Clark and Edgar Counties) the enthusiasm is not as great as I expected." [23]

It is interesting to note that Reinhard Luthin's "Indiana and Lincoln's Rise to the Presidency," [24] Charles Roll's "Indiana's Part in the Nomination of Abraham Lincoln for President in 1860," [25] Charles Zimmerman's "The Origin and Rise of the Republican Party in Indiana from 1854 to 1860," [26] and Russell M. Seeds' *History of the Republican Party of Indiana* (Indianapolis: The Indiana History Co., 1899) make no mention of John G. Stephenson as having had a role in Indiana politics or the formation of the Republican party.

We must assume, nevertheless, that he spent much more of his time practicing politics than medicine. While his business card as physician and surgeon does appear in the *Terre Haute Journal* in 1851, the *Terre Haute City Directory* for 1858, and the *Terre Haute Business Directory* for 1858--

59, his name is not given in the *Transactions* of the State Medical Society of Indiana (Indianapolis: Elder & Harkness, 1861), listing all those who had been members of the society since its organization. Nor is he mentioned in G. W. H. Kemper's *Medical History of the State of Indiana* (Chicago: American Medical Association, 1911), C. N. Combs' *Terre Haute Physicians* (unpublished), or H. C. Bradsby's *History of Vigo County* (Chicago: Nelson, 1891), although the chapter "Medicine" does list physicians of the 1850's. The latter work includes the names of four doctors who in 1861 signed a letter to President Lincoln endorsing Stephenson for the position of Librarian of Congress.[27]

While in Terre Haute, Stephenson was also active in temperance activities. A note in the October 12, 1858, issue of the *Terre-Haute Daily Union* announcing a meeting of the "Terre-Haute Division No. 94 Sons of Temperance" is signed by J. G. Stephenson, Patriarch.

After Lincoln's election, Stephenson decided to use his political connections to obtain a patronage position: that of Librarian of Congress. We can only speculate as to his reasons for choosing to leave Terre Haute and the medical profession. By his own admission, the primary factor appears to have been financial.[28]

His brother Reuben Henry was at this time librarian of the Young Men's Mercantile Library in Cincinnati and his knowledge of the Library of Congress may have influenced John to seek the position. The first letter in his campaign to become Librarian is dated as early as November 27, 1860, when a supporter wrote Lincoln that "Dr. Jno. G. Stephenson of Terre Haute is a candidate of Librarian of Congress, is a true Republican, and will make a faithful and competent officer should he receive the appointment, and I recommend him to your favorable consideration."[29]

During the winter of 1860 and the spring of 1861, a number of individuals wrote to Mr. Lincoln on behalf of the doctor. In representative letters, Stephenson is described as "distinguished for his agreeable manners,"[30] "an earnest and persevering laborer in the cause of Republicanism,"[31] "a learned and urbane gentleman,"[32] "a Republican of the working kind,"[33] and "well-fitted by education, congenial tastes and experiences to discharge the duties of the position for which he asks."[34] Nine physicians and one dentist, six of whom are listed in the 1858 *Terre Haute City Directory*, wrote in support of Stephenson declaring that they felt him to be "parcularly fitted for the office of Librarian of Congress."[35]

Joseph W. Calvert, a delegate to the Chicago convention from the third district of Kentucky, also wrote to Lincoln in January of 1861 to urge the appointment of Stephenson, stating that in "April last his influence was exerted, to the extent of his ability in . . . setting forth your claims for the nomination in Chicago, and making plain to the delegation of our state, the importance of your nomination."[36] Senator Henry S. Lane of Indiana assured Lincoln that Stephenson's nomination would be more than acceptable. "The Dr. is a gentleman of fine education, pleasing manners and of superior business qualifications & his character for honor and honesty is above all question. His appointment would give great pleasure to the Republicans of his neighborhood and to none more than myself."[37]

Stephenson came to Washington[38] and wrote to President Lincoln, in a letter dated May 7, 1861, urging his own appointment. At the outset, he directed Lincoln's attention to the fact that the

near approach of a session of Congress renders it expedient, that the question of a change in the office of "Librarian in the Library of Congress" should be considered without necessary delay;—so that the new incumbent of that office (if there should be one) may so familiarize himself with his position before the meeting of Congress, that by the order and energy of his administration of its affairs, he may bring credit to himself and the power that appoints him—and convince protesting Senators that they erred in their protest against a change in that office.

He then advanced his own claim, stating that his qualifications were "ample" and that he had been "amongst the earliest advocates in Indiana of your nomination to the Presidency by the Republican Party" and "an earnest and continuous laborer in the Cause that triumphed in your election." Stephenson further pointed out that nearly all prominent Republicans in Indiana, including Senator Lane, Governor Morton, and the Hon. Caleb B. Smith, had endorsed him.

The Hon. Wm. P. Dole will be able to inform you that I have made no inconsiderable sacrifice of time and business (and of means to the full extent of my ability) whenever and wherever the friends of our cause have desired, so that I am now in a pecuniary condition that will greatly be relieved by your granting the application that is made in my behalf.[39]

In a letter to Dr. Davis, dated May 14, 1861, William P. Dole, Lincoln's commissioner of Indian affairs, writes:

I have just left Mr. Lincoln. I found him alone this evening and had a good old fashioned talk as I frequently have and always, when he has leisure . . . Mr. Lincoln is very kind to me and has given me not only what I have asked for myself but so far nearly anything I have asked for my friends . . . and promised me to appoint Dr. Stevenson Congressional Librarian tomorrow. You know that the Dr. is not heavy mettal but he has worked hard for us & is poor and can hand down books to M. C. as well & as gracefully as any one and besides he is a Wabash man and I am for *him. You know I never forget friends.*[40]

It is not known how many rivals Stephenson had for the position of Librarian, but at least three individuals wrote to President Lincoln advocating the candidacy of Hezekiah L. Hosmer of Toledo.[41] Senator James A. Pearce, chairman of the Joint Committee on the Library, wrote to Lincoln on March 8, 1861, recommending the retention of John Silva Meehan as Librarian of Congress:

I have been Chairman of the Library Committee on the part of the Senate for fifteen years and have had therefore opportunity to judge the competing fitness and merits generally of the librarian and his assistants. The latter are appointed by the Librarian. During all that time no change has been made in these appointments, the President having always deferred to the wishes of Congress and neither House having desired any change. The present officers understand and perform all their present duties with singular care, fidelity and ability. They *know* the Library which now contains nearly 70,000 volumes, can refer . . . to any desired books and understand the character of the collection as no one could do who had not been long engaged in these duties—any new librarian or assistant would require a considerable time to learn what the others already know. . . . They are not politicians but men of books, devoted to the specialty and singularly well qualified in their duties, writing and knowledge, great security of manners and accuracy of habits. I trust they may still be as they heretofore have been, unaffected by political changes, & safe from the influence of political partisanship which has heretofore had no influence in the republic of letters. . . .[42]

Senator Pearce's sentiments were endorsed by fellow committee members William Fessenden of Maine and Jacob Collamer of Vermont.[43] Stephenson's letter to Lincoln of May 7, 1861, indicates that he is aware of the Joint Committee on the Library's attitude toward the appointment of a new Librarian of Congress.

Despite the reservations of these Senators, President Lincoln wrote the State Department for Stephenson's commission,[44] and his appointment bears the date of May 24, 1861.[45] His name was entered on the payroll as Librarian of Congress on June 1, 1861.

Thus, at the age of 33, John Gould Stephenson became the fifth Librarian of Congress. During his first summer in that office he scrutinized his subordinates and determined that a changing of the guard was in order. The ensuing transformation in the staff so alarmed Senator Pearce, chairman of the Joint Committee on the Library, that on September 23, 1861, he wrote to one of his committeemen:

While at Bedford the Librarian wrote me that the service of the Library required the removal of all assistants & Robert Kearin (who was called a messenger though in fact an assistant) except young Meehan in the Law Library. This letter I recd. only about 5 Sept. & soon after I heard of the removal of H. & K., A. was next removed. . . . The Librarian complains of disorder & neglect in the Library which I think be fancies. If there has been anything wrong it has been because the officer's have been unable to compell members to return all the books they have taken out. I think L is disposed to take too much authority on hand in the purchase of books. He has no right to purchase any book without the order of the committee or chairman wherein however I learn he has sometimes done. . . .[46]

A letter of the same date from President Lincoln to Caleb Smith indicates that some confusion with regard to the Library's present staff did exist: "Has Dr. Stephenson, Congressional Librarian, resigned? Is there any vacancy of Assistant Congressional Librarian?"[47]

Stephenson's 1861 report makes note of the Joint Committee's concern over his clean sweep:

A due respect for the Committee and for their opinions as expressed in their communication touching the subject of removals from office in the Library, impels the Librarian to state that the reasons for the several removals . . . was his conviction, induced by several months of trial and observation, as well as by the facts as to the condition of the Library already recited, of their incapacity for their several posts. No alternative was left him, in carrying out the reforms he had determined to introduce in the Library, but to select new and more competent assistants, holding himself rigidly responsible for their fitness and fidelity. In filling the vacancies created by those removals, he deems it proper to state that he has been guided neither by personal nor political favoritism, but has sought for capacity and industry alone as the indispensable qualifications of his appointees. Whether he

BREAD-OVENS UNDER THE CAPITOL.

The War Department set up bakeries in the basement of the Capitol to help feed the troops stationed in the area. Smoke from the ovens deposited soot "everywhere" throughout the Library. Harper's Pictorial History of the Civil War *by Alfred H. Guernsey and Henry M. Alden, vol. 1 (Chicago: Star Publishing Co., 1894).* LC–USZ62–57284

has suceeded in securing them, time and practical conduct of the Library will determine.

As Stephenson hoped, time has indeed shown that at least one of his changes was most fortunate. Stephenson's choice of Ainsworth Rand Spofford as his first assistant has been called his single greatest contribution to the development of the Library of Congress.[48]

Spofford, a good friend of Stephenson's brother Reuben Henry and an admirer of Lincoln, was working in Washington as a war correspondent for the *Cincinnati Daily Commercial*. The Librarian realized that Spofford, a bibliophile, could provide the expertise he himself lacked, and, as Spofford indicated in a letter, the two men understood each other well. Spofford described the Librarian as a "thorough good fellow—liberal—high-minded—& active—but with no special knowledge of books—& having to put up with most of the former assistant librarians, he called me to his aid for my experience & bibliographic knowledge." [49]

Spofford, in the same letter, describes the Library of Congress in 1862:

The Library of Congress is a collection of 72,000 vols. embracing all departments of literature & science, & is the only national Library at the Capitol. The public uses it precisely as the Astor in N.Y. & members of Congress & of the gov't only draw out books. The Library is a magnificent room in the central front of the Capitol & a great resort. The Librarian (who is appointed directly by the President) receives $2160 salary. There are three asst. Librarians . . . a messenger . . . and two laborers. . . . The Law Library (which is kept in the old Supreme Court Room) is under the charge of one of the three assistant librarians—who has been many years in that department. The two remaining assistants—whose position is equal in every particular—have charge of the administration of the miscellaneous Library, under the general direction of the Librarian. Practically, the last amounts to little, as Dr. S. between whom & myself there is a thorough good understanding, leaves pretty much all to my management, and I have actually been doing the work of both assistant Librarians ever since I have been here (6 months)—keeping the other assistants in the Catalogue. Now for the duties of the place. They are exceedingly light—consisting of attendance daily from 9 am to 4 or 5 during the sittings of Congress—& 9 to 3 in the vacations which are usually more than half the year. Under no circumstance is the Library open after dark—the room being iron-cased & fire-proof, without gas fixtures. The labor consists of becoming familiar with the contents & location of the various chapters into which books are arranged—supplying the calls of readers, occasionally aiding Members of Congress—writing an occasional letter—keeping a few simple a/c's, & cataloguing the new purchases as they come in. All this divided between three persons—besides the Librarian & the porters. The annual increase in the collection is about 3000 vols.—Congress appropriates every year $5,000, & $2,000 for miscellaneous Books. [50]

Spofford makes no mention of the problems caused from the bakeries set up in the basement of the Capitol by the War Department to help feed the troops stationed in the area. The smoke from the ovens deposited soot on the volumes and tables in the Library. Dr. Stephenson vigorously protested the existence of the bakeries in the Capitol building:

I am pained to see the treasure intrusted to my care—a treasure that money cannot replace—receiving great damage from the smoke and soot that penetrate everywhere through that part of the Capitol which is under my charge, without any means at my command to prevent it. I am now satisfied that there is no remedy, except the removal of the circle of bakeries that hems us in and those directly under the library. [51]

B. B. French, commissioner of public buildings, concurred with Stephenson and suggested that the War Department move the bakeries to the Old Gas House just west of the Capitol. [52] The Senate took cognizance of the nuisance, and Senator Solomon Foot requested that a previous resolution regarding the bakeries be reconsidered. [53] In the House, Representative Charles Russell Train tried to convince that body to agree to the removal of the bakeries from the Capitol, citing the fact that it was impossible to heat the Library of Congress when the bakeries were in operation because the military had built a flue into the flue of the Library furnace.

The wheels of government turned slowly. Nearly a year passed before the offending ovens were finally removed from the basement of the Capitol late in October of 1862, and then only after the intervention of the President himself. [54]

Shortly after the episode of the bakeries, Stephenson urged fireproof rooms for the Library. [55] And soon thereafter the announcement was made that the commissioner of public buildings had recommended an enlargement of the Library of Congress. [56]

Only two reports from the Librarian to the Joint Committee on the Library during the Stephenson years have survived. The first report was filed December 16, 1861, less than six months after Stephenson assumed office. While the 1861 report appears to be in Stephenson's handwriting, it was not signed. David Mearns considered it to be the work of an assistant. [57] John Y. Cole believes the report to have been written by Ainsworth R. Spofford.

Reduced to its essentials, the Library of Congress in 1861 consisted of four rooms, seven people, and 70,000 books. The scarcity of extant records makes it almost impossible to tell how energetically Stephenson entered upon the duties of his new office. [58] Much of the correspondence was signed by his assistants, Spofford and Edward B. Stelle. We do know from the Library's letterbooks and from the 1861 annual report that Stephenson sent medals damaged by the fire of 1851 to the Smithsonian Institution to be repaired, [59] that he reestablished communication with Edward Allen, the Library's book agent in London,[60] and that he closed the Library from September 9 to October 1, 1861.[61] Stephenson's report of 1861 deplored the lack of modern reference works, the inadequacy of the newspaper file, the accumulation of duplicates, the large number of missing volumes, and the dirty carpet. "That no Encyclopedia, less than twenty years old, is to be found in the Library of Congress is matter of constant surprise and inconvenience to members and others seeking the latest statistical and scientific information," Stephenson noted. Another impediment was the lack of a complete file of some American newspaper "furnishing a full, current history of the times for the last twenty years."

Material available in the National American Woman Suffrage Association Archives and Stephenson's 1861 report to the Joint Committee on the Library indicate that Stephenson had staffing problems.

Spofford, with reference to the dismissal of Assistant Librarian George Blackwell, writes:

The week which has elapsed since Dr. Stephenson's strange & sudden dismissal of George has only confirmed my feeling expressed to you in my last hurried note. It is so far as I can see a most unaccountable freak, absurd or at least unreasonable in its origin, & unjust in its consequences. As George will have fully possessed [?] you of the ostensible grounds of the Dr.'s displeasure, I need not recount them. How much to attribute to his own real feelings of dissatisfaction, & how much to the influence of female back-biting I do not know. But the act of dismissal altho he admitted it to be hasty & "perhaps" unjust, evidence a prejudice in his mind that is probably invincible. . . . The Doctor has shown a weakness of character in the whole matter . . . he has shown himself to me in a new light. I knew that he was a man of strong impulses—somewhat quick, & prone to act upon half views—but I have never before (fortunately) been compelled to see & suffer from an exhibition of his prejudices. He has left me so free to act in all things after my own judgment, & has himself been so prone to consult mine, that his action in this case without reference to me both surprised and pained me.[62]

Stephenson's report to the Joint Committee on the Library, dated January 7, 1863, states that the Library was then the fourth largest in the United States and contained 79,214 volumes. He calculated that the Library's holdings would increase at a rate of six or seven thousand volumes per year. To improve the transfer of books "to and from the houses of members," he asked for authority to "employ an additional messenger and to keep a horse and wagon for the purpose."

Many of the volumes reported as missing during the last session had been recovered, but Stephenson was convinced that some would never be returned. Every effort had been made to restrict the loan of books to those government officials specifically authorized by statute, and to a considerable extent, the effort had been successful. Nevertheless, the report continues, "some books are taken from the Library for the use of persons not entitled by law to have them."

On a trial basis, Stephenson had sent his assistant Ainsworth Spofford to New York, Philadelphia, and Boston to purchase books for the collections. The average cost of books purchased by the Library Committee's agent since December 1860 had been, including binding, $3.25 per volume. Mr. Spofford's journey proved successful. The Library could now purchase books, including the cost of binding and transportation, at $1.70 per volume, a substantial savings.

Cleanliness, organization, and efficiency were attributes held in high regard by Stephenson; it is not surprising therefore that he noted in the report:

It is with some degree of pride that I ask the attention of the Committee to the present cleanliness and order of the Library—to the ability, energy and fidelity of its subordinate officers—and to the promptness with which the wants of members of Congress are supplied—and that I express my confident expectation of giving the management of this library an efficiency not surpassed anywhere.

James Alfred Pearce, chairman of the Joint Committee on the Library for 17 years, had died on December 20, 1862. Dr. Stephenson quite appropriately concluded his report with a tribute:

The records of the Committee and the history of the Library declare him to have been the friend and guardian of this library. He has selected all or nearly all the books that have been ordered since the fire, has ever manifested a jealous care for its safety, and has had more than any man the control and direction of the library, for which his high literary attainments well fitted him. He has left his mark on the Library ineffaceably. The elegant courtesy of his manners and the kindness of his feeling made his presence in the Library always a pleasure to everyone employed there. By his death the interests of the Library have lost their best advocate, and the officers have lost a valued friend and counsellor.

During the Civil War period, when so many individuals from Indiana were stationed in Washington, the *Indianapolis Journal* ran a series of articles describing the city and its Hoosier inhabitants. Among these is a description of the Librarian and the Library of Congress in 1863.

The Congressional Library is now an interesting institution to a Hoosier, as the Librarian, Colonel J. G. Stephenson, is a Hoosier, formerly of Terre Haute, and the principal assistant is Mr. Spofford, formerly of the *Cincinnati Commercial,* who was made by nature for a librarian. Mr. Stephenson has completely broken up the "old fogy" crust which had hardened and thickened over the Library during the twenty or thirty years of the administration of his predecessor. It is a moving thing now, with a spirit and aim which in a very few years will make it the best library in the nation. He has selected his assistants with a merciless disregard of all considerations but fitness, and has thus obtained the means to add to the Library greatly while administering it satisfactorily. Mr. Spofford, who knows the size, dress, appearance and contents of more books than any twenty of the usual class of erudite men, is always watching for available purchases, in Europe and at home, and has already secured several, of which there are but one or two duplicates at all on this side of the Atlantic.

The Library contains now 82,875 volumes, exclusive of duplicates, public documents, and everything but those works which are usually meant in speaking of a library, and the Law Library contains over 18,000 volumes, arranged as conveniently as the confined quarters assigned them in the building will admit, in a number of small rooms and passages adjacent to the main hall, and in the main hall of the library, but no arrangement can show them to advantage without light and more convenient space. . . .

Mr. Stephenson is working his way as rapidly as possible to complete a convenient arrangement of all the unplaced books, and a general re-arrangement and enlargement of the Library, and when he succeeds, as he surely will, there will be few better in the country.[63]

As the article implies, Stephenson apparently left most of the duties of the Library to his competent assistant Spofford. War raged around the capital, and Stephenson, the doctor, undoubtedly felt that his own skills could be put to better use in the hospitals and on the battlefields.

On September 23, 1861, in one of his last dispatches to the *Commercial,* Spofford noted Stephenson's medical assistance to the members of the 119th Indiana Regiment:

There is a scarcity of surgeons in the army, and some are graciously volunteering . . . to attend the numerous cases of illness in the army and in hospitals. The 119th Indiana Regiment is the one which has suffered the most hitherto from chills and fever . . . Dr. J. G. Stephenson, late of Terre-Haute, has generously devoted a large share of his time to these sufferers, a temporary hospital for whom has been established in the Patent Office.[64]

Margaret Leech, in her *Reveille in Washington, 1860–1865,* describes the Patent Office Hospital in 1862:

Since the preceding year, the Patent Office had been used as a hospital. One thousand more beds were placed on the second floor and on the gallery which ran around the lofty hall. At night, in the glare of the gaslight, it was a curious scene. Like some new exhibit of ghastliness, waxy faces lay in rows between the shining glass cabinets, filled with curiosities, foreign presents and models of inventions. The nurses' heels clicked on the marble floor, and over all lay the heavy smell of putrefaction and death.[65]

A young soldier, wounded at Gainesville, Va., August 28, 1862, and a patient of Dr. Stephen-

Army of the Potomac on the march to Chancellorsville, passing along the north bank of the Rappahannock on the way to Kelly Ford, April 30, 1863. Pencil drawing by E. Forbes. Prints and Photographs Division. LC–USZ62–542

son's, wrote a short note from Washington, D.C., to his parents on September 11, 1862:

I will now try and write you a few lines. You must not expect much. . . . My wound is getting along finely so Dr. Stephenson says. It is still quite painful and still continuous running. I find my expenses are going to be a great deal more than I thought. I have to pay for washing the sheets . . . I have nothing more to say now. Give my love to al

Affectionately yours,
T. H. Benton [66]

A letter to Mr. Benton's father from an army nurse, Mary Roche, to whose home Benton had been taken, reports the young sergeant's death:

Your son appeared to improve, had good appetite and was very cheerful. On Thursday evening Doctor Stephenson said he was threatened with the inflammation of the lungs from the exposure on the Battlefield. Friday he seemed a little better. On Saturday I began to feel a little more anxious and the Doc staid the most of the day with him . . . Doctor Stephenson dressed his wounds three and four times a day [and] was with him from Saturday afternoon until he died at half-past-one on Sunday noon . . . Doct. Stephenson after hs death opened his purse and found $20. He paid me $10 . . . his bed had to be changed twice a day . . . the Doctor paid for all his medicine. . . .[67]

In addition to tending the Civil War wounded and "giving to the management of the Library an efficiency not surpassed anywhere," [68] Stephenson found time to write to Gov. Oliver Morton on behalf of Captain Brasher of the 14th Regiment Indiana Volunteers, who was wounded by a musket shot at the Battle of Antietam:

I have know Capt. Brasher for ten years and have no hesitation in saying that his past character and habits and his distinguished gallantry and discretion in this war entitle him to consideration at the hands of the Executive of our State.[69]

It is probable that the governor heeded Stephenson's request, for he served as a member of the governor's military staff with the rank of colonel. The *Report of the Adjutant General of the State of Indiana, 1861–1865* lists Jno. D. Stephenson as a special aide-de-camp with assignment to the relief soldiers of the Army of the Potomac.[70]

The unpublished notes in the Lancaster Historical Society corroborate the fact that Stephenson was active in politics in Indiana and Illinois, that he served on the staff of Governor Morton with the rank of colonel, and that he carried important dispatches to the commanding officer of the Army of the Potomac before the Battle of Gettysburg.

Stephenson, in his resume, states:

I never enlisted, and never was commissioned in the military service of the United States, but during a part of 1861 served as acting naval surgeon of the 19th Ind. Vols. and in 1863 served with the Army of the Potomac as a volunteer aid de camp with my Militia rank of Colonel, participating in the battles of Fitzhugh Crossing, Chancellorsville, and Gettysburg.[71]

The part he played in the first two battles is not known, although notes in the Lancaster Historical Society's collections indicate that he was "entrusted with important dispatches" on more than one occasion. The society's material includes the fact that "Stephenson was one of three persons recommended by General Doubleday for bravery and promotion." Maj. Gen. Abner Doubleday, commanding the Third Division, First Army Corps, stated in his report: "Colonel Stephenson, Librarian of Congress, acted as a volunteer aide to General Meredith. He exposed himself freely on all occasions, and rendered many valuable services." [72] That Stephenson had been in the thick of the fighting during the Battle of Gettysburg may be presumed from the fact that the First Brigade of the First Division, commanded by General Meredith, suffered 1,153 casualties.[73]

In *The Iron Brigade at Gettysburg,* William Dudley writes, "Special mention is made of the gallant service of Capt. J. D. Wood, A.A.G., and Col. J. G. Stephenson, a volunteer aid, and Lieut. Samuel Meredith, A.D.C., all of whom rendered brilliant and effective services throughout the day." [74]

Brig. Gen. Solomon Meredith wrote President Lincoln on behalf of Colonel Stephenson within a week of the Battle of Gettysburg:

To his Excellency
Abraham Lincoln
President of the U.S.
Sir:
This will be presented by Col. John G. Stephenson, Congressional Librarian, who has been serving on my Staff as Volunteer Aid, for the past two months. His services have been valuable in the field and his desire to do all in his power for his country in this her hour of need is great.
If there is any position you could give him where he could render service in the field it would be worthily bestowed.

I am Sir
Very Respectfully
Your Obt Svt.
S. Meredith
Brig. Gen'l.[75]

It is interesting to note that John G. Stephenson's name does not appear in the definitive work chronicling the medical history of the Civil War, Abner Doubleday's own major book on Gettysburg, or Alan Nolan's *History of the Iron Brigade* (New York: Macmillan, 1961).

On December 22, 1864, John G. Stephenson submitted his resignation as Librarian, effective December 31, and Ainsworth Rand Spofford was commissioned as of this date.[76] The reasons behind his resignation are cloudy. It has been written that Stephenson was a participant in "speculations created by the War," [77] but no details have been found, except for a possible connection with an act of 1872 compensating Edward G. Allen, the Library's London agent, for the sum of $1,480, "of which sum he was unjustly defrauded by the conduct of the Librarian in the year eighteen hundred and sixty-three." [78]

The Lancaster, N.H., Historical Society's records indicate that Stephenson went south after resigning the position of Librarian. There is also a note in the society's files that his assistant Spofford assumed the office.

In a letter dated April 8, 1880, addressed to the secretary of war and signed by A. Grant, the individual in whose home John G. Stephenson would later die, a statement is made to the effect that Stephenson would have received another patronage position had Lincoln lived but a month or two longer:

My dear Sir:

Dr. Jno G. Stephenson, whom you doubtless recollect, desires to be appointed a clerk in the office of the Surgeon General.

His learning, mature years and business experience eminently well qualify him for the place he seeks.

His services to the soldiers during the rebellion (when he was Librarian of Congress) and his unwavering devotion to the Republican party since its first organization, entitle him to some consideration. If Mr. Lincoln had lived another month, Dr. S. would have been amply provided for.

I shall esteem it a personal favor if you will give him the position he asks for.

Cemetery Hill previous to Pickett's charge at the Battle of Gettysburg, July 3, 1863. Drawing by A. R. Waud. Prints and Photographs Division. LC–USZ62–160

I will take the liberty of calling on you within a few days.[79]

We can only assume, given the contents of this letter, that Stephenson had been engaged in some kind of activity of direct benefit to the Republican party and Mr. Lincoln. The doctor was given the position he wanted.

Stephenson states in a letter dated September 29, 1881, addressed to the Hon. S. J. Kirkwood, secretary of the interior: "I was . . . Librarian of Congress from June 1861 to Jan. 1865, when I resigned that office; from that time to Sept. 1880, was employed in various capacities as a clerk not in the service of the United States; was a clerk in the Record and Pension Division of the Surgeon General Office from Sept. 1, 1880 to March 30, 1881, when I was discharged—cause not stated." [80]

Stephenson gives no specific information as to his whereabouts during the years 1865 to 1880. The District of Columbia census for 1870 lists Stephenson in ward 4; *Boyd's Directory of Washington, Georgetown, and Alexandria for 1871* lists John G. Stephenson, physician, as residing at 306 4½ Street, N.W.[81] The obituary notice for his older brother, Reuben Henry Stephenson, states that Bryant, John, and Oliver were all living "in the far west" at the time of Reuben Henry's death in January 1881.[82]

It does not appear that Stephenson was, as his obituary notice reads, "very largely known." *The Dictionary of American Biography* does not mention him among the Americans who achieved fame. The historical societies of New Hampshire, Indiana, and the District of Columbia contain virtually no material on Stephenson, either as a politician, physician, or Librarian of Congress. The Indiana State Library has one reference to him in its card file; this is to Johnston's one-page resume of the Stephenson years.[83] The Indiana State Archives has one Stephenson letter in its Morton Collection. The Lancaster Historical Society and the National Archives have but meager offerings. Books on life in Washington during the Civil War and local, county, and state histories of the places in which Stephenson lived and worked yield almost no information about him.

Since his appointment to the post of Librarian of Congress was "one of the minor spoils which accrued to the Republican Party by its capture of the national administration in the election of 1860," [84] it seems reasonable to assume that his name would appear in major, or at least regional, works on Republican politics before the election. Allan Nevins' reference to Stephenson as a "well-informed politician," [85] Stephenson's letter of March 25, 1860, to Lyman Trumbull,[86] and the few letters to Lincoln, already noted, are the only evidence we have that Stephenson was actively engaged in partisan politics. Even his nephew, Nathaniel Wright Stephenson, a Lincoln scholar and Civil War historian, makes no mention of his uncle, a Lincoln appointee, in his writings.

While he may not have been "very largely known," we do have some evidence that he was "much liked." A letter from W. T. Dennis, appearing in the *Quaker City Telegram*, reads:

Our Indiana citizens are nobly devoting themselves to the work of mercy, many giving their whole time and their means as far as they are able. Dr. John G. Stephenson, librarian to Congress, has devoted his whole time and his fine professional skill to the relief not only of our own sick and wounded, but to those of other States. As an evidence of their appreciation of his services, several wounded officers and privates of New York regiments, whom he attended, have presented him with a beautiful set of sleeve buttons and shirt studs elegantly set with diamonds.[87]

Another letter, this one in the *Indianapolis Journal,* praises Stephenson's courage and concern at Gettysburg: "Col. Stephenson, who all the day had been serving in the hottest of the fight as aid to Meredith, relieved a wounded Colonel, and strove to rally his regiment." [88]

Records in the National Archives show that Stephenson consulted a physician as early as August 1883, complaining of an inability to sleep for days at a time. As of October 16, 1883, he was too ill to continue his work as medical examiner in the Pension Office, a position he had held since July of that year.[89] The *Washington Post* obituary makes note of the fact that "he had been ailing for a month and on Friday called Capt. Grant, who invited him to stay at the house for a day or two until he felt better. . . . his death was so unexpected that Dr. Bliss preferred an autopsy should be made, while believing it resulted from heart disease." [90]

Resident members of the old First Army Corps met at the office of Colonel Dudley on November 13 and passed a resolution expressing their regret at the death of Dr. J. G. Stephenson, who had served with them in the corps during the war.

A committee was appointed to make arrangements for the funeral, which took place in the Metropolitan Presbyterian Church on Capitol Hill, November 14, 1883.[91]

John Gould Stephenson, physician, politician, and Librarian of Congress from 1861 to 1864, lies buried in an unmarked grave in Washington's Congressional Cemetery.[92]

NOTES

[1] *Washington Post,* November 12, 1883, p. 1.

[2] Washington *Evening Star,* November 12, 1883, p. 1.

[3] Cohasset, Mass., *Vital Records of Cohasset, Massachusetts to the Year 1850* (Boston: Wright & Potter Printing Company, 1916), p. 98.

[4] Scituate, Mass., *Vital Records of Scituate, Massachusetts, to the Year 1850* (Boston: New England Historic Genealogical Society, 1909), 2:266.

[5] Amos Newton Somers, *History of Lancaster, New Hampshire* (Concord, N.H.: Rumford Press, 1899), pp. 260, 406–7, 464, 535, 537–39.

[6] Ibid., pp. 129, 416.

[7] James Brackett, *Historical Sketch of Lancaster, New Hampshire* (n.p., 1876?), p. 21.

[8] Somers, p. 167.

[9] Ibid., pp. 418–19.

[10] Dartmouth College, *Dartmouth College and Associated Schools: General Catalogue, 1769–1940* (Hanover, N.H., 1940), pp. 908–9.

[11] Frederick C. Waite, *The First Medical College in Vermont, Castleton, 1818–1862* (Montpelier: Vermont Historical Society, 1949), p. 231.

[12] Personnel File of John G. Stephenson, December 1881, Record Group 84, Office of the Secretary of the Interior, 2712–1881, National Archives and Records Service.

[13] Dartmouth College, *General Catalogue of Dartmouth College and the Associated Schools, 1769–1900* (Hanover, N.H., 1900), p. 200.

[14] Stephenson to Lincoln, May 7, 1861, Lincoln Collection, Library of Congress, XLIV, 9790–91.

[15] *Terre Haute City Directory and Business Mirror, for 1858* (Terre Haute, Ind.: R. H. Simpson, 1858), p. 81.

[16] Unpublished records in the Lancaster, N.H., Historical Society supplied by Mrs. Jane Hunter and Mrs. Cecile Costine.

[17] William P. Dole to Lincoln, March 16, 1861, Lincoln Collection, XXXVII, 8185.

[18] Thomas H. Nelson to Lincoln, March 13, 1861, Lincoln Collection, XXXVII, 8072.

[19] J. W. Calvert to Lincoln, January 4, 1861, Lincoln Collection, XXV, 5723.

[20] Terre Haute *Wabash Express,* February 22, 1860.

[21] Allan Nevins, *The Emergence of Lincoln,* vol. 2, (New York: Charles Scribner's Sons, 1950), p. 239.

[22] Stephenson to Lyman Trumbull, March 25, 1860, Trumbull Papers, LC.

[23] Stephenson to Lyman Trumbull, June 2, 1860, Trumbull Papers.

[24] Reinhard H. Luthin, "Indiana and Lincoln's Rise to the Presidency," *Indiana Magazine of History* 38 (December 1942): 385–402.

[25] Charles Roll, "Indiana's Part in the Nomination of Abraham Lincoln for President in 1860," *Indiana Magazine of History* 25 (January 1929): 1–13.

[26] Charles Zimmerman, "The Origin and Rise of the Republican Party in Indiana from 1854 to 1860," *Indiana Magazine of History* 13 (September 1917): 211–69; 13 (December 1917): 349–412.

[27] Letters to Lincoln, March 1861, Lincoln Collection, XXXIX, 8601.

[28] Stephenson to Lincoln.

[29] S. B. Gookin to Lincoln, November 27, 1860, Lincoln Collection, XXI, 4672.

[30] W. Gilpin to Lincoln, March 30, 1861, Lincoln Collection, XXXIX, 8499.

[31] E. B. Allen to Lincoln, February 18, 1861, Lincoln Collection, XXXIII, 7401.

[32] Ibid.

[33] James H. McNeely, editor of the *Evansville Journal,* to Lincoln, April 3, 1861, Lincoln Collection, XL, 8727.

[34] Gilpin to Lincoln.

[35] Letters to Lincoln, March 1861.

[36] Calvert to Lincoln.

[37] Henry S. Lane to Lincoln, May 7, 1861, Lincoln Collection, XXXV, 7825.

[38] Richard C. Wood, "Librarian-in-Arms: The Career of John G. Stephenson," *Library Quarterly* 19 (October 1949): 263–69.

[39] Stephenson to Lincoln.

[40] William P. Dole to Dr. Davis, May 14, 1861, Dole Collection, Indiana Historical Society Library.

[41] Richard Mott to Lincoln, March 11, 1861, Lincoln Collection, XXVI, 7981; Kinsley Bingham to Lincoln, March 30, 1861, XXXIX, 8487; R. G. Corwin to Lincoln, March 9, 1861, XXXVI, 7932.

[42] Senator James A. Pearce to Lincoln, March 8, 1861, Lincoln Collection, XXXV, 7914–17.

[43] Jacob Collamer to Charles Lanman, November 17, 1864, Lanman Papers, LC.

[44] Lincoln to Secretary of State, May 23, 1861, Department of State Appointment Papers, National Archives.

[45] List of Librarians of Congress, Department of State

Miscellaneous Officers' Letterbook, no. 1, p. 164, National Archives.

[46] J. A. Pearce to William P. Fessenden, September 25, 1861, Correspondence of William P. Fessenden, LC, vol. 2, March 17, 1861–November 2, 1863.

[47] Roy P. Basler, ed., *The Collected Works of Abraham Lincoln,* vol. 4 (New Brunswick, N.J.: Rutgers University Press, 1953), p. 537.

[48] Lucy Salamanca, *Fortress of Freedom; the Story of the Library of Congress* (Philadelphia: J. B. Lippincott, 1942), p. 197.

[49] Ainsworth R. Spofford to Henry B. Blackwell, May 2, 1862, National American Woman Suffrage Association Archives, LC.

[50] Ibid.

[51] *Senate Misc. Doc. No. 8* (37th Cong., 2d sess., ser. 1124), p. 2.

[52] Ibid., pp. 2–3.

[53] U.S. Congress, *Congressional Globe* (February 3, 1862): 607.

[54] B. B. French to E. M. Stanton, October 23, 1862, Commissioner of Public Buildings, National Archives.

[55] Stephenson to French, November 20, 1862, Librarians' Letterbooks, LC.

[56] *National Intelligencer,* January 29, 1863.

[57] David C. Mearns, *The Story up to Now; the Library of Congress, 1800–1946* (Washington: Library of Congress, 1947), p. 71.

[58] Wood, p. 265. According to Wood, only one letter received in the period 1861–64 is extant in the Library of Congress Archives.

[59] Stephenson to Joseph Henry, August 6, 1861, Librarians' Letterbooks.

[60] Stephenson to Edward Allen, August 20, 1861, Librarians' Letterbooks.

[61] *National Intelligencer,* September 26, 1861.

[62] Ainsworth Spofford to Henry B. Blackwell, September 22, 1862, National American Woman Suffrage Association Archives.

[63] *Indianapolis Journal,* November 28, 1863, p. 2. Material from this newspaper and from the *Quaker City Telegram* was brought to my attention by A. D. Gaff, who is writing a history of Company B, 19th Indiana Regiment.

[64] *Cincinnati Daily Commercial,* September 23, 1861, p. 1.

[65] Margaret Leech, *Reveille in Washington, 1860–1865* (New York: Harper & Brothers, 1941), p. 206.

[66] T. H. Benton to his parents, September 11, 1862, Indiana Historical Society Library. This letter and the following one were both brought to my attention by Tom Rumer, Reference Librarian, Indiana Historical Society Library.

[67] Mary Roche to T. H. Benton's parents, October 20, 1862, Indiana Historical Society Library.

[68] Annual Report to the Joint Committee on the Library, January 7, 1863.

[69] Stephenson to Oliver Morton, December 21, 1862, Archives Division, Morton Collection, Indiana State Library.

[70] Indiana. Adjutant-General's Office, *Report of the Adjutant General of the State of Indiana, 1861–1865,* vol. 2 (Indianapolis: W. R. Holloway, 1865), p. xi.

[71] Personnel Records of John G. Stephenson.

[72] U.S. War Department, *The War of the Rebellion: A Compilation of the Official Records of the Union and Confederate Armies,* series 1, XXVII, pt. 1, p. 256.

[73] Mearns, p. 71.

[74] William W. Dudley, *The Iron Brigade at Gettysburg: Official Report of the Part Borne by the 1st Brigade, 1st Division, 1st Army Corps, Army of the Potomac, in Action at Gettysburg, Pennsylvania, July 1st, 2d, and 3d, 1863* (Cincinnati: Privately Printed, 1879), p. 13.

[75] Solomon to Meredith Lincoln, Record Group 94, 519–S–CB–1863, National Archives.

[76] List of Librarians of Congress, p. 164.

[77] William Dawson Johnston, *History of the Library of Congress,* vol. 1 (Washington: Library of Congress, 1904), p. 383.

[78] *Statutes at Large,* XVII, p. 686.

[79] A. Grant to Alex Ramsey. Application file of John G. Stephenson, Record Group 107, War Department, National Archives.

[80] Personnel File of John G. Stephenson.

[81] William Andrew Boyd, comp., *Boyd's Directory of Washington, Georgetown, and Alexandria for 1871* (Washington: R. L. Polk & Co., 1871), p. 328.

[82] *Cincinnati Daily Gazette,* January 14, 1881, p. 5.

[83] Johnston, p. 383.

[84] Mearns, p. 82.

[85] Nevins, p. 239.

[86] Stephenson to Trumbull, March 25, 1860.

[87] Richmond, Ind. *Quaker City Telegram,* September 29, 1862, p. 2.

[88] Chaplain Thomas Barnett in the *Indianapolis Journal,* July 9, 1863, p. 2.

[89] Personnel File of John G. Stephenson.

[90] *Washington Post,* November 12, 1883, p. 1.

[91] Washington *Evening Star,* November 14, 1883, p. 6.

[92] Grave No. 244, Range 6, Records of the Congressional Cemetery.

A. R. Spofford
1849

Ainsworth Rand Spofford

The Valiant and Persistent Librarian of Congress

by John Y. Cole

The transformation of the Library of Congress from a legislative library into an institution of national significance was, in large measure, the achievement of one individual: Ainsworth Rand Spofford, Librarian of Congress from 1864 to 1897. From the day he started work at the Library, Spofford assumed that it *was* the national library, and he spent the rest of his life making that conviction a reality. In the process, he provided his successors at the Library of Congress with the comprehensive collections and spacious building necessary for the development of a truly modern American national library.[1]

Spofford's 47-year career at the Library of Congress was a step-by-step progression toward his goal. As Assistant Librarian from 1861 to 1864, when the Library of Congress was a small legislative library in the west front of the U.S. Capitol, he carefully prepared the way for its future growth. His appointment as Librarian of Congress by President Abraham Lincoln on December 31, 1864, inaugurated a six-year period of unprecedented expansion that resulted not only in the Library's becoming the largest library in the United States but also in its emerging into a position of national preeminence. Spofford's most important

collection-building achievement was the centralization of all U.S. copyright activities at the Library of Congress, which brought into the Library two copies of each copyrighted book, pamphlet, map, photograph, print, and piece of music. Moreover, the 1870 copyright law eventually made a separate building a necessity, even though it took 26 years of pleading and planning by Spofford before it was completed. That Italian Renaissance structure, located across the east plaza from the Capitol, is truly the capstone of Spofford's effort, for its monumental nature permanently ensured the Library's national role. On July 1, 1897, four months before the new building was opened, the 72-year-old Librarian willingly stepped down to assume the duties of Chief Assistant Librarian. He served in that post until his death in 1908.

Ainsworth Spofford was a self-educated, old-fashioned bookman whose personal and profession-

Spofford posed for this photograph in 1849, shortly after he had helped organize the Literary Club of Cincinnati. Courtesy of the Literary Club of Cincinnati.

John Y. Cole is chairman of the Librarian's Task Force on Goals, Organization, and Planning.

al interests were inseparable. His reputation as a reliable source of information for both official and unofficial Washington made him a well-known figure in the nation's capital for nearly half a century and greatly enhanced his national library efforts. Industrious and fair-minded, he was respected by all, even though his formal and somewhat abstract manner was not always understood or appreciated. To the dismay of many, he was also an exceedingly stubborn individual. Spofford's successes, however, can be attributed to the same single-mindedness that occasionally disturbed his contemporaries. He never lost sight of his principal purpose—the transformation of the Library of Congress into the American national library—and he was a shrewd politician and propagandizer in the pursuit of that goal.

Spofford was a prolific essayist, editor, and compiler; in truth, almost a compulsive popularizer of knowledge. Since he felt that a librarian should be an educator, the primary purpose of his many compilations was to select and summarize what he considered to be the best or most useful information, whether it be statistical facts or literary essays. His annual *American Almanac and Treasury of Facts, Statistical, Financial, and Political* (12 vols.; New York and Washington: American News Company, 1878–89) is one example. Other typical, multivolume compilations which he edited include *The Library of Choice Literature* (8 vols.; Philadelphia: Gebbie & Co., 1882; 2d ed., 10 vols., 1888) and *The Library of Historic Characters and Famous Events of All Nations and All Ages* (10 vols.; Philadelphia: F. Finley & Co., 1894–95). In the last decades of the 19th century Spofford became so well known as a compiler and official source that in 1900 his principal publisher, Gebbie & Co. of Philadelphia, promoted a standard Rand McNally atlas under the title *Spofford's Cabinet Cyclopaedia Atlas of the World*.[2]

Throughout his life, Spofford actively participated in local cultural societies. In 1849, as a young man, he was the principal organizer of the Literary Club of Cincinnati, which is still in existence. In later years he called his 12 years of membership in the Literary Club "the most valuable part of my education."[3] In the capital, he frequently presented papers before the Washington Literary Society and played a major role in the founding of four important organizations: the Columbia

Historical Society and the District of Columbia Library Association in 1894, the Public Library of the District of Columbia in 1896, and the library school at Columbian College (now the George Washington University) in 1897. He was a principal officer in the literary, historical, and library associations, a member of the board of trustees of the public library, and the director of the library school.

Spofford's personal interests were perhaps most accurately described in the formidable title of his only full-length monograph: *A Book for All Readers, Designed as an Aid to the Collection, Use, and Preservation of Books, and the Formation of Public and Private Libraries* (New York and London: G. P. Putnam's Sons, 1900). Although *A Book for All Readers* is a relatively complete—and surprisingly entertaining—compendium of Spofford's lectures and thoughts about libraries and librarianship, it cannot be claimed that it was the culmination of years of continual learning, because Spofford's opinions on these subjects had been formulated decades earlier. For example, his observations about binding, preservation, reference collections, bibliography, periodical literature, and the Library of Congress as the American national library are essentially the same views he expressed in the five articles he contributed to the 1876 U.S. Office of Education compilation *Public Libraries in the United States*.[4] But the origins of Spofford's views on these subjects can be traced back even further, to the period between 1845 and 1861 when he was a bookseller and newspaperman in the thriving city of Cincinnati.

Spofford in Cincinnati, 1845–61

Born in Gilmanton, N.H., on September 12, 1825, Ainsworth Rand Spofford was the sixth child of Rev. Luke Ainsworth Spofford and Greta Rand Spofford.[5] Luke Spofford, a Presbyterian pastor, served eight different congregations in New Hampshire and Massachusetts between 1825 and 1845, the years of Ainsworth's birth and boyhood, which was spent in Chilmark, Mass., on Martha's Vineyard. Since poor health prevented Ainsworth from attending Amherst College, he was tutored at home. He developed an insatiable appetite for reading and, for all practical purposes, educated himself—a fact of which he was quite proud. In 1882 Amherst, which claimed his father Luke and older brother Henry as alumni, awarded Ainsworth an honorary LL.D.

As a youth, Spofford became interested in book-binding and his father arranged for him to serve a brief apprenticeship in a local bindery. The isolation of Martha's Vineyard, however, soon forced the Spoffords to leave the island. A tubercular condition spread within the family in 1843 and was aggravated by severe weather and the inability to obtain adequate medical help. After two members of the family died, Luke Spofford decided to move. In 1845 the Spoffords and their two daughters left for Newburgh, N.Y., Henry went to Louisiana, and Ainsworth migrated west to Cincinnati where he soon found congenial employment as a bookstore clerk in the firm of E. D. Truman, bookseller and publisher.

E. D. Truman was Elizabeth D. Truman, whose husband, William T. Truman, a well-known publisher, had recently died. Until 1843 William had been in a partnership with Winthrop B. Smith, and together they launched the popular "Eclectic Series" of texts that soon included the famous McGuffey Readers. Elizabeth Truman, struggling to continue her husband's business, welcomed Ainsworth's eager help and, according to a contemporary, his "energy, great memory, and knowledge of books soon made him indispensable for the business and he was sought for by those entering the store." [6] Spofford continued his own reading at night, studying languages and devouring the works of his favorite authors, especially Ralph Waldo Emerson, Theodore Parker, and Nathaniel Hawthorne. Largely because of his interests, Mrs. Truman's bookstore became an informal literary center and Cincinnati's leading importer of the works of the New England transcendentalists. Politically, Spofford and his friends took a strong antislavery stand and became ardent "free-soilers." But it was his son's religious view that truly disturbed the Reverend Luke Spofford, who on November 23, 1848, confided to his brother Jeremiah:

But I must frankly say that, if he (Ainsworth) were half as correct in his *religious* creed as he appears to be in his political, it would give great joy to my heart. But alas, he has gone far away from the truth as it is in Jesus, & yet seems firmly persuaded in his own mind that he is a real Christian, & destined to future & immortal bliss! . . . This, I can assure you, is one of the greatest trials, if not *the* greatest, which I have ever experienced. And yet this son is remarkably kind both to me & all the family—offering us pecuniary aid whenever needed.[7]

Spofford's experiences at E. D. Truman, which became Truman & Spofford in 1851, were of great practical value to him when he eventually came to the Library of Congress. It was at the bookstore that he developed his lifelong interest in acquisitions and book selection and enhanced his knowledge of binding and other booktrade skills. Between 1851 and 1859, Truman & Spofford published at least 15 books and pamphlets, which familiarized him with the publishing world and the copyright laws. On behalf of the firm, he made semiannual book-buying trips to Boston, where he met many booksellers and publishers and attended lectures by Emerson and Parker.[8]

The organization of the Literary Club of Cincinnati on October 29, 1849, was a natural culmination of the Truman & Spofford gatherings. There already was a literary society in Cincinnati, but it was too genteel for the young radicals from the bookstore. They formed their own club, pledging themselves to debate the controversial issues of the day. Lively discussions, catawba from the local vineyards, and good fellowship were characteristics of the Literary Club from its first days, but its most important function for Spofford was educational. The club widened his intellectual horizons and enhanced his self-confidence. His closest friends were always fellow Literary Club members; two of them, Reuben H. Stephenson and Rutherford B. Hayes, later were of great importance in his career at the Library of Congress. Stephenson, librarian of the Young Men's Mercantile Library Association in Cincinnati, was indirectly responsible for Spofford's acceptance of a position at the Library of Congress. In 1861 Spofford visited Stephenson's brother, Librarian of Congress John G. Stephenson, who soon persuaded him to take the job of Assistant Librarian of Congress. Rutherford B. Hayes, as a Congressman from 1865 to 1867, served as chairman of the Joint Committee on the Library and worked closely with his old friend, who was then Librarian of Congress, during the important first stages of Spofford's national library efforts.

Ainsworth Spofford was not only the principal organizer of the Literary Club but also its most frequent debater and essayist. In addition to his other roles, in the early years of the club Spofford

became a literary entrepreneur, and a most successful one. This phase of his career began in April
1850, when he invited his intellectual mentor,
Ralph Waldo Emerson, to visit Cincinnati on a
lecture tour sponsored by the club. Impressed by
Spofford's petition of 99 signatures and his pledge
of $150, Emerson accepted. In the next few years,
Spofford was also responsible for arranging the
lecture tours that brought Theodore Parker and
Bronson Alcott west for the first time.[9]

Spofford's adventures in literary entrepreneur-
ship were valuable training for the future Librarian of Congress. He became a skillful practitioner
of the art of persuasion, successfully convincing lec-
turers, sponsors, and audiences of the potential
value of different lecture series. Once a speaker
was committed to come to Cincinnati, Spofford
persistently took care of all details—renting the
hall, selling tickets, advertising, and guaranteeing
a good audience. He also demonstrated his practical sense by using the lectures to increase the
sales of Truman & Spofford, even selling books to
the speakers themselves. Finally, since the lecture
tours he arranged were invariably successful, Spofford's self-confidence and reputation were enhanced. Even Senator Salmon P. Chase was impressed. In a letter on March 10, 1852, to E. S.
Hamlin, the Senator recommended that he discuss with Spofford, "a gentleman of talent, principle, and business qualities," the possibility of establishing a liberal newspaper in Cincinnati. Chase
admitted to his friend that he did not know Spofford personally, but he had "formed a high opinion
of him from the reports of others." [10]

Not surprisingly, the first book published by the
new partnership of Truman & Spofford consisted
of two essays recently read before the Literary
Club. The first, which asserted the right of human
conscience to transcend the written law—especially when that law was the Fugitive Slave Law—was
delivered by Spofford on February 1, 1851. The
second, a rebuttal from an unknown club member,
was presented on April 5, 1851. The anonymous
112-page book, titled *The Higher Law Tried by
Reason and Authority: An Argument Pro and Con,*
was published shortly thereafter. The fairness
shown in publishing both sides of the argument
was characteristic of Spofford, who carefully noted
in the preface: "Both essays are now published in
accordance with a proposal made by the writer

of the first essay, that an article maintaining the
opposite view should be published side by side
with his own." Such fair-mindedness apparently
had its limits, however. Shortly after the Truman &
Spofford edition appeared in Cincinnati, the New
York firm of S. W. Benedict published Spofford's
54-page essay without the rebuttal from his friend.
It would appear that the enterprising Spofford
arranged for the publication of his essay in New
York soon after its Cincinnati appearance.[11]

The proud author sent a copy of the book to his
friend Emerson, who in response went so far as to
claim that Spofford's essay had so influenced his
own discourse on the subject that:

> though I have tried again & again to scratch out your
> part of it, I have only succeeded in a degree, and fear
> I shall not hide the most unblushing plagiarisms, if I
> print it, as they say I must.[12]

Thus encouraged, Spofford continued his writing. In the October 1855 issue of *North American
Review* he published a long essay on the works of
Victor Hugo and, three years later, he turned to
Emerson for assistance in having an essay titled
"Napoleon's Nemesis" published. Although he did
not find in it the "high merit" of Spofford's
Higher Law, Emerson nevertheless sent the essay
to Francis Underwood, editor of the recently established *Atlantic Monthly* magazine. It was rejected, but Emerson broke the news in a kind note
that concluded: "It is a solid comfort to me to
know that you are always there fast abiding in your
convictions, & inevitably a power for good in that
important community." [13]

Spofford's attempt to have this essay published
was more than a Literary Club exercise, for by
1858 Truman & Spofford was in financial trouble
and he was looking for other types of work. The
need was somewhat urgent because by then he was
a family man: on September 15, 1852, he had married Sarah Partridge, a schoolteacher, formerly
from Franklin, Mass., and they now had two sons,
Charles and Henry.

Truman & Spofford had always been more successful as a literary center than as a business ven-

*The Spofford family about 1870. Standing in the back
row, from left to right, are sons Charles and Henry.
Seated, left to right, are Sarah Spofford, daughter
Florence, and Ainsworth Spofford.*

ture. Moreover, most of the books published by the firm can be easily identified as catering to Spofford's friends or to his personal interests. For example, in addition to *The Higher Law,* he published the *Catalogue* of his friend Reuben H. Stephenson's Mercantile Library, three volumes of sermons by his friend the Reverend Moncure D. Conway, two abolitionist novels, and several books concerning the teaching of languages. The store was hurt by the economic depression of 1857 and gradually evolved into a wholesale textbook and stationer's store. In early 1859, despite his continued efforts to keep it solvent, the firm of Truman & Spofford failed.

In mid-July of 1858, Spofford began writing strongly partisan letters about Ohio politics for the New York *Evening Post*, cloaking his identity under the pseudonym "Sigma." To his delight, in October the *Cincinnati Daily Commercial*, a Republican newspaper, reprinted three of his letters with favorable comment. It was a good omen, for in January 1859 Spofford became the *Commercial*'s associate editor and chief editorial writer.

In the 1850's, the owner of the *Commercial*, Martin D. Potter, had closely aligned the newspaper with the young Republican party. In 1856 he sent his talented editor Murat Halstead to Philadelphia to report on the party's first national convention. A year later Halstead was dispatched to Washington to report on the inauguration of President Buchanan. Halstead developed a national reputation, and, by the time Spofford was hired, the *Commercial* was one of the most frequently quoted western newspapers, boasting the highest circulation of any newspaper in the Ohio Valley. Spofford's political opinions and literary skills were well known to Potter as well as to Halstead, who was a fellow Literary Club member.

When Spofford joined the *Commercial*, his friend Halstead, now designated editor in chief, traveled to Washington to report on the opening of the 36th Congress. The first Spofford editorial, published on January 11, 1859, entitled "A Bibliologist," was an attack on the naive book-buying practices of the city librarian. Other editorials during his first month on the *Commercial* also dealt with subjects he knew well: the higher law; antislavery and political parties (entitled "Partyism and Piracy"); the lecture system; historians and "national history"; modern literary style and taste ("The Spasmodic School of Writing"); international copyright; practical affairs and intellectual activity ("Material Progress"); and the U.S. copyright system. During the next two years, Spofford continued to present *Commercial* readers with his opinions on an extraordinary wide range of political and literary topics. In 1883 Halstead commented that his associate editor had "completed his education," for Spofford's "marvelous knowledge of books was not less comprehensive and searching than now and he had a fine faculty for producing an endless supply of editorials." [14]

As an editorial writer, Spofford was never reluctant to promote his personal causes or, on occasion, to lash out against his enemies. One example of the latter was an editorial on April 16, 1860, in which he characterized Senator Louis T. Wigfall, a secessionist from Texas, as "the chief of the boors and blackguards" in Congress, a "social buffoon and political ignoramus" best known for his "boozy rant and rambling ineptitudes." But most of his editorials illustrated his concern with educating his audience and, above all, his ardent sense of purpose.

Spofford's intense personal interest in books naturally led him to write frequently about reading, libraries, and related topics. Therefore, by the time he arrived at the Library of Congress, his opinions about the proper use of libraries and the importance of books and reading had been not only formulated but also articulated in the columns of the *Commercial*. One recurrent theme was the selection of the "best" literature—the books worthy of permanent retention. He also discussed, at great length, the Ohio school library laws. This topic led him to the subject of the English public library system. In an editorial published on February 21, 1860, entitled "A Popular Free Library System," Spofford described the library movement in England and included the complete text of the British Public Libraries Act of 1855. After advocating a similar law for the state of Ohio, he concluded with a description of public libraries in various English cities, admiring especially the Liverpool Library, which he labeled a true "people's university."

On December 5, 1860, nearing the end of his two-month career as the *Commercial*'s chief editorial writer, Spofford's long article on the art of reading was printed. In it he combined a discussion of his favorite topic with personal advice. The editorial, like many others, contains opinions basic to Spofford's view of life—in this instance, his stern refusal to waste time in purposeless activity, thereby leaving one free for essential purposes. He succinctly posed both the problem and the solution:

How to combine the advantages of both the permanent and the periodical literature—how to study the past without becoming confirmed disciples of Dr. DRY-AS-DUST, and how to absorb the present without frittering our minds away on trifles, is the practical question for most of us. We have but a small modicum of leisure, against a *plenum* of literature. . . . To read much and to much profit, we must be able to make the time given to it the most available. It must not be spent on a deliberate effort to absorb all the words which we go over. This effort should be kept for the few things which are worth reading thoroughly. . . . The true art is to read for ideas—not words.

In early 1861 Spofford, rather than Halstead, was sent to Washington to report on the opening of the 37th Congress and the inauguration of President Lincoln. On January 16, 1861, the *Commercial*'s new political correspondent arrived "in the city of mud & politicians," as he described it to his wife, Sarah.[15] With his usual energy and enthusiasm he plunged into the national political scene. During his first week in the capital, he produced six telegraphic dispatches and wrote five lengthy letters for *Commercial* readers—all signed Sigma. Strongly partisan, he praised the abolitionists and scorned the Democrats, especially the southern Democrats. Sigma's February correspondence reflected the increasing excitement over President-elect Lincoln's impending arrival. In the March 5, 1861, issue of the *Commercial,* portraying Washington on the eve of the inauguration, Spofford mentioned the Library of Congress for the first time: "At the Congressional Library, a herd of sight-seers press continually around, gazing into the quiet, well-stored alcoves, and reading aloud the titles of books they never saw or heard of." In all, Spofford's accounts of Lincoln's inauguration and the events surrounding it filled over a dozen columns in the *Commercial,* and the correspondent made no effort to conceal his admiration for the new President.[16]

After a three-month return to Cincinnati, during which Fort Sumter was fired upon and the Literary Club formed its own infantry company,

Spofford was again sent to Washington. This time he was the *Commercial*'s war correspondent. As the hot summer days progressed, Sigma became increasingly irritated by the inaction of the Union Army. Suddenly, however, he found himself reporting on the Battle of Bull Run, where, as he told Sarah, it was necessary for him to use "them legs." In closing his letter, he indicated that he expected to return to Cincinnati as soon as Congress adjourned, probably in about a week. But several days later Spofford was confronted with a new possibility—becoming the Assistant Librarian of Congress. He explained to Sarah that he was doing less writing for the *Commercial,* leaving him "two or three hours leisure every day to devote to the rich stores of the Congressional Library. You know my passion for books. Dr. Stephenson gives me full range, & has even intimated a desire that I should consider the offer of a position as assistant Librarian."[17]

Dr. John G. Stephenson, a physician from Terre Haute, Ind., had recently been appointed Librarian of Congress by President Lincoln at the behest of Senator Henry S. Lane of Indiana.[18] A political appointee with little interest in his role as Librarian, Stephenson was looking for a knowledgeable assistant. His brother's friend, with his impressive knowledge of books, intellectual zeal, obvious energy, and Republican credentials, was a likely candidate.

Three days later, on August 5, Spofford received a definite offer from Dr. Stephenson. The possibility of a general pay reduction for all *Commercial* employees and the long hours Spofford was forced to spend at the job, especially at night, made the Library offer especially attractive. In a long letter written to Sarah immediately after he received the offer, Spofford outlined no fewer than 17 reasons "favoring" the job but could only find nine reasons that reflected "the other side." Besides escape from the *Commercial,* other positive rea-

In a letter to his wife, dated August 5, 1861, Spofford carefully outlined the "Reasons Pro and Con" with regard to his accepting the position of Assistant Librarian of Congress. The reasons themselves amply illustrate his preference: the seventeen pro considerations apparently offset all the reasons offered on "The Other Side," except possibly the ominous "A Change of Profession—usually an evil." LCMS–40972–1

Reasons Pro and Con.

1. Less Laborious Employment –
8 to 9 hours per day, during sessions
of Congress, which last from Dec.
to March or May, and 6 hours of
every other day during recess of
Congress, being 7 or 8 months y year.

2. No Evening nor night work, with
saving of eye-sight, & time for family.

3. No Exhaustion of brain.

4. As consequence of last 3 particulars,
lengthening of life by some years perhaps.

5. A congenial intellectual occupation, keeping mind alert without
severely taxing the powers.

6. Largely increased opportunities
of acquaintance, especially
with public men, editors & scholars

7. Fine Scenery of Washington, &
Advantages of Public Institutions & children

8. Time for occasional recreation
and travelling

9. Superior Advantages from Library
& leisure toward accomplishing any
literary work whatever

10. One whole holiday per week the
year round with no thought of business

11. Ability to increase salary several
hundred dollars by correspondence.

12. Deliverance from anxiety, hurry & rush
about "going to press".

13. Removal from old associations
of failure in business.

14. Escape from disagreeables of a coal-smoke
city

15. Superior opportunities for finding future literary or newspaper employment.

16. Less Sedentary & more active employment — more standing & moving about — no stooping to write.

17. Greater facility of seeing & being seen by family relatives.

The Other Side

1. Less Positive Fixed Salary by $200.

2. Contingency of Removal in 1865. (4 years)

3. Less Field for Distinction or Ambition

4. A Change of Profession — usually an evil

5. A Subordinate Station — nominally

6. Greater Expense of Living in Washington

7. Sacrifice by Removal — Furniture, &c

8. Total Change of Social & Family

9. Possibly More Unfavorable Climate

Probably I shall think of a good many more things before I get through. At all events, I cant decide it without your help. So turn it over — but not in the least anxiously — for we shall be taken care of. If I should not get orders from home to return before next week, I may telegraph you to meet me somewhere on a certain day. You had better take your time tho. To make a good visit rather than hasten, even to return with me. You may, if you choose, write me one more line here as to this. And tell me whether a dispatch sent care John W. will reach you the Same day. Truly Yours always Ainsworth

128 LIBRARIANS OF CONGRESS, 1802–1974

sons listed by Spofford included "a congenial intellectual occupation, keeping mind alert without severely taxing the powers," and "largely increased opportunities of acquaintance, especially with public men, editors & scholars." [19] After returning to Cincinnati in mid-August, Spofford accepted Stephenson's offer. A year later, on May 2, 1862, he informed his friend Henry B. Blackwell that he had accepted the job "chiefly to escape the severe night-work which was very wearisome to my energies without ministering specially to my intellectual growth or ambition." [20]

The new Assistant Librarian of Congress could not assume his duties until the latter part of September, since the editor Halstead had already scheduled another assignment for his traveling correspondent in St. Louis. It was also necessary to arrange for a new Washington correspondent to take over the daily telegraphic dispatches, even though it was agreed that Sigma would continue to write weekly letters to the *Commercial*. Two weeks before he was to begin work at the Library, Spofford was back in Washington. He informed his readers on September 14 that he was house hunting; moreover, "after a somewhat extensive perambulation," he had discovered that there were few houses available for rent, which seemed to deny the prevailing notion that there was a " 'stampede' of inhabitants from Washington, under stress of fear of the sacking of the city by Beauregard's army. . . ."

Sigma's last telegraphic dispatch to the *Commercial* was dated September 22. On or about September 23, 1861, the former Cincinnati newspaperman, tired of the daily rigors of journalism and eager for a more "congenial intellectual occupation," began his new duties as Assistant Librarian of Congress.

Assistant Librarian of Congress, 1861–64

Spofford always assumed that the Library of Congress was the American national library. His view notwithstanding, in 1861 the Library's collection was undistinguished in quality and meager in quantity, being surpassed in size by Harvard, New York's Astor Library, the Boston Public Library, the Boston Atheneum, and Yale. Nor had Congress shown much interest in transforming its Library, which it considered a legislative library, into the national library. Whenever such an expansion

was proposed by a Congressman or journalist, as happened on occasion, the idea was quickly dismissed. Members of the Library's governing board, the Joint Committee on the Library, as well as the various Librarians of Congress before Spofford, generally had been content with the institution's status. Nevertheless, by virtue of its establishment in Washington in 1800 and the strong interest shown in it by Thomas Jefferson, whose 6,000-volume library served as its foundation, the Library of Congress had substantial claim to a national role. Until Spofford arrived, however, no one had the interest, skill, or perseverance to capitalize on that claim.

Ainsworth Spofford saw no conflict between the functions of a legislative and a national library; in fact, he thought the functions were complementary. He felt, as did Thomas Jefferson, that a comprehensive collection covering all subjects was as important to Congress as it was to scholars and the general public. Spofford's belief in the positive value of reading for character development led him to insist on liberal access to the Library for all.

The notion of an American national library claimed many advocates before Spofford. By the middle of the 19th century, such New England intellectuals as Rufus P. Choate and George P. Marsh considered a national library to be a cultural necessity, without which the United States would be incapable of establishing its intellectual independence from Europe and the Old World. During the congressional debates that resulted in the creation of the Smithsonian Institution in 1846, Choate and Marsh urged that the Smithsonian bequest be used to establish such a library. Charles Coffin Jewett, the Smithsonian librarian from 1849 to 1854, went further: he tried to mold the Smithsonian into not only a national library but also a national bibliographic center. However, Joseph Henry, the secretary of the Smithsonian, was adamantly opposed to this concept and instead saw the Smithsonian as an institution which would encourage the "increase and diffusion" of scientific knowledge. Since Jewett's plan was not compatible with the secretary's, Henry dismissed his librarian in 1854, thus eliminating the possibility that the Smithsonian might develop into the national library. Jewett became head of the Boston Public Library and subsequently lost interest in his national library designs. Ironically, the idea was kept alive in the 1850's by Joseph Henry himself, who favored such an institution so long as it did not affect the Smithsonian. Once the ambitious Ainsworth Spofford arrived at the Library of Congress, Henry lent not only his personal support but also that of the Smithsonian Institution to the cause of the Library of Congress as the national library.[21]

Spofford and Jewett shared several ideas relating to a national library; in particular, both recognized the importance of copyright deposit. Yet there was one major difference in their views. Spofford never envisioned the Library as the center of a network of American libraries, a focal point for providing other libraries with cataloging and bibliographic services. Instead, he viewed it as a unique, independent institution—a single, comprehensive collection of national literature to be used both by Congressmen and by the American people.

Spofford's Cincinnati experiences—his book-trade skills, knowledge of books and libraries, and political acumen—were of great importance for the future of the Library of Congress, since they enabled the Assistant Librarian to begin his national library efforts immediately. His accomplishments as Librarian of Congress, particularly remarkable during his first seven years (1865–72), were the direct fulfillments of efforts begun when he was Assistant Librarian.

For all practical purposes, Assistant Librarian Spofford directed the Library of Congress from 1861 to 1864, during Librarian Stephenson's term of office. In fact, Stephenson embarked on the first of his many extended absences from the Library on the day Spofford arrived and did not return for two months.[22] Stephenson spent much of his time as a battlefield surgeon, and his Assistant Librarian was quite happy to be left in charge. Writing to Henry Blackwell in 1862, Spofford informed him that since Dr. Stephenson had "no special knowledge of books," as his assistant he felt quite "free to act in all things."[23] With an experienced entrepreneur in charge, the Library of Congress began its transition from a small legislative library into a national institution.

Spofford found himself truly dismayed at the Library's state of neglect. He occasionally used his weekly Sigma letters to the *Commercial* to describe Library events and he did not hesitate to express his uninhibited opinion about its neglect.

The best evidence, however, of Spofford's immediate absorption in the problems of the Library is an 18-page, 3,500-word handwritten manuscript titled "Annual Report of the Librarian, December 16, 1861." [24] Although unsigned, it obviously is Spofford's first extended plea on behalf of the Library of Congress as the national library. Since the report is extremely critical of the Library's condition, Spofford prefaced it with a careful assurance of his motives, appealing in polite yet firm language for the support of the Joint Committee on the Library:

The undersigned, in submitting the following Report upon the condition of the Library of which he is made by law the Custodian, deems it proper to state that the facts and suggestions which it embodies are the fruit of careful labor and observation, and solicits the attention of the Joint Committee on the Library as calculated to repair its deficiencies and to promote its usefulness to those who are entitled to its benefits.

Within the Library, he reported that nothing was right: the entire place was coated with dust, the books needed repair and binding, and there were "remarkable deficiencies in the collections, which were especially in need of up-to-date encyclopedias, statistical references, and newspapers." For example, "that no Encyclopedia, less than twenty years old, is to be found in the Library of Congress is matter of constant surprise and inconvenience to members and others. . . ."

Continuing unabated, Spofford urged the committee to take more pride in the Library's appearance. In recommending a new marble floor to replace the dust-catching carpet, he compared the Library to other national libraries, noting that the floor of the British Museum was slate, "except that of the reading room, which is of solid oak, embedded in cement." Lamenting "the absence of nearly all the publications, new & old, of the Government of the United States," Spofford reminded the committee that the Library of Congress was, after all, the "Library of the Government."

Finally, the zealous Assistant Librarian attached the following eight separate appendixes to his report, supporting his criticisms, and outlining proposed remedies: 1) a current statement of expenditures; 2) a roster of institutions and individuals to whom complimentary copies of the newly published Library catalog should be sent; 3) a list of publications which should be forwarded for the purpose of international exchange; 4) a memorandum comparing amounts paid for the Library's books with the lower prices obtainable if the Library would deal directly with a selected group of publishers in Boston, New York, and Philadelphia; 5) a proposed set of rules and regulations governing all aspects of the Library's operations; 6) a status report on the publication project of the U.S. Exploring Expedition, administered by the Library; 7) a list of urgently needed books and periodicals; and 8) an itemization of requisite U.S. government publications.

On January 31, 1862, Emerson was in Washington and Spofford welcomed his friend to the Library. He did not hesitate to show Emerson examples of shocking neglect in the Library during the past years, explaining that it "had been under Southern domination, and as under dead men." For this reason, the collections of medicine and theology were very large, while that of modern literature was "very imperfect." [25]

During the early months of 1862, using his Sigma pseudonym, Spofford continued his criticism of Congress and of politicians in general. In the February 12 issue of the *Commercial* he complained:

And if there is any good reason for paying $3,000 per annum . . . for a third of a year's attendance, in Washington, of a body of men, two-thirds of whom could not earn as much in a whole year at home, it has not yet been satisfactorily shown.

Describing his Sigma letters to Henry B. Blackwell, Spofford admitted that they could be risky, especially since "too severe reflections upon individual Congressmen might give rise to unpleasant personal relations." It apparently was a chance that he was willing to take, however. In the same letter to Blackwell, dated May 8, 1862, Spofford admitted his aversion to politicians and described the purposeful way he spent his leisure time:

For myself, despising, perhaps unduly, the whole tribe and generation of politicians, I have systematically avoided social opportunities and engrossed myself in intellectual pursuits connected more-or-less intimately with acquiring a thorough knowledge of a great Library and accumulating materials for future use in literature. [26]

A second handwritten annual report, still bursting with criticism, albeit carefully worded, is dated January 7, 1863. [27] Although signed by the Librarian, it follows the same pattern as the first report and is obviously Spofford's work.

In this report, Spofford began his skillful appeal for congressional support by pointing out that although the Library's collection of nearly 80,000 volumes was the fourth largest in the United States, "in its collective value it is second." Unfortunately, however, there probably was "no library in the country as poorly provided with means for the safe keeping of its more valuable parts" than the Library of Congress. A remedy to the situation, the expansion of the Library's rooms, was then proposed. Spofford also described important accomplishments since the first annual report, presented a year earlier. For example, retracing the path he had followed during his book-buying trips for Truman & Spofford, the Assistant Librarian had visited book stores and publishers in Boston, New York, and Philadelphia. Utilizing his past skills, he had succeeded in obtaining books at an average cost of $1.70, whereas the average cost of books purchased by the agent of the Joint Committee on the Library since December 1, 1860, was $3.27. The Library's binding work was now being performed by two firms in Philadelphia at 15 percent less than the costs in Washington, and the quality was "much superior." Finally, there was a lengthy explanation of a new recommendation, that borrowing privileges be extended to include the "Judges and Solicitor of the Court of Claims." Spofford never stopped pressing the committee for the extension of library privileges to various categories of noncongressional users and for the extension of hours of service. He felt a library was worthwhile only if it was used, and he was never too particular about who used it.

Despite his personal misgivings about politicians in general, Spofford carefully cultivated the congressional support that he knew was necessary for his eventual success. His two annual reports as Assistant Librarian exhibited the same tactful, persuasive arguments that he was to use in his dealings with Congress for the rest of his career. While the reports were frank statements which outlined the Library's problems in detail, their tone was positive. Blame for past conditions was not assigned; instead, Spofford looked to the Library's future. Throughout his career, and despite his strong personal feelings, Spofford assiduously avoided name-calling—at least in public. All personal opinions about individual Congressmen and controversial public issues were expressed only behind his Sigma pseudonym. Spofford's reputation for neutrality and fairness in public matters aided his personal efforts immeasurably. In spite of his political beliefs, after 1861 he was rarely identified with the Republican party and never with any special interest group. In the minds of Congressmen and the public he was identified only with the Library of Congress and his personal crusade to expand it into a national library.

Spofford's arguments on behalf of the Library, as outlined in the two annual reports, exhibited the same characteristics contained in his future annual reports as Librarian and in his many personal letters to Congressmen and other officials in support of the Library. In his national library arguments, Spofford invariably: 1) assumed the Library of Congress already was the national library; 2) presented his proposals as practical, relatively inexpensive alternatives which would enable Congress to perform its own tasks more efficiently; 3) appealed to both national and congressional pride; and 4) flattered Congress, optimistically predicting that, in its wisdom and genuine concern for the Library and what it represented, it would approve his proposed action. He was rarely disappointed.

Continuing his efforts to obtain additional funds for the Library, on October 8, 1863, Spofford made his first direct appeal to an Ohio friend. On that date he explained to Secretary of the Treasury Salmon P. Chase that an additional $1,000 in the contingency fund was requisite so the Library could acquire necessities which previous administrations had neglected, including new furniture and catalog card drawers.[28] The increase was approved.

Spofford began to serve as a book purchasing agent for a few Ohio Congressmen, all personal friends, in 1864. He selected the books himself and passed along the Library's discount. On September 19, 1864, for example, Senator John Sherman wrote from Mansfield, Ohio, that he was most pleased with the books recently selected and shipped to him by Spofford. For the next few years Sherman provided him with $400–$500 annually to purchase books.[29] At the same time, the busy Librarian also bought books for the personal libraries of three other prominent Ohio friends: Rutherford B. Hayes, Salmon P. Chase, and James A. Garfield, then a Congressman. All these gentlemen strongly supported Spofford's national library

efforts. Garfield, in particular, developed a close relationship with Spofford and the Library of Congress; in fact, before he succeeded in obtaining franking privileges for the Library, Spofford used Representative Garfield's frank for official mail. Garfield also was one of the Library's most frequent users, and apparently relied on its resources for, among other purposes, the preparation of speeches. When he was in Cleveland in 1873 and trying to compose two speeches to deliver there, he lamented in his diary: "Every day I miss Spofford and our great Library of Congress." [30]

Somehow the busy Assistant Librarian also managed to compile a new catalog of the Library's contents, which was based on an entirely new system of arrangement. Earlier Library of Congress book catalogs had been arranged according to the Library's classification system; Spofford published a catalog that was arranged alphabetically by author. He felt that this was the most practical system for finding the desired books quickly. His opinion was succinctly expressed in the preface to the new four-volume catalog, which was published in September 1864:

In the arrangement of any catalogue of books, the chief desideratum, next to accuracy of description, is facility of reference, and to this end all minor considerations should be sacrificed.[31]

In the late autumn of 1864, it became apparent that Librarian Stephenson was going to resign. In spite of his accomplishments, it was not certain that Spofford would be promoted to the position of Librarian. His principal competitor was Charles Lanman, a local writer and a former librarian of the House of Representatives, who had the support of Senator Reverdy Johnson of Maryland, the second-ranking member of the Joint Committee on the Library. Although he knew that he had the support of the committee chairman, Senator Jacob Collamer of Vermont, Spofford decided to fight for the position, and he soon overwhelmed the opposition. The Assistant Librarian actively solicited endorsements from every Representative and Senator, and their response was impressive. On November 11, 1864, Spofford forwarded 16 letters favoring his promotion to the librarianship to President Lincoln, explaining that the endorsements were necessary because he had "no special (i.e., recent) political claims," having made it his business "to attend to the duties of my position the engrossment even of my leisure time." Eight more letters and a petition were forwarded to the President on December 22, the date of Stephenson's resignation. The aggressive Assistant Librarian explained to Lincoln that these papers, together with those sent in November, "make up 22 Senators and 87 Representatives who have signified their preference in the matter." President Lincoln, on December 31, 1864, appointed Ainsworth Rand Spofford fifth Librarian of Congress.[32]

Librarian of Congress, 1865–97

While serving as Assistant Librarian, Spofford gained the confidence of most members of the Joint Committee on the Library and began the expansion of the Library's collections and its national role. Once he was promoted to Librarian, Spofford was able to deal directly with individual committee members in an official capacity, and before long the members deferred to the Librarian in virtually all Library matters. The consistent support of the committee was of considerable importance in his endeavors. Spofford never presented the committee with the precise definition of a national library or a formal program for the development of the Library, but he repeatedly expressed his opinion in correspondence, in journal articles, and in his published annual reports (1866–96). He believed that the American national library, situated at the Library of Congress, should be a permanent, comprehensive collection of national literature used by Congress and those whom Congress represented. It was the sole library of the American government and the American people, a unique and an independent institution.[33]

Spofford's relatively narrow view of the role of a national library helped him achieve his goal. Taking advantage of a favorable post-Civil War intellectual and political climate, between 1865 and 1870 he gained congressional approval for several critical expansions of the Library. With the exception of the $100,000 appropriated in 1867 for the purchase of the Force library, each was accomplished at little expense to the government. In all, there were six legislative acts which ensured a national role for the Library of Congress: 1) an appropriation providing for an expansion of the Library within its location in the Capitol, approved in 1865; 2) the copyright amendment of 1865, which brought copyright deposits into the Library's

collection; 3) the transfer, at Joseph Henry's suggestion, of the 40,000-volume library of the Smithsonian Institution to the Library of Congress; 4) the 1867 purchase of the nation's outstanding collection of Americana, the private library of the archivist and historian Peter Force; 5) the international exchange resolution of 1867, which provided for the continuing development of the Library's collection of foreign public documents; and 6) the copyright law of 1870, centralizing all United States copyright registration and deposit activities in the Library and requiring the deposit of two copies of each copyrighted book, pamphlet, map, photograph, print, and piece of music. In five years Spofford had gathered his "national collection," or at least the beginnings of it, and had provided for its continued growth. The Library of Congress had suddenly become the nation's largest library. Furthermore, this rapid and permanent expansion made a separate Library building a necessity. In his 1872 annual report, Spofford presented a recommendation and a detailed plan for a separate structure, beginning an effort that was to last a quarter of a century.

Although the six legislative acts and the plan for the new building were closely related and individually important achievements, the centralization of copyright activities and the successful campaign for a separate Library building were Spofford's most significant national library accomplishments and, for that reason, bear closer examination.

Before 1870, copyright registration and deposit functions in the United States were divided among the Department of State, U.S. district court offices, the Smithsonian Institution, the Library of Congress, and the Patent Office.[34] Spofford, like Jewett, believed that copyright deposits provided the most practical channel for accumulating a comprehensive collection of American publications. After struggling with the problem for five years, in 1870 Spofford proposed that all registration and deposit activities be centralized at the Library of Congress. According to his plan, two deposit copies—one for legal record and the other for library use—would be sent to the Library. The Librarian would be responsible for registering the works, enforcing the deposit stipulation, and keeping the copies deposited as legal evidence separate from the general collections.

Early in 1870, Spofford presented his ideas for the centralization of copyright activities to Representative Thomas A. Jenckes of Rhode Island, whose Committee on Patents was about to report out a bill for the revision and consolidation of the patent laws. Spofford already had obtained the support of Samuel S. Fisher, the recently appointed commissioner of patents. Fisher, a patent lawyer from Cincinnati, had been a member of the Literary Club of Cincinnati, and Fisher and Jenckes had corresponded on the subject of patent law reform before Fisher came to Washington. Assured of the support of the Patent Office, which was the copyright registration agency and legal custodian of the deposit for record, Spofford wrote a 1,600-word letter on April 9, 1870, to Representative Jenckes, in which he outlined the arguments favoring the centralization of all copyright activities at the Library.[35]

Less than a week later, on April 14, 1870, Jenckes skillfully condensed Spofford's eight pages of arguments into a short, effective speech advocating the transfer of the copyright business to the Library, and he attached the proposal to his pending bill to revise the patent laws. Jenckes' bill passed Congress easily, and when it was signed into law by President Ulysses S. Grant on July 8, 1870, the Library of Congress became the first central agency for copyright registration and for the custody of copyright deposits in the United States.

Spofford began his efforts to expand the Library's space in the Capitol in 1863 when he was Assistant Librarian. The approval of that expansion in the appropriation act of March 2, 1865, was his first significant legislative victory as Librarian. That achievement was extremely important, for it established a precedent for the future enlargement of the Library to house its growing collections. It also enabled the Librarian to acquire two collections that contributed greatly to the Library's national stature, the Smithsonian and the Force libraries.

While these two collections nearly filled the new wings authorized in 1865, it was the copyright law of 1870 that made additional space imperative. During 1871, the first full year of the law's operation, approximately 20,000 books, periodicals, musicial and dramatic compositions, photographs, prints, and maps were acquired exclusively through copyright. Assuming that "the constant and rapid growth" of the Library left Congress with no alternative except to provide additional space, in his annual report for that year Spofford suggested a separate Library building. In his 1872 annual report he insisted on it, urging the Joint Committee on the Library to recognize the "absolute necessity of erecting a separate building for the Library and the copyright department conjoined."

In fact, over half of Spofford's 1872 report is devoted to delineating the desirable features in the building he envisioned. This annual report is the most important document in the history of the Library building, for it outlines the basic idea behind the structure, which itself would not be completed until 1897. That Spofford's conception of the building should survive after a seemingly endless architectural competition, countless congressional arguments about its design and location, and several changes of architects and engineers is a considerable tribute to his foresight, tenacity, and political skill.[36]

What the Librarian termed "the Library building question" dominated his annual reports as well as his thoughts until April 15, 1886, when the matter was finally settled. On that date President Grover Cleveland approved an act to erect a new Library of Congress across the east plaza from the Capitol, utilizing a modified version of the originial Italian Renaissance design of Smithmeyer & Pelz. Although the building was not completed for another 11 years, Spofford achieved what he wanted: a monument that both expressed and enhanced the national purpose of the institution it housed. Furthermore, the widespread publicity he obtained in newspapers and popular magazines during those years helped his national library efforts considerably.[37]

Spofford did not allow lack of space to halt his collection-building efforts. Of particular note was a precedent he established in May 1882 for the acceptance by the Library of gifts to the nation from private citizens. The citizen was the Washington physician Joseph M. Toner, and the gift was his 40,000-volume private library, which Spofford had been eyeing for several years. The legal basis for accepting the gift was essentially an informal agreement between Spofford and his friend from Ohio, Senator John Sherman, who was then serving as chairman of the Joint Committee on the Library. On March 25, 1882, during the initial negotiations, Spofford informed Toner:

While the Chairman of the Library Committee conceives that there is full power vested in the Committee under existing laws, to receive and provide for the separate custody of any donations of books, acting as the official organ of Congress, he suggests that it would be eminently proper that a special act should be passed, recognising and accepting the gift in behalf of the Government. . . .[38]

The necessary joint resolution was approved on May 19, 1882, and the collection was acquired, even though space in the overcrowded Library could be found only "by partitioning off a portion of the crypt" under the Capitol rotunda. In his 1882 annual report, Spofford nevertheless proclaimed his hope that "this first example of the gift of a large private library to the nation will be an incentive to other similar donations or bequests."

For the most part, Spofford operated quite independently from the American library movement and the American Library Association itself.[39] The primary reason was, quite simply, that he did not have the time to participate. By 18/6, when the American Library Association was founded, Spofford's Library of Congress already was the leading library in the United States and he was completely absorbed in the struggle for a new building. Spofford was a charter member of the ALA but could not get away from Washington to attend many of its annual meetings. At the 1896 congressional hearings on the Library, he explained that because of "this onerous business of copyrights," he had been able to attend only four of the annual meetings—and at two of those he had been the host in Washington! About the same time, in response to a letter from the trustees of the John Crerar Library asking him to recommend a candidate for librarian of that institution, Spofford bluntly stated: "My range of acquaintance with the skilled men of the profession is limited by my very engrossing official duties to comparatively few." He suggested that the trustees consult either Melvil Dewey or Justin Winsor, since they "would have far wider knowledge of men worthy of consideration than myself."[40]

Spofford's independence from other libraries and librarians was accentuated by his idea of a national library as well as by his personal temperament. He believed the Library should be, essentially, a comprehensive accumulation of the nation's literature, the American equivalent of the British Museum and the other great national libraries of Europe. He did not view it as a focal point for cooperative library activities and was not inclined to exert leadership in that direction. Furthermore, his personal enthusiasms were acquisitions and bibliography, while many younger librarians were interested in problems of library organization.

Because Spofford's administration between 1872 and 1897 was dominated by the unceasing flow of materials into cramped quarters, other Library activities suffered. To the dismay of many, Spofford's carefully conceived scheme for a complete index to the documents and debates of Congress was abandoned about 1877, after several years of work. In 1880 he was forced to cease publication of the Library's alphabetical catalog after only two volumes (A–Cragin) had been published. The Library gradually fell behind in its exchanges and in all aspects of its daily business. Historians as well as librarians complained. For example, in a letter to his friend O. H. Marshall, Francis Parkman confided: "They say I am the worst correspondent in the world; but they lie. Spofford beats me all hollow. I sometimes answer a letter; he never does."[41] Parkman may have been exaggerating but his complaint became common in the late 1880's.

It appears that during this same period Spofford was also forced to forgo most Library recordkeeping, including that of the copyright department. This situation led, in 1895, to a Treasury Department investigation of the copyright accounts; the Librarian was completely exonerated of any intentional wrongdoing, but he was deeply embarrassed.[42] Another unhappy event was the 1896 theft of valuable manuscripts from Spofford's office by two Library employees. The worst part, perhaps, was that the Librarian did not know that the manuscripts—which included George Washington's diary—were missing until a New York manuscript dealer got in touch with the Washington police.[43] These events, along with Spofford's

Spofford at his cluttered desk in the old Library of Congress in the Capitol. This photograph was taken about 1896, a year before the spacious new Library building opened. LC-USZ62-44185

advancing age and intellectual stubbornness, created restlessness, if not unhappiness, among the leaders of the profession. They looked to the Library of Congress for a new type of leadership. While cognizant of Spofford's problems and appreciative of his accomplishments, the ALA leadership was anxious to influence the expansion of the role and functions of the Library. As the magnificent new Library building neared completion, the Joint Committee on the Library provided the association with the perfect opportunity.

The committee's hearings on the condition of the Library were held from November 16 to December 7, 1896, before the move into the new building. The purpose was to recommend a new organization plan. Although Spofford was the principal witness, the ALA sent six librarians to testify, including its president, William H. Brett, librarian of the Cleveland Public Library; Melvil Dewey, director of the New York State Library; and Herbert Putnam, librarian of the Boston Public Library. The testimony of Dewey and Putnam on the desirable features of the Library of Congress was of special interest. Both men avoided direct criticism of Spofford, but it was obvious that their view of the proper functions of the Library differed from that of the aging Librarian of Congress. Putnam wholeheartedly endorsed Dewey's description of the necessary role of a national library: "a center to which the libraries of the whole country can turn for inspiration, guidance, and practical help." Centralized cataloging, interlibrary loan, and a national union catalog were among the services described.[44]

Immediately after the end of the hearings, Putnam supplemented his comments in a letter in which he summarized the testimony of the ALA witnesses. The future Librarian of Congress found that:

On one point in particular we were very strongly in unison . . . an endeavor should now be made to introduce into the Library the mechanical aids which will render the Library more independent of the physical limitations of any one man or set of men; in other words, that the time has come when Mr. Spofford's amazing knowledge of the Library shall be embodied in some form which shall be capable of rendering a service which Mr. Spofford as one man and mortal can not be expected to render.[45]

Putnam was stating, tactfully, that not only was it time for the Library of Congress to modernize, but also its services should be expanded far beyond those offered by the Library under Spofford.

However, the restructuring of the Library's functions could not wait for the final report of the Joint Committee on the Library. Provisions for reorganization were included in the legislative appropriations for fiscal year 1898, approved February 18, 1897, three weeks before the hearings and report of committee were published. The appropriations act gave the Librarian of Congress the authority to establish the Library's rules and regulations, increased the staff from 42 to 108, and recognized the Library's national role through the expansion of all aspects of its operations. The committee therefore declined to recommend any organization plan when its hearings and report were published on March 3, 1897, pointing out that the Librarian himself now had the authority to make all rules and regulations, a power heretofore held, at least technically speaking, by the committee itself.[46]

Chief Assistant Librarian, 1897–1908

When the new law went into effect on July 1, 1897, President William McKinley appointed a new Librarian of Congress, bringing to a close Spofford's 32-year career as Librarian. The President, as well as the library profession, felt it was time to replace the 72-year-old Librarian with a younger and more skilled administrator; all were relieved when Spofford himself agreed and cheerfully stepped down. The new Librarian, the veteran journalist and diplomat John Russell Young, immediately appointed Spofford Chief Assistant Librarian.[47] Spofford frequently served as Acting Librarian during Young's short but productive term of office, which lasted only until January 20, 1899, when Young died after a brief illness. Retaining to a remarkable degree the physical and mental vigor of his earlier years, Spofford also served as Chief Assistant Librarian in Herbert Putnam's administration, which began on April 5, 1899.

As Chief Assistant Librarian, Spofford was freed from most of the administrative duties that he had found so burdensome. Once again he could concentrate on his first love: developing the Library's collections. He made two trips to Europe primarily for this purpose. He also found more time for writing, editing, and lecturing. An especially memorable occasion was his return to Cincinnati in October 1899 to help celebrate the 50th anniversary of the founding of the Literary Club. In his address before the club on October 28, he restated his belief in the Library of Congress as the national library and reaffirmed his personal idealism:

The president has referred, in terms all too complimentary, to my chosen vocation as a librarian and to my connection with the magnificent new library building at Washington. While I take no personal pride in it, I am delighted to have lived to see its completion and to enjoy its many utilities, freed from the grinding cares which so long vexed my weary soul amid the frightful congestion of the nation's books in the narrow and overcrowded Capitol building. The removal to that airy and spacious edifice was like being suddenly translated from purgatory into paradise. I call it the "the book palace of the American people," in which you all have equal rights with me. It is our great national conservatory of books, in which the works of all of you will be welcomed and forever preserved. . . .

Finally, permit me to say, as one who has lived long and tasted much of the sweet and the bitter that are mingled in the cup of life, that I adhere evermore to that belief in the best, which, amid all the trials and disappointments of life, should never be surrendered. Amid the prevalent overweening worship of wealth, the tyranny of fashion, the baseness of politics, and the false luster of worldly glory, let us, brothers of the Literary Club, hold fast by the unmeasured powers of the mind. We need no higher ambition than that our names may stand always for fruitful labor and fair play, for personal independence and for useful life.[48]

Spofford was also able to devote time to local library affairs, including becoming the director of Columbian College's new library school. In addition to his official reports as Librarian and his lectures, Spofford wrote several articles on a wide variety of subjects and edited nearly a dozen multivolume reference works. He maintained that a librarian was primarily an educator who must be constantly concerned with the diffusion and use of knowledge, not merely with its custody. His many unofficial writings, especially the multivolume reference compilations intended for a popular audience, were a consequence of this philosophy. So were his many affiliations with literary and historical societies, where he presented papers and debated with the same fervor that characterized his Literary Club days.

Spofford's crucial role in the shaping of the Library of Congress was fully appreciated by his friend and successor Herbert Putnam. Putnam greatly expanded all aspects of the Library's activities, especially its national services. Among other innovations, he established a new classification system, inaugurated the sale of printed catalog cards to other libraries, and initiated an interlibrary loan system. Putnam's overall view closely resembled that of Charles Coffin Jewett many years before: a national library should not only cooperate with other libraries but also assume a position of leadership in the library world. Putnam accurately observed, however, that the national library services and the remarkable expansion of the Library during his administration could not have occurred without the Library's comprehensive collection of Americana and its spacious building, both the result of Spofford's efforts between 1861 and 1897.[49]

William Warner Bishop, superintendent of the reading room from 1907 to 1915, called Putnam's treatment of Spofford "a never failing delight," describing it as "deferential, affectionate, kindly, and considerate."[50] It was also protective; for example, when Spofford naively became involved in an embarrassing business scheme promoting former Congressman James D. Richardson's *Messages and Papers of the Presidents* (1897), Putnam skillfully intervened on behalf of his Chief Assistant.[51] Spofford's life was inseparable from the Library that he did so much to mold, and thanks largely to Putnam, the last years were fruitful and pleasant. Still in the service of the institution he joined in 1861, Ainsworth Rand Spofford died on August 11, 1908, at the age of 83.

Spofford's Lasting Influence

Putnam paid his friend a final official tribute in the Librarian's 1908 annual report, first noting that Spofford truly had served as Librarian Emeritus during his last decade, then concluding:

His most enduring service—the increase of its collections—continued to the last few weeks of his life, and continued with the enthusiasm, the devotion, the simple, patient, and arduous concentration that had always distinguished it. The history of it during its most influential period will be the history of the Library from 1861 to 1897. This will in due course . . . appear.

The copyright laws and the new building were Spofford's most singular accomplishments in bringing his vision of an American national library to fruition. Later Librarians, of course, have greatly expanded the Library's functions and services, but their achievements have been based on Spofford's fundamental premise that a national library was a great national collection universal in both its range and its usefulness.

Spofford was the Librarian of Congress who permanently established the dual nature of the Library: during his administration it became, and it remains today, both a legislative and a national library. Convinced that the Library that served the American national legislature *was* the national library of both the government and the people, he expanded its collections and functions accordingly. Since the turn of the century, critics have maintained that the national library should be in the executive branch of government, where its primary purpose would be service not to Congress but to the nation as a whole. Others have felt that Congress should officially designate the Library as the National Library of the United States. Spofford never felt called upon to debate either of these questions, concentrating instead on obtaining the "liberal support" of Congress for the growth of the institution.[52]

Spofford was the first Librarian of Congress to assume the responsibility for selecting books for the collections; before his administration the function had been carried out by the chairman of the Joint Committee on the Library. With his bookstore experience and interest in acquisitions, it would have been unthinkable for Spofford to defer to others. Moreover, the first two committee chairmen under whom he served, Senator Jacob Collamer of Vermont and Representative Rutherford B. Hayes of Ohio, were delighted that the Librarian took this initiative. Spofford never let a challenge to this authority go unanswered, as a new chairman, Senator Edwin S. Morgan of New York, learned in 1868 when he questioned two of the Librarian's book selections. Spofford responded quickly to Morgan's inquiry, clearing up at least one misunderstanding and firmly, but politely, informing him why the two books had been purchased:

I bought "The Lover's Dictionary"—lately published by Harper & Bros., because it is the largest dictionary of quotations of poetry, alphabetically arranged, ever published, and as such, indispensable to answer the questions continually arising in every library as to the authorship of particular sentences. . . . The other work to which your inquiry extends, De Miller's "Abuses of the Sexual Function," I bought because it is a new treatise, by an eminent physician, on a subject in which the Library of Congress has every important work issued in English & French.[53]

Since he dominated the Joint Committee on the Library so thoroughly, Spofford also assumed other important responsibilities previously in the committee's domain, such as setting the Library's budget, establishing its rules, and hiring and dismissing its employees. Therefore when Congress, in its February 18, 1897, reorganization of the Library, stipulated that the Librarian should assume sole responsibility for making the "rules and regulations for the government" of the Library, it was only sanctioning what had already taken place during Spofford's administration.

Finally, Spofford's basic role in the administrative reorganization of the Library should be recognized. There were seven employees in the Library when he assumed the position of Assistant Librarian in 1861, and the collections totaled approximately 70,000 volumes. By 1897, those collections numbered nearly 900,000 volumes and uncounted thousands of maps, musical works, prints, and photographs. At that time there were 42 employees, but Spofford admitted that 26 of them worked fulltime on the copyright business, which also took up 75 percent of his time. Obviously a separate copyright department and a full-time register of copyrights were desperately needed, and Spofford recommended both in his 1895 annual report.

Primarily because of the chaos created by the overcrowded conditions, there was no particular organization pattern in the Library during Spofford's long term as Librarian. Yet in his own mind Spofford visualized how the Library should be organized once it occupied the new building, and he began preparing for this arrangement in the 1870's. In addition to a separate unit for the administration of copyright, there were several classes of material received through copyright that constituted natural administrative units, namely printed books, maps and charts, graphic arts, and music. Through the acquisition of the Force library, Spofford became increasingly interested in American historical manuscripts and, in his 1875 annual report, he asked Congress to authorize the employment of a "competent historical scholar" to arrange and index manuscripts.

In Spofford's view the Smithsonian library, acquired in 1866, formed a natural foundation for the Library's science collections. He also planned on separate cataloging, binding, and periodical units and, of course, a reading room service operating out of the great central reading room—deliberately patterned after the British Museum.

This basic organizational plan was discussed at great length by Spofford in a special report to Congress in 1895, in congressional hearings during November and December of 1896, and in a statement early in 1897 on the use of the Congressional Library.[54] Virtually all of Spofford's suggestions, including those for a greatly increased staff, were accepted by Congress and incorporated into the reorganization plan that became effective with the beginning of the new fiscal year, on July 1, 1897. In this sense, Spofford provided his successors not only with a magnificent collection and building but also with a basic administrative structure.

Ainsworth Rand Spofford was Librarian of Congress for 32 years; Herbert Putnam served for 40 years, from 1899 until 1939, when he then became, in name as well as function, Librarian Emeritus of Congress. In his "Remarks at a dinner honoring the 150th anniversary of the Library of Congress, December 12, 1950," Putnam's thoughts turned back to the man whom he had succeeded more than half a century before:

Very few executives have had the fortune to live with their posterity and to be welcomed with a eulogy instead of an elegy. But if you are summoning shades of the past, you must not fail to summon one shade and keep *him* contemporary—the valiant, persistent . . . "forecasting," "foretelling," "prophesying," shade . . .—Ainsworth Spofford.[55]

NOTES

[1] For a detailed account of Spofford's influence on both the Library of Congress and American librarianship, see Ainsworth Rand Spofford, *Ainsworth Rand Spofford: Bookman and Librarian,* ed. John Y. Cole (Littleton, Colo.: Libraries Unlimited, Inc., 1975). See also John Y. Cole, "Ainsworth Spofford and the 'National Library,'" (Ph.D. diss., George Washington University, 1971).

[2] A bibliography of Spofford's writings is in Spofford, *Ainsworth Rand Spofford: Bookman and Librarian,* pp. 187–99.

[3] Spofford to the Literary Club, October 25, 1886, Archives of the Literary Club of Cincinnati, Cincinnati, Ohio.

[4] U.S. Bureau of Education, *Public Libraries in the United States of America; Their History, Condition, and Management.* Special Report, Part I (Washington: Government Printing Office, 1876), pp. 253–61, 673–78, 679–85, 686–710, 733–44. Spofford not only was a major contributor to the volume but also aided in its inception and organization; see Francis Miksa, "The Making of the 1876 Special Report on Public Libraries," *Journal of Library History* 8 (January 1973): 30–40.

[5] See Jeremiah Spofford, *A Genealogical Record . . . of the Descendants of John Spofford and Elizabeth Scott* (Boston: Alfred Mudge and Sons, 1888).

[6] John W. Herron, "Biographical Sketch of Spofford," June 30, 1894, Archives of the Literary Club of Cincinnati.

[7] Ainsworth Rand Spofford Papers, Library of Congress.

[8] For information on Parker, see John C. Broderick, "Problems of the Literary Executor: The Case of Theodore Parker," *Quarterly Journal of the Library of Congress* 23 (October 1966): 261–73.

[9] For details, see Louise Hastings, "Emerson in Cincinnati," *New England Quarterly* 11 (September 1938): 443–69, and C. Carroll Hollis, "A New England Outpost; as Revealed in Some Unpublished Letters of Emerson, Parker, and Alcott to Ainsworth Spofford," *New England Quarterly* 38 (March 1965): 65–85.

[10] Salmon P. Chase Papers, LC.

[11] A copy of the Truman & Spofford edition is in the Minnesota Historical Society, Minneapolis, Minn. The Library of Congress owns the S. W. Benedict edition.

[12] May 23, 1851, Spofford Papers.

[13] July 1, 1858, Spofford Papers.

[14] "History of the *Cincinnati Commercial*" (1889), Murat Halstead Papers, Cincinnati Historical Society.

[15] Spofford Papers.

[16] Spofford's 1861 Sigma correspondence is quoted at greater length in David C. Mearns, *The Story up to Now; the Library of Congress, 1800–1946* (Washington: Library of Congress, 1947), pp. 79–84.

[17] July 23 and August 2, 1861, Spofford Papers.

[18] Richard G. Wood, "Librarian-in-Arms: The Career of John G. Stephenson," *Library Quarterly* 19 (October 1949): 263–69.

[19] Spofford Papers. For a full account of Spofford's appointment, see John Y. Cole, "A Congenial Intellectual Occupation," *Manuscripts* 26 (Fall 1974):247–53.

[20] National American Woman Suffrage Association Archives. Hereafter cited as NAWSA Archives.

[21] For a discussion of early efforts to establish a national library in the United States, see John Y. Cole, "Of Copyright, Men, and a National Library," *Quarterly Journal of the Library of Congress* 28 (April 1971):114–36.

[22] Stephenson's letters for late 1861 are in Librarians' Letterbooks, LC. In his *Story up to Now,* Mearns concludes that Stephenson did the Library of Congress neither harm nor good during his administration, an assessment apparently shared by Wood in his "Librarian-in-Arms."

[23] May 2 and September 22, 1862, NAWSA Archives.

[24] Library of Congress Archives. This important document is discussed at greater length in Cole, "Ainsworth Spofford and the 'National Library,'" pp. 72–75, and is reproduced in Spofford, *Ainsworth Rand Spofford: Bookman and Librarian,* pp. 55–63.

[25] Ralph Waldo Emerson, *Journals of Ralph Waldo Emerson,* ed. Edward Waldo Emerson and Waldo Emerson Forbes, 10 vols. (Boston and New York: Houghton Mifflin Co., 1909–14), 9:395.

[26] NAWSA Archives.

[27] LC Archives.

[28] Librarians' Letterbooks.

[29] Sherman to Spofford, September 19, 1864, and April 28, 1869, Spofford Papers.

[30] Spofford to Chase, October 6, 1868, Chase Papers; John Peters to Hayes, March 26, 1870, Rutherford B. Hayes Papers, Hayes Library, Fremont, Ohio; Spofford to I. S. Derby, July 10, 1867, Garfield Papers, LC; and Spofford to S. I. Bowen, May 27, 1867, LC. Diary of James A. Garfield, June 25, 1873, Garfield Papers.

[31] U.S. Library of Congress, *Alphabetical Catalogue of the Library of Congress; Authors* (Washington: Government Printing Office, 1864), p. 4.

[32] Record Group No. 59, General Records of the Department of State, National Archives and Records Service.

[33] A summary of Spofford's view is found in his "The Function of a National Library," in *Handbook of the New Library of Congress,* comp. Herbert Small (Boston: Curtis and Cameron, 1897), pp. 123–28.

[34] See discussion in Cole, "Of Copyright, Men, and a National Library," pp. 114–36.

[35] Librarians' Letterbooks.

[36] The relevant portions of the 1872 annual report are reproduced in Spofford, *Ainsworth Rand Spofford: Bookman and Librarian,* pp. 74–79. For a detailed account of the architectural competitions and problems, see John Y. Cole, "Smithmeyer & Pelz; Embattled Archi-

tects of the Library of Congress," *Quarterly Journal of the Library of Congress* 29 (October 1972):282–307.

[37] Spofford's role in the planning and construction of the new building is described in John Y. Cole, "A National Monument for a National Library; Ainsworth Spofford and the New Library of Congress, 1871–1897," in *Records of the Columbia Historical Society,* vol. 48 (Washington: Published by the Society, 1973), pp. 468–507. For additional details about the building, see Helen-Anne Hilker, "Monument to Civilization; Diary of a Building," *Quarterly Journal of the Library of Congress* 29 (October 1972):234–66.

[38] Librarians' Letterbooks.

[39] John Y. Cole, "LC and ALA, 1876–1901," *Library Journal,* October 15, 1953, pp. 2965–70.

[40] Letter from Spofford to Messrs. Jackson, Blatchford, & Keith, Trustees of the Crerar Library, February 25, 1895, reproduced in *The John Crerar Library, 1895–1944* (Chicago, 1945), p. 36.

[41] Francis Parkman, *Letters of Francis Parkman,* ed. Wilbur R. Jacobs, 2 vols. (Norman: University of Oklahoma Press, 1960), 2: 149–50.

[42] The episode was thoroughly reported by the press. See the Washington *Evening Star,* July 10 and August 21, 1895; the *Washington Post,* December 10, 1897; and the New York *Herald Tribune,* December 11, 1897.

[43] See Fred Shelley, "Manuscripts in the Library of Congress," *American Archivist* 11 (January 1948): 11–14.

[44] U.S. Congress, Joint Committee on the Library, *Condition of the Library of Congress, March 3, 1897,* 54th Cong., 2d sess., Senate Report 1573, pp. 139–68, 179–203, 216–28.

[45] Ibid., p. 228.

[46] Ibid., pp. i–ii; 29 Stat. 538.

[47] Young would not accept the post without Spofford's consent, and the appointment of Spofford as Chief Assistant Librarian was agreed upon before President William McKinley's nomination of Young. See John Russell Young to Melvil Dewey, Librarians' Letterbooks, August 13, 1897, and the Washington *Evening Star,* June 30, 1897.

[48] *The Literary Club of Cincinnati* (Cincinnati: Ebbert & Richardson Co., 1903), pp. 16–18.

[49] See Herbert Putnam, "A Librarian Past: Ainsworth Rand Spofford—1825–1908," *The Independent,* November 19, 1908, pp. 1149–55.

[50] William Warner Bishop, "The Library of Congress, 1907–1915; Fragments of Autobiography," *Library Quarterly* 18 (January 1948):6.

[51] The episode is described in Robert D. and Helen C. Stevens, "Documents in the Gilded Age: Richardson's Messages and Papers of the Presidents," *Government Publications Review* 1 (Spring 1974):233–40.

[52] For an outline of the views of Spofford and subsequent Librarians of Congress concerning the legislative

and national roles of the Library, see John Y. Cole, "For Congress & the Nation; the Dual Nature of the Library of Congress," *Quarterly Journal of the Library of Congress* 32 (April 1975): 118–38.

[53] February 5, 1868, Edward S. Morgan Papers, New York State Library, Albany.

[54] U.S. Congress, Joint Committee on the Library, *Special Report of the Librarian of Congress, December 3, 1895,* 54th Congress, 1st sess., Senate Doc. 7; U.S. Congress, *Use of Congressional Library. January 18, 1897,* 54th Cong., 2d sess., Senate Doc. 65.

[55] Herbert Putnam Papers, LC.

John Russell Young

The Internationalist as Librarian

by John C. Broderick

John Russell Young. The name *almost* sounds familiar, as if its owner were one of those Boston Brahmins who wrote sentimental-didactic poetry that everyone used to memorize.

On the contrary, Young was the farthest remove from the Boston Brahmins: an immigrant from Ireland who was brought to the United States in his infancy. His sickly father, who settled in Philadelphia, was a weaver unable to provide adequately for his family. After the death of Young's mother in 1851, the four surviving children were dispersed, Young becoming the ward of an uncle in New Orleans where he continued his meager formal schooling. He returned to Philadelphia at age 15 and apprenticed himself to another relative, who was a printer, and soon became able to gather his brother and sisters into one household, of which he was the chief support.

Thousands upon thousands of American boyhoods began this way in the 19th century, but, despite Horatio Alger, few were preliminary to an adult life spent in the highest circles of journalism, politics, business, and diplomacy. John Russell Young's life, however, followed unexpected and unpredictable patterns. For example, few thought of him in 1897 for the position of Librarian of Congress. Rumors had Young accepting another diplomatic post or even a Cabinet appointment. Nevertheless, the appointment, when it came, seemed so eminently right that Young was confirmed the same day, a fact in which the new Librarian took special pride. His tenure was to be the briefest in the 175-year history of the Library of Congress, a scant 18 months, but it was hardly the least significant.

Materials for the study of Young's life are abundant. With their aid we may readily understand the course his life took, the ways in which the Librarianship was a culmination (as well as a personal disappointment), and even, as one of those New England poets put it, "what might have been."

Young apparently owed nothing to Ireland, where he was born November 20, 1840, the son of George and Eliza Rankin Young. He visited Ire-

John Russell Young as he appeared in 1897, shortly before assuming the position of Librarian of Congress. LC–USZ62–6011A

John C. Broderick is chief of the Manuscript Division.

land only twice, in 1879–80, and may even have sought to obscure his Irish birth.[1] Of Scots lineage and Presbyterian background, he was not a typical "Irish" immigrant of the 1840's. The Young family sailed to America in 1841 and settled first in Downingtown, Pa., moving three years later to Philadelphia, where Young began his education at the Harrison School.

Of many formative influences upon Young, four may be singled out: his mother; her New Orleans surrogate after her death, Mrs. Hagenbach; his mentor in journalism, John W. Forney; and the city of Philadelphia itself.

About Young's mother, who died June 21, 1851, little is known except for her son's recollections. Nearly 20 years after her death Young wrote in his diary, "That summer day is in my brain as yesterday." [2] Eliza Young seems to have inspired in Young an extraordinary bookishness.[3] She may also have inculcated the driving ambition which was a large part of his character. No doubt the family dislocations that occurred after her death gave added significance and poignance to the event. When Young visited his birthplace, the village of Dunnamanagh in County Tyrone, his relatives remembered his mother as "a highly remarkable and superior woman." [4]

In New Orleans Young became acquainted with a French instructor in his school, Mrs. Hagenbach, whose letters to Young, especially after his return to Philadelphia, set a high standard of accomplishment for the young man. Her letters are the earliest bits of correspondence in the John Russell Young papers in the Manuscript Division, and Young's preservation of them for nearly 50 years indicates their importance to him. In retrospect, they seem oppressive and not entirely healthy—full of complaints about Young's neglect and, later, disparagement of his adolescent interest in girls, which is made to seem disgraceful. On the positive side, the letters assume that there is no role which Young cannot fill—if he will only be selfless enough. In the earliest letter, December 12, 1854, after reproaching Young for his failure to write, Mrs. Hagenbach continues: "But a *cameleon* [i.e., Young, then 14 years old] never will make a useful or famed statesman—far from it, it can only become defamed in history; and by his contemporaries—and I will hope that mon Jean will not be the like—but become great in good-

ness—great for his own benefit which will consist as real greatness does—in the good he can do for his country and his fellow creatures in general." The letter concludes: "O John become great." [5]

Although the career which Mrs. Hagenbach forecast for Young was statesmanship, Young himself very early settled on journalism, to which his apprenticeship in his cousin's print shop was more immediately allied. Early in 1856 Young apparently wrote to the famous editor Horace Greeley about how to prepare himself for a career as a newspaper editor and whether an opening existed on Greeley's *New-York Tribune*. It was a natural enough question and, for a 15-year-old apprentice, indicated thoughtfulness as well as ambition. Greeley's reply (May 13, 1856) was insufferable in its sanctimonious brutality. It read in part:

3. You seem to me to be laboring under the delusion that somebody's favor . . . can be of material service to you. When you are older, you will realize that, under God, nobody but yourself can do you much good or favor.

4. I do not like the way you speak of your personal ties and associations. There seems to be a varnish of sentimentality covering an abyss of selfishness. Beware of it. [6]

In 10 years Young would be Greeley's managing editor at the *Tribune*.

In August 1857 Young secured a position of copyboy on the *Philadelphia Press,* chiefly through his demonstrated ability to decipher editor John W. Forney's crabbed hand. He almost immediately submitted a dramatic notice of a performance of *Richard III*, in which he pontificated on the work of various Shakespearean actors of the 19th century. Very shortly thereafter, he became a reporter and subsequently managing editor and editor of newspapers published in Philadelphia and Washington by Forney, who more and more valued Young's ability. The association with Forney was fortuitous. Given widespread credit for the nomination of James Buchanan, Forney was just beginning his most influential decade when Young went to work for him. In addition to

Young's conscientiousness and precocious sense of responsibility for his family, even at age 16, are evident in a letter to his father and brother, October 1, 1857, written at 2 a.m. after a long night of work at the Philadelphia Press. *LCMS–46584–1*

[1857]

Phila. October 1. 1837.
Two O'clock in the morning.

My Dear Father & Brother,

I am very sleepy. But
I take these few moments before I go to
bed to write You a few lines. Mary Ann
arrived here yesterday, and I was very much
Surprised to See her, I Can assure You.
I was just getting up, when she arrived,
although it was dinner-time. I am a
late riser I can assure You, since I came
to work for Col. Forney. I was astonished
to see Mary Ann here and no one
along with her. I was hoping You
had come,— and was sorry when I heard
You had not. I hope, however to
See You in a few days.
I am glad to hear of Your
Success at House Keeping in St Clair.
Mary Ann has been telling me ever
since she arrived about her fine times,
her nice cakes— her good bread,—
And what a mischievous boy Jimmy
is. I hope he will be good though

Mary Ann is very anxious to go to house keeping here. She wants me to go and hire a house, and get Uncle Jimmy Rankin. I won't do any such a thing. I would not ask any thing better than for us all to live together once more, — but I do not want to depend entirely on Uncle Jimmy, or on any body else. I am not going to rent a house till you come to town. You know more about such matters than Mary Ann, Uncle Jimmy or I. You have had experience which we have not. You can get things cheaper, and do every thing better. You could earn from 6 to 7 dollars a week, I from 3.½ to 4 dollars, and between us we can get along. Provisions are getting cheaper, — and though Work is very scarce yet you can always get something to do. Now is the time to get a house, — get in coal and flour, potatoes and provisions before the winter comes in. Every day you lose now, so much the worse in the end. I am sick and tired of boarding

and would get along twice as comfortable
among my own friends and in my own
home. I am in a good place to work
at. Have a steady job, as long as I behave
myself — and am getting along very well.
All I want now is a home of our own,
and the only way we can get that is
by your coming to town right away, and
hiring a house. If you put it off
two or three weeks winter will be on
us, — and what then can we do?

I expect Uncle James Young of
New Orleans home from Europe in a
week or two, — and as he will stop
in Philadelphia you could get some
assistance from him. Mary Ann tells
me you have no work in St. Clair,
and I think you have a better chance
of getting work here than in a small
town like that. Mary Ann says you
will come down on Saturday. I expect you on Tuesday or Monday and
if you do not come I shall feel disappointed. We can do nothing till
you come. Mary Ann is running around
no one to mind her, — I cannot, working

working as I do all night and half the day. Without some one to keep an eye on her, — what will she come to.

If You intend coming here, — and nothing would please me better. The cold weather is two or three weeks of us, and we have hardly time to prepare for it.

I am sorry Jimmy is such an unruly boy, — if all Mary Ann tells me is true. I am sorry he does not treat his father with more respect. He will be better I hope, — and if he comes to town, see how good he can be. ~~Eliza~~ Lizzie is sick with the croup. But I hope will soon recover. She sends her love to You all.

I am so sleepy, I cannot see to write. Come to Philadelphia soon, unless You are going to spend the winter near Pottsville. Write soon, and let Jimmy write, I can read his writing better. Mary Ann sends her love to you. As do all your friends. I am your sleepy affectionate son till death,   John F. Young.

his printing empire, Forney served as Clerk of the House of Representatives 1851–57, 1860–61, and Secretary of the Senate 1861–68. In 1861 he founded the *Washington Chronicle,* of which Young was in charge for a time. By the time the Civil War broke out, Young was Forney's closest assistant and, because of Forney's legislative duties, soon in operational charge of his enterprises.

From Forney, whom he later described as "my first master," [7] Young acquired fierce antislavery and pro-Union sentiments. Through Forney he gained access to national political and military leaders, including President Lincoln, to whom Forney was an adviser and confidant. Young also may have been misled by Forney's example into too secure an opinion about the power of the press, since Forney's political influence did not derive from his successful journalism, but rather vice versa.

Less easy to demonstrate but pervasive throughout Young's career was the sense that Philadelphia and the opinion of its leading citizens were the measure of a man's importance. After two days in New York City in 1859, Young wrote: "Glad I am home for after all, there is no comparison between the metropolis of Pennsylvania and that of New York." [8] Forty years later, after a career which centered in New York for many years, Young wrote in his diary (March 14, 1898): "N.Y. is nothing but a Babylon to me, & I leave it without any sentiment." Throughout his life Young was essentially a Philadelphian, maintaining business interests, club memberships, and lifelong friendships in the city from which his career required him almost perpetually to absent himself.

Young first came to national attention through his account of the Confederate victory and Union retreat at the Battle of First Manassas (Bull Run), published in Forney's *Philadelphia Press* July 22, 1861. As an eyewitness observer, Young was able to give substance and credibility to his report through numerous human details:

As we drew nearer the field evidences of death were more striking. About half a mile from the immediate scene of hostilities the first shelter for the wounded had been obtained. A low, white frame house stood on the side of a road, covered with a few trees, surrounded by a garden of blooming roses, and neatly enclosed in rough white palings. It was the house of a plain Virginia farmer, but the necessities of war converted his home into an hospital. The well in front was guarded by sol-diers. The chambers, the kitchen, the parlor, the porch, and the shade under the trees were occupied by wounded men, some moaning sadly, some bearing their agony in heroic silence, and others beseeching the doctor to place them out of the reach of pain, and occasionally one asking faintly for a cup of water. In the meantime the doctors ran hither and thither, binding, trepanning, amputating, probing, and soothing, assisted by the old Virginian, a blunt specimen of a son of the Old Dominion, who, assisted by his family, was assiduous to relieve the miseries of that fearful day. The soldiers had crawled round his well, and broken in his fences, and overrun his house. The flowers no longer bloomed in the garden, but, crushed and broken, they gave forth their fragrance under the bruising feet of the soldiers. Where the roses had grown in the morning dead men lay in noon. [9]

There were many reputations in journalism made during the Civil War. The names of Whitelaw Reid and Charles C. Coffin come to mind. Young was just such a beneficiary as these.

With the increase of managerial and editorial responsibilities, Young's writing was limited to anonymous "leaders." However, he did some special reporting at times. In the spring of 1864 he traveled to Louisiana to report on Gen. Nathaniel P. Banks' ill-fated Red River campaign. [10] In that same year his industrial journalism for the *Press* was printed separately as *A Visit to the Oil Regions of West Virginia, Ohio and Pennsylvania* (Philadelphia: Ringwalt & Brown, 1864).

In 1865, following a disagreement with Forney, Young was employed by the Philadelphia financier Jay Cooke, who had been appointed a fiscal agent of the Treasury Department to sell government securities at 7.30 percent (hence the designation of Cooke's "seven-thirties"). Young was one of several journalists employed to "put over" the sale, without which the national government faced fiscal crisis. Cooke's firm sold $600 million worth of securities in less than six months in 1865, to supplement his disposal of $500 million worth of securities earlier in the war. Young moved to New York to carry out his publicity work for Cooke and began to submit special articles to Greeley's *New-York Tribune* and attempt to crack the serious magazine market. [11] He had also helped found the *Philadelphia Morning Post,* in which he maintained a strong financial and editorial interest, to his eventual sorrow.

Changes in his family situation had reinforced Young's own natural ambitions to intensify his dreams of success and active pursuit of it. On

October 18, 1864, Young had married in Washington Rose Fitzpatrick, daughter of a longtime employee of the U.S. Senate. Their son "Johnny" had been born July 27, 1865. The marriage was to be marked by sadness. Until her death in 1881, Mrs. Young was frequently ill, and all three children of the marriage died in childhood.

Before the year 1865 was out, Young had earned a regular position on the *Tribune* staff and in mid-1866 he was named managing editor, succeeding Sydney Howard Gay, the first to bear that title, who had resigned because of ill health. Young thus became, at age 25, the operational head of one of the country's leading newspapers, in charge of a large staff that included such men as George Ripley, who had founded the Brook Farm transcendental community in Massachusetts before Young was born.

Despite his youth, Young was resolute and decisive as managing editor of the *Tribune* 1866–69. He was innovative and perceptive as well. He suggested that George W. Smalley become a permanent correspondent in London, a position Smalley was to occupy with great influence over the next 40 years. Young employed Henry M. Stanley as a travel writer and secured Samuel L. Clemens' sketches of the tour to the Holy Land, to be published in 1869 as *Innocents Abroad*. Thirty years later, after reading a biography of former *Tribune* writer Bayard Taylor, Young remarked in his diary (November 22, 1898): "How much I did for *The Tribune* & yet how much I am out of its history. It bears the impress I made upon it." Except for the passions released by the impeachment and trial of Andrew Johnson, Young might have continued his role at the *Tribune* and secured his rightful place in its history.

Young's antipathy toward President Andrew Johnson was almost instantaneous. On August 25, 1866, he wrote to John Hay that "the best of Presidents has been succeeded by the worst." [12] Over the next two years Young carried his opposition to the President to unreasonable lengths, overcoming admonitory restraints by Horace Greeley and his own initial caution. Young's first *Tribune* editorial on "The Impeachment of the President" appeared January 8, 1867, following introduction of articles of impeachment by Congressman William Ashley. Young thought impeachment complex and involved, likely to win sympathy for

Johnson, and uncertain in its sequel. Nevertheless, he did not oppose impeachment in January 1867; he merely urged caution. "Let us walk slowly, and survey the ground as we go." Later that month a Philadelphia friend, Sam Wilkeson, wrote: *"Impeachment is dead sure.* The Tribune will make a capital mistake if it opposes it." [13] As the year 1867 progressed, Young was less and less inclined to oppose impeachment. Moreover, Horace Greeley's frequent absences gave Young considerable freedom in use of the *Tribune* editorial columns.

On June 11, 1867, Young editorialized on "Reconstruction," an article which brought him a four-page letter from Chief Justice Salmon P. Chase, dated June 28. Chase was the *Tribune's* (certainly Greeley's) strong favorite for the Republican nomination in 1868 and the presidency. Chase took note of Young's abuse of President Johnson in the June 11 article but did not wish to comment in writing. "On this subject I should like to exchange views with you in a friendly talk." On the substantive questions, however, "I must say frankly that I see no ground for thinking that the President has not intended to carry out the Reconstruction Acts in good faith: or that the Attorney General has not honestly sought to ascertain & state their true meaning." [14]

Horace Greeley, meanwhile, in Albany for the New York state constitutional convention, was sending Young encouraging, but admonitory messages. "I have not written to direct you, because you were doing very well, and because too much dictation seems to me to take the courage out of almost any one. . . . I trust we shall be able to exert a good influence on the progress of Reconstruction." [15] Greeley was fixed in his opposition to Grant for President. "I don't want any man for President who *ever* gets drunk. Andy Johnson should suffice of that sort for at least fifty years yet." [16] Nevertheless, he advised Young to use caution. "Get all the information you can about Johnson's projects and doings, but I would speak of them all with love, dignity and moderation. We must not destroy our ability to speak with power at the proper instant." [17] Early in September Greeley, still in Albany, wrote Young: "I would not go so far against Johnson that the Ashleys can quote us in pushing impeachment. Johnson is as useful to us as the devil is to Orthodox theology. We can't afford to get rid of him till we have elected our

President. Were he expelled from the White House, we should all be by the ears. Be wary on this point." [18] But Young was headstrong and determined to bring about impeachment. In mid-September Greeley had to veto an article favoring impeachment, already set in type. "Let it stand till we see more clearly what ought to be done. Nothing can be gained by printing it." [19] In November Greeley wrote: "Be careful not to let bitter things be said that will be quoted by the Obstructives at the South." [20] Despite these warnings, Greeley frequently in these months pronounced himself "more than satisfied" with Young's conduct of the *Tribune.*

Although Greeley's influence was restraining Young, others were egging him on. Two of these were Wendell Phillips and Speaker of the House Schuyler Colfax. Young would remember Phillips, the Brahmin abolitionist orator, as "in many respects the most charming figure I ever knew in public life." [21] He had illusions about Colfax ("there was nothing in Colfax but the franking privilege") or the self-interest which prompted his support of Young's radicalism. Nevertheless, he intrigued with Colfax and others in Washington to further impeachment. "Go ahead. We'll follow your plume," Phillips urged Young.[22] In January 1868 Phillips wrote, "You are leading the public thought & purpose grandly & have every morning our fresh thanks for your fidelity & fresh joy that your position makes it so effective." [23] From Colfax: "Your Editorials have rung like a trumpet throughout the land." [24] Daniel Sickles was another who thanked Young for the "powerful articles" in the *Tribune.*[25]

The year 1868 was crucial to the fortunes of the presidency, the nation, and John Russell Young. He began the year with the article "Concerning Popularity," which *Tribune* publisher Samuel Sinclair thought would cost 10,000 subscribers.[26] Nevertheless, on January 13 the *Tribune* stockholders met, reelected Greeley editor, and approved Young's management of the paper. Early in February Greeley went west for a month of lecturing. In his absence Young put the *Tribune* firmly into the impeachment camp with three editorial articles February 24, including one entitled simply "The President Must Be Impeached." [27] There was, he argued, "no avoiding this conclu-

sion . . . no explaining it away. There is no middle course." The President must be "swept out of office" for his "treachery."

Young found his "impeachment *coup d'etat,*" as he designated it, "very successful," though he was "anxious to hear from Greeley." [28] He heard from others. Colfax wrote from Washington: "The Tribune *is* magnificent these days, thanks to your prompt & decided action. Its white plume is at the head of the column, just where I am delighted to see it. I have heard scores of eulogies on Monday's grand paper. Said a Member to me, 'Never did its bugle blast sound more cheerily to us all.' " [29]

From that point until the decision in the Senate in May, Young was unrelenting in his editorial onslaughts. He was in and out of Washington during the spring, to the extent that Greeley was "vexed" by his absence from New York. He was in the Senate gallery as the impeachment trial began, and, as the first crucial vote approached, he published "The Statesmanship of Impeachment," in which he argued:

> It is therefore impossible to escape Impeachment. The Senate must convict Mr. Johnson, or assume the responsibility of his succeeding policy, and share with him the odium of his past career. The Republican Senators have voted a hundred times that he is an enemy of the country! Any Republican vote now, but one of Impeachment, is therefore a lie. . . . We could wish a unanimous vote on Impeachment, but the partisanship of the Democrats forbids it. So it becomes the high and solemn mission of the Republican party. . . . Impeachment is loyalty, patriotism, statesmanship. The Republican who votes against it seeks a lot with the men who have warred and plotted for the destruction of the Republic.[30]

Edwin M. Stanton wrote Young: "The hour of judgment is nigh at hand, and should the great criminal be condemned, the national deliverance will be due to you, more than any one else. Yours has been the White plume of Navarre." [31]

The "great criminal," of course, escaped condemnation by one vote, and thus Young was denied the coveted role of national deliverer, which leading actors in the impeachment drama assigned to him.[32] He took the news of the impeachment verdict on the first crucial vote "quite tranquilly being prepared therefor." His diary for the last two weeks of May, however, seems that of a sleepwalker. He fired one more salvo in the *Tribune,* "The Tainted Verdict," May 27, and then subsided. His interest turned instead toward the nomination and election of Grant and Colfax, for whom, he wrote Adam Badeau, he was "doing all we can." [33]

In the midst of the impeachment crisis, Young took on a responsibility far removed from his daily journalistic routines. He was chairman of the committee arranging the great press dinner at Delmonico's April 18, 1868, in honor of Charles Dickens. Dickens' first visit to the United States in 1842 had led to his severe criticism of American manners and institutions (especially slavery) in his *American Notes* (1842) and a resulting paper warfare across the Atlantic. Twenty-five years later, however, almost all was forgiven, and the English novelist's widespread public readings in the United States (1867–68) were a financial bonanza, though in their strenuousness they may have shortened his life. (Dickens died June 9, 1870.) Planning and arranging the Dickens dinner took a great deal of Young's time in early 1868, its compensation lying in the opportunity to secure an intimate acquaintance with one of the great men of the 19th century, always a compelling motive for the hero-worshipping Young. The dinner itself was somewhat anticlimactic. Dickens, already feeling the effects of his rigorous tour, became ill and had to leave the dinner before its completion. His letters of thanks to Young, however, are genuine and authentic. His last words in the United States, reported by the *Tribune* staff member who accompanied the ship down the bay, were, "Tell Mr. Young I shall never forget his kindness." [34]

The most graphic account of Young's triumphant era as managing editor of the *Tribune* appears in two articles in *Packard's Monthly* in October and November 1868.[35] The author was Amos J. Cummings, city and political editor of the *Tribune,* who after his subsequent dismissal by Young was employed as the first managing editor of Charles Dana's *New York Sun* during the period when the *Sun* attacked Young at every opportunity. In 1868, however, Cummings was Young's subordinate, who professed to regard his chief as "a literary comet," though the tone of Cummings' description verges more than once toward disbelief and ridicule:

. . . What! this blue-eyed boy the Managing Editor of the most influential journal in America! You can hardly believe it. In personal appearance Mr. Young is the most insignificant person about the office. He is light-complexioned, has a large, sloping head, thatched with brown hair, a clear forehead, and a prominent nose, and is as quick of motion as a sparrowhawk. He is of medium height—say five feet eight. His words flow from his lips in rapid succession, as if each one was struggling to get out of his mouth ahead of the other. And this man has flashed upon the journalists of New-York like a literary comet. Twelve years ago he was a printer's devil; when South Carolina sprouted into Secession he was a reporter in Philadelphia; one year more found him a Dramatic Critic on *The Washington Chronicle;* six years ago he was the Managing Editor of *The Philadelphia Press;* two years after this he was with General Banks during the Red River expedition; next we find him an agent of Jay Cooke's in 7.30 times. While at this business, in his leisure hours, he wrote editorials for *The Tribune.* They were unusually spicy and argumentative, attracted the attention of Mr. Greeley and Sidney Howard Gay, and now that printer's devil is a newspaper autocrat—the peer of statesmen, and a potent power in the land. At first sight he appears common-place, but when you talk with him, and partly fathom the depth of that wonderful blue eye, and the decisive cut of the nose and the mouth, you recognize an impress of a peculiar intellectual vitality, a fertility of resource, a quickness of comprehension, and a nervous energy, that stamps him as a steam-engine among newspaper men. His attire is neat, but not foppish. He wears one of those little round-topped hats, with a small, circular rim, and this increases his boyish appearance. His room is lined with books of reference. . . . Young writes by spasms. He pays strict attention to the business details of the office. Every letter, every bill, every rejected communication is filed. He is able to furnish, at a moment's notice, a filed voucher for every cent of expenditure during his administration. Such strict attention to business requires a vast amount of time. But when a great national emergency arises, especially during the absence of H. G., he throws himself into the breach with a characteristic energy, and the columns of *The Tribune* are red-hot with his short, sharp, ringing sentences, until the storm has passed. His were the stinging editorials on the Philadelphia Convention, his were the columns of invective poured over the Impeachment renegades, his were the fierce attacks upon the far-born movement to nominate Grant before the General had defined his position, and his are the showers of sarcasm launched upon John T. Hoffman. The phrase, "Impeachment is Peace," is Young's; so are the words "Let us have Peace." He it was who called Grant "a sashed and girded sphynx." He it was who wrote the brilliant book reviews on Buchanan's "Defence of his Administration," Greeley's "American Conflict," and Richardson's "Life of Grant." There are no lazy hairs in his head; each one seems to be inspired with electric energy. As Butler was the author of the word "Contraband," applied to the slaves of Rebels, so is Young the author of the word "Copperhead," as applied to the members of the Democratic party.[36]

Cummings goes on to comment upon Young as a disciplinarian. (Cummings' sport with a

Young edict against office profanity was apparently the root cause of his subsequent dismissal.) He continues with an account of a typical 2 p.m. editorial meeting, in which Young "nervously dances around his desk for forty seconds," and then takes up the items one by one, rebuking Cummings for letting the *World* get the better of the *Tribune* on a murder story, characterizing an Associated Press dispatch as "a Rebel lie," ordering a telegram sent in cipher to Smalley in London, instructing him to send a man to Romania to check on reports of an insurrection there. Despite the less than deferential handling of Young, Cummings concludes by acknowledging: "During the past two years the old readers of *The Tribune* have noticed a marked improvement in the paper. Its columns have grown more sparkling and fervent, and it has conducted the present Presidential campaign with an energy and skill heretofore unsurpassed." [37] The years referred to were simultaneous with Young's tenure as managing editor.

In mid-January 1869 Young went to Washington to take some soundings (engage in "chin-music," as he phrased it) about the probable character of the Grant administration ("if I can fathom the mysteries of the inscrutable Ulysses"). He left Whitelaw Reid in charge of the *Tribune* during his absence as he had done with more and more frequency since Reid joined the New York office staff in September 1868. For some reason Young rather dreaded the trip and in a letter to Reid, January 17, 1869, reported that his preference would be to "instantly seek out the genial [A.R.] Spofford and drink Sherry wine with him in the alcoves of the Library [of Congress] . . . and read his immense black-letter books." [38] Nevertheless, he remained in Washington a full week and was well satisfied with Reid's handling of the *Tribune* during his absence. The paper had been *"provokingly good,"* he wrote Reid. Early in February, Reid, perhaps grown accustomed to authority, took umbrage at an order by Young which he construed as a personal rebuke. Young, unfortunately, was insensitive to Reid's objection. "I have about a dozen vexations every calendar month to which it does not compare. And about which I never write." [39] Reid responded, and Young wrote again, in a somewhat more conciliatory way, but still rather stiff-necked. "Any additional assurance to my former note I cannot give.

That I only renew." [40] It was the beginning of an alienation that became embittered in the 1870's but which both men put behind them with the passage of time. [41] Reid, of course, assumed Young's duties later in the year and survived a fight for control of the *Tribune* following Greeley's death in 1872, eventually to establish Reid family control of the newspaper until its demise in 1966. There is no evidence to suggest that Reid was part of the "cowardly conspiracy" leading to Young's resignation, but he was its beneficiary, so much so that one is tempted to cast Reid and Young in the roles of Gilbert and Sullivan's "happy undeserving A" and "wretched meritorious B."

To do so would oversimplify and distort the situation. Young was victimized by circumstances, but his own arrogance and self-righteousness, exemplified in his onslaughts on Andrew Johnson the year before, prepared him for a fall. Young's power and authority to some extent went to his head. A young man, still in his twenties, he spoke easily of attacking Senators "severely," as he had instructed Reid about Senator Harlan the preceding year.

If Young was guilty of hubris, he was soon brought low enough to satisfy the most fastidious Aristotelian. Charles A. Dana's *New York Sun* for April 27, 1869, began the first in a month-long series of attacks on Young, which led to his resignation from the *Tribune* May 19. In the April 27 issue, four and a half columns were devoted to publication of some of Young's private correspondence, largely to a Philadelphia friend, Charles McClintock, with interspersed commentary. The charges against Young were that he subverted the *Tribune* office, replacing veteran staff members with his own Philadelphia entourage (including his brother, who "was given the Washington plum" at $3,000 per annum); that he surreptitiously sent Associated Press dispatches received by the *Tribune* to the *Philadelphia Morning Post,* which was not entitled to them; that he used the influence of the *Tribune* to benefit the *Post;* and that he generally intrigued against his employers, whom he characterized as "old fogies," including *Tribune* publisher Samuel Sinclair. The commentary and headlines were pointed and personal. Young was called "the Richelieu of the press." His head was said to be "phrenologically well developed in the region of secretiveness and rather low in the vicinity of cautiousness." According to the *Sun,* Horace Greeley had been shown the letters April 23, four days before publication. Three weeks later the *Sun* would contend that if Greeley had then signified an intention to control Young, the letters would not have been published.[42]

Young retaliated by having Dana arrested and instituting a $100,000 libel suit against Dana, with similar actions against newspapers which reprinted the *Sun*'s dispatches. Although the suits were not brought to trial, he later consoled himself with the fact that he had "silenced" Dana, but his days were numbered at the *Tribune.*[43] The suits themselves merely provided the *Sun* with additional copy for this journalistic thrice nine-days' wonder. The *Sun* published 17 articles, editorials, and dispatches on the Dana-Young controversy over the next month. Even after Young's resignation from the *Tribune,* the *Sun* pursued him for more than a decade, referring to him usually as the "sneak news thief," attacking Young's short-lived *New York Standard* (1870–72) as "Thieves' Own," and ridiculing James Gordon Bennett for employing Young as a foreign correspondent.[44]

The *Sun* attacks on Young were in keeping with roughneck personal journalism of the era, smack of New York newspaper rivalries (Dana also attacked Greeley and Reid), and have a political dimension as well, Dana generally opposing Grant and Young then emerging as his chief defender. Some of Young's correspondence printed in the *Sun* could be called the exuberant indiscretions of youth. Nevertheless, there is much that cannot be explained away despite Young's longtime hostility to the Associated Press as a "copperhead" organization and his contention that AP's refusal to include the *Philadelphia Post* in its network constituted a monopoly on a commodity of general public value—the news. Young blundered badly and was too proud and sensitive to ride out the storm.[45]

Although Young secured backing to launch the *Standard,* chiefly from Benjamin Butler, and sought to keep it alive to provide U. S. Grant with journalistic support in New York City, it was a "desperate" venture and doomed from the outset. Young also fostered an American Press Association, of which he was for a time president, as an alternative to the Associated Press, but this too made little headway. His own Philadelphia business affairs were not prospering, and Young in

1870 was undoubtedly at low ebb.[46] He reached 30 that year and, except for the height from which he had fallen, had many assets for the future, not least of which was his growing friendship with President Grant.[47] Moreover, Young was on the verge of a decided shift in the ordinary routines of his life.

Young's two decades of predominantly foreign residence began in 1871, when he undertook a confidential mission to Europe for Secretary of State Hamilton Fish concerning the settlement of the Alabama claims. He was therefore once again in the right place at the right time to witness a historic event, the fall of the French Commune in late May 1871. Young wrote a lengthy, widely admired dispatch for his *New York Standard* [48] and the following year began a long-term association with the *New York Herald* that finally ended only with his death. Throughout the mid-1870's Young was chiefly in Paris, London, Vienna, and Madrid, but his duties and travels took him across Europe for the next five years. In 1876 he was back in the United States, spending the early months in the South and mid-1876 in New York and Philadelphia (July 4 in Philadelphia, of course). By late September, however, he was on his way back to London.

Once more Young was well situated. It was natural that he should give a press dinner in London for former President Grant when that old friend and dignitary arrived in June 1877. And it was equally natural that Grant should invite his friend to accompany him on the extensive travels he was just beginning. It was a journalistic coup for Young and the *Herald,* but Young's service to Grant would be at least equal to the opportunity. As Young's former *Tribune* colleague, George W. Smalley, wryly remarked, Grant captivated "the

The rivalries of New York editors and publishers were caricatured in an 1870 cartoon in Punchinello, which depicted the editorial disputes as washday squabbles. On the right, Charles A. Dana of the Sun *shakes his fist in the face of a rather passive John Russell Young of the* Standard. *On the left, Manton Marble of the* World *glares at George Jones of the* Times, *the two separated by Horace Greeley of the* Tribune. *In the background, Hugh J. Hastings of the* Commercial Advertiser *seems oblivious to the baneful glance of Theodore Tilton of the* Independent. *LC–USZ62–34334*

versatile and fertile journalist who had acted as a sort of civil and political aide-de-camp in his recent journeys, and who works the press for him with untiring energy." [49]

Around the World With General Grant is Young's ample, bountifully illustrated, two-volume account of the former President's two-and-a-half-year progress through the Northern Hemisphere after leaving office in March 1877.[50] Young was with Grant for virtually the entire journey, in which Grant and his small party crisscrossed Europe and the Middle East for more than a year and a half and then struck out for Asia in January 1879, spending the better part of that year in India, Southeast Asia, China, and Japan. Once the Grant party returned to the United States, Young proceeded on to the East Coast.

The book is based on Young's dispatches to the *Herald,* published from time to time during the travels. Once published, however, the dispatches were fair game for competitors, and Young and his publisher had to rush his own book into print

to get his fair share of its rightful market. As a result, the book is uneven and its scale inconsistent. Young will often hurry Grant ("an intense and merciless traveler") through several towns and cities on a page, then spend an entire chapter on a single ceremonial dinner. There were many such dinners, culminating in a 50-course extravaganza in Nagasaki in June 1879, the bill of fare of which made a small volume.[51]

Despite its imperfections, *Around the World With General Grant* is a remarkable achievement. It is full of lively observation, independent judgment, obiter dicta of wit and freshness, and some unforgettable vignettes, including some of primary historical interest, such as the account of Grant's conversations with Bismarck and those with the emperor of Japan. Young also embellished his narrative with several chapters recording his own conversations with Grant, largely about Civil War history and the government of the United States during Reconstruction. Despite what Young called the general's "long-conceded

187

PUNCHINELLO.

MAY 28. 1870.

EDITORIAL WASHING-DAY IN NEW-YORK.
(See paragraph on opposite page.)

supremacy" at silence, Grant could be very talk-
ative about his favorite subjects.

The book is at its liveliest in description of the
American expatriate, especially in Paris and London where Young had observed him for several
years. Occasionally Young will break into his
travel narrative with a witty sketch, as in the following account of a 19th-century Kilroy:

> It was here [Karnac] we came across the tracks of the
> name-writing donkey. There are traces of the animal in
> other parts of the world, but in Egypt they reach the
> highest form of development. The stone is soft, and
> travelers who come here have time to spend, and it is
> only an hour or two to cut your name deep in the stone
> which for thirty centuries has borne the story of a
> nation's power. You look at a fine range of carving and
> follow the story of the legend, and suddenly you are ar-
> rested by some name hacked in the walls—Brown, or
> Smith, or Thompson. These inscriptions go back, some
> of them, a long time. There are Greek names that belong
> to the days of the Lower Empire. I saw many French
> names, belonging to the expedition of Bonaparte in 1799,
> twenty at least, especially on top of the pylon at Et Foo.
> One name, "John Gordon, 1804," is frequently repeated.
> I suppose John Gordon has answered for his sins by this
> time, and let us hope that the recording angel reminded
> him of the way he hacked the walls at Luxor and
> Dendereh. But the greatest donkey of the tribe—the
> monumental donkey of the age—is "Powell Tucker" of
> New York. If Powell Tucker reads these lines he will
> learn that his name is the theme of repeated execrations
> throughout Egypt. Powell, as the story goes, did not
> content himself with carving his name on the walls—
> that, perhaps, would have been too much trouble. So
> he carried a sailor with him, and this sailor had a pot
> of black paint and a brush. Whenever Powell came to a
> monument the sailor painted in large black letters,
> "Powell Tucker, New York, 1870." Sometimes it is only
> "P. T.," but the tracks are here and there all over Egypt.
> The authorities in charge of the antiquities have tried to
> rub out this and other marks of vandalism. But Powell's
> sailor painted deep, and we voted unanimously that
> America was again in the ascendant; that whatever the
> American did he excelled the world, and that in a country
> where you see the name-writing donkey of all species—
> Greek, Arab, French, Italian, British—the monumental
> name-writing donkey of the age is Powell Tucker of New
> York. I hope Powell is alive, that he may enjoy this well-
> earned fame. I would like to see him—to look at him—to
> see with my own eyes a gentleman who could wander
> through this land of beauty, fable, and historic renown—
> this land of temples and tombs—and here, where genera-
> tions of a forgotten age had in patient faith and humility
> carved the legends of their faith and their history—there,
> in the sanctuary where the gods were worshiped, to have a
> sailor, with a pot of black paint, to smear his name! Let
> us all be proud of Tucker. In his own department of
> usefulness as a name-writing donkey he has given America
> a conceded although scarcely an enviable renown.[52]

Young's style, as the excerpt above indicates, is
clear and dry, but not clinically so. Before the
ruins at Karnac or the Taj Mahal his rhetoric is
equal to the impressive occasion. *Around the
World* easily avoids the guidebook clichés of much
travel literature of the 19th century and their
opposite, the bumptiousness of Mark Twain's con-
temporaneous *A Tramp Abroad*. With more time
for its preparation, Young might well have recognized and improved the prosaic patches and
brought the work to a level consistent with that
of its best parts.

The trip with Grant was, in Young's final estimation, "an experience that one can never hope
to see again." It would in time affect his life and
his career immeasurably. But, in the meantime,
he had to get on with both.

It was Young's custom to write in the flyleaf
of his pocket diaries his various addresses for the
year. Often these were numerous. The list in the
1879 diary concludes: "And around the world."
It was literally true. He began the year in London
before setting out on the Asian travels with Grant.
The party returned to the United States in September, and Young remained for a month in
California, at the end of which he received word
of his father's death in Philadelphia. He proceeded
east, arriving in Philadelphia October 18. During
the next month he worked furiously at his book,
but by Thanksgiving day he was at sea again, on
his way to England. He spent 10 days in Paris,
conferring with Bennett, but he ended the year
where he began it—in London.

Young was homesick. Mrs. Young had not accompanied him on his travels with Grant, and she
had remained in Philadelphia when he returned
to Europe in late 1879. In the early spring of 1880,
Young was able to send her word that he was
"coming home," James Gordon Bennett having
approved his reassignment to New York. Before
going, perhaps under the mistaken assumption
that his international travel was drawing to a close,
he went to Ireland "on a visit I have often wanted
to make to the homes of my ancestors."[53] He
visited various villages in Northern Ireland, met
numerous uncles and cousins, and heard their
recollections of his mother and father. That venture over, he embarked for the United States.

In September Young's third child died. Her
mother meanwhile had contracted malaria in Cali-

fornia, where Young had hoped to establish some business interests. Rose Fitzpatrick Young died in New York January 4, 1881, before her 40th birthday. Hers had been a difficult life beset by illness, long separations from her husband, and the loss of all three of her children.[54]

Young resumed his international career in mid-1882, returning to the Far East as United States minister to China. More than a year earlier, former President Grant had urged his appointment to a diplomatic mission. In a letter to President-elect James A. Garfield, February 18, 1881, Grant spoke of Young specifically as minister to Japan: "The United States has a grand mission in the East and Mr. Young is the best equipped man in America to commence it."[55] Grant's interest was genuine, in the mission as well as the man. His views on the Orient, as Young had made them widely known in *Around the World With General Grant,* were welcome in the Eastern capitals since Grant emphasized amity between China and Japan as a means of avoiding oppression by foreign nations, especially European. One diplomatic historian attributes to Young "the creative force" behind Grant's views on policy in eastern Asia, views so enlightened and in advance of events that Grant's failure to secure the presidency in 1880 meant that "American policy in the Far East suffered a distinct and even deplorable loss."[56]

Despite Grant's urging, President Garfield did not act upon the recommendation, and it was left to his successor, Chester A. Arthur, to enlist Young in the diplomatic service by a ministerial appointment March 15, 1882.[57] Ten days later *Harper's Weekly* hailed the appointment. "The nomination and prompt confirmation of Mr. John Russell Young as United States Minister to China is a compliment to one of the most brilliant of American journalists, and has promptly evoked the commendation of the press of the country irrespective of party. . . . Mr. Young's appointment is one eminently fit to be made."[58]

On April 25 Young remarried. His second wife was Julia Coleman, whom he described as "the most accomplished and beautiful woman I have ever known."[59] The bride, the niece of wealthy former Connecticut governor Marshall Jewell, was 22 years old. Young was 41.

Young reached China in late summer after a long stopover in Japan. Julia Young was frequently ill during the first year of her marriage, a condition attributed to the Asiatic climate. Early in the new year it was decided that she should go to Paris to await the birth of their child, expected in the summer of 1883. Young accompanied her to Shanghai, and on April 19 she sailed for Marseilles and Young returned to his post at the American legation in Peking. On August 2 he received a dispatch informing him of the birth of a son, who a subsequent message from James Gordon Bennett assured him was a "fine boy." Mrs. Young did not prosper, however, and by mid-October fell dangerously ill. She died in Paris October 22, age 24. The body was returned to Hartford for funeral services, and the boy, Russell Jewell Young, was placed in the care of his mother's family in that city.

Despite these personal griefs, Young was an active minister, one whose role was strengthened by the esteem in which he was held by high officials of both China and Japan, especially Li Hung Chang, principal viceroy of China, who had been Young's friend and correspondent since the 1879 visit with Grant. Almost simultaneously with Young's arrival in China, there was an international incident, the gravity of which Young realized and sought to convey to the Department of State. In July and August 1882 uprisings by Korean soldiers in Seoul resulted in the burning of the Japanese legation and the flight of its members. The uprising was quickly quelled, but the Japanese sought an indemnity of $500,000 as redress. They sought it, moreover, by a treaty with the king of Korea, traditionally bound in loyalty to the Chinese emperor. A separate treaty with Korea had a precedent in that which Commodore Robert Shufeldt had negotiated May 23, 1882, and which was before the Senate for ratification as Young took up his duties.

In a long dispatch to Secretary of State Frelinghuysen, October 2, 1882, Young delineated the subtleties of the situation in almost prophetic terms:

Whether Corea is a dependency or a sovereignty, China can never look without natural apprehension upon any infringement of her territorial integrity. The maps will show the military importance of Corea. A Russian or a Japanese army in that country would be a grave menace to China.[60]

He urged the United States to persuade Japan to modify the language of its treaty to acknowledge the special relationship between Korea and China.

Young also used his office effectively during the dispute between France and China in 1884, but for the most part his service in China involved protection of some American business interests, discouragement of opium traffic, and furthering westernization in China. Nevertheless, one diplomatic historian gives Young extremely high marks:

All things considered, it is fair to describe John Russell Young as among the three or four most competent American diplomatic representatives in the Far East in the nineteenth century. Although cast by the circumstances for a minor part he was the peer of Caleb Cushing at Macao, and he had a world wide political view far superior to that of either Burlingame or Townsend Harris. All his experience previous to his services in Peking had contributed to make him a really finished diplomat. His trained powers of observation and his skill as a reporter, added to rare literary ability, made his despatches rank among the best received at Washington. His long political career had developed a sense which served him well in a court enveloped in political intrigue. His journalistic and editorial experience, and his tour of the world with General Grant, put him well at ease in the field of diplomacy. Finally, the remarkable reception given to General Grant in Peking and Tokio, together with the intimate and very cordial personal relations established by both Grant and Young, enabled Young to go to his post in Peking already more familiar with the pressing problems than was usual in those days or even later.[61]

Following Grover Cleveland's election, Young resigned because, as he later explained to the President, a post "so important as this, should be filled by one, who possesses your entire confidence.—Upon this, I have no claim, as I do not know you personally.— and I am not a politician,

but a journalist." [62] He left China in the spring of 1885 and returned to the United States, resuming his connection with the *Herald*. The year 1886 found Young in England for several months, but he returned to Philadelphia in the fall, only to end the year seriously ill. The year 1887 was a rarity for Young, spent entirely within the geographical limits of the United States. These years immediately following his service in China had no particular focus as Young sought to resume his journalistic career and pursue some business schemes. His inner life was restricted to concern for his sister Mary (Mrs. John Blakeley of Philadelphia) and her seven children. He also managed to visit Hartford periodically to see his son, Russell.

In late November 1888 Young returned to Europe, primarily to assist in the establishment of a London edition of the *New York Herald,* of which it was expected that Young would be editor.[63] The Paris edition of the *Herald* was thought to be costing James Gordon Bennett $100,-000 a year, but he was ready to launch a London edition as well.[64] Young wanted to proceed to London quickly, but Bennett detained him in Paris until late January 1889, less than a week before the first issue of the London edition would be published. As a consequence, the beginnings of the newspaper were disorganized. After a week or 10 days of furious effort, Young predictably fell ill and was confined to his rooms for a week or more. Young remained abroad throughout 1889, principally in London, but in mid-October he was recalled to Paris. From late January to early May 1890 he and his fiancée, Mrs. May (Dow) Davids, were the guests of James Gordon Bennett on a tour of the Riviera, the Mediterranean, the Suez Canal, the Red Sea, and the Indian Ocean. Young returned to the United States in late May 1890, ending 20 years of extensive travels in Europe, Africa, and Asia.

Young resigned from the *Herald* November 4, and on November 18 at New York's Astor House took as his third wife, Mrs. Davids. Their son, Gordon Russell Young, born December 14, 1891,

Former President Ulysses S. Grant and Chinese viceroy Li Hung Chang during Grant's visit to Tietsin, May and June 1879. Young's friendship with the two international figures did much to determine the shape of his career. LC–USZ62–7606

was to become a prominent military engineer and a commissioner of the District of Columbia.

Young thus arrived at age 50 (November 20, 1890), having distinguished himself in journalism and diplomacy. He was not in good health and had put on weight over the years, nearing 200 pounds. Whereas he had seemed surprisingly young for the responsible positions he held in the 1860's, he aged rapidly in his middle years. About this time (January 28, 1889) Walt Whitman described Young to Horace Traubel as "lymphatic—of course not thin: rather stout, brisk, compact—it might be said, a strong man. . . . Young was of the [Edmund] Gosse type—is still, I suppose: combed, cleaned, polished, brushed, exact." Traubel asked if Young lacked finesse. Whitman replied: "Hardly: I had reference to the outer man—the social man. Gosse is eminently scholar—all scholar: the university man: all refined, bookish, made up. Young was not so developed: not in that direction: had more native grit." [65]

In the 1890's Young resumed his place in Philadelphia. He had given up his regular position with the *New York Herald* though he continued to write extensively for Bennett's newspaper to the end of his life. He was able now to contribute more effectively to the *Philadelphia Evening Star,* the Young family newspaper, and to other outlets. Within a year of his return to Philadelphia he took a leading position in the Union League and shortly thereafter achieved the pinnacle of social success, the League presidency. And in the summer of 1898—in the midst of his tenure as Librarian of Congress—Young was under some Republican party pressure to run for mayor of Philadelphia.[66]

In 1892 Young served as a director of the Union League of Philadelphia, in the formation of which 30 years earlier he had been the youngest of the founding members. At the end of that year he was elected president of the League for 1893 and a year later was reelected. Young's elevation to the presidency of the influential, though not yet venerable, Philadelphia institution signified his acceptance by the established and socially and financially prominent. On the day he assumed the presidency, Young wrote in his diary: "Feel a sense of deep responsibility. The honor as great as one could have in a social sense in Philadelphia. I could not hope for more." [67]

The Union League had been formed in the

closing weeks of 1862 when concerned Northerners had reason to doubt that the fragile Union would survive Confederate military victories crowding in succession upon their ill-prepared consciousness. Its first article of association defined the condition of membership as "unqualified loyalty to the government of the United States, and unwavering support of its efforts for the suppression of the Rebellion." [68] At its organizing meeting the charter members briefly considered whether membership in the Republican Party itself should not be a requirement. While other Democrats and former Democrats, including Young's mentor, John W. Forney, sat silent, Daniel Dougherty objected: "Not for me! Not for me! I am for the Union—not for any Republican President." A compromise was reached, in which support of the Union was the sole condition of membership. Young later wrote that he considered the speech by Judge J. I. Clark Hare in support of the compromise position "the foundation of the Union League." [69]

This ancient controversy surfaced 30 years later on the very night of Young's election to the League presidency. The date was December 12, 1892, little more than a month after Grover Cleveland's election to a second term over the incumbent, Benjamin Harrison. Many believed that Harrison's defeat was due to Republican defections. And some defections had apparently occurred even in the party bastion, the Union League of Philadelphia.

At the 1892 meeting a resolution was introduced to require members to sign the following pledge:

I am a Republican. My political sentiments and principles are in harmony with the national policy as advanced by the Union League. I voted the Republican ticket at the preceding national election. If I change my politics I will at once resign my membership; and in the event of my not doing so, and sufficient proof is adduced that I have broken this pledge, The Union League is hereby authorized to expunge my name from the roll. [70]

After considerable debate the question was referred to a special committee for report at the 1893 meeting, as it could not be acted on earlier because of provisions of the League by-laws.

The 1893 annual meeting—the first over which Young presided—was one of the stormiest in the League's history and one of the most far-reaching in its implications. The special committee offered a resolution in these terms:

Candidates for membership must be of good character and repute, and politically affiliated with the Republican party, and in harmony with its principles as recognized and supported by The Union League. Failure at any time, after the admission to membership, to maintain these qualifications shall subject the member to suspension, as hereinafter provided for acts or conduct hostile to the objects of the League. [71]

The heated and acrimonious debate which followed lasted more than two hours. Civil War veteran Gen. Louis Wagner, former commander-in-chief of the G.A.R., spoke for the committee. He made no attempt to conceal his contempt and ridicule for the opposition. When some lawyers present raised technical objections, General Wagner replied that he did not know that any members of his committee were lawyers. "Probably it was for that reason we were so unanimous, so prompt and so effective in the conclusion we reached—probably, I say." When another member sought to interrupt, Wagner remarked: "Patience, brother, patience! . . .—if a man who is not a lawyer dare call a member of the bar 'brother.'" The basis for the grievance was made quite evident in the remarks of another member who complained of "gentlemen who had been admitted as Republicans, and who had declared that they were Republicans," who nevertheless announced their pleasure that Cleveland had been elected, "glad of that which had put sorrow in the hearts of at least nine tenths of our membership." He urged adoption of the resolution so that "if gentlemen differed with the majority of this League, let them keep their feelings to themselves and not flaunt them around here in the faces of others." According to the minutes, the remark was followed by "long-continued applause."

Toward the end of the debate, one courageous defector, George Gluyas Mercer, took the floor.

For the commemorative photograph of the reunion at Gettysburg, April 1893, Young stands at the left in stovepipe hat and light, rather rumpled overcoat beside one-armed Gen. O. O. Howard. General Longstreet, with full white sideburns, stands in the position of prominence at the center. Major General Daniel Sickles, who lost his leg at Gettysburg, is seated beside him. At the far left, leaning on his umbrella, is the governor of Pennsylvania, Robert Pattison. LCMS–46584–2

His appearance was greeted with catcalls and abuse. The minutes record the scene as follows: "(Note.—Here the expressions of disapprobation from the audience which accompanied the speaker's remarks swelled into a volume of cries of 'The question,' 'Sit down,' and hisses.)"[72] His next attempt was met by "Prolonged cries of disapprobation."

Despite the tenor of the meeting and the majority sentiment in behalf of the resolution, the vote did not reach the necessary two-thirds. A change of only 18 votes out of a total of about 500 would have provided the necessary margin. After the failure to adopt General Wagner's stringent resolution, the League unanimously approved a watered-down version, "that the Directors ought not to admit to membership any applicant not politically affiliated with the Republican party."[73] In the words of the League historian, the compromise principle, although never made part of the bylaws, "has been adhered to ever since." [74]

Young's conduct of the meeting was firm and fair, and, although he cannot be said to have maintained order, the character of the meeting was such that it probably could not have been kept in stricter control. Once the membership question was disposed of, Young relinquished the chair for the remainder of the long evening, at the conclusion of which his reelection was announced by the largest vote in League history to that time. Although Young was no longer the arrogant doctrinaire of the 1860's, it is impossible to understand him fully outside the context of a fierce and sometimes savage partisanship for the Republican cause, of which the Union League debate is an example.

Despite the satisfactions and tributes which his presidency of the Union League brought him, Young himself was undoubtedly most gratified in these years by the two-day 30th anniversary reunion at Gettysburg of Confederate and Union officers in April 1893.[75] It was, as the *New York Times* (May 1, 1893) acknowledged, a decidedly personal triumph:

The party was brought together by John Russell Young, and it is doubtful whether any other man in the country

could have gathered together so many persons living at remote points and representing so many varied interests. The Pennsylvania Railroad placed a special train at Mr. Young's disposal, including a hotel car and a combination baggage and smoking car, under the personal charge of Mr. J. P. McWilliams of its passenger department.

General James Longstreet was the central figure of the gathering, but Generals O. O. Howard, E. P. Alexander, William Mahone, D. McMurtrie Gregg, Daniel Sickles, Pennsylvania Governor Robert E. Pattison, and many other lesser known military men made up the party of 40. In his diary for April 28, Young wrote: "Never had a more interesting day & this the end of so much negotiation, pulling & hauling." The second day's activities were somewhat curtailed by a rainstorm, but a commemorative picture was taken, in which Young, standing between General Howard and Governor Pattison, looks as "tired" as his diary entry for that day (April 29) revealed him to be.

The excursion to Gettysburg was facilitated by Young's position as president of the Union League and a vice president of the Philadelphia and Reading Railroad. Before the year was out, however, changes at the Reading led to Young's departure, and he faced the new year with his customary anxieties. "I have had more cares than usual," he wrote in his diary December 31, "& perhaps never entered a new [year] with more anxiety. The gap in my affairs from the Reading overthrow has been a serious one. But I have done the best. I have many reasons for gratitude to God. . . . I look forward with hope—without fear."

In addition to his journalism and activities associated with the Union League, Young was occupied in the mid-1890's with several publishing projects. The most ambitious was the two-volume memorial history of Philadelphia, which he edited.[76] The first volume, which appeared in 1895, was dedicated to Robert Todd Lincoln "with the friendship and esteem of the editor." Young also contributed a 16-page introduction to James P. Boyd's biography of James G. Blaine, published in 1893.[77] Throughout the period plans were also afoot for a chronicle of the Union League, which Young had planned as chairman of the League committee on publication. Like many of his enterprises, this work reached print after his death, and with the signs of his paternity obscured.[78] Young also began to lay plans and make preparations for a biography of Ulysses S. Grant, an occupation of a decade, according to his estimate.

A visit to Mexico in late 1895 and early 1896 had serious consequences. He returned to Philadelphia February 8, 1896, "very ill." He was convalescent for nearly two months, in the midst of which his doctor died. By early April Young was well enough to travel to Hartford and New York to see his son Russell confirmed in the Congregational Church. Later that month he was in Harrisburg for the Republican state convention, which endorsed four reform bills prepared by a special committee, of which Young had been chairman, bills providing civil service for state and local governments.

The year 1896 was, of course, a national election year, one in which the Republicans expected to resume their stewardship of the presidency as they had regained control of Congress in 1894. Throughout the spring the candidacy of William McKinley gained momentum. Young wrote in his diary (May 5): "The McKinley movement seems a land slide. I cannot comprehend it, except upon grounds that one cannot but regret in politics." The grounds were the influence of wealth, and Young's hope was that a vice-presidential nominee would be chosen acceptable to the Grant faction of the party.

For 10 days in mid-June, while the Republican national convention met in St. Louis, Young was in Canton, Ohio, where he was entertained by McKinley and had several private talks with the Ohio governor. Although characteristically acerbic about the place ("There is nothing in Canton but the air"), Young secured a better opinion of McKinley and described him as "the best type of the eminent American." McKinley's opinion of Young was also high. The approaching election and its consequences, therefore, were of great interest to Young, not merely as an influential practicing journalist, but as an adviser and confidant of those in the highest party circles. In addition, his younger brother, James Rankin Young, was not only to make his first race for Congress successfully later that year but to lead the Republican ticket in Pennsylvania.

Before the election, however, there occurred the kind of ceremonial occasion in which Young found repeated delight. His old friend Li Hung Chang, principal viceroy of China, made a formal visit to the United States on his return from the coronation of Czar Nicholas II. In tribute to Young, Li consented to be entertained at the Union League as well as to make a private and informal visit to Young's own home. Young went to New York City to meet Li on August 28. The following day he was present at the home of W. C. Whitney in honor of Li, a gathering which included President Cleveland, several Cabinet members, and former ministers to China. On August 30 Young assisted Mrs. Grant in a reception for Li. Two days later he accompanied Li to West Point. On September 3 Li visited Philadelphia, seeing Independence Hall and attending a reception at the Union League, in addition to making his private visit with Young and his wife and their son Gordon.

McKinley's election in November brought about profound changes in Young's way of life, some immediate and some remote. By February 1897 he had made Washington his base of operations (though not his residence) for his special articles for the *New York Herald* and the *Philadelphia Evening Star*. Until the President-elect took office in March, there would be intense speculation about appointments. Young himself was among those frequently mentioned. In his diary for February 22, he wrote: "All manner of rumors about my going into the cabinet." The Philadelphia newspapers reported that Young was under consideration as assistant secretary of state, secretary of the navy, and as a minister to one or more countries. Young himself would have liked to be named minister to Spain, which he knew well, a post earlier held by literary men, Washington Irving and James Russell Lowell. However, he was apparently thought of diplomatically only in connection with a return to China, which did not attract him.

On January 21, 1897, Young recorded in his diary receipt of *"a very important communication from Mr. McKinley."* Such a communication is not present in the Library's McKinley papers or Young papers, but about this time Henry Watterson, Alexander McClure, and James M. Carson, among others, were pressing Young's claims upon McKinley. Nevertheless, Young was not to receive an appointment before organization of the new government in March. On May 4 Young called on the President, who "said that he would have

an important nomination very soon:—namely that of the Librarian of Congress.—Would like to nominate Mr Spofford, but was afraid he could not—I presume he had me in mind,—but I made no suggestion.— Would rather be paralyzed than in any way disturb Spofford—." [79] Spofford's well-known mishandling of Library accounts (which Young would later hear characterized as "criminal neglect") effectively prevented his appointment. Over the next few weeks Young satisfied himself that Spofford was not a possible candidate, and by June 1 his own own appointment was expected. It came June 30, and the Senate confirmed the new Librarian the same day. Young took great satisfaction in the immediate confirmation, which he believed to be "unprecedented." The newspaper accounts of Young's appointment were followed by the printing of a face-saving letter from Spofford to the President, dated June 28, 1897, disavowing his own candidacy to continue in the position.

John Russell Young was Librarian of Congress from July 1, 1897, until his death January 17, 1899, long enough to prepare two annual reports, issued in December 1897 and 1898, respectively, and covering Library developments through the preceding June 30. (In fact, the reports covered many developments occurring up to the date of writing, which in those days was very shortly before publication.) Young was better satisfied with the first report than the second, which was more a "record" than an "anticipation."

Both reports together provide evidence of the Young way of dealing with things and touch on six fundamental aspects of Young's Librarianship: the administrative transition, relocation of the library, appointments, reorganization, development of the collections, and innovative steps by the new Librarian.

After a few months in office Young concluded, "All of the antecedent affairs appear in confusion," [80] but his public references to his predecessor showed forbearance. The muddled state of copyright finances is papered over thus: "Amount of copyright fees reported by Mr. Spofford from July 1, 1896, to April 30, 1897, with receipts for May and June estimated, no accounts therefor having been rendered." [81] In his diary (March 3, 1898), on the other hand, after a conversation with Secretary of the Treasury Lyman Gage and

Representative Alexander Dockery, Young reported the impression (whether his or Dockery's is not clear) that Spofford's handling of Library appropriations for 1896 and 1897 had been "criminal neglect." Nor was he satisfied with the Library's holdings. The collections of the Library constituted "a good working library of authorities" but not "a universal library" capable of "satisfying the wants of scholars." Nevertheless, he acknowledged that Spofford had "long striven in vain for appropriations to secure [the Library's] natural growth." [82] Young always treated Spofford with the respect due an old friend and predecessor in office, but he left no doubt in the minds of the staff that a new administrative day had dawned in the Library of Congress. [83]

The tenure of John Russell Young as Librarian will always be associated with the opening of the elegant Washington landmark which to many is "the" Library of Congress. The story of its construction has been told elsewhere. [84] It had been expected that the relocation of the Library holdings from the Capitol to the new building would occur between March 4 (the customary beginning of a long congressional adjournment) and July 1, 1897. The first session of the 55th Congress, however, began March 15 and continued until July 24, 1897. As a consequence, the move was delayed. The old Library closed a week after congressional adjournment, except for copyright business. The relocation of the books was the occupation of virtually the entire staff over the next three months. The new Library opened to the public November 1, although some work was still in progress on the building and its contents. In his 1897 *Report* (p. 6) Young paid tribute to "the care, foresight, and industry of the staff" which not only permitted movement of the Library's "manifold and various treasures" in 10 weeks, but did so "without the loss or apparent misplacement of a volume."

Things were not quite as rosy as the *Report* implied. For example, there had been a robbery in the Law Library in mid-August. Young was also still much concerned about the theft of manuscripts in early 1896 by two employees, Philip McElhone and Lewis Turner. But in the physical arrangements of the Library's holdings he took satisfaction, privately as well as publicly.

One problem, however, Young did not obscure.

His commentary in the annual reports on appointments may lack the frantic eloquence of his diaries and correspondence on the subject, but it is candid and to the point. The Library was authorized to increase its staff from 42 to 108 on July 1, 1897. Until completion of the move, Young delayed many appointments though he made the key staff appointments as soon as possible. Young's problems with appointments were dual: the number of applicants and the advocacy of Senators and Representatives for particular candidates. Eventually, the whole question became so oppressive that Young lost all sense of proportion. In his diary for September 2, 1898, he wrote: "I cannot make the Library an almshouse. I cannot appoint incompetent people. I cannot put a thousand pegs in a hundred holes. It is all a miserable, teasing, harrowing business, and 'wears out the soul.' " Three weeks later he thought there "never was a more perplexing problem." [85]

Although such comments reveal more about Young than the Library, the new Librarian was under great pressure, from both applicants and their congressional sponsors. On the average, there were more than 40 applications for every vacancy. Giving due consideration to such numbers was the first problem. Most of the applicants, moreover, seemed to have at least one congressional advocate. Young consequently became involved in an endless round of correspondence, fending off importunate job-hunters and keeping their sponsors at bay. The following letter, to Senator John M. Thurston, November 1, 1897, is typical:

> I deeply regret that any action of mine should give you cause for "just criticism." The problem with which I have been struggling has been that of putting five thousand pegs into a hundred holes. I have considered, primarily, fitness for library work. This I had to do, or the Library might as well close. . . .
>
> You say, further, that you are "justified in believing that most of the appointments in the Library are secured through considerations of favoritism, with an utter disregard of the just claims of Republican Senators from certain of the Western States." As this is rather a criticism than a statement of fact, it is difficult to answer it. So far as "favoritism" is concerned, I have broken life-long friendships because I did not appoint favorites. I had no one to serve when I became the Librarian. Never sought the office, resigned larger emoluments to accept it. I have as much personal interest in the appointments as I would have in a game of chess. . . . [86]

On January 6, 1898, Young called upon President McKinley and urged him to put the Library under civil service. The President said "he would do it, as soon as I was ready." Young's congressional advisers, however, were opposed. On February 4 he discussed the subject with Senator Eugene Hale, who "had some doubts as to the Civil service, so far as the Library is concerned. Thought one department should be free." Ten days later Young saw the President again, who indicated his willingness to bring the Library employees into civil service within 30 days, but on the same day Representative Henry H. Bingham told Young that "the law did not permit" the President to enact civil service in the Library. Young's diary fell silent on the subject for several months, and his annual reports do not mention it. However, on December 23, 1898, his diary records that he "sent message to Mr. McKinley in regard to civil service reform." Young died barely three weeks later. At the confirmation hearings of his successor, Herbert Putnam was asked if he favored civil service for Library employees. Putnam equivocated, but generally opposed it for the Library of Congress. The 1901 annual report, Putnam's first extensive report, states succinctly (p. 203): "The appointments are not subject to the provisions of the civil-service law, which applies only to the Executive Departments of the Government." So much for civil service.

The appropriations act for fiscal 1898, which was the instrument for establishing the organization of the "new" Library, contained the following clause: *"Provided,* That all persons employed in and about said Library of Congress under the Librarian . . . shall be appointed solely with reference to their fitness for their particular duties." [87] To verify "fitness," Young appointed a three-man board (the Chief Assistant Librarian, the register of copyrights, and the superintendent of the reading room) to examine applicants for Library positions. The candidates included many Library employees on probationary appointment. The examination took place April 20, 1898, and consisted of about a dozen questions on each of the departments. The appendix to the 1898 *Report* includes the questions, which ranged from the technical ("What is meant by the word 'entry,' as used in cataloguing?") to the historical ("Who was Peter Force?"). The examining board was Young's chief reliance in answering congressional criticism, whether by individuals or that contained in a Senate resolution of December 17, 1897. In his 1898 *Report,* partially in reply to that resolution, Young stated flatly: "There have been no removals and no appointments for political reasons." [88] Young, of course, had been a lifelong Republican partisan, and the *Library Journal* had criticized his own appointment as an example of political preferment, which in part it was. Nevertheless, his sturdy sense of integrity and his resistance to patronage requests preserved, at a crucial time for the Library, the spirit of civil service even though the letter had been denied him.

For key positions Young appointed Spofford as his Chief Assistant Librarian: Thorvald Solberg as register of copyrights, a position he was to occupy for more than 30 years; J. C. M. Hanson, who was in charge of the Catalogue Department for 13 years before concluding his career at the University of Chicago; and, as first chief of the Department of Manuscripts, Herbert Friedenwald, who was to win fame for his activity in the American Jewish Historical Society and editor of the *American Jewish Yearbook.* Young also advanced staff members within the Library, such as the cartographer, P. Lee Phillips, and Spofford's chief assistant, David Hutcheson, who was made superintendent of the reading room. Young brought A. P. C. Griffin, formerly of the Boston Public Library, and Arthur R. Kimball, state librarian of New Hampshire, to the staff later. His intention in his principal appointments was to have all sections of the country represented, befitting the national character of the Library. Hence Thomas H. Clark, former speaker of the Alabama legislature, was named law librarian. [89] Hanson, from Wisconsin, was named after another midwesterner, Alexander J. Rudolph, had declined to be considered. As David Mearns put it in *The Story Up to Now,* "It was a good team. It was a good start." [90] The *Library Journal,* which had initially (July 1897) deplored Young's appointment as "a matter of regret and disappointment," grudgingly admitted two months later: "Nothing can do more to justify the selection of Mr. Young than the admirable appointments he has made for the leading positions." [91]

Young also sought a balanced staff in what would now be called the hiring of minorities. Approximately 10 percent of the staff were black employees, more than half of whom Young appointed. As Librarian's messenger he appointed Louis Alexander, who had been employed in his own Philadelphia household. Another interesting appointment was that of Paul Laurence Dunbar, whom Young identified in a note to Senator George F. Hoar as "the well-known young colored poet." [92] Young seems to have taken a special interest in Dunbar, who had been recommended to him by Robert Ingersoll, "for long, long years" one of Young's "most honored and valued friends." [93] When Dunbar fell ill in late 1898, Young gave him the maximum leave allowed by law (60 days) and assured him that his position was secure and would be awaiting his return January 1. However, on January 1 Young was on his deathbed and Dunbar did not resume his position.

As a result of his appointments, about one-quarter of the staff during Young's tenure were women. This proportion was the result of his conscious effort to employ women in substantial numbers. Young later came to regret the action because the work was too strenuous, he thought, especially during the transition period. He made the appointment of women the subject of a paragraph in the 1897 *Report,* expressing the hope that "in a year or two" there would be more "gentle and useful offices suitable for women." In private, Young was by turns oppressed and philosophical over the problem. To J. W. Babcock, he wrote, October 18, 1897: "The lady applicants have given me a great deal of anxiety. So many hundreds who have every accomplishment but aptitude for library work—so much sorrow—such sore distress—a hundred sad tales a day." The next day, however, he wrote to Senator George P. Wetmore: "There is a universal impression that the Library is a Garden of Eden, especially designed for ladies. I am the angel with the flaming sword barring the entrance. On the contrary, the work is severe— must be for a year or so, until we are reorganized." [94]

Reorganization was a major concern of the new Librarian. To the President's secretary, John Addison Porter, Young wrote on September 14, 1897: "There is chaos in the Library and each department has had to be reorganized from the ground up." Until shortly before Young's appointment, the Library was organized into two departments: general and law. Appropriations for the increase of the general department were under the direction of a joint committee of three Senators and three Representatives; those for law, under the direction of the Chief Justice. The President "solely" had authority to "appoint from time to time a Librarian to take charge of the Library of Congress." A concurrent resolution of the Senate May 5, 1896, called upon the Joint Committee to investigate "the condition of the Library of Congress, and to report upon the same at the next session of Congress, with such recommendations as may be deemed advisable; also to report a plan for the organization, custody, and management of the new Library building and the Library of Congress." The Joint Committee took testimony from a number of witnesses (including Melvil Dewey and Herbert Putnam), to the extent of 279 printed pages.[95]

Before the Joint Committee could make its recommendations, however, the full House acted on appropriations for fiscal 1898 and, in doing so, preempted the field by establishing the organization of the new Library and specifying its officers and staff. The law as amended and signed by President Cleveland February 19, 1897, provided for a catalog department, a copyright department, a manuscript department, a music department, a periodical department, and the following administrative units, which were the equivalent of departments: reading room, art gallery, hall of maps and charts, congressional reference library at the Capitol, and law library. These departments were to have "superintendents," except that the principal officers of the reading room, catalog department, and copyright department were designated assistant librarian, chief, and register of copyrights, respectively. There was also to be a Chief Assistant Librarian. The act also established the position of superintendent of the Library building and grounds, coequal with the Librarian in compensation and alike subject to Presidential appointment and Senatorial confirmation.[96]

That was the organizational scheme which, along with some subsidiary units, Young inherited as Librarian of Congress. During his tenure he effected some administrative changes (creation of an order department and a mail and supply department and establishment of a pavilion for the blind) and proposed others (a circulating department, a restoration and binding department, a juvenile department). Young was initially opposed to a circulating department but apparently acceded to Spofford in requesting it. Before its establishment, however, creation of a public library for the District of Columbia made it unnecessary. Despite the proliferation of departments, which was probably unavoidable in the shakedown period of Young's tenure, the Librarian himself was of quite another mind. He would have preferred fewer departments, "condensation," as he phrased it.[97] In his diary for August 11, 1898, Young wrote: "The main trouble with these departments is that each wishes to become a small kingdom in itself & rule independent. The bill should be changed so as to reduce them all into three important departments—Copyright, Catalogue [, and] Administration."

No phase of the Library concerned Young more than development of the collections. On June 12, 1898, he confided to his diary: "I am trying to build the library far into the future, to make it a true library of research." To accomplish this end, he sought increased appropriations, private gifts, and exchanges, all within the context of firm bibliographical control of the collections.

Young sought significantly increased appropriations for development of the collections ("The only interests in the Liby which concern me are what pertains to its development.").[98] On January 14, 1898, however, a few days before the House Appropriations Committee hearings, he learned that there would not be "much effort to give the Liby money, that it will be rather on Spofford's lines." Senator William B. Allison "said that next year there would be more chance of doing something in the way of buying new books." The funds for books (general) for fiscal 1898 had been a mere $4,000, of which Young managed to spend all but 71 cents. For the following year he asked for $30,000 plus $5,000 additionally for manuscript purchases, of which he was granted only $15,000, with nothing specifically for manuscripts. To one as keenly aware of the Library's needs as Young was, the result was disappointing. In his 1898 *Report* (p. 6), he wrote: "While the Librarian is grateful for the recent increased appropriation of $15,000, it would be wise to increase this so as to broaden the Library in every phase of progress." The Library, he reminded the Congress, is "an asset, not an expense."

Senator George Hoar of Massachusetts was, in Young's words, "one of the best friends of the Library," one who believed that the Library should have a fund of $200,000 "from which to draw in the way of getting at books."[99] The two men worked closely on the most notable private gift during Young's tenure, the art collection and library of Gardiner Greene Hubbard, along with the promise of a bequest of $20,000 for the increase of the collection following Mrs. Hubbard's death. Young was attentive in negotiating for the Hubbard collection and made several trips to "Twin Oaks," the spacious Hubbard estate, later to be the Washington home of the Hubbards' daughter and son-in-law, Mr. and Mrs. Alexander Graham Bell, and still later the Chinese embassy. The negotiation was delicate because Mrs. Hubbard wanted the collection housed in a designated room in the Library to be thereafter called "The Gardiner Greene Hubbard Library." She so stipulated in her letter offering the collection March 21, 1898. Although Young acquiesced in this phase of the request in his transmittal letter of March 30 to the Joint Committee, privately he thought that it "would have been better to have given the works & left the arrangement to the Librarian."[100] The Senate also objected to calling parts of public buildings after the names of individual citizens. It was Senator Hoar who secured the compromise by means of which the collection, but not part of the Library of Congress, was to bear Mr. Hubbard's name. The revised resolution of acceptance passed the Senate June 27, 1898, and the House July 7.[101]

Young's extensive international travel and his contacts in the diplomatic service led to the preparation of a circular letter to diplomatic and consular representatives of the United States in behalf of the Library. Prepared and distributed by Young in consultation with Secretary of State William R. Day, the letter was dispatched February 16, 1898. An appendix (p. 83–87) to the 1898 *Report* lists the first fruits of that effort, nearly 300 volumes and pamphlets from 20 embassies and consulates. "Under a reciprocal and considerate policy," Young wrote in the 1898 *Report* (p. 6), "the Library by the mere processes of administration could be largely increased in value." Young also sent the curator of manuscripts, Dr. Friedenwald, to Cuba in early January 1899 to locate and acquire library materials. After Young's death on

January 17, Spofford summarily recalled Frieden-wald to Washington. Despite the abbreviated venture, Friedenwald secured 126 manuscripts and some 300 books and pamphlets for the collections. The favor with which the Chinese regarded Young as a result of his travels with Grant, his ministry in the 1880's, and, above all, his friendship with Li Hung Chang is evident in the arrangement Young made with the Chinese ambassador, Wu Ting-fang, for employees of the embassy to catalog Chinese books in the Library, largely acquired through purchase of the library of Caleb Cushing. One of the most widely traveled men of his generation, Young showed that he was keenly aware of the need to internationalize the Library's collections, to supplement the Americana derived from gifts and copyright deposits.

Among the hidden evidences of Young's contributions to internationalize the Library of Congress is the series of gifts by William W. Rockhill of Orientalia, chiefly, Chinese books. The Librarian's annual reports for 1901 and 1902 record the extent to which the Library was indebted to Rockhill, assistant secretary of state, for the growth of its Chinese collections. What such reports do not record was that Rockhill was one of Young's "boys" in the State Department, having served as secretary of the legation when Young was minister to China. Young and Rockhill were frequent correspondents from the mid-1880's to the late 1890's, and Young's letters to Rockhill in Harvard's Houghton Library document a close and personal friendship, which undoubtedly laid the basis for Rockhill's benefactions so soon after Young's death and in a field of particular interest to both men.

In his 1898 *Report* Young sought to sensitize the Congress and the citizens to the national role of the Library. "If the American felt the same interest in his national library as the Englishman in the British Museum, in a few years we should have one of the three great libraries of the world. The fact that we depend almost alone upon the accretions of the Copyright Department and the modest appropriations of Congress narrows our scope and limits our usefulness." [102] In his diary, Young recorded his discouragement. Shortly after completing the 1898 *Report*, he wrote (December 5, 1898) : "The Library will grow as a slow development, and be governed by the appreciation of the people & the good will of the Congress. I depend more upon the copyright, the exchanges than private support, & yet I know of no monument that could do more good & assure a more enduring fame than such a gift as Mr. Rockefeller could make. Such an impetus would sweep it ahead." If Young had lived, appeals for massive private support may have been his tack.

John Russell Young was an innovative Librarian of Congress. His best known innovation was development of a "pavilion" for the blind, in which he had gathered the Library's holdings "in pointed and raised letters" and an assistant put in charge. Young also initiated a series of readings for the blind, beginning November 8, 1897, one week after the opening of the new Library. Young anticipated only one or two readings a week, but during the first year there were daily readings, Sundays excepted, and approximately 10,000 visitors to the pavilion, which was located in the northwest pavilion, present site of Music Division and Personnel Operations offices. [103] The Librarian in his first *Report* (1897) also called for transfer of historical manuscripts from other government departments to the Library of Congress, especially the historical archive in the Department of State, which contained personal papers of early Presidents and other officials, purchased by the government throughout the 19th century. [104] Six years later, by Act of Congress and Executive Order, the transfer was accomplished. Young also began the reassembly of the library of Thomas Jefferson, the contents of which had been intermingled throughout the Library's collections and, in Young's words, "entombed and forgotten." In order to "perfect the tribute it is proposed to pay to an immortal name," Young began the task of locating books and forming a special collection. He included a history of the Jefferson library as an appendix to the 1898 *Report*. [105] The culmination of Young's initiatives appears in one of the Library's noblest bibliographical monuments, *Catalogue of the Library of Thomas Jefferson,* a five-volume catalog edited by E. Millicent Sowerby and published 1952–59. In a preface to the first volume, Librarian of Congress Luther H. Evans remarks that efforts to reassemble the library began "at the turn of the century." Young's name is not mentioned. The beginnings of a uniform classification system and the opening of a public card catalog, both in

1898, were other initiatives which his successors developed.

William Dawson Johnston, who wrote the definitive account of the early years of the Library of Congress, left notes and preliminary chapters toward a second volume on the Library's history. In that unpublished manuscript is an authoritative survey of John Russell Young as Librarian of Congress:

Mr. Young entered the Library profession without technical training; but with what is better, a broad cultivated mind with an intelligent discernment of the mission of the Library and a capacity of adapting means to ends. His methods were simple and direct, guided by a mind abhorent of complicated and circumrotary processes. In this he was in unconscious sympathy with the methods of that peerless Librarian the lamented [Justin] Winsor. Under Mr. Young's guidance the Library was fast becoming a living force and rapidly gaining in public appreciation. The inert books were transformed into active agents of usefulness; scholars, students, and the humblest inquirers were encouraged by him and the policy of the widest use of the books consistent with safety was enjoined upon his subordinates.[106]

Young died January 17, 1899, after a three-week illness, the only Librarian of Congress to die in office. His funeral services were held Saturday, January 21, at St. John's Church in Lafayette Square. The Chinese embassy staff attended the funeral en masse, a mark of distinction said to have been rarely conferred before, if ever. The Library of Congress was closed for the day. A special train from Philadelphia brought a large group from the Union League, where Young's presidential portrait was draped and the flag in front of the League house remained at half-staff. Tributes to Young's leadership and laments over the untimeliness of his death vied for space in the Washington, Philadelphia, and New York newspapers. One tribute, however, stands out from the rest.

I have known him since [1865]. I served with him on the New York Tribune, when he was managing editor and I was city editor and night editor. I think he was one of the most brilliant newspaper writers the country ever produced. Horace Greeley regarded him as a marvel, and was very fond of him. James Gordon Bennett was also much attached to him, and for many years Mr. Young had great influence with Mr. Bennett.

Mr. Young was doing magnificent work in the Library. No man could appreciate that fact more than myself, and I bear cheerful witness to it. If any author went to the Library to make some researches, he was given a room, writing material, messengers to wait on him, and he could keep that room as long as he wanted. That just shows one of the little details of his management, all tending to make the Library the grand institution which it has become. I regard it as a great misfortune to the country that he should die before he could carry out all the plans he had for the Library. Socially he was genial, companionable, bright and witty. He was prophetic in political matters, thoroughly acquainted with the politics of the country, and knew every great politician intimately.[107]

The author of those sentiments was Amos Jay Cummings, political editor on the *Tribune* under Young, author of the graphic but irreverent *Packard's Monthly* article about Young's managing editorship, a casualty of Young's discipline, later managing editor of the *Sun* and implacable journalistic nemesis of Young for more than a decade. By a twist of fate too curious for fiction, Cummings had entered politics, been elected to Congress, and served as Representative from New York during Young's tenure as Librarian and as a member of the Joint Committee on the Library. It is somehow symptomatic of Young's career that his early death permitted his old adversary to wax noble about Young's life and work.

The accomplishments of John Russell Young in his brief tenure as Librarian of Congress were far from negligible. Moreover, they were coincident with an active schedule of journalistic writing for the *New York Herald* and other outlets.[108] Seen in this light, they were remarkable. It is only when we consider the state of Young's health during his Librarianship that his achievements verge on the incredible. How the man did what he did, feeling as he did, almost defies belief.

Notwithstanding his vast reading, his voluminous writing, and his far-flung travels, Young was not robust. Even as a young man he was troubled with insomnia, headaches, fatigue, rheumatism, neuralgia, and sundry ailments, including urological problems. Young was also subject to depression. The death of his two-year-old son "Johnny" in 1867 oppressed him for years. The death of his sister Mary on February 8, 1898, afflicted Young's own final year of life. The course his life took was not calculated to check a natural tendency toward self-pity, and his depression and hypochondria were self-fulfilling and mutually supporting. On November 14, 1890, four days before his third marriage, he was "taken suddenly & violently ill, with fever, pain, & congestive chill." He went ahead with the marriage November 18, but was "very ill & retired after the ceremony." This is merely one of many instances in which his physical and emotional states were apparently intermingled.

Young's first weeks as Librarian came during a period of good health. On August 20, 1897, indeed, he wrote a friend that he had "not been ill for a moment" since arriving in Washington the preceding January. One ominous occurrence, however, was a severe fall from a trolley car in early November, ominous in that Young had a history of such falls. By December, he was complaining of various ailments, especially pain in his feet.

The record of his physical and emotional ills became a litany in 1898. He consulted several doctors, went on a milk diet, took various unspecified medicines, and eventually underwent electric shock treatments—all to no avail. He feared mental collapse and thought he detected its early signs, such as forgetfulness, strange dreams, and visions. A week at Atlantic City in mid-June had not improved his condition, and in mid-July his doctor ordered him to leave for the country *"at once."* He made the train trip to Buena Vista, Pa., his servant Louis Alexander "fanning me all the way up." [109] There was some improvement, but in mid-August, shortly before he was to return to Washington, Young suffered another attack, the "suddenness & severity" of which alarmed him, as did "the same hallucinations & depression of spirits." [110] The return to Washington on August 15 was even worse than the trip to Buena Vista. Young "trembled so could hardly get on the train," and, after an unfortunate delay because of a missed connection in Baltimore, "trembled from nerves head to feet as I climbed the stairs at home & tumbled into bed." [111] Dr. Friedenwald of the Manuscript Department had accompanied Young on the return trip, and soon, A. R. Spofford reported, the Library was full of rumors about Young's condition. There was speculation within Young's family as well, leading him to "morbid moods" against which he tried to fortify himself. "Have been thinking of [Roscoe] Conkling & his end, & note some of the symptoms that attended his end. But it may be a fancy. Am ready." [112] Despite family concern, Young found little peace and quiet at home, which he characterized as "the domestic circus, musical & otherwise." [113]

The next attack ("the severest I have ever had") occurred in early October and lasted a week. In late November he complained of a "constant pain in my side." Early in December he fell again, this time on the Library's marble steps, injuring his knee. The stomach pains returned shortly before Christmas and led to further uneasiness. "I leave such things to nature as I never had a satisfactory talk with any doctor," he wrote on December 21. By Christmas Eve, however, Young was in better spirits and "feeling very well." The year, he thought, was closing "pleasantly." He left the Library earlier than usual that afternoon in order to help Mrs. Young with the Christmas tree, "but as I was going into the house, when I slipped and fell & received a severe stunning smashing blow on the face." The diary entry ends incoherently. The final entry in his diary occurred December 27, 1898: *"Token govt. Very ill."* Three weeks later he was dead.

It is obviously mistaken to contend (as some standard authorities do) that Young's death occurred from complications following the Christmas Eve fall. The fall was merely a final evidence of increasing debility, physical and mental, during his year and a half as Librarian. Perhaps all his symptoms related to Bright's disease, of which he had evidenced some signs in his twenties and to which the attending physician ascribed his death. In any case, John Russell Young while Librarian of Congress was a very sick man.

Men and Memories: Personal Reminiscences (New York and London, 1901) was posthumously compiled by Young's widow, largely from his published newspaper and magazine articles, with some letters to and from Young included. Poorly done, it is full of elementary errors in names, dates, etc. In substance, however, it is meaty. In a foreword, Alexander McClure expressed the belief that Young's "intimate acquaintance with eminent men exceeded that of any other one man in the entire century" (p. ix). Few readers of *Men and Memories* will be disposed to doubt it. Young's career offered him splendid opportunities for friendship with the celebrated men of his time, literally all over the world, and he did not neglect them. Here are first-hand accounts, based on intimate acquaintance, of Charles Dickens, Horace Greeley, Walt Whitman, Edwin Forrest, James Gordon Bennett, Roscoe Conkling, Li Hung Chang, Henry

George, U. S. Grant, of course, and many, many other 19th-century notables.

Even as a truncated and substitute memoir, however, it has one glaring deficiency. Although it traces many of Young's movements and records some of his associations, it reveals little of Young himself. Young was self-effacing, by nature and by profession. Whether his vantage point was a ridge overlooking the Battle of Bull Run, a place "at the side of Lincoln" as he delivered the Gettysburg Address ("in a high key, voice archaic, strident, almost in a shriek," according to Young),[114] on a hotel balcony on the Rue de la Paix when the Paris crowd toppled the Vendome Column, in the company of Grant and Bismarck as they discussed the professions of arms and government, or in the American legation in Peking, Young was an observer par excellence. He wrote abundantly and well; he left a series of diaries and preserved much of his voluminous private correspondence; he seems to have left a strong impression on many notable men; but Young himself remains elusive.

The Librarianship of Congress, therefore, was as important to Young as he was to the Library. He did not seek the position and, at first, even declined it. He would have preferred to be made minister to Spain "and taken a more active part in public affairs" than his "tranquil position" as Librarian permitted. His annual salary of $5,000 represented a financial sacrifice, he thought. Nevertheless, he accepted the position and fulfilled its responsibilities with insufficient regard for his own health and well-being. What Young would in time have made of the Librarianship is speculation at best. His accomplishments in 18 months were significant, but his principal service was to confer upon the Library his own prestige and some of his best characteristics. Although his appointment was criticized as "political," Young sought scrupulously to make the Library apolitical. Thenceforward, it was reasonable to expect a singular person, not a functionary, to fill the position and to grant the Library a freedom to pursue its mission free of political pressure.

The most regrettable aspect to Young's brief incumbency, however, is that, despite his achievements, he was able to make merely a start. It was a good start, to be sure, but the observer of his career would require more to bring Young from the periphery and background to the forefront, where his contemporaries were convinced he belonged.

In another sense, however, the imagination does not rebel at Young's early death and the brevity of his Librarianship. He was a man of the 19th century. Barely into his twenties, he was thrown into contact with the politically and journalistically powerful. The Civil War and Reconstruction were his milieu, and his heroes were the prominent men of that era. As each one fell in the 1880's and 1890's, Young's habit was editorially to memorialize them and to refresh the tints on fading mental pictures of the past. Although he recognized current problems and devised effective lines of action to solve them, his mind dwelt upon the great political issues of the past and his imagination upon the heroic struggles which bred them.

For a new century, a new Librarian of Congress, a younger and healthier Librarian of Congress, would not be amiss.

NOTES

[1] In Young's lifetime and shortly thereafter, he was represented as having been born in Downingtown, Pa., in 1841, rather than Ireland in 1840. Since one of the sources giving such information was the *Memorial History of Philadelphia,* which Young edited, and a memorial sketch appended to the *Report of the Librarian of Congress,* 1899, one suspects Young's complicity in the mistake. The correct information appears in John Russell Young, *Men and Memories: Personal Reminiscences,* ed. May D. Russell Young, 2 vols. (New York and London: F. Tennyson Neely, © 1901), 1: xiii, and in the sketch of Young in the *Dictionary of American Biography.* Among Young's many animadversions against the Irish, see his article "The Election for the Presidency," *Macmillan's Magazine* 35 (January 1877): 244–55.

[2] John Russell Young, Diary, March 6, 1870, John Russell Young Papers, Library of Congress. Subsequent quotations from Young's diaries, if sufficiently identified through references in the text, will not necessarily receive a footnote citation. All diary quotations are from originals in the Young Papers unless otherwise identified.

[3] In his diary for January 10, 1898, on the occasion of his son Gordon's first day at school, Young reminisced: "How well I remember my own first visit,—to school,—

the day snowy, father carrying me on his back, school on Marlborough street. Miss Wilson the teacher,—my small bible in simple words.—not six, but admitted under age because I could read. . . ." In a letter to T. V. Cooper, July 15, 1898, Young characterized himself at age 21 as "full of books and bookishness." Librarians' Letterbooks, Library of Congress.

[4] Young to Mary Young Blakeley, April 18, 1880. Copy in manuscript biography of Young, pp. 2–4, Young Papers.

[5] M. H. to Young, December 12, 1854, Young Papers. The writer is identified by annotations on her letters as "Madame Hagenbach," the designation used by the unknown author of the unpublished manuscript biography in the Young Papers (probably May D. Young). All the letters are signed "M. H.," "M. H. B.," or "M. Hagenbach." Most of the letters are datelined "Opelousas," about 100 miles from New Orleans.

[6] Greeley to Young, May 13, 1856, Young Papers.

[7] Young, "Men Who Reigned: Bennett, Greeley, Raymond, Prentice, Forney," *Lippincott's Monthly Magazine* 51 (February 1893):196.

[8] Diary entry quoted in the manuscript biography, p. 53, Young Papers. Young's original diary for 1859 is not in the Young Papers.

[9] *Philadelphia Press,* July 23, 1861, p. 2.

[10] See "The War in the Southwest," *Philadelphia Press,* April 12, 1864, p. 1, and "The Campaign in Louisiana," ibid., April 25, 1864, p. 1.

[11] See his letters to *North American Review* editor Charles Eliot Norton in the Houghton Library, Harvard University.

[12] Young to Hay, August 25, 1866, John Hay Papers, John Hay Library, Brown University.

[13] Wilkeson to Young, January 21, 1867, Young Papers.

[14] Chase to Young, letterpress copy, June 28, 1867, Salmon P. Chase Papers, LC.

[15] Greeley to Young, June 20, 1867, Young Papers.

[16] Greeley to Young, July 23, 1867, Young Papers.

[17] Greeley to Young, August 12, 1867, Young Papers.

[18] Greeley to Young, September 4, 1867, Young Papers.

[19] Greeley to Young, September 22, 1867, Young Papers.

[20] Greeley to Young, November 20, 1867, Young Papers.

[21] Diary, July 7, 1898, Young Papers. The comment on Colfax below is also of this date.

[22] Phillips to Young, August 24, 1867, Young Papers.

[23] Phillips to Young [January?] 1868, Young Papers.

[24] Colfax to Young, September 4, 1867, Young Papers.

[25] Sickles to Young, November 18, 1867, Young Papers.

[26] *New York Tribune,* January 2, 1868, p. 4. Diary, January 2, 1868, Young Papers.

[27] The others were "The Forbearance of Congress" and "Moral Causes for Impeachment." He followed these with "The Impeachment of the President" and two other impeachment editorials, February 25, and "Impeachment Is Peace," February 26—seven editorials on the subject in three days, at least five of them of Young's authorship, along with numerous news dispatches, etc.

[28] Diary, February 24, 1868, Young Papers. Young later described the results and Greeley's reaction thus: "The *Tribune* leaped and bounded. The circulation swept onwards. There was joy in the exchequer. Greeley returned in grief from the Minnesota woods. He did not believe in impeachment. 'Why hang a man who was bent on hanging himself?' " Greeley also objected to introducing "these crazy, reprehensible French methods into a composed American legislature." Young, "Men Who Reigned," p. 190.

[29] Colfax to Young, February 25, 1868, Young Papers.

[30] *New York Tribune,* May 9, 1868, p. 4.

[31] Stanton to Young, May 10, 1868, Young Papers. It is at least curious that Colfax, Phillips, and Stanton should all adopt the "white plume" to signify Young's moral leadership. It is an allusion, conscious or otherwise, to Thomas B. Macaulay's historical poem, "Ivry," about King Henry of Navarre.

[32] Young's editorials may, in fact, have been counterproductive. That at least was the view of J. W. Schuckers, private secretary to Chief Justice Salmon P. Chase and a frequent correspondent of Young's. See the fragmentary manuscript by Schuckers, which begins: "It is my entirely fixed opinion—I may say that it is almost within my certain knowledge,—that if it had not been for the terrific infamous onslaughts made upon one of the doubtful Senators by Republicans high and low, everywhere in the country, by letters, telegrams, individual visitors, deputations and by newspaper attacks,—particularly by Mr. Greeley in The Tribune,—that that Senator would have voted otherwise than he did vote." J. W. Schuckers Papers, LC.

[33] Young to Badeau, July 17, 1868, Adam Badeau Papers, Houghton Library, Harvard University.

[34] See the account in *Men and Memories,* 1:120–48. The *Tribune* devoted its entire front page and part of page 2, April 20, 1868, to the Dickens dinner. Dickens' manager, George Dolby, called the dinner "one of the most brilliant of its kind ever held in the Empire City" in *Charles Dickens As I Knew Him: The Story of the Reading Tours in Great Britain and America (1866–1870)* (London: T. Fisher Unwin, 1885), p. 303. Another account of the dinner appears in Kate D. Sweetser, "Dining with Dickens at Delmonico's . . . ," *Bookman* 49 (March 1919):20–28.

[35] "How Newspapers Are Made. The New York Tribune," *Packard's Monthly* 1 (October 1868):87–89; (November 1868):105–9.

[36] Did Young coin the word "Copperhead," as Cummings asserts? The origin of the usage is unsettled. Paul H. Smith, "First Use of the Term 'Copperhead,' " *Amer-*

ican Historical Review 32 (July 1927):799–800, attributed the usage to the *Cincinnati Gazette,* July 30, 1862. Joe Skidmore, "The Copperhead Press and the Civil War," *Journalism Quarterly* 16 (December 1939):345, attributed the usage to the *Detroit Free Press* in 1861, an attribution accepted by Frank L. Mott, *American Journalism . . .* (New York: Macmillan, 1941), p. 355. If Young deserves credit for the coinage, it should be looked for in the columns of Forney's *Philadelphia Press* in early 1861.

[37] Cummings, "How Newspapers Are Made," p. 109.

[38] Young to Reid, January 17, 1869, Reid Family Papers, LC.

[39] Young to Reid [February 13, 1869], Reid Family Papers.

[40] Young to Reid [February 19, 1869], Reid Family Papers.

[41] Young's magnanimity was put to the test in early 1889 when he was establishing the London edition of the *New York Herald.* The publisher, James Gordon Bennett, instructed him to give editorial support to the anticipated nomination of Reid as ambassador to Great Britain. In his diary (March 2, 1889) Young remarked that he would do so "as well as I can. Reid's coming here would mean the most implacable enemy of the *Herald* & myself. I have always been on civil terms with Reid although in the early sixties we were intimate. He chose to dissolve the intimacy by allowing his ambition to lead him into an act of perfidy & there has been no time since when he could do me an injury when he has missed the opportunity." Reid was named minister to France instead by President Harrison. In the early 20th century he served as ambassador to Great Britain.

[42] The *Sun* attacks appeared on the following dates: April 27, p. 2; April 28, pp. 1–2; April 29, p. 2; May 1, p. 1; May 2, p. 2; May 7, p. 2; May 8, p. 2; May 10, p. 2; May 12, p. 2; May 16, p. 2; May 17, p. 2; May 18, p. 2; May 19, p. 2; May 20, p. 2 (two items); May 21, p. 2.

[43] Greeley defended Young in the *Tribune,* May 1, 1869, p. 6, but agreed that the Associated Press matter deserved investigation. Meanwhile, Young made some attempt to discredit the *Sun* charges. See, for example, his letter to Adam Badeau, May 3, 1869, Badeau Papers, Harvard University, in which he asked Badeau, President Grant's secretary, for a letter from Grant, to be privately shown to Greeley, exonerating Young of the charge of having sought an office from Grant.

[44] Candace Stone, *Dana and the Sun* (New York: Dodd, Mead, 1938), pp. 125–26.

[45] Young was popularly thought to be discredited by the *Sun* attacks. See Frederic Hudson, *Journalism in the United States* (New York: Harper & Bros., 1873), pp. 560, 682–84, for a near-contemporary account. Hudson (p. 560) attributed Young's downfall to the journalistic

"mania" to double and treble oneself—a mania which Young was said to have shared with Forney, James Gordon Bennet, and others.

[46] Late that year he wrote Secretary of State Hamilton Fish that he would like to live in Washington, his wife's birthplace, but not at the cost of seeking an office from the President. "I shrink from the whole range of Washington offices,—with irresistible antipathy." Young to Fish, November 14, 1870, Hamilton Fish Papers, LC.

[47] Years later, Young would recall Grant as his "most dear & honored friend, whose memory grows in splendor as the years go on. No such friend as Grant." Diary, January 9, 1897, Young Papers.

[48] *New York Standard,* June 15, 1871, pp. 1, 4. Young's dispatch was reprinted in the *Philadelphia Star.* The *Standard* version is represented by the appropriate pages filed with the correspondence in the Young Papers.

[49] *New York Tribune,* July 17, 1877. Quoted in Joseph J. Mathews, *George W. Smalley* (Chapel Hill: University of North Carolina Press, 1973), p. 85.

[50] *Around the World With General Grant: A Narrative of the Visit of General U. S. Grant, Ex-President of the United States, to various Countries in Europe, Asia, and Africa, in 1877, 1878, 1879. . . .* 2 vols. (New York: American News Co., © 1879). According to Ellis Paxson Oberholtzer, *A History of the United States Since the Civil War,* vol. 4 (New York: Macmillan, 1931), p. 58, Young's book was "one of the most widely circulated books in the history of the publishing trade in America."

[51] Young was not overwhelmed by the occasion. "The first serious dish was composed of crane, sea-weed, moss, rice bread and potatoes, which we picked over in a curious way, as though we were at an auction sale of remnants, anxious to rummage out a bargain." *Around the World,* 2:486.

[52] *Around the World,* 1:301–2.

[53] Diary, April 16, 1880, Young Papers.

[54] See the obituaries, January 5, 1881, in the *New York Times,* p. 5, and the *New York Herald,* p. 10.

[55] Grant to Garfield, February 18, 1881, James A. Garfield Papers, LC.

[56] Tyler Dennett, "American Choices in the Far East in 1882," *American Historical Review* 30 (October 1924):86.

[57] In regard to the appointment, Young had written to Adam Badeau, February 13, 1882: "I really do not care for it, and have only considered China or Japan in the light of a possible public duty. I expect, if I should be named, to be horribly abused, and perhaps assailed in the Senate by the enemies of the General as well as my own. But I shall not fly from the ordeal." Badeau Papers.

[58] *Harper's Weekly* 26 (March 25, 1882):187. The magazine also included (p. 188) a quarter-page portrait of Young, reproducing a photograph by I. W. Taber.

[59] Diary, October 22, 1883, Young Papers.

[60] Printed by Dennett, "American Choices," pp. 96–97. Many of Young's dispatches are printed in appropriate volumes of *Foreign Relations of the United States*: 1883, pp. 123–211; 1884, pp. 46–104; 1885, pp. 144–69.

[61] Dennett, "American Choices," pp. 84–85. See also Merle Curti and John Stalker, " 'The Flowery Flag Devils'—The American Image in China, 1840–1900," *Proceedings of the American Philosophical Society* 96 (December 1952): 663–90.

[62] Young to Cleveland, March 29, 1885, Grover Cleveland Papers, LC.

[63] See clipping from unidentified London newspaper in Young's diary for February 3, 1889, which states that Young was "for many years the chief leader-writer on the *Herald* in New York, and was at one time the best-paid journalist in the world. . . . if anybody can make such an experiment successful, he is the man."

[64] It has been estimated that the younger Bennett made and spent $30 million from the *Herald* during his lifetime. Mott, *American Journalism*, p. 421.

[65] Horace Traubel, *With Walt Whitman in Camden*, vol. 4, ed. Sculley Bradley (Philadelphia: University of Pennsylvania Press, 1953), p. 40.

[66] Young's reply, as recorded in his diary, June 17, 1898, had been: "I do not think I would accept if the town were thrown into the bargain." A day earlier he had written in his diary that "there was scarcely a duty in the office that would not be very distasteful to me."

[67] Diary, December 13, 1892, Young Papers. Henry Watterson, in a memorial tribute to Young in his *Louisville Courier-Journal*, called the League presidency "the highest social distinction which a citizen can attain to in our country." See reprint in the *Washington Post*, February 12, 1899, p. 21.

[68] *Chronicle of the Union League of Philadelphia 1862–1902* (Philadelphia: The Union League, 1902), p. 58.

[69] Young, *Men and Memories*, 1:46.

[70] The Union League of Philadelphia, *Proceedings*, 1892 (Philadelphia, 1893), pp. 8–9.

[71] *Proceedings*, 1893 (Philadelphia, 1894), p. 8.

[72] Ibid., p. 37.

[73] Ibid., p. 43.

[74] Maxwell Whiteman, *Gentlemen in Crisis: The First Century of the Union League of Philadelphia* (Philadelphia: The Union League, 1975), p. 157.

[75] This does not seem to have been a Union League function, but Young entertained General Longstreet and others at the Union League before departing for Gettysburg.

[76] *Memorial History of the City of Philadelphia . . .* , ed. John Russell Young, 2 vols. (New York: New-York History Co., 1895–98).

[77] James P. Boyd, *Life and Public Services of Hon. James G. Blaine . . . .* (n.p., Publishers' Union, 1893).

[78] See note 68.

[79] Diary, May 4, 1897, Young Papers.

[80] Diary, January 27, 1898, Young Papers.

[81] *Report of the Librarian of Congress*, 1897 (Washington: Government Printing Office, 1897), p. 3.

[82] Ibid., pp. 44–45.

[83] To P. Lee Phillips, the map librarian, Young wrote on December 22, 1897: "I know of no rules as to the government of the Library other than my own." Librarians' Letterbooks. Letters by Young as Librarian are from this source unless otherwise identified. If dated in text, they will receive no footnote citation.

[84] Helen-Anne Hilker, "Monument to Civilization: Diary of a Building," and John Y. Cole, "The Main Building of the Library of Congress: A Chronology, 1871–1965," *Quarterly Journal of the Library of Congress* 29 (October 1972): 234–70.

[85] Diary, September 28, 1898, Young Papers.

[86] Young to Thurston, letterpress copy, November 1, 1897, Librarians' Letterbooks.

[87] *Report*, 1901, p. 202. The "Constitution" of the Library is surveyed on pp. 198–208 of the 1901 *Report*, with many provisions of law excerpted.

[88] *Report*, 1898, p. 42. Young's letter in reply to the resolution was printed as Senate Document 42, 55th Cong., 2d sess. Young was also staunch in his support of Library employees and defended Thorvald Solberg several times in reply to congressional criticism.

[89] Young, influenced perhaps by reputed regional distinctions, wanted to "go South" for a law librarian, he wrote Chief Justice Melville Fuller, August 22, 1897, Librarians' Letterbooks.

[90] David C. Mearns, *The Story Up to Now* (Washington: Library of Congress, 1947), p. 153. Forms part of *Annual Report of the Librarian of Congress*, 1946.

[91] *Library Journal* 22 (August 1897): 379. References to Young in *LJ* over the next two years were progressively complimentary, although great credit was usually given to his "able assistants."

[92] Young to Hoar, December 20, 1897, Librarians' Letterbooks.

[93] Young to Dunbar, August 18, 1897, Librarians' Letterbooks.

[94] Young to Babcock, October 18; to Wetmore, October 19, 1897, Librarians' Letterbooks.

[95] *Report*, 1901, pp. 200–201. See also Mearns, *The Story*, pp. 138–42.

[96] *Report*, 1901, pp. 200–203. See also Mearns, *The Story*, pp. 142–47.

[97] Diary, January 18, 1898, Young Papers.

[98] Diary, January 14, 1898, Young Papers.

[99] Diary, February 23, 1898, Young Papers.

[100] Diary, April 7, 1898, Young Papers.

[101] See *Report*, 1898, p. 54.

[102] Ibid., pp. 6–7.

[103] Ibid., pp. 40–41.

[104] *Report,* 1897, p. 29.

[105] *Report,* 1898, pp. 63–66.

[106] Johnston, notes on history of Library of Congress: J. R. Young, pp. 5–6. William Dawson Johnston Papers, LC.

[107] *Philadelphia Public Ledger,* January 18, 1897. Clipping from Bernard R. Green Papers, LC.

[108] Young remarked in his diary for June 2, 1898, following receipt of a telegram from James Gordon Bennett that *Figaro* had printed his letter, "So I am in the position of addressing the public opinion of Paris, New York, London & Washington on the same day."

[109] Diary, July 15, 1898, Young Papers.

[110] Diary, August 13, 1898, Young Papers.

[111] Diary, August 15, 1898, Young Papers.

[112] Diary, September 29, 1898, Young Papers.

[113] Diary, November 1, 1898, Young Papers.

[114] Young, *Men and Memories,* 1:70.

Herbert Putnam

The Tallest Little Man in the World

by Edward N. Waters

Herbert Putnam, more than any person I can think of, deserves a full-length biography. To write such a work would demand years of research, the reading of many books, and the examination of countless documents and letters. The brief bibliography appended to this "appreciation," indispensable as the works it cites are, can record only the highlights of his career. Each title is individually valuable, but I must single out two items that I call invaluable—those written by David Chambers Mearns, distinguished historian and librarian, who served on the staff of the Library of Congress for half a century. Any one searching for these under the author's name in a library catalog might not find them. *The Story up to Now* appeared as a substantial portion of the 1946 *Annual Report of the Librarian of Congress* (then Luther H. Evans). And it was a subsequent Librarian of Congress, L. Quincy Mumford, who disclosed Mr. Mearns' authorship of the lengthy essay *Herbert Putnam and His Responsible Eye* which constituted the major share of *Herbert Putnam, 1861–1955: A Memorial Tribute* (Washington, Library of Congress: 1956). To the latter Mr. Mearns appended a detailed chronology of the chief events and awards in Herbert Putnam's life. I am deeply grateful to all the authors mentioned, quoted, and listed in the ensuing pages, but my deepest and most unrestrained gratitude must go to that eloquent and perceptive scholar David Chambers Mearns, my colleague and superior for some 35 years. He was forced to decline this privileged assignment—but you and I can imagine what he would have done with it.

*　　*

On April 5, 1899, a great event happened in the Library of Congress. On that day Herbert Putnam took office as Librarian. Short of stature and slight of build, at the age of 37 he was a young man for such a responsible post, and it may well be doubted that he anticipated 40 years of service in what became one of the greatest libraries, perhaps the greatest, in the world. Under his "responsible eye" (his own expression) it flourished and grew and extended its influence to every corner of America; its preeminence was acknowledged abroad; its resources permitted its collections to come alive. All

Herbert Putnam, Librarian of Congress, 1899–1939.
BH833–32

Edward N. Waters is chief of the Music Division.

The Evening Star.

WASHINGTON, D. C., WEDNESDAY, APRIL 5, 1899—FOURTEEN PAGES.   TWO CENTS.

No. 14,384.

THE EVENING STAR,
PUBLISHED DAILY, EXCEPT SUNDAY,
AT THE STAR BUILDING,
Pennsylvania Avenue, 1101 Pennsylvania Avenue,
The Evening Star Newspaper Company,
s. H. KAUFFMANN, Pres't.

New York Office, 66 Tribune Building.

THE WASHINGTON EVENING STAR
has a larger home and household
circulation in the city of publication, in proportion to population,
than any other newspaper in the
world. That is, it is regularly delivered by carriers to permanent
subscribers in the largest percentage of residences in the city.
It is a pointer of value to ad-
vertisers. Householders and members of family circles are the people who want things and pay for
them.

POSTED IN MANILA

Proclamation to Filipinos in Three Different Languages.

WELL RECEIVED BY THE PEOPLE

English Bankers Optimistic as to American Policy.

AGUINALDO'S FORCES

TO BE CHIEF OF ORDNANCE

Appointment of Colonel Buffington by the President.

Designers of a Career of Improve-ments—His Career in the Army—The Resulting Promotions.

THE NEW LIBRARIAN

Mr. Herbert Putnam Takes the Oath of Office.

ENTERS UPON HIS DUTIES TODAY

A Brief Talk With Him as to the Work Laid Out.

WILL PROCEED SLOWLY

REFUSED TO ANSWER

W. D. Wilson Before Pennsylvania Bribery Investigating Committee.

HE HAD BEEN OFFERED A BRIBE

Declined to Say if John R. Byrne Was the Man.

GIVEN TIME TO CONSIDER

AT THE WHITE HOUSE

The President Will Attend a Grant Monument Unveiling.

BIG TIME EXPECTED IN PHILADELPHIA

A Filipino Caller Gives His Views on Affairs.

EXECUTIVE CLEMENCY

PAY OF ARMY OFFICERS

An Important Decision by the Comptroller of the Treasury.

"Troops Are Operating Against the Enemy" and Emoluments Correspond.

PREFERENCE TO SOLDIERS

Civil Service Commission's Response to Inquiry Respecting Appointments.

IN PINK AND WHITE

Beautiful Decorations at the Sloane-Hammond Wedding.

BRIDE, NIECE OF THE VANDERBILTS

Ceremony Celebrated at St. Bartholomew's Church, New York.

GROOM, GEN. HAMMOND'S SON.

this occurred under Herbert Putnam's aegis, and continues today. The Library of Congress of the present and future exists as a nearly anonymous monument to him.

What did the press think of the appointment? The *Evening Star* of April 5, 1899, after the usual eye-catching headlines, reported:

This morning Mr. Putnam appeared at the library and Acting Librarian Spofford escorted him to the commodious quarters set apart for the librarian. The oath of office was taken before a notary in the Capitol building, after which Mr. Putnam signed the oath and sent the document to the Secretary of State.

The remainder of the day was spent in becoming acquainted with the heads of departments in the library and the principal employes. Mr. Spofford introduced the new librarian to his subordinates and went with him through the building, pointing out the location of the departments, and giving him a bird's-eye view of the working branches.

Mr. Putnam is a young-looking man, when one considers the work he has done and the results he has accomplished. His most striking characteristic is reserve of manner, not reserve which suggests coldness or haughtiness, however, for, on the contrary, he is very genial. His personality is attractive and would impress one as a man who makes friends easily and without much effort upon his own part.

. . . Mr. Putnam is venturing cautiously upon his work, and, as might be expected, is not in a position at this time to talk very specifically about the library or his own intentions. When questioned upon his general policy respecting the library, he said:

The Washington Evening Star *on April 5, 1899, described Herbert Putnam's first day as Librarian of Congress. "Mr. Putnam feels that he has a large undertaking before him, and that he cannot at this time grasp it as a whole. Necessarily he must take it in detail, and a detail which can only be worked out day by day. He must come to know his subordinates thoroughly, to know the demands of their positions, and to have his own work unfolded to his understanding by daily experience.*

"He is very chary of promising sweeping innovations at this time. It is probably a pretty good guess that he will not talk much along this line until he is ready to do something, and it is likely that one would not be far wrong in surmising that Mr. Putnam's own mind is not altogether made up upon reforms to be effected. He says himself that he has theories and ideas about the library, but he realizes that now he will have to consider facts, and he will weigh his theories carefully and consider them in the light of the conditions which surround him before he exploits them."

"I am not insensible to the consideration of a policy, but if I were asked the direct question as to what it shall be I would have to reply that I have administered a library in Minneapolis, I have administered a library in Boston, but I have never administered the Library of Congress. The policy, I imagine, will be a question of the future."

. . . The impression which one gets from Mr. Putnam at this stage of the proceedings is that he is a conservative and cautious man, going slowly about his business, understanding it thoroughly. He will apply the knowledge that he has gained in other fields to the work before him, but with a regard for the conditions existing here, which may differ from those surrounding his labors heretofore. He says that in a great library the results of a mistake made at the outset becomes more embarrassing as time passes on and the library grows, and he has found it advisable to be absolutely certain before going ahead.

Mr. Putnam does not seem at all like a man who would be solicitous to make a great public show of his accomplishment of duty, and he realizes that in this case it may be a year or more before the results of his labor come to the surface. He loves hard work, he says, and has come to Washington with full appreciation of the fact that there is plenty of hard work before him.

This man who loved hard work, who refused to formulate or adopt a policy prematurely, was born George Herbert Putnam on September 20, 1861, in New York. He was the sixth son and tenth child of George Palmer Putnam and Victorine Haven Putnam. His early education was obtained in the city of his birth at James H. Morse's English and Classical School. He then entered Harvard, where, in his second year, he was awarded honors in classical studies. In 1883 he graduated *magna cum laude,* wearing the coveted Phi Beta Kappa key. The following year he studied law at Columbia University and then became a librarian. Surely at that time he had no idea what a hold he and librarianship would have on each other.

Continuing his legal studies he accepted the invitation to become librarian of the Minneapolis Athenaeum and began his work in October of 1884. Minneapolis was a young and vigorous city at that time. Culture was exerting a strong attraction, and the Athenaeum had been founded in 1860 with funds derived from a lecture by Bayard Taylor. As yet, however, there was no public library there, the Athenaeum being maintained by stockholders and subscribers. But public sentiment had been aroused and a municipal library was highly desired. Miss Gratia A. Countryman has described the situation vividly:

Just at this time the Athenaeum directors appointed a cultured young Harvard man as librarian. Mr. Herbert Putnam came with an unusually fine background of book knowledge, and with an acquaintance with eastern libraries and their methods. He began his new work . . . with energy and enthusiasm.

He could not have entered the city at a more opportune time, and the Athenaeum directors could not have found a man with more ability to solve their problems. He identified himself at once with all of the educational projects of the city, and brought the vigor and keenness of his active mind to the solution of his own task with a clear vision of its possibilities.

There were other active movements besides the library going on in the city. The Minnesota Academy of Science was discussing the necessity of a building to house its growing museum. The directors of the Society of Fine Arts, which had been organized the previous year and had held a very successful loan exhibition, were considering how and where they could establish a permanent art exhibit.

. . . It needed the work of a leader to bring committees from each of these organizations together to discuss the possibility of a common building to house them all, and later to propose to the city council that it be made a municipal undertaking. He [Putnam] was that leader.

No more than two months elapsed before the directors of the Athenaeum abandoned plans for a new building of their own. If a public library was to be established, the Athenaeum was willing to share. And the Academy of Science and the Society of Fine Arts came to similar agreement. The essential legislative act was passed on February 28, 1885, and the public library became a legal entity.

The public library building, however, was still some years off, and Putnam had to perform his duties as the Athenaeum librarian. Working in a small upstairs room he modernized antiquated methods, revised the charging system, initiated a new system of cataloging and classification, and gave readers access to alcoves so they could find desired volumes for themselves. He provided a breath of fresh air in a stale, old-fashioned environment. In 1888 he was charged to make a trip to Europe to purchase books for both the Athenaeum and the new public library, having been elected public librarian that same year.

He held this double job when the new public library was opened in December of 1889. It was thronged by Minneapolitans, driven by desire to read and by avid curiosity, and it is not surprising to learn that some confusion resulted. Unexpected demands exhausted the inadequate supply of books, and a new and inexperienced staff provided delays and disappointments. Miss Countryman reported: "Only the tact and the sympathetic hearing and explanation of Mr. Putnam saved the reputation of the new library service during that first winter. . . . He modified rules and simplified methods and red tape whenever it could be done to the advantage of readers without weakening service."

Putnam was also such a believer in the benefits of libraries that he opened two branches in Minneapolis during his first year in office and established a third branch the year after. If financial resources had been more plentiful and personal circumstances more favorable he would doubtless have accomplished much more than he did.

Even so, his achievement was notable, both professionally and romantically. The year following his arrival in Minneapolis he was admitted to the Minnesota bar, and the year after that he married Charlotte Elizabeth Munroe of Cambridge, Mass. Ahead of them lay 42 years of happy married life. And their two daughters were both born in the midwestern metropolis—Shirley in 1887, Brenda in 1890.

A great misfortune befell Minneapolis at the close of 1891. Putnam resigned on December 31, and the family returned to the East. Mrs. Putnam's mother was ill, and the family deemed it advisable to be near her. Miss Countryman is again our witness in testifying to the dismay felt throughout the city when it learned that their librarian was leaving. And the board of the public library expressed its appreciation in these terms:

His knowledge of books, his patient attention to all the details of official duty, his unfailing courtesy, his readiness to attend to the wishes of all the patrons of the library, have made him a most excellent librarian, have commanded the admiration of the Board and have endeared him to the people of our city.

Barely in his thirties, young Putnam was well on his way to becoming the tallest little man in the world. Arriving in Minneapolis at a most auspicious moment and exercising his vision and wisdom in forming a coordinated muncipal institution, he exerted a permanent influence in Minneapolis which will not soon be forgotten.

Back in Massachusetts Putnam was quickly admitted to the bar of Suffolk County and practiced law for several years, but he had already made his mark as a librarian, a profession he would soon reenter and never leave. One opportunity he shunned, undoubtedly most wisely. In 1893 he was invited to become the librarian of Brown University, but he chose not to accept. He waited two more years and then, not yet 34, on February 11, 1895, he became director of the Boston Public Library. In the words of Congressman Lawrence Lewis, in a stirring tribute offered in 1939:

"With no solicitation . . . on his part, . . . [he was] selected by the trustees because of his proved capacity and briliant executive reputation. . . ." This old institution had struggled along without a director for 2 years and had fallen into a condition approaching disorganization. The new building on Copley Square, "that superb palace of books, beautified by Puvis de Chavannes, Sargent, Abbey, St. Gaudens, and MacMonnies," had been recently completed, but it was to be Dr. Putnam's task to open it and make it available for public use. This he did with marked success.

The young librarian was a few inches taller!

It was Charles F. D. Belden, himself a successor of Putnam as director of the Boston Public Library, who eloquently described Putnam's achievement in Boston:

In casting about for the man who should take the library at this juncture and lead it into a larger life worthy of the noble building just completed, the trustees were fortunate in discovering Mr. Putnam, then engaged in the practice of law in Boston, after seven years of library work in Minneapolis. This opportunity was a unique one. The first great municipal library building in the country was placed in Mr. Putnam's hand, as a frame into which the oldest of large American public libraries was to be fitted. Thanks to his wisdom and skill, in a brief period of four years, the library expanded to fill the frame and almost outgrew it; and in making a modern institution of the Boston Public Library, he pointed the way for other libraries all over the country. From the time of his appointment, Mr. Putnam was given a free hand and the wholehearted support of the Board of Trustees. His four years of administration gave daily proof of the wisdom of his selection. Quiet, alert, industrious, he saw unerringly the next thing to be done; he inspired confidence in both trustees and staff, and his power of achievement always kept pace with his vision.

Apparently Putnam left no aspect of the institution's work untouched. He established a children's room, surely one of the earliest in America; he increased the flow of books between headquarters and the branches; he extended and encouraged interlibrary loans with other libraries; he added an hour—until 10 p.m.—to the library's

working day; he organized a Special Libraries Department and opened a separate newspaper room. A smattering of statistics will testify to the city's library health: in 1894 home circulation amounted to 832,113; in 1898 it jumped to 1,245,842. In 1894 the Boston Public Library claimed to hold 610,375 volumes; four years later the claim was advanced to 716,050.

His relations with the staff were particularly harmonious, and a peculiarly modern note is found in Belden's description: "The extension of greater recognition to women in library work was a significant feature of Mr. Putnam's administration. Women were freely advanced or appointed to positions which, a few years previously, they were thought to be incapable of filling." He freely and firmly assigned responsibility where it belonged. He was frankly but kindly critical. He stimulated his senior officers and other employees to their best efforts, and all who worked for him experienced a rare satisfaction. His reward was lasting admiration and generous homage.

The new and magnificent Boston building, with all its beautification, was not an unmixed blessing. Splendid though it was, many elements proved inefficient, and in his last year in Massachusetts, Putnam, supported by his trustees and municipal authorities, effected numerous changes. These greatly improved all aspects of library work.

Belden concluded his laudatory remarks by quoting the official tribute of March 24, 1899, given by Putnam's Boston Trustees when they knew he was leaving:

In accepting the resignation of Mr. Herbert Putnam as Librarian, the Trustees of the Public Library of the City of Boston desire to put upon their records the following votes:
That they recognize the harmonious and helpful relations between the Librarian and the Trustees from the day he accepted the office; the remarkable administrative qualities he has shown—in directing the alterations by which the Library Building has been so well fitted for its purposes—in increasing to so large a degree the interest the public takes in the Library, until today it has a larger constituency than any other—in instituting so successfully the work of the Public Library in connection with the Public Schools—and in making the public realize that this institution created and supported by it, really belongs to it, and needs its ever-enlarging patronage and generosity.
That they appreciate the feeling which leads Mr. Putnam, at much personal sacrifice, to give up his position here to take charge of the Congressional Library at

Washington, and his desire to make it the culmination of the Library system of this country, and in time one of the great Libraries of the world.

That their highest regard goes with him in the difficult work he is about to assume, and their faith in his gifts to bring it to the most successful issues.

And then Belden was impelled to add this expressive coda: "The Public Library of the city of Boston takes pride in the thought that it gave him to the nation, and that his fruitful four years in Boston helped in training him for his great career of service in Washington."

With little thought of ever taking charge of the Library of Congress Putnam had been called to Washington, under the terms of a Senate resolution of May 5, 1896, to give his views as to the Library's future. The new and still magnificent building across the street from the Capitol was nearing completion; it would open the following year. A new Librarian was needed, and Congress wanted the best advice possible regarding its leadership and development. Among the persons testifying were Ainsworth Rand Spofford, Librarian of Congress from 1864 to 1897, Bernard Green, superintendent of the building, Melvil Dewey, George H. Baker, William I. Fletcher, Rutherford P. Hayes, W. H. Brett, W. T. Harris, S. P. Langley, and Herbert Putnam. According to a bill in the House of Representatives the new Librarian, when selected, would have "complete and entire control of the Library proper, including the copyright business"—incorporated in the Library of Congress in 1870—and would "prescribe rules and regulations under which his assistants are to be employed and have the custody and management of the Library." This last provision changed completely the earlier law which gave such authority to the Joint Committee on the Library. The Legislative Appropriations Act, approved February 19, 1897, put the Librarian in charge of the reorganized Library of Congress.

The 34-year-old Putnam explained the operations of the Boston Public Library, how he made appointments, how the cataloging was done, and how the library formulated policy for bibliographical service and activity. His testimony and advice included his views on the qualifications of the Librarian and the mission of the Library.

The first necessity for the Library of Congress, Putnam maintained, was adequate staffing by persons expert in their fields. When asked about the older system of appointments being made by the joint committee, he replied: "I believe in centering responsibility. I should say that if the Librarian of Congress is absolutely free from political control in the selection of his men, if he will not have to recommend persons who are forced upon him, then it is safe to leave it to him. . . ." And he submitted the following statement respecting the qualifications of the Library of Congress's chief executive:

This should be a library, the foremost library in the United States—a national library—that is to say, the largest library in the United States and a library which stands foremost as a model and example of assisting forward the work of scholarship in the United States. And you will be spending for it a sum that must be nearly $500,000 a year to make it what your committee seem to purpose that it should be made. I should suppose that you would have to have for the administration of that library a force exceeding numerically 200 employees, perhaps 250. I should suppose that the man who is to have the final administration of that library must have above all things else administrative ability—the same kind of man who is to manage the property or interest of any large corporation, is to handle large funds, is to manage a large force of employees; such a one should have administrative capacity. It is as much required in a library as anywhere else. . . . I do not believe that your chief administrative officer, attending properly to the business problems of the library, need be a profound bibliographer or need to know the most of all the persons in the library as to what the library contains. I should regard him as bearing a relation to the library something similar to that corresponding to, or borne by, the president of a university to the several departments of that university. . . . I presume that the modern college president considers that his chief function is to secure the best men for each department, and to administer on a large scale this business, and see that the business is conducted properly, and to secure great efficiency, and more especially at the beginning, to consider and determine the scope of the work to be undertaken, to form plans on a large scale which might serve as recommendations to the committee . . . with reference to the larger service to be rendered. I don't say a knowledge of specialties, in addition to these capacities, would be inconsistent with them, but it seems to me that those capacities are undoubtedly necessary, and that the chief executive must have them preeminently. (Lucy Salamanca, pp. 240–41)

Back in Boston Putnam reflected on his remarks and wrote to the joint committee to correct "inadvertences which were certain to occur in such testimony given offhand." He admitted that his statement might have been "ill-balanced," that perhaps he laid too much stress on the quality of the head librarian being a "man of affairs . . . rather than the man of books." He had slighted the latter quality, and he wanted the Congress to understand that its new Librarian "should know enough of the literary side of the Library, of bibliography, etc., to appreciate intelligently the needs of the several departments of specialized work."

In stressing the necessity of order and systematization Putnam paid tribute to Ainsworth Rand Spofford, soon to become the Chief Assistant Librarian. "In other words," said Putnam, "the time had come when Mr. Spofford's amazing knowledge of the Library shall be embodied in some form which shall be capable of rendering a service which Mr. Spofford as one man and mortal can not be expected to render." (Lucy Salamanca, pp. 241–42). In 1908, when Spofford died, Putnam offered another, more extensive and more glowing tribute to his predecessor once removed.

It will be noticed that in his testimonial statement Putnam anticipated the Library of Congress being defined as the "national library," and he frequently referred to it as such in reports and addresses. In effect it is the national library, and Putnam's instincts were right as he used this early appellation.

On July 31, 1897, the Library of Congress in the Capitol was closed, and the onerous task of moving the contents to the new building was begun. Thirty days earlier, on July 1, John Russell Young, 57 years old, was appointed Librarian of Congress, and Ainsworth Rand Spofford, 75 years old, became Chief Assistant Librarian. On November 1 the move was completed and the public admitted. The present was bright and the future most promising. But on Christmas Eve, 1898, the new Librarian suffered a fall from which he failed to recover, and on January 17, 1899, he passed away. J. C. M. Hanson described what happened immediately:

Again, there swooped down on the President [McKinley] and Congress a host of aspirants to a position which many of them must have considered one of comparative leisure, a sinecure in which they might pass their declining years amid pleasant and dignified surroundings, holding occasional intercourse with authors living and dead, and meeting statesmen, diplomats, and other distinguished and representative people from various parts of the country and the world. . . .

Among the librarians who finally rallied to the aid of the library, perhaps no one stood out more prominently than Richard R. Bowker. He was not only a bibliographer and librarian, but a business executive, an author, a journalist, and a man of affairs, who knew just what to do under the circumstances and how to do it. No better man could have been secured to sponsor the cause of the library and librarians at the Executive Mansion than he. With William C. Lane, President of the A. L. A., and other members of its Executive Board, he went to Washington and secured action which has had a far-reaching effect on education and librarianship in America.

So Herbert Putnam, now 37 years old, was nominated Librarian of Congress on March 13, 1899, began his active duties on April 5, while Congress was in recess, and was confirmed by the Senate on December 12. The story of other aspirants to the job, particularly that of one Samuel J. Barrows, is diverting, but scarcely part of this essay. Putnam was young, highly intelligent, without library training but with ample library experience, and ready to battle for the future of—a national library. He was also a man of affairs. Shortly after coming to Washington he was elected to membership in the Cosmos Club on May 8 and a month later delivered the commencement address at the Johns Hopkins University in Baltimore (June 13). The present was still bright, and the future was ever more promising.

What did he find as he entered his new office? He tells us in his article "The National Library: Some Recent Developments" (in *Bulletin of the American Library Association,* September 1928):

It is the recent period which I am to review. But to explain it . . . I should first remind you of the conditions existing when the collections entered the new building thirty-one years ago, and indeed still substantially existing when I viewed them with a responsible eye. . . .

The printed collections lacked (1) a systematic classification, (2) a shelf-list, (3) a catalog, save a manuscript author-list on cards as compiled at the Capitol by an inadequate staff, without adequate bibliographic apparatus. There was the beginning of an organization for classification, shelf-listing and cataloging; but for those three processes and the accession work also, the staff numbered but twenty-seven persons. The entire roll apart from the building force, but including the Copyright, comprised but 130.

The annual appropriation for increase was $30,000; for printing and binding, $25,000. And the total annual appropriations were about $300,000.

Quoting from the same source Lawrence Lewis also drew from Putnam's own words:

The building stood as planned: the outside quadrangle, the octagonal reading room centered within it, and the three main book stacks radiating from it—north, east and south—to the quadrangle itself. For the accommodation of material there were those three stacks, providing for about 1,800,000 volumes; for the accommodation of readers the main, and the periodical reading rooms; and for the accommodation of the service, besides the Copyright Office, spaces and equipment there and there in the outside quadrangle. The printed books and pamphlets had been shelved in the stacks; the manuscripts were cased in a corner pavilion; but the maps, music, and prints remained still on the floors or on packing cases.

Lewis then proceeded to enumerate Putnam's triumphs over the next quarter century and the benefits they brought to the American library system.

Putnam, of course, could not have gained his triumphs alone. He needed and depended on expert help and advice. William Warner Bishop wrote of Putnam's good fortune in finding some first-rate men on the job and his knack for selecting equally good men as operations and influence expanded.

Herbert Putnam found some remarkable men on the staff of the library in 1899. It is to his lasting credit that he saw and proved their power, fitted them to the work for which each was most suited, and sustained them in their daily service. Solberg, Hanson, Martel, Griffin, Phillips, Hutcheson, are names which have meant much to American librarianship. To them he added with the years others—Sonneck, Engel, Martin, Ford, Hunt, Ashley, Hastings, Boyd, Meyer, Parsons, Slade, Harris, and now Jameson, to mention but a few. And he gave them helpers. Adamant to political pressure . . . he drew to the library an array of skilled librarians unequaled in America. In the years of the World War this force suffered much depletion. Happily it has recovered and the newer classification of government employees gives it a reasonably sound professional status. The salaries have never been high, but there has always under Dr. Putnam been distinction in working in the Library of Congress, a distinction which has brought and kept a strong staff.

In those early days of Putnam's administration the Librarian welcomed new staff members in person. An affectionate reminiscence is provided by Harriet Wheeler Pierson, who arrived in Washington on May 31, 1900:

"Washington" called the conductor as the train slid into the old Pennsylvania Station at 6th and B Streets, N.W. . . . The cataloger stepped down from the car with mixed feelings. . . .

It was the custom for those newly come to the Library to report at the office of the Librarian. . . . Ushered into the room of simple and appropriate elegance, embarrassment was banished for the timid cataloger by the genial smile of the Librarian, whose brief word was to be remembered through all future years, "We expect great things of you." "Great things of *me*?" thought the cataloger. "I must not fail him. I will do my best, whatever that may be; not great things, for I am not capable of that, but—my best."

Such was the inspiration the Librarian engendered.

Another of the first and greatest needs of the Library was a new or vastly revised classification scheme. Having heard that Melvil Dewey was revamping the decimal classification, Putnam wrote to his elder colleague in Albany on April 6, 1900, asking for further particulars. He also asked for permission to make certain modifications rendering the Dewey system more practicable to the needs of the Library of Congress. But after months of intensive investigation he concluded that the Dewey system was not suitable, that no existing scheme could be applied without considerable change, and he determined that an entirely new schedule should be drafted. As a result the Library of Congress classification came into being, generally acknowledged to be the best for libraries of great size.

After nearly a year in office Putnam read in the

Putnam (fifth from left) and his staff on the steps of the first Library of Congress building, 1914. Included are officers of the Library. Front row, from the left: Thorvald Solberg, register of copyrights, Allen R. Boyd, chief clerk, Jessica L. Farnum, secretary of the Library, Appleton P. C. Griffin, Chief Assistant Librarian, Putnam, Bernard R. Green, superintendent of buildings and grounds, and John V. Würdemann, captain of the watch.

Second row: Francis H. Parsons, assistant in charge of the Smithsonian Deposit, Gaillard Hunt, chief of the Division of Manuscripts, Hermann H. B. Meyer, chief of the Division of Bibliography, William Warner Bishop, superintendent of the Reading Room, David E. Roberts, assistant in the Division of Prints, Oscar G. T. Sonneck, chief of the Division of Music, Charles H. Hastings, chief of the Card Division, and Oswald Welti, assistant in the Division of Maps.

Back row: William Adams Slade, chief of the Division of Periodicals, Arthur Kimball, in charge of the Binding Office, Israel Schapiro, in charge of the Semitic Division, Henry J. Harris, chief of the Division of Documents, Ernest Bruncken, assistant register of copyrights, J. David Thompson, in charge of the Legislative Reference Service, Frederick W. Ashley, chief of the Order Division, Samuel M. Croft, in charge of the Mail Division, Charles Martel, chief of the Catalog Division, and Clarence W. Perley, chief classifier. LC–USZ62–6013A

Washington Post of March 25, 1900: "A number of rare and costly books forming a part of one of the most valuable collections of the Congressional Library, were stolen on Thursday night from the Library reading room," also that "thefts of books are becoming more and more frequent, and—hardly a week passes without several volumes being stolen." Putnam was not a man to miss an opportunity and he wrote a letter the next day to the joint committee. He admitted the possibility of the theft of *one* book—which was promptly recovered. He pointed out the difficulty of finding desired volumes and said there was no place a reader could peruse a rare volume except in the Librarian's office. And he persuaded the Congress to grant the estimates requested in that year's appeal for appropriations!

Early in 1900 he could say that the Library of Congress, in sheer accumulation of holdings, exceeded any library in the Western Hemisphere. It contained 850,000 printed books; 250,000 pamphlets; 26,000 manuscripts; 50,000 maps; 277,000 musical compositions; over 70,000 prints, as well as an estimated 140,000 volumes and pamphlets still undigested from the Copyright Office. But these were just the beginning of the collection which Putnam envisioned as being richly and comprehensively international and capable of serving Congress and scholarship as no other single institution could. On October 20, 1900, he made a valiant effort to obtain the famous John Carter Brown Library to grace his shelves, and he failed. It went instead to Brown University in Providence, R.I. But as Mr. Mearns wrote in reviewing the situation: ". . . it is not as exemplifying an essay in futility that Mr. Putnam's eloquent pronouncement has been transcribed. It is, rather, because of its magnificently accurate projection of the Library of Congress and its future stature in the world of learning that it has been recovered from the

oblivion to which it was consigned more than fifty-five years ago. As prophecy it commands respect, because what it foretold has come to pass. As an illustration of his assurance, awareness, aspiration it is unexcelled." (*Herbert Putnam, 1861–1955;* p. 33.)

Service, too, was uppermost in Putnam's mind. In 1901 the Library of Congress was authorized to lend books outside of the District of Columbia, and interlibrary loan was a fait accompli. That same year Putnam initiated steps leading to the sale of printed cards to libraries all over the country. Within two years (according to Charles A. Goodrum, p. 39) the Library was producing cards at the rate of 225 titles daily. Libraries throughout the United States were rapidly learning to depend on the Library of Congress for most of their cataloging.

On October 15, 1901, the Librarian ventured to send a long message to President Theodore Roosevelt stressing the importance of the Library of Congress, the role it should play in the fields of education and scholarship, its recent growth, its present organization, and its position as a national investment. Near the close he asked this question: "Has not the time come for some reference to it in a statement which includes a summary by the Chief Executive . . .?" The President responded by including two paragraphs in his first annual message to Congress, on December 3, 1901:

Perhaps the most characteristic educational movement of the past fifty years is that which has created the modern public library and developed it into broad and active service. There are now over five thousand public libraries in the United States, the product of this period. In addition to accumulating material, they are also striving by organization, by improvement in method, and by co-operation, to give greater efficiency to the material they hold, to make it more widely useful, and by avoidance of unnecessary duplication in process to reduce the cost of its administration.

In these efforts they naturally look for assistance to the Federal library, which, though still the Library of Congress, is the one national library of the United States. Already the largest single collection of books on the Western Hemisphere, and certain to increase more rapidly than any other through purchase, exchange, and the operation of the copyright law, this library has a unique opportunity to render to the libraries of this country—to American scholarship—service of the highest importance. It is housed in a building which is the largest and most magnificent yet erected for library uses. Resources are now being provided which will develop the collection properly, equip it with the apparatus and service necessary for its effective use, render its bibliographic work

widely available, and enable it to become, not merely a center of research, but the chief factor in great co-operative efforts for the diffusion of knowledge and the advancement of learning. (*Herbert Putnam, 1861–1955;* pp. 35–36)

Almost immediately after his inauguration Putnam was deluged with offers of honorary degrees and invitations to be a speaker at college commencements. He accepted quite a few. On June 3, 1903, he spoke at the commencement of Columbian University (now George Washington University) of Washington, D.C., and in his remarks, inimitably phrased, he proved that he was not a conventional librarian but a champion of intellectual freedom and independent thought. Libraries, after all, are only a means to an end. On that day he said:

I have kept my promise to abstain from the trite theme of the uses of books. You know more of these than I can tell you,— or than you yourselves will ever know again. This occasion is for you the apex,—the summit of the hill of knowledge, —unsullied by experience. It is not merely a parting of the ways,—it is a parting of the wise. You will never be so wise again. You will know more; but you will never again be so wise. You will never again have the interest in books that you have had in the past few years, nor the confidence in their solution of the problems of life that you have today. The book which is now to concern you is the book of life. The book of life isn't easy reading. And it has no index. Rather, I should say, it has an index, and the index is where indexes should be—at the end. But it is shut to you till you reach the end. Indeed it is a book which each of you must not merely read but must write for himself. Write it fairly, write it sturdily, and it will be a book to last, even though it never find a publisher. It will at least form a section of that artful ledger, kept by the unerring accountant, which is to yield up its debits and credits against you at the final commencement day.

Cotton Mather used to oblige his children "to retire and ponder on that question 'What should I wish I had done if I were now dead.' " A salutary but somewhat sombre diversion,—to which I shall not now invite you, though I might find precedents. The world is a cheerful world today; and the most interesting world that ever was; and the book that your life is to write may if you like be a cheerful and interesting book, and a helpful one; for full of service as the world appears, help is still needed.

It is a fashion of commencement addresses to advise you how to write it. I am not the one to advise you, and I shall not try. I have undertaken rather to say something of the opportunities which you are leaving than of those which lie before you. If I should say anything of these latter, it would be only to urge you to apply to them the ideals, the standards, and as many as possible of the methods for which the academic life stands. *Freedom* is one: the academic freedom, which follows an argument to its consequences, however inconvenient; freedom to form an opinion, and to hold, and to alter it, even though it differ from your neighbor's; *tolerance* for his opinion though it differ from yours; *respect* for the accumulated judgment of the past as against the whim or emotion of the present.

Throughout his career as Librarian of Congress Herbert Putnam was careful about his appointments. He wanted expert subject specialists and highly trained technicians. He skillfully rejected patronage applicants, but was happy to receive recommendations for eligible candidates. An elite staff was his great objective. And when a position was of critical importance he vigorously sought a salary for it which would be commensurate. Mr. Mearns quotes from a communication in this vein which Putnam sent to the secretary of the treasury: "This position [Chief of the Division of Manuscripts] became vacant September 1st [1901]. I am holding it vacant until the salary shall be placed at a sum which will enable me to secure for it a thoroughly adequate person. This division deals with the material which forms one of the two greater divisions in a national library. . . . The interests involved are altogether too important to be entrusted to a second-rate man." (*Herbert Putnam, 1861–1955;* p. 34)

Equally desirous of strengthening the Library's international holdings Putnam successfully negotiated the purchase of Gennadius Vasilievich Yudin's fabulous collection of Slavica in 1907. His "responsible eye" was never closed.

In 1908 Putnam instinctively responded with humanitarian sympathy to the passing of Ainsworth Rand Spofford, who died on August 11. His fair and laudatory article appeared in two journals that fall, November 19 in the *Independent* and December in the *Library Journal*. Spofford was in the unique position of having been Librarian of Congress, from 1864 to 1897, then becoming the Chief Assistant Librarian. The following two paragraphs convincingly show how Putnam and Spofford both profited from the situation.

To give over to another the accustomed reins of authority is at no time easy; to give them over at the moment when the institution is emerging from a pinched and narrow to a spacious and glorious life; from the life which has been a struggle to the opportunities for which one has struggled: to give them over then, and with them the prestige and the privilege of the office; such a surrender is hard indeed. The man who, like Dr. Spofford, can make it without a murmur, before *or after*,

is of incredible rarity. The man of his years who, having for two generations been chief executive, can not merely subordinate, but endear himself to his successor, and never waver in fidelity to the institution nor enthusiasm for its interests—such a man has achieved a feat beside which mere feats of memory are of trivial moment.

With him, however, this was not a feat, but nature; the ordinary expression of a nature absolutely loyal, consistently unselfish, enduringly childlike. It will be a sad day for any profession when such a nature is referred to as merely "quaint," as if an anachronism. Particularly will it be a sad day for our profession, with its present stress upon system and mechanism. The age, indeed—our calculating age—requires these: the masses of material to be dealt with, the number and variety of needs to be met, the demand that they be met with promptness and precision. System and mechanism are now necessary auxiliaries; but they cannot be substitutes. And I, associated with them, under duty to promote them, shall not cease to be grateful for the nine years which have given me near contact with one who signified so much and so deeply without regard to them. To me, indeed, Ainsworth Spofford was more than an individual; he was an institution. And with him the continuity has been broken, an order has past, for which no "new order," however efficient, can compensate.

Putnam was no mean poet, and to his eulogy he appended these stanzas:

A. R. S.
1825–1908

———

The Epilogue

He Toiled long, well, and with Good Cheer
In the Service of Others
Giving his Whole, Asking Little
Enduring patiently, Complaining
Not at all
With small Means
Effecting Much

*   *

He had no Strength that was not Useful
No Weakness that was not Lovable
No Aim that was not Worthy
No Motive that was not Pure

*   *   *

Ever he Bent
His Eye upon the Task
Undone
His Soul upon the Stars
His Heart upon
The Sun

*   *

Bravely he Met
His Test
Richly he Earned
His Rest

Putnam was never one to forget or neglect the literary hobbies of persons in high authority. Knowing President Woodrow Wilson's penchant for reading mystery novels he sent a supply to the White House, and May 22, 1913, the Chief Executive penned him an appreciative note saying: "Thank you sincerely for your courtesy in personally attending to my modest wish for detective stories. I am sure those that you sent me will keep me going for some time." (*Herbert Putnam, 1861–1955;* pp. 85–86)

In 1911 Congress seemed to think that its Library was somewhat deficient in supplying the legislative assistance it had a right to expect. When several bills were introduced for the creation of a legislative reference and bill-drafting bureau, Putnam prepared a special report which was clear and to the point. He suggested that the Library had, for many years, rendered the service commonly sought from a legislative office. It had prepared bibliographies and reading lists on all sorts of legislative questions; it had been ever ready to advise Congressmen on the best sources of information; it was eager to make available all of the Library's vast resources to the nation's lawmakers. And he gave precise details of the operations a legislative reference bureau must perform:

It undertakes not merely to classify and to catalogue, but to draw off from a general collection the literature— that is, the data—bearing upon a particular legislative project. It indexes, abstracts, compiles. It acquires extra copies of society publications and periodicals and breaks these up for the sake of the articles pertinent to a particular subject. It clips from newspapers; and it classifies the extracts, the compilations, the articles, and the clippings in a scrapbook, or portfolio, or vertical file, in such a way that all material relating to that topic is kept together and can be drawn forth at a moment's notice. To printed literature it often adds written memoranda as to fact and even opinion as to merit, which it secures by correspondence with experts.

The above work, which organizes and concentrates all the data pertinent to a question in such form as to be readily responsive, is beyond the abilities of the Library with its present organization. The Library would gladly undertake it; it could undertake it without additional appropriation for the material itself, so far as this is in printed form; but it would require for it an enlargement of its present Divisions of Law, Documents, and Bibliography, and in addition the creation of a new division under the title of a Legislative or Congressional Reference Division.

In transmitting his report to Congress he wrote a letter which emphasized certain important principles. Perhaps the most significant one was:

That for the work to be scientific (i.e. having only truth as its object) it must be strictly nonpartisan; and that, therefore, whatever the appointing or administrative authority, the selection of the experts and the direction of the work should by law and in fact be assuredly nonpartisan.

For several years the matter was unsettled, but action was finally taken in 1915 when the appropriation bill for that fiscal year included authorization for the establishment of a Legislative Reference Service. (Mearns: *The Story up to Now;* pp. 199–200)

It was also in 1915, though his interest was years older, that Putnam carried further his endeavors in magnificently enlarging the Library's collection of oriental literature. And his zeal remained constant. Before long he could boast of having accumulated the largest collection of Orientalia outside of the Far East.

The United States entered the First World War in the spring of 1917. Putnam became the general director of the American Library Association's Library War Service, and he performed his duties nobly. His concern, his surprise, and his gratification are apparent in the foreword he provided to T. W. Koch's *War Service of the American Library Association.* There he wrote:

If, visiting a camp library, you should ask for a list of the books issued on a given day you would find some surprise. I have before me a typical such list. It leads off with Sullivan's American business law, followed by Moss' Applied Miner Tactics and Barker's Red Cross in France. Next come five volumes on physics, four on electricity, two on chemistry, one on physiology, three on aviation, one on military signaling, one on agriculture, three on motors, ten—including Gerard and Gibson— on the war itself. Among other miscellaneous titles are Kipling's Departmental Ditties, Service's Rhymes of a Red Cross Man, Taylor's Practical Stage Directing, a life of Grant, a history of Missionaries and—The Iliad of Homer! And the fiction which forms half the list (less than it would at an ordinary library) is by no means

On September 29, 1921, President Warren Harding signed an executive order to have the original manuscript copies of the Declaration of Independence and the Constitution of the United States transferred from the Department of State to the Library of Congress. The next day, Secretary Charles Evans Hughes delivered the documents to the Librarian. LC–USZ62–00399

negligible in quality; for it includes at least, Doyle, Fox, Wister, Conrad, Locke, London, Poe, Dumas and Mark Twain. For the matter of that the actual selection of fiction in the Camp Libraries is of a higher grade than that in the average public library.

At one typical camp a single day's circulation included books on the following: French history, mechanics, topography and strategy in war, self propelled vehicles, hand grenades, field entrenchments, bridges, chemistry, physics, astronomy, hydraulics, electricty, mediaeval history, calculus, civil engineering, geography, American history, surveying, materials of construction, general history, masonry, concrete. About three fourths of the books taken out were non-fiction.

And the reason for all the wartime library service was: "To make better men of the soldiers as well as to make better soldiers of the men."

The First World War had its own impact on the Library of Congress, and the Librarian was keenly aware of it. He wanted to maintain and bolster morale, which was suffering under economic strain and emotional upset. Miss Pierson, who had vowed to do her best when she joined the Library force years earlier, reproduced a letter Putnam wrote, on July 25, 1918, "to the Loyal Staff of the Library of Congress." Some of its passages cry for quotation:

A word, which, if I could, I would say to each of you individually:

You have much to discourage you in the present situation. Your expenses are increasing; your salaries aren't.

Meantime you see numerous of your associates going to positions elsewhere at salaries not merely higher than they were paid here, but higher than you are getting here for work of a higher grade. . . .

If you can't live on your salary here you can't be blamed for taking a higher one elsewhere. But don't for a moment believe that—outside of the fighting ranks themselves—there is any "war work" more necessary than that you are doing here. It is our country as a whole which is at war; it is our government *as a whole* which is its agent. And it needs to bring to bear in the conflict every one of the elements, every one of the forces, which makes for its efficiency. . . .

The Library has its part to play—an indispensable one. Its efficiency *must* be maintained. And you who, resisting temptations elsewhere, are aiding to maintain it, can as justly say that you are doing "war work" as any of those who leave it for a bureau with a military title.

You can feel also that in "standing by your job," patiently, steadily, at a serious personal sacrifice, you are proving a loyalty as unselfish—as fundamentally patriotic—as any shown in this crisis.

To thank you for it would seem to imply that it is a loyalty to me or to the Library, whereas it is the higher loyalty to a cause and a principle. But I want you to know how clearly I realize it, how deeply I value it, and how sure I am that in the end, and upon the final reckoning, it will secure the recognition it deserves.

On February 28, 1924, Putnam, happily and solemnly, placed the two manuscripts most precious to the history of the United States on exhibit. The Declaration of Independence and the Constitution, engrossed on parchment, had recently been

transferred from the Department of State. Actually almost two and a half years had elapsed since President Harding signed the Executive Order, September 29, 1921, releasing the invaluable documents to the Library's custody. It included this paragraph:

This Order is issued at the request of the Secretary of State [Hughes], who has no suitable place for the exhibition of these muniments and whose building is believed to be not as safe a depository for them as the Library of Congress, and for the additional reason that it is desired to satisfy the laudable wish of patriotic Americans to have an opportunity to see the original documents upon

which rest their Independence and their Government.
Warren G. Harding

Putnam himself brought the manuscripts to the Library and witnessed their being placed in a heavy steel safe where they reposed until they were displayed to the public. He described the unveiling ceremony briefly and with telling effect:

The installation of them, in the presence of the President, the Secretary of State, and a representative group from Congress took place on February 28 [1924], without a single utterance, save the singing of two stanzas of "America"—in which the entire company of onlookers joined. The impression upon the audience proved the emotional potency of documents animate with a great tradition.

President Calvin Coolidge and his wife, Grace Goodhue Coolidge, attended the dedication, on February 28, 1924, of the "shrine" where the parchment copies of the Declaration of Independence and the Constitution were protected while in the keeping of the Library of Congress. Visitors were impressed, according to the Librarian's report of 1924, with "the provision for safeguarding the documents from touch and from injurious light, while insuring their complete visibility without formality." Also in attendance at the dedication were the secretary of state and representatives from Congress. National Photo Co. LC–USZ62–57285

And there they remained for more than a generation, until they were once again transported to their final and logical resting place, the National Archives, in special cases long in planning and long in construction. (Cf. Mearns: *The Story up to Now;* pp. 203–4.)

It was at this time, too, that Putnam responded to a congressional bill, enacted March 4, 1923, "to provide for the classification of civilian positions" in the federal service. It was a highly necessary act,

and Putnam had to submit recommendations to a commission representing the Bureau of the Budget, the Bureau of Efficiency, and the Civil Service Commission (Mearns: *The Story up to Now;* pp. 204–6). Mr. Mearns states clearly the complications confronting Putnam as he prepared his presentation. It consisted of five stages: "(1) Initial allocations by the several chiefs of divisions; (2) a review and revision of these by a commission of seven staff officials by the Chief Assistant Librarian; (3) opportunity to the several chiefs to submit further representations in support of decisions negatived; (4) a final review by Mr. Putnam; and (5) the submission by Mr. Putnam of a formal communication to the Personnel Classification Board."

Stressing the uniqueness of the Library in terms of size, skills, and service, Putnam succinctly summarized its needs and his hopes:

As our National Library, and with . . . [its] varied responsibilities, it can not afford to have less than the best obtainable—
(1) Knowledge, experience, and judgment in the development of its collection;
(2) Technical perfection in its processes—classification, cataloguing, and the other treatment of material;
(3) Skill, training, and experience in reference work, bibliography and interpretation;
(4) In its consultative service (e.g., in law, art, music), specialists who are authorities in the subject matter;
(5) In its service to our highest tribunal and its bar, not merely the most comprehensive law library, but the most competent administration and interpretation;
(6) In its legislative service—effective apparatus as to all legislation enacted in every country, and experts who will digest it, the law, the facts, the authorities in matters of opinion: experts comparable at least to those who are employed by the interests seeking legislation.

A year later he wrote:

It was not to be expected . . . that the first applications of a scheme so comprehensive, on a basis professedly philosophic, could be free from inconsistencies, from discrepancies, and from individual hardship. All have been experienced. In the aggregate, however, they are not to be weighed against the vast benefits of the scheme itself—the decision for it, the adoption of it, the progress under it, and the acceptance by Congress of the resulting decisions.

Mr. Mearns points out that 20 years would have to pass before the inconsistencies and discrepancies and hardships were eliminated, and then concludes that Putnam "had fought a fight which was good."

The quality of Putnam's division chiefs had al-

Elizabeth Sprague Coolidge (1864–1953), whose endowment to the Library ensures the performance of music there as well as furthering the study and appreciation of it. LC–USP6–1532A

ways been distinguished. Oscar G. T. Sonneck, appointed chief of the Music Division in 1902, was the first of a noteworthy line of musicologists to give preeminence to the Library's music holdings, and he was followed by Carl Engel, who was succeeded by Oliver Strunk and Harold Spivacke. Engel, head of the Music Division from 1922 to 1934, occupied the post when an event occurred which, with the wholehearted support of the Librarian, led to the Library's unofficial designation as "world center of chamber music." This title, still unofficial, continues to apply.

Mrs. Elizabeth Sprague Coolidge (1864–1953), under the auspices of the Library of Congress, sponsored three concerts of chamber music in the Freer Gallery of Art on February 7, 8, and 9, 1924. Distinguished artists presented programs of mixed content. The way was paved to untold progress and riches and artistry. Herbert Putnam and Carl Engel figured in the program.

Mrs. Coolidge, a thoroughly trained musician as pianist and composer, already nationally known as a munificent patroness of music, had sponsored festivals of chamber music in Pittsfield, Mass., since 1918. She described her advent to the Library of Congress in the following words:

After seven yearly festivals in Pittsfield and following an ever-widening area of musical experience and contacts, I came to realize that the activities begun on South Mountain ought to be perpetuated and that the best—perhaps the only—way to do that would be to institutionalize them. . . .

I received a suggestion which led to the solution about the future of my Festival. I had asked Frank Bridge and his wife to remain awhile in America and, for relaxation after our strenuous three days, to take a motor trip with me. After a visit to southern Virginia, we stopped at Washington, and, as sight-seers, were invited to take luncheon at the "Round Table," a gathering of the Chiefs of Divisions in the Library of Congress, presided over by its wonderful Librarian, Dr. Herbert Putnam. Naturally the conversation turned to the recent Berkshire Festival. I happened to be seated next to a certain Dr. Moore [Charles Moore, Manuscripts Division], who, while chatting about my musical affairs, rather pointedly asked me if I might not consider giving some such music to the Library of Congress. The only equipment for such a prospect seemed, at that time, to be an upright piano upon which, in the basement, music might be tried out or practiced.

Herbert Putnam organized the Round Table, a semiprofessional luncheon group, shortly after becoming Librarian. The regular partakers and the visitors all had one thing in common—a consuming interest in matters of intellectual and artistic concern. This interest engendered what would become the regularly scheduled chamber music festivals, as Mrs. Coolidge explained:

However, when, the following Spring, I sent to the Library two [actually three] chamber programs, Dr. Putnam borrowed from the Smithsonian Institution a delightful little auditorium in the Freer Gallery, and there my Pittsfield players opened a series of three concerts which, later, led to the establishment of the Coolidge Foundation and thus found a way to insure the perpetuation of my Festivals; the little Coolidge Auditorium . . . was built into a corner of one of the courts of the Library; a fund was accepted by President Coolidge and the Congress, and our first Washington Festival was given in October 1925. (Let me add—that both the Librarian and the Congress had to be persuaded; the former by a warm friend of mine and of music; the latter by the Librarian himself!)

In September of 1924 Putnam attended the chamber music festival which Mrs. Coolidge sponsored in Pittsfield. And it should be noted that the marble plaque on the east wall of the foyer of the Coolidge Auditorium, a striking likeness of Mrs. Coolidge, is a creation of the Librarian's daughter, Brenda Putnam.

Mrs. Coolidge's interest and purpose were quickly and permanently fulfilled. The auditorium was built, festival succeeded festival, all of the chamber music manuscripts commissioned by her or given to her were added to the Library's collections, and great artists and ensembles appear in the Library regularly. Generous patrons and patronesses have followed her example. She and Putnam achieved a revolution in library service that is still increasing in effectiveness as other libraries follow their initiative.

Far from the least result of her venture was the creation of the Library of Congress Trust Fund Board, authorized by Congress on March 3, 1925, to accept endowments and to pay to the Library a rate of interest which will last as long as our government endures. The Trust Fund Board was particularly dear to Putnam's heart. One of his ideals of library service was the rendering of interpretative assistance. He wanted consultants and holders of "chairs" who, familiar with the collections and with the fields they embraced, would aid the researcher in extracting all they had to offer. Endowments from private resources now made this possible.

Sometimes the collections blossomed out in unexpected directions, and Putnam, as gardener, was not one to inhibit their growth. A notable example occurred in 1926 when the famous magician Harry Houdini (born in 1874, his real name was Ehrich Weiss) died, bequeathing his famous collection to the Library of Congress. It was a notable acquisition, certainly off the beaten track and offering investigators esoteric fields to explore and cultivate. With the exception of his dramatic collection, all the fruits of his magic curiosity became the property of the American people. He was a student as well as a showman, and he had spent many years researching in libraries, browsing in bookshops, consulting catalogs, and advertising for long-sought titles. The Librarian's annual report for 1927 quotes Houdini's own description of the collection he had formed:

"I have spent a goodly part of my life in study and research," he wrote in his book "A Magician among the spirits." "During the last thirty years I have read every single piece of literature on the subject of spiritualism that I could. I have accumulated one of the largest libraries in the world on psychic phenomena, spiritualism, magic, witchcraft, demonology, evil spirits," etc.

Such a bequest was fully appreciated by Librarian Putnam.

Financial assistance from John D. Rockefeller, Jr., made possible the beginning of the National Union Catalog, announced by Putnam the following year, 1927. The Librarian of Congress was steadfastly pursuing his goals: augmenting the bibliographic apparatus and increasing the service to the nation's scholars. Additional financial aid from the same benefactor also made possible the acquisition of source materials—in copies and facsimiles—necessary for the penetrating study of American history.

On October 26, 1927, Putnam sent a communication to the president of the American Library Association. It had to do with censorship in public libraries and is a statement of which every American should be proud:

In the case of History—which isn't an exact science,—it [i.e., the public] has a right to expect there a representation of all serious views decently expressed. To provide it is the essence of the service of a public library in a free community. And to eject from a public library a sincere book, by a reputable author, on the ground that its views are erroneous, is to tyrannize over public opinion. Our American public wouldn't stand for it.

Applied generally and carried to an extreme, it would leave our libraries the expression of nothing but the prejudices which happen to be in authority at the moment. With the Democrats in authority it would bar books supporting the Republicans, with Catholics in authority it would bar the literature of Protestantism, with free trade in authority it would bar the literature of protection, with the empiricists in authority it would bar the literature of dogma, with an anarchist temporarily in authority it would eject the literature of law and order. The emasculated collection would represent nothing but the whim, the passion, or the self-interest temporarily in control, and be wiped out by the whim, the passion, or the self-interest that succeeds it. (Herbert Putnam papers, Manuscript Division)

On the eve of celebrating his 30th anniversary as Librarian of Congress Putnam modestly disclaimed what had already been achieved and boasted only of the Library's chief virtue. In an essay entitled "The National Library" he declared: "We have far to go, and many levels still to reach. In even the fundamentals 'our house is not yet in order' and won't be till we have caught up with the classification, the cataloging and the production of the cards. There is, in fact, no single particular, save one, in which we are not defective. But that one is an asset. It is—optimism."

In his annual report for 1928 Putnam announced the initiation of another activity of vital importance to the American people. Thanks to the generosity of several individuals—Andrew Mellon, Mrs. Adolph C. Miller, Mrs. Alvin C. Parker, John Barton Payne—there was established a program "for the acquisition of American folk-song." Now called the Archive of Folk Song, it is the section of the Music Division which preserves and promotes the people's heritage of music, dance, and games, foreign as well as domestic. The collections have grown enormously both in mechanical recordings and in manuscripts, and the archive's success surely led to the creation of the Music Division's Recorded Sound Section, a development which followed Putnam's retirement. The Librarian was, however, always interested in recordings of every kind—classical, popular, and folk—and early encouraged the collecting of cylinders and discs.

As he entered his fourth decade as Librarian of Congress he was given a surprise party and presented with a festschrift entitled *Essays Offered to Herbert Putnam by His Colleagues and Friends on His Thirtieth Anniversary as Librarian of Congress, 5 April 1929*. Notable Congressmen, scholars, and librarians paid admiring and affectionate tribute to their subject, emphasizing the past without neglecting the present and the future. Fantasizing that future, Carl Engel, then chief of the Music Division, contributed an essay called "Concert A.D. 2025 in the Library of Congress," and he imaginatively recalled 20th-century events as though they were the happenings of a hundred years before. Most succinctly he wrote:

A third name [after Coolidge and Sonneck] must be associated with our commemoration tonight: that of Herbert Putnam. It is too well known, too well beloved by everyone who is familiar with the annals of this institution to require more than proud and thankful mention. Human events are shaped by personalities. The very things we are commemorating here tonight could not have come to pass, one hundred years ago, without the vision and the tact of Herbert Putnam, without the qualities of mind and character that made him a great Librarian of Congress because he was a great person.

Later in 1929 Putnam was able to create an Aeronautics Division, and in 1930 he won the long sought authorization for the construction of the Library's Annex. His boasted—but not boastful—optimism seemed to be wholly justified.

And it was also in 1930 that Putnam gained one of his greatest triumphs, the acquisition of the Library's Gutenberg Bible, one of the three perfect copies in existence and often referred to as a landmark in the history of civilization. The most important part of a most valuable collection, this volume will always be one of the Library's truly priceless treasures. The Librarian's account of obtaining it, in his annual report for 1930, deserves

Otto H. F. Vollbehr's collection of 15th-century books included a vellum copy of the Gutenberg Bible and 3,000 other items. It was acquired by the Library of Congress in 1930. Dr. Vollbehr (on the right) was a retired scientist who collected this incunabula after World War I. LC–USZ62–57287

to be quoted at some length. Once again his modesty comes to the fore.

The outstanding acquisition of the year . . . was that of the (Otto H. F.) Vollbehr collection of fifteenth century books (3,000 miscellaneous items, together with a copy on vellum—one of three perfect copies existing—of the Gutenberg forty-two-line Bible).

The history of this acquisition is singular and notable. The main collection, gathered by Doctor Vollbehr after the war and when conditions were peculiarly favorable, had for several years been in this country, having been brought here by him for exhibit at the Eucharistic Congress in Chicago. For the Gutenberg Bible he had with the Benedictine Monastery at St. Paul, in Carinthia, a contract of purchase entered into in 1926. Doctor Vollbehr—not by vocation a dealer in books, but a retired scientist, who, after an accident, had been exhorted to take up "collecting" as a diversion—had ambitions for the collection quite apart from considerations of profit to himself, although, like other collectors, a profit to himself through a sale of it was a warrantable expectation. He desired to see it remain in this country, the permanent possession of some research library, and preferably the Library of Congress. As time elapsed this latter disposition of it became almost an obsession with him, accentuated by his gift to us of two special collections (one of printers' marks, one of woodcuts) of great scope and practical value.

Representing as it did the investment of practically his entire fortune, the collection of incunabula could not be tendered as a gift. He conceived the idea, however, that some American citizen might contribute one-half the commercial value of it (which he then without the Bible reckoned at $3,000,000); in which case he professed willingness to forego the remaining half.

For nearly two years, assisted by admirers of the collection, he sought such a citizen. By last autumn the quest had failed, and the collection was to return to Europe to be auctioned off. On December 3, 1929, however, Representative Collins, of Mississippi, introduced in Congress a bill for the acquisition of it through special appropriation, describing it, however, as consisting of 4,500 items (for he included 1,500 upon which Doctor Vollbehr had merely an option) plus the vellum copy of the Gutenberg, for which Doctor Vollbehr was under contract to pay a sum which, including interest, services, and export duty, would exceed $300,000.

Incidentally, the bill proposed that when placed in the Library the collection should be known as the Herbert Putnam Collection of Incunabula.

Quite irrespective of the embarrassing compliment to me which I regarded as but a friendly gesture on the part of a legislator warmly interested in the Library, such a proposal caused me consternation. I feared its effect not merely upon my general repute with Congress for moderation but upon recommendations then pending, including the regular appropriation bills and a bill to authorize an expenditure of over $6,000,000 for the construction of the Annex. I felt, therefore, obliged not merely to abstain from any advocacy of the measure but to keep entirely aloof from the discussion upon it, save to recognize the extraordinary interest of the material, to agree that the possession of it by the Library would greatly enhance its prestige and abilities, and to concede that the acquisition of it by Congress upon its own initiative would greatly impress the world of culture, and would favorably influence many a collector of rarities to choose the Library as the donee or legatee of them. This attitude I preserved until the passage of the bill by the House.

Mr. Collins persisted, and speedily brought to the support of his bill not merely a considerable interest among his colleagues but a "public opinion" expressed in the press and in numerous letters, not merely from people with passion for the rare and curious but from citizens at large whose sentiment and emotion seemed to be stirred by the prospect that our Congress might by its enactment demonstrate a sensibility to "things cultural" with which neither it nor our country is habitually credited.

The volume and intensity of this opinion was increased by a speech of Mr. Collins in the House on February 7, of which copies were widely diffused. On March 10 a hearing upon the bill was given by the Committee on the Library (to which it had been referred) at which numerous librarians, bibliographers, and other experts testified to the significance of the collection and of incunabula in general, and expressed enthusiasm for the acquisition. On June 4 the bill (revised, simplified, and omitting the reference to myself) was reported, but without recommendation, and with a statement carefully balanced between appreciation of the merits of the collection and the perils in prospect through the initiation of what seemed a new policy in the expenditure of Government funds for projects purely "cultural." On June 9 the bill was, upon motion of the leader of the Republican majority (Representative Tilson), called up under suspension of the rules, and passed, with only incidental comment. On June 16 I appeared before the Senate committee in definite support of it, explaining my own earlier hesitations, a portion of which had been quieted by the enactment of the appropriation bill, and (on June 9) of the bill to provide for our annex building; and submitting my opinion that the failure of the Collins bill, especially if ascribed to the indifference of the Library Committee and the Librarian, would be a calamity.

On June 18 the committee reported on the bill with a favoring recommendation. On June 24 it was passed by unanimous consent.

Owing to the legislative congestion it was not, however, actually approved by the President until the final day of the session, July 3, on which day also the final deficiency bill became law, carrying the requisite appropriation.

The 3,000 items constituting the main collection being already in this country were susceptible of prompt delivery to us, subject only to release of certain claims against Doctor Vollbehr which constituted a lien upon them. By July 15 all were cleared and under our roof, awaiting only the check of them with his catalogue, already in our possession. The Gutenberg Bible was still at the Monastery of St. Paul (in Austria) awaiting payment by Doctor Vollbehr of the final installments of the purchase price ($250,000) which, with interest since 1926, the export duty ($25,000), and certain other charges amounted then to approximately $325,000. A month later, with the aid (rendered through the American Legation at Vienna) of advances by the Library upon its own transaction with him, Doctor Vollbehr was enabled to free the three volumes from any further claim of the monastery, and on August 16 delivered them to the American minister, who accepted them in our behalf, later forwarding them by a special courier to our embassy in Paris whence in turn a special courier delivered them to me on the deck of the *Leviathan* at Cherbourg.

By the 3d of September they also were safely within the walls of the Library at Washington.

Putnam's claim to optimism and philosophy of assurance seemed thoroughly justified. Endowments were encouraged and gratefully received; new divisions were established; in 1931 positive action was taken to benefit the blind; chairs and consultantships were increased. Thus the eminent historian James Truslow Adams penned this tribute to the Library of Congress in his Epilogue to *The Epic of America*, published in 1931 (Boston: Little, Brown, and Co.):

The foundation established by Gertrude Clarke Whittall (1867–1965) provides funds for chamber music concerts played on the Stradivari instruments she presented to the Library.

Like the country roads, our whole national life is yet cluttered up with the disorderly remnants of our frontier experience, and all help should be given to those who are honestly trying to clean up either the one or the other. But the frontier also left us our American dream, which is being wrought out in many hearts and many institutions.

Among the latter I often think that the one which best exemplifies the dream is the greatest library in this land of libraries, the Library of Congress. . . .

The Library of Congress . . . has come straight from the heart of democracy, as it has been taken to it, and I here use it as a symbol of what democracy can accomplish on its own behalf. Many have made gifts to it, but it was created by ourselves through Congress, which has steadily and increasingly shown itself generous and understanding toward it. Founded and built by the people, it is for the people. Anyone who has used the great collections of Europe, with their restrictions and red tape and difficulty of access, praises God for American democracy when he enters the stacks of the Library of Congress.

But there is more to the Library of Congress for the American dream than merely the wise appropriation of public money. There is the public itself, in two of its aspects. The Library of Congress could not have become what it is to-day, with all the generous aid of Congress, without such a citizen as Dr. Herbert Putnam at the directing head of it. He and his staff have devoted their lives to making the four million and more books and pamphlets serve the public to a degree that cannot be approached by any similar great institution in the Old World. Then there is the public that uses these facilities. As one looks down on the general reading room, which alone contains ten thousand volumes which may be read without even the asking, one sees the seats filled with silent readers, old and young, rich and poor, black and white, the executive and the laborer, the general and the private, the noted scholar and the schoolboy, all reading at their own library provided by their own democracy. It has always seemed to me to be a perfect working out in a concrete example of the American dream—the means provided by the accumulated resources of the people themselves, a public intelligent enough to use them, and men of high distinction, themselves a part of the great democracy, devoting themselves to the good of the whole, uncloistered. (Mearns, *The Story up to Now;* pp. 217–18)

In 1935 a sprightly little lady, emulating but not imitating Mrs. Coolidge, approached the Librarian directly and offered a dazzling gift: two violins, a viola, and a violoncello, all made by Antonio Stradivari and each one accompanied by a bow crafted by François Tourte. They were promptly accepted, as were a third Stradivari violin and a fifth Tourte bow in the following year, plus an endowment to ensure their preservation, care, and use. The donor was Mrs. Gertrude Clarke Whittall (1867–1965), whose intense enthusiasm for chamber music led her to this splendid exercise in generosity. Indeed, she did far more. In 1937 she provided the means to construct the Whittall Pavilion as the permanent home of the Strads and from time to time augmented her endowment. Her benefactions continued long after Putnam's retirement and death, but they were initiated during his most fruitful administration. He had a way with donors, male or female, which was irresistible.

As his term in office was drawing to a close Putnam had still another occasion to prepare a room, designed for a specific purpose by Paul Cret. The Librarian announced it, in his annual report for 1938, in words that showed its provenance: "On the further wall of the reading space a tablet recognizes the contributory relation with its prospective collection and service, of the Hispanic Society of America, through its President, Mr. Archer M. Huntington." This legend is engraved on the tablet:

The Hispanic Foundation
In
The Library of Congress
This Center
For the Pursuit of Studies
In Spanish, Portuguese and Latin-American Culture
Has Been Established
With the Generous Cooperation of
The Hispanic Society of America
In Extension
Of Its Service to Learning

And in his report Putnam added: "With its appropriate physical features and its remarkable collection (enhanced through the Huntington fund and by gifts and deposits from the Hispanic Society . . .) this room is certain not merely to serve important uses and to have wide distinction, but to exercise an important influence upon our diplomatic and cultural relations with the communities represented."

Having served nearly 40 years, with a brilliant record of accomplishment back of him, Putnam rejected an enticing proposal to write his autobiography. Mearns (in *Herbert Putnam, 1861–1955*; p. 91) quotes from Putnam's letter of November 18, 1938, to Col. Theodore Roosevelt of Doubleday, Doran & Co.: "I have kept no records; and I am not given to reminiscence, my habitual concern having been always of today or tomorrow rather than of yesterdays." The world is the poorer for this characteristic decision.

The 5th of April 1939 was approaching, and many realized the significance of that date. One eminent group, the American Council of Learned Societies, directed by Dr. Waldo Gifford Leland and then located in Washington, D.C., tendered Putnam a festive dinner on January 27 of that year. It presented to him a glowing statement hailing his achievement of 40 years and mentioning the fields of learning and culture into which he had guided the Library to preeminence. In acknowledging the tribute Putnam opened his appreciative remarks in this whimsical fashion:

I have been absorbed in the recital, awed by the amount of research it represents; but somewhat dizzy from the elevation to which it exalts me; and apprehensive. At such a height one's in danger of losing his equilibrium—his sense of proportion between himself and his job, the job and the universe. There was, you remember, Theudas, who, according to Gamaliel [allegedly the teacher of the Apostle Paul; see Acts 5:34–36], "boasted that he was somebody"; and came a cropper.

On April 5 itself the Librarian's famous and exclusive Round Table proffered him a luncheon followed by a program at which a bronze bust of the Librarian, sculpted by Brenda Putnam, was unveiled. On this occasion, too, the following letter from the President of the United States was read:

The White House
Washington

March 28, 1939.

My dear Dr. Putnam:

I wish it were possible for me to be with my friends of the "Round Table" on April fifth. But I expect to be away from Washington at that time. I do want, however, to congratulate you on the fortieth anniversary of your librarianship.

The completion of two score years of service in making the great resources of the Library of Congress serve the needs of the American people is an event of outstanding importance. Under your direction our national library has become one of the great libraries of the world.

I think Carlyle's saying that the true university is a collection of books is of greater force today than when the Sage of Chelsea uttered it. I have an unshaken conviction that democracy can never be undermined if we maintain our library resources and a national intelligence capable of utilizing them.

I believe the library has become universal in scope and national in service.

Very sincerely yours,
[signed]   Franklin D. Roosevelt

Dr. Herbert Putnam
Librarian of Congress
Washington, D.C.

That same day, April 5, 1939, marked the official opening of the Annex, so desperately needed and so valiantly struggled for by the soon-to-become Librarian Emeritus.

The fifth of April had come and gone, and Herbert Putnam was still Librarian of Congress, albeit unwillingly. Nearly a year earlier, on June 15, 1938, he had written to President Roosevelt: "I shall be prepared 'on or after July 1,' to turn over the administrative duties to my successor as Librarian, and to facilitate his entrance upon them." Five days later an act unique in the

Library's history was approved which provided "that upon separation from the service, by resignation or otherwise, on or after July 1, . . . Herbert Putnam, the present Librarian of Congress . . . shall become Librarian Emeritus, with such duties as the President of the United States may prescribe, and the President of the United States shall thereupon appoint his successor. . . ."

No action was taken, and on March 27, 1939, the Librarian again wrote to the President: "Under the appended act and my immediate assurances to you, my retirement to the office of Librarian Emeritus and the nomination of my successor as Librarian might have taken place on any date since last July. Your delay in proceeding under it has been a compliment which I have appreciated, as would any executive. On April fifth, however, I shall have completed forty years of my service here. If by then you are prepared to name my successor, my retirement and his nomination as of that date would seem especially appropriate and welcome." This prompted President Roosevelt, on March 28, to send the following reply: "I need not tell you that I have been glad to have you continue in such fine spirit in the office of Librarian. And I can understand your wish to become Librarian Emeritus after your historic years of service on April 5th. However, I cannot fill your place on that date—principally because it is such an extremely difficult place to fill. Therefore, I must leave it to your good judgment either to stay on for a month or two or to retire and let your first assistant carry on until such time as I can find your successor. I know you will understand." (*Herbert Putnam, 1861–1955;* pp. 91–92)

The President did not long delay his selection of a new Librarian. On June 7, 1939, he nominated Archibald MacLeish to that position, and the Senate confirmed him on June 29. Putnam officially became Librarian Emeritus of Congress on the first of October (Mearns, *The Story up to Now,* p. 219). He retained a private office in the Main Building, came to the Library daily, and generously gave sage advice and counsel to all who sought him out. The Library of Congress, now more than seven times as large as 40 years earlier, faced a completely new era.

The Librarian's annual report for 1939 offered the following statistical summary, estimated, of the institution's holdings:

Printed books and pamphlets	5, 828, 126
Maps and views	1, 421, 285
Music (volumes and pieces)	1, 221, 333
Prints (pieces)	548, 622

No attempt was made to estimate the number of manuscripts in the Manuscripts Division. Perhaps it could only be guessed at. In quantity as well as quality Putnam's 40-year administration had been impressively productive.

Two more encomiums may fittingly be inserted here. On April 5, 1939, Justice Felix Frankfurter wrote to Putnam: "From the viewpoint of ultimate contribution to the enduring values of civilization, I know of no public servant who has contributed more during these last forty years than you have." And that same year Wilhelm Munthe, director of the University Library, Oslo, made this statement in *American Librarianship From a European Angle:* "To me the Library of Congress is like a giant orchestra, in which each member is a virtuoso or a specialist on his own peculiar instrument. In front of them stands that little musical enchanter who directs without the help of a baton—and under his spell they produce the world's most remarkable library symphony" (*American Librarianship* [1939; reprint ed., Hamden, Conn.: Shoe String Press, 1964], p. 95).

Putnam died on August 14, 1955, at Woods Hole, Mass., at the age of nearly 94. What a monument he left the nation!

The title of this little appreciation comes from an obituary written by Jens Christian Bay and published in *Libri,* vol. 6, no. 2, 1956. What kind of a person was this tallest little man in the world, a phrase which so appropriately contrasts his mental and spiritual height with his diminutive stature? I served under him for eight years, knew him only slightly, saw him infrequently. I knew him somewhat better as Librarian Emeritus than as Librarian. I revere and love his memory, and this affection increases with each passing year.

Let us turn to David C. Mearns (in *Herbert Putnam, 1861–1955;* p. 43 ff.) once more for some insight into Putnam as person.

By common assent Herbert Putnam was a Patrician. . . . Certainly there *was a* lofty, Olympian quality in his bearing. . . .

That he was subjected to an impenetrable dignity cannot be denied. He possessed no gifts for glib or sudden intimacy. He rarely gave or asked a confidence. He kept his own counsel. His emotions were indiscernible.

No associate ever called him by his given name. . . . The vulgarities of slang, he dismissed as "F Street" language. He was temperate in all things—passionately temperate and fastidious.

But it were foolish to think of him as being cold, and more foolish to think of him as seeking to promote that belief. . . .

Between the staff and Herbert Putnam, the Librarian of Congress intervened. It was due neither to indifference on the one hand, nor to diffidence on the other. It was the result of a carefully cultivated concept that the Library was invested with a composite personality of all the personalities who served it. . . . It is doubtful that he understood these forces, separating him from his subordinates. There was evidence of this at the observance of his thirtieth anniversary, April 5, 1929, when he composed an encyclical:

"The encomiums upon me personally [he wrote] went so far that, while accepting as one does, the sheer kindness of them in the spirit in which it was meant, I was obliged to protest an excess which I felt to be *rationally* inadmissible. It consisted, not in overpraise of the Library in what it has become, not in over-valuation of its aims, not even in a too-liberal appraisal of the services I have rendered—but in a disproportinate view of my function in relation to the Library as an organism.

"The protest was not made out of modesty . . . but because of my urgent concern that the personality to be considered significant is the personality of the institution itself, of which the personalities of the staff, including myself, are merely components.

"It is, I say, that embracing personality which is my main concern. It must, even more especially, be yours. For though I may attempt definitions of it, and from time to time secure resources for the freer realization of it, the actual development of it rests chiefly with you. The major task will be yours; and the *will* for it must be yours.

"And therefore, in sharing with you the commendations of these days, and the new zests which they inspire, let me ask you to give still freer exercise to those qualities in you without which, in spite of building, books, and apparatus, the Library will never express or fulfill its proper nature.

"And I ask it of you, not as subordinates, serving under me, but as associates, serving *abreast* of me."

There was no condescension, however unconscious, in this exhortation; it was addressed: "To my Immediate Family—All Six Hundred of You." On the contrary, there is every reason to believe that, on his own part, Herbert Putnam felt a sense of close kinship with his appointees. . . .

. . . He was venerated. He was endowed with extraordinary gifts. He was changeless and timeless. . . . His actions were sometimes inexplicable, incredible, inscrutable, but there was confidence in his wisdom, in his judgment, in his foresightedness.

He was stern. He exacted the highest standards of professional and personal conduct. . . . But he was not unjust, not easily provoked, not recklessly, impetuously, incensed. . . .

Of course, the staff's pride in him was inordinate: pride in his urbanity, suavity, courage, understanding, prescience. There was pride in his wit; in his intellectual gaiety and exuberance. . . . There was pride in his eloquence, his idiom, the faultless style of his compositions. . . . The Putnam legacy is a wisp of grandeur.

I cannot resist the temptation or impulse to relate the incident which permanently endeared Putnam to me. I had a glimpse of the man which few were privileged to receive. I cannot document the event of nearly 40 years ago, more's the pity, but I can vouch for its essential truthfulness and how happy it made me.

Easter Sunday of 1939 fell on April 9. On that day Marian Anderson sang to an uncounted multitude from the steps of the Lincoln Memorial. It was a triumphant climax of right over prejudice, of justice over injustice.

Marian Anderson had been engaged to appear in Constitution Hall, the official headquarters of the Daughters of the American Revolution. However, her performance was canceled by the DAR. There was a hue and cry throughout the city and the country from those who appreciated her musical and artistic achievements and the significance of her efforts to obtain social equality for fellow members of her race, but the Daughters of the American Revolution stood by its decision. As soon as the cancellation was firmly announced, arrangements were made for Marian Anderson to sing elsewhere—at $5 per ticket.

At that time Putnam called me to his office, handed me a $20 bill, and instructed me to obtain four tickets for him. I took the money with the greatest pleasure and promised to execute his errand promptly. Fortunately for all concerned, the very next day it was announced that Marian Anderson would sing *free* in front of the Lincoln Memorial.

I returned the $20 to Putnam immediately, but as I handed him the money I had to express my own deep pleasure and satisfaction in his desire to support Marian Anderson and to ally himself with the protest. His reply was brief and simple— how I wish I could remember his exact words. He said that he was highly indignant over the unfair stand taken by the Daughters of the American Revolution and he wished to participate in the only way he could to see that justice was done.

It was indeed a privilege to serve abreast of Herbert Putnam.

References

American Council of Learned Societies. "To Herbert Putnam, Librarian of Congress, 1899–1939. An Address in Appreciation of His Services to Scholarship and to the Advancement of Knowledge. . . ." Washington: The Council, 1939.

"Remarks by Dr. Herbert Putnam at the dinner . . . Hotel Washington, January 27th, 1939 . . . ," pp. [11]–[14].

Ashley, Frederick W. "Three Eras in the Library of Congress." In *Essays Offered to Herbert Putnam by His Colleagues and Friends on His Thirtieth Anniversary as Librarian of Congress, 5 April 1929 . . .* , pp. 57–67.

Bay, Jens Christian. "Herbert Putnam, 1861–1955." In *Libri; International Library Review and Communications* 6 (1956): 200–207.

Belden, Charles F. D. "The Library Service of Herbert Putnam in Boston." In *Essays Offered to Herbert Putnam by His Colleagues and Friends on His Thirtieth Anniversary as Librarian of Congress, 5 April 1929 . . .* , pp. 10–14.

Bishop, William Warner. "Thirty Years of the Library of Congress, 1899 to 1929." In *Essays Offered to Herbert Putnam by His Colleagues and Friends on His Thirtieth Anniversary as Librarian of Congress, 5 April 1929 . . .* , pp. 24–34.

Coolidge, Elizabeth Sprague. *Da Capo; a Paper Read Before the Mothers' Club, Cambridge, Mass., March 13, 1951*. Washington: Library of Congress, Elizabeth Sprague Coolidge Foundation, 1952.

Countryman, Gratia A. "Mr. Putnam and the Minneapolis Public Library . . . ." In *Essays Offered to Herbert Putnam by His Colleagues and Friends on His Thirtieth Anniversary as Librarian of Congress, 5 April 1929,* pp. 5–9.

Essays Offered to Herbert Putnam by His Colleagues and Friends on His Thirtieth Anniversary as Librarian of Congress, 5 April 1929. Edited by William Warner Bishop and Andrew Keogh. New Haven: Yale University Press, 1929.

Goodrum, Charles A. *The Library of Congress*. Praeger Library of U.S. Government Departments and Agencies. New York, Washington: Praeger Publishers, 1974.

Herbert Putnam, 1861–1955; a Memorial Tribute. Washington: Library of Congress, 1956.
Includes Mearns' "Herbert Putnam and His Responsible Eye."

Herbert Putnam, Librarian of Congress, Fortieth Anniversary, 1899–1939. Washington, 1939.
"The Programme."

Herbert Putnam, Librarian of Congress, Fortieth Anniversary, 1899–1939. Washington: W. F. Roberts Co., 1939.

Johnston, William Dawson. *History of the Library of Congress.* Vol. 1, 1800–1864. Washington: U.S. Government Printing Office, 1904.

Koch, Theodore Wesley. *War Service of the American Library Association.* With a foreword by Herbert Putnam. Washington: A.L.A. War Service, Headquarters: Library of Congress, 1918.
Foreword: pp. 3–8.

Lewis, Lawrence. *A Tribute to Dr. Herbert Putnam, Librarian of Congress.* By Hon. Lawrence Lewis of Colorado before the House of Representatives, February 17, 1939. Washington: U.S. Government Printing Office, 1939.

The Library of Congress. *The Gutenberg Bible in the Library of Congress.* Washington: Library of Congress, n. d.

MacLeish, Archibald. "The Reorganization of the Library of Congress, 1939–44." *Library Quarterly,* October 1944, pp. 277–315.

Mearns, David Chambers. "Herbert Putnam and His Responsible Eye." In *Herbert Putnam, 1861–1955; a Memorial Tribute.*

Mearns, David Chambers. "Herbert Putnam: Librarian of the United States." *D.C. Libraries,* pp. 1–24. Washington: issued by the District of Columbia Library Association, January 1955.

Mearns, David Chambers. "The Story up to Now." In the *Annual Report of the Librarian of Congress, June 30, 1946.* Washington: Library of Congress, 1947, pp. 13–227.

Pierson, Harriet Wheeler. *Rosemary; Reminiscences of the Library of Congress.* Washington: 1943.

Putnam, Herbert. . . . *Address of Herbert Putnam . . . Librarian of Congress, at the Eighty-Second Annual Commencement of the Departments of Arts and Sciences, June 3, 1903, at the National Theater, Washington, D.C.* Washington: Judd & Detweiler, printers, 1903.

Putnam, Herbert. "The Great Libraries of the United States." *Forum,* June 1895, pp. 484–94.

Putnam, Herbert. "A Librarian Passed: Ainsworth Rand Spofford—1825–1908." *Independent,* November 19, 1908, pp. 1–6.

Putnam, Herbert. . . . *The Library of Congress as a National Library.* Reprinted from the *Proceedings of the Conference of the American Library Association,* Portland, July 4–7, 1905. Boston: A.L.A. Publishing Board, 1905.

Putnam, Herbert. "The National Library: Some Recent Developments." *Bulletin of the American Library Association,* September 1928, pp. 346–55.

Salamanca, Lucy. *Fortress of Freedom; the Story of the Library of Congress.* With a foreword by Archibald MacLeish. Philadelphia, New York: J. B. Lippincott Co., 1942.

Waters, Edward N. *The Music Division; a Guide to Its Collections and Services.* Washington: Library of Congress, 1972.

Archibald MacLeish

The Poet Librarian

by Nancy L. Benco

Archibald MacLeish, poet, playwright, journalist, teacher, lawyer, and government official, served as Librarian of Congress from 1939 to 1944. In his brief tenure, he instituted an administrative reorganization that affected virtually every operation and every employee of the Library. The modernization helped the Library survive the severe disruptions in services and personnel which occurred at the outbreak of the Second World War. As a leading spokesman in the fight for democracy and as a distinguished poet, he brought to the Library an intellectual and cultural recognition it had not known before.

Archibald MacLeish was born on May 7, 1892, in Glencoe, Ill., the son of a Scottish merchant who had settled in Chicago in 1856. Andrew MacLeish was for 40 years manager of the retail store he had founded for Carson, Pirie, Scott & Company. As a founder and trustee of the University of Chicago and several other schools, he exerted a strong influence on the city's educational development. MacLeish's mother, Martha Hillard, the daughter of a Connecticut Congregational minister, was a Vassar graduate and instructor. She became president of Rockford College in Rockford, Ill., while still in her twenties. After her marriage in 1888, Mrs. Mac-

Leish worked for many years with the Woman's Foreign Mission Society in Chicago and with many other public service organizations, educational and social, including particularly Hull House.[1]

MacLeish grew up at Craigie Lea, the family place on Lake Michigan. At a young age he left the Midwest to study at Hotchkiss preparatory school in Connecticut. In 1911 he entered Yale, where he began a lifelong pattern of doing many different things well. He wrote poems and prose for the Yale literary magazine, which he eventually edited, played football and water polo, delivered the class poem, and earned a Phi Beta Kappa key. After his graduation, he went to Harvard Law School. During World War I he enlisted in the army as a private, served with the field artillery in France, and was discharged two years later as a captain. He returned to law school, where he was an editor of

Archibald MacLeish during his first year as Librarian of Congress. Washington Press-Photo Bureau, Washington, D.C. LC–W26–1531–3

Nancy L. Benco is a public information specialist in the Information Office.

the *Harvard Law Review,* and graduated in 1919 with the Fay Diploma.

In 1920 while teaching part-time at Harvard, he joined the Boston law firm of Choate, Hall & Stewart and practiced law for three years, gaining a reputation as a successful trial lawyer. His law work, however, left him no time to write the poems he wanted to write, and in 1923 he quit the law and went to Paris with his wife, Ada, a Connecticut girl and a singer whom he had married in 1916, and their two small children.[2] For the next five years he read and wrote, publishing several collections of verse, among them *The Happy Marriage and Other Poems* (1924), *The Pot of Earth* (1925), *The Hamlet of A. MacLeish* (1928), and *New Found Land* (1930). While living on the Left Bank, he established close ties with Ernest Hemingway, John Dos Passos, and other young Americans writing in France in the 1920's. During this period he traveled to Persia with a League of Nations mission and, on his return to the United States in 1929, to Mexico, where he followed the route of Cortez' army in preparation for writing his narrative poem *Conquistador,* which won a Pulitzer Prize (1932).

In the United States he and his family settled on a farm in Conway in the Hoosac Hills of Massachusetts. As the Great Depression deepened, MacLeish's friend Henry Luce invited him to join the staff of *Fortune* magazine, which, ironically had begun publication on the eve of the crash of 1929. MacLeish accepted and worked at *Fortune* for nine years, writing articles on political, social, and cultural subjects. His research took him across America and to Europe, South America, and Japan. In an amiable arrangement with Luce, he worked on the magazine long enough each year to pay his bills and then went back to Conway to his own writing. Much of the poetry and drama which he produced during this period was concerned with political and social issues: *Public Speech* (1936), a volume of verse, *The Fall of the City* (1937), a verse play for radio, *Air Raid* (1938), also a verse play for radio, *Frescoes for Mr. Rockefeller's City* (1933), a collection of verse, and *Panic* (1935), a verse play. Politically a liberal, MacLeish, along with other American writers (notably Hemingway), supported the Loyalist cause against the Fascist coup in Spain. Eventually, as *Fortune*'s character changed, MacLeish grew restless and in 1938 he accepted President James B. Conant's invitation to set up the Nieman Founda-

tion for journalism at Harvard.

MacLeish met Franklin Roosevelt early in his first term and shortly thereafter took Luce to the White House.[3] For the December 1933 issue of *Fortune,* MacLeish wrote a lengthy and laudatory article on the President's New Deal program. Later he and another writer, Robert Sherwood, called on the President to protest the American failure to support the Spanish government. On December 15, 1938, Roosevelt summoned MacLeish, professors Felix Frankfurter and Samuel Morison, librarians Randolph G. Adams and Julian Boyd, and other prominent scholars to a White House luncheon to discuss the President's plans for a library at Hyde Park. It was reported at the meeting that "Dr. Adams had remarked to Dr. Boyd on the astonishing absence of the Librarian of Congress, and Dr. Boyd had replied that in his opinion the prospective holder of that august place must be present in the room." [4]

Speculation over the post had been growing since Herbert Putnam, after 40 years as Librarian, announced in the summer of 1938 his plans to retire as soon as a successor was chosen. Eager for a voice in the decision, the American Library Association immediately began making strenuous, but ultimately unsuccessful, efforts to consult with Roosevelt. Its requests for meetings with the President were denied. In December the association submitted, unsolicited, the name of its executive secretary Carl H. Milam. Milam's candidacy, however, was never publicly announced.[5] John Vance, law librarian at the Library of Congress, had announced his own candidacy without ALA's support.

Roosevelt was looking for his own man, someone outside the library profession. In the spring of 1939 he sent a memorandum to Felix Frankfurter, whom he recently had appointed to the Supreme Court, asking for help in the matter:

> I have had a bad time picking a Librarian to succeed Putnam. What would you think of Archie MacLeish? He is not a professional Librarian nor is he a special student of incunabula or ancient manuscripts. Nevertheless, he has lots of qualifications that said specialists have not.
>
> What do you think? You might consult with Sam Morison and any other Twentieth Century minds you think useful. I assume you will not revert to the Nineteenth Century in making your recommendation! [6]

Frankfurter thought that MacLeish was an excellent choice for the Library. He had known the writer "in his various manifestations" for nearly 25 years. MacLeish had studied law under Frankfurter at Harvard, had solicited articles from him for *Fortune,* and in 1939 was editing a collection of Frankfurter's writings for publication. The friendship between Frankfurter and MacLeish, as evidenced by their correspondence in the Library of Congress manuscript collections, remained close until Frankfurter's death in 1965. In his May 11 letter to Roosevelt, Frankfurter described his concept of the librarianship as a cultural and intellectual position:

What is wanted in the directing head of a great library are imaginative energy and vision. He should be a man who knows books, loves books and makes books. If he has these three qualities the craftsmanship of the librarian's calling is an easily acquired quality. But only a scholarly man of letters can make a great national library a general place of habitation for scholars, because he alone really understands the wants of scholars. . . .

He [MacLeish] unites in himself qualities seldom found in combination—those of the hard-headed lawyer with the sympathetic imagination of the poet, the independent thinker and the charming "mixer." He would bring to the Librarianship intellectual distinction, cultural recognition the world over, a persuasive personality and a delicacy of touch in dealing with others, and creative energy in making the Library of Congress the great center of the cultural resources of the Nation in the technological setting of our time.[7]

Frankfurter sent a copy of his letter to MacLeish and urged him to accept. In a lengthy reply on May 15, the poet explained why he could not take the job. He needed, he said, long periods of free time to

On May 28, 1939, MacLeish wrote to President Roosevelt declining the offer of the Librarianship of Congress. Four days later, after a second visit to the White House to discuss the matter, MacLeish reconsidered and wrote Roosevelt: "I should be very proud indeed to serve as director of the Congressional Library should you wish to name me." The Franklin D. Roosevelt Library.

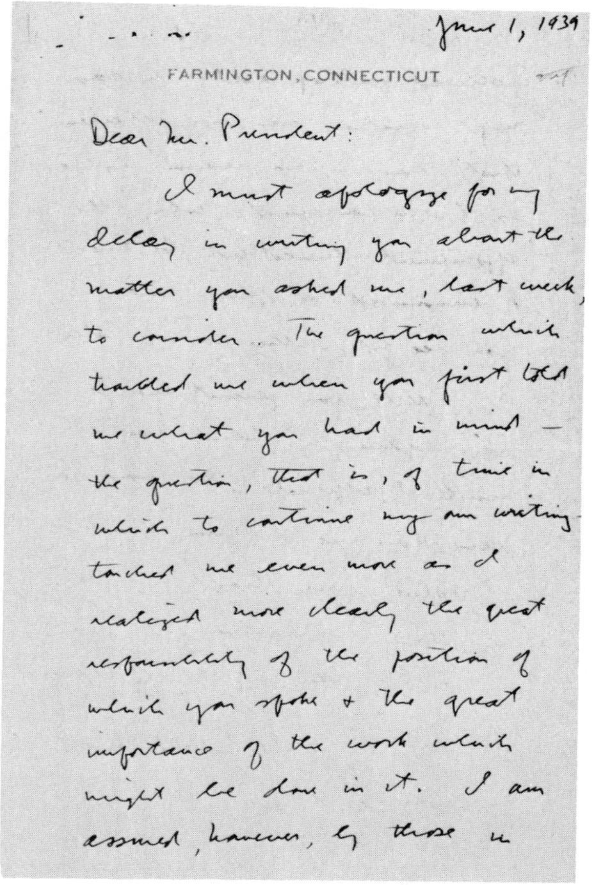

June 1, 1939

FARMINGTON, CONNECTICUT

Dear Mr. President:

[handwritten letter]

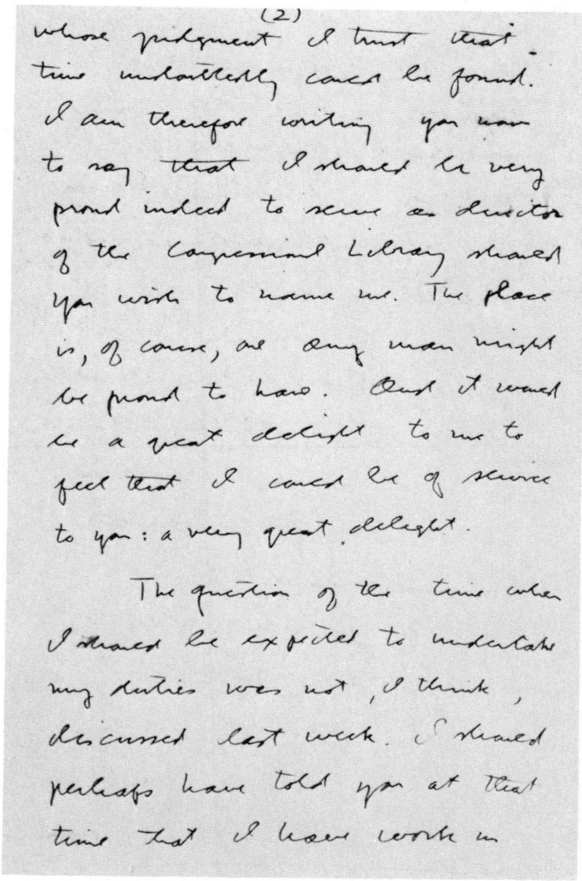

(2)

[handwritten letter, continued]

write, and for this reason he had, with a great deal of personal suffering, given up law practice and his editorship at *Fortune*. He told Frankfurter: "I understand . . . your enthusiasm for a non-technical librarian as head of that great library, but even such a man would have to give a close and almost day-by-day attention to the library. . . . As it is, I have never wanted to write as much as I do at the moment and have never had so many things which demanded to be written. I am afraid they would never be written in the Library of Congress or with the Library of Congress as the principal interest in my life." [8]

They were prophetic words; for during the years he served as Librarian, MacLeish wrote only one poem. The frustration he frequently felt was expressed in his correspondence over the next five years. Nevertheless, he did write numerous speeches, articles, and radio scripts as Librarian.

At Frankfurter's urging, the poet traveled to Washington on May 23 to discuss the appointment with the President, but still uncommitted, he returned to Conway to talk the matter over with his wife. On May 28 he wrote to Roosevelt declining the offer. The Librarianship, he said, was not a task which "a man with an art to practice could fairly undertake." Moreover, he wrote, "the job is pretty much a permanent job. A man would hardly be much good at it for three or four years and it would be unfair of him to leave until he had passed his apprenticeship and served for many years thereafter. I should therefore feel, in taking it, that I have given up my own work pretty much for the rest of my life." [9]

(3)

. . . hard to which I am deeply committed which will require some matters to clean up. It is hard to foresee the precise time required. I should probably be out of deep water by the end of the summer — say October first. But I should deeply appreciate any further time I might be allowed as I am quite certain I should have to devote myself entirely to the Library for a considerable period after taking over.

I trust this fact will not seem an inconvenience.

(4)

I should perhaps add — in case my situation has any relevance — that there is no reason, so far as I am concerned, why the appointment should not be made, or announced, at any time you see fit, either now or later.

Will you permit me to say again in closing how much I appreciate the honor you have done me, & how much I value your thought of me in this connection.

very respectfully yours

Archibald MacLeish

To
The President
Washington, D.C.

A few days later MacLeish was invited back to the White House and this time the President was able to convince the poet to accept the appointment. In a four-page, handwritten letter dated June 1, MacLeish told Roosevelt:

The question which troubled me when you first told me what you had in mind—the question, that is, of time in which to continue my own writing—touched me even more as I realized more clearly the great responsibility of the position of which you spoke and the great importance of the work which might be done in it. I am assured, however, by those in whose judgment I trust that time undoubtedly could be found. I am therefore writing you now to say that I should be very proud indeed to serve as director of the Congressional Library should you wish to name me. The place is, of course, one any man might be proud to have. And it would be a great delight to me to feel that I could be of service to you: a very great delight.[10]

Roosevelt's response was one of decided relief. In a manner typical of much of the subsequent Roosevelt-MacLeish correspondence, the President replied in a jocular vein:

It is one of those curious facts that when I got your first letter I took to my bed with a severe attack of indigestion—and that when your second letter came I found myself able to rise and resume my normal life. . . .

It is perfectly all right about your taking office after the Summer is over—say the end of September or the first of October. And I am also very clear that you will be able to take "time off" for writing, especially if you like travel to distant parts where you could also improve your knowledge of ancient literature. For example, as Librarian of Congress, you should become thoroughly familiar with the inscriptions on the stone monuments of Easter Island—especially in their relationship to similar sign writing alleged to exist on ancient sheepskins in some of the remoter lamaseries of Tibet. If you go on such a trip I would like to go along as cabin boy and will guarantee that I will not interrupt the Muse when she is flirting with you![11]

At the end of a press conference on June 6, Roosevelt announced his nomination of MacLeish as Librarian. The President told newsmen that although the post had been difficult to fill because of its many requirements, he had found what he wanted in MacLeish—"a gentleman and a scholar . . . who, in every nation of the world, would be known as such."[12]

The announcement launched a storm of controversy. The following day in Congress, Representative J. Parnell Thomas accused MacLeish of being a "fellow traveler" of the Communist party. His allegations, based on the poet's participation in 1937 in the leftist-dominated Second American Writers

Congress, were subsequently denied by MacLeish to the satisfaction of the Senate Library Committee.

That same day ALA president Dr. Milton J. Ferguson sent telegrams to librarians across the country urging them to oppose confirmation. In a statement to the press, he charged that MacLeish lacked the necessary training and experience to direct the largest library in the world. "I have the highest regard for Mr. MacLeish as a poet," he said, "but I should no more think of him as librarian of Congress than as chief engineer of a new Brooklyn Bridge."[13]

President Roosevelt responded enthusiastically to MacLeish's acceptance of the Librarianship. In his letter dated June 6 the President assured MacLeish that he would "be able to take 'time off' for writing." Lent to the Library for reproduction purposes by Archibald MacLeish.

THE WHITE HOUSE
WASHINGTON

June 6, 1939.

Dear Archie MacLeish:-

It is one of those curious facts that when I got your first letter I took to my bed with a severe attack of indigestion -- and that when your second letter came I found myself able to rise and resume my normal life.

You make me very happy and the nomination will go to the Senate in a few days. I will take care of the matter of approval by the Senators from your State.

It is perfectly all right about your taking office after the Summer is over -- say the end of September or the first of October. And I am also very clear that you will be able to take "time off" for writing, especially if you like travel to distant parts where you could also improve your knowledge of ancient literature. For example, as Librarian of Congress, you should become thoroughly familiar with the inscriptions on the stone monuments of Easter Island -- especially in their relationship to similar sign writing alleged to exist on ancient sheepskins in some of the remoter lamaseries of Tibet. If you go on such a trip I would like to go along as cabin boy and will guarantee that I will not interrupt the Muse when she is flirting with you!

As ever yours,

Franklin D. Roosevelt

Archibald MacLeish, Esq.,
Farmington,
Connecticut.

The protest gathered strength at ALA's annual conference which opened on June 18 in San Francisco. At the first general session, librarians by an overwhelming vote endorsed a letter sent by the association council a few days earlier to the President, the Vice President, and the Senate. The letter charged that MacLeish's confirmation "would be a calamity." It continued:

> Mr. MacLeish could not qualify for the librarianship of any college or public library in America which attempts to maintain professional standards. . . . He most certainly is not qualified to be the librarian of the largest and most important library in the world.
> The administration of the Library of Congress is not a simple task which can be learned quickly. It is complex and highly professional. . . . The appointment of a man as a figurehead would do no honor to the appointee. It would, however, be a denial of the value of professional training and experience.[14]

More than 1,400 librarians protested the nomination through petitions forwarded to the Senate Library Committee.

Although ALA claimed that it represented 90 percent of the profession, many librarians gave their support to MacLeish. Members of the New York Public Library staff association and the Metropolitan Library Council urged immediate confirmation. M. Llewellyn Raney, director of the University of Chicago Libraries, denounced ALA's campaign as "irregularly launched, and marked with such persistence and intolerance as to awaken the resentment in Washington and revulsion among the soberer, scholarly element at San Francisco." [15]

The controversy spread into the public press, where opinion was similarly divided. In an editorial entitled "A Shocking Nomination," the *New York Herald Tribune* on June 9 charged that MacLeish was "completely unequipped" for the post. The New York *Sun* on June 10 claimed that the nomination was "the eccentric favoring of a personal friend of Mr. Roosevelt." Supporting MacLeish in two editorials, the *Boston Herald* on June 10 contended that noncareer librarians like Putnam and John Russell Young had "made more enduring contributions to library administration and upbuilding than the career men." The *Boston Daily Globe* on June 8 predicted that with MacLeish as Librarian, the "work may be expected to extend in directions not yet guessed."

On June 20 the Senate Library Committee, which had met informally with MacLeish and an ALA delegation, voted unanimously to recommend confirmation. Following a two-hour debate on June 29, the Senate overwhelmingly approved the nomination by a 63 to 8 vote. Two days later a *New York Times* editorial noted that the vote accurately reflected the small proportion of opposition against MacLeish.

The ALA immediately took steps to make amends with the new Librarian. Its newly elected president, Ralph Munn, offered the association's "complete and most friendly cooperation" in a letter dated July 1. "We all regret," he wrote to MacLeish, "that our attempt to secure a professionally trained librarian had to take the form of a protest against your confirmation. I am sure you realize, however, that your lack of library training and experience was the sole basis of our action." [16] In his reply, MacLeish said that he bore no resentment over the protest. "It is my earnest desire to extend library service through the Library of Congress and through the libraries of the country. I shall need the aid, counsel, and advice of the librarians of the country in any attempt to realize that hope. I, therefore, accept your offer of cooperation as warmly and sincerely as I know you make it." [17] Although MacLeish's ties with the ALA never grew close, the library profession soon looked to him for leadership.

Many of the reasons which led to the protest against MacLeish recurred 36 years later when historian Daniel J. Boorstin was nominated for the post. Professional librarians criticized both men for their lack of library training, experience, and administrative capabilities. Both were questioned by Congress on their political views. Both were, of course, eventually confirmed. Unlike Boorstin, however, who was sworn in as Librarian at a stately ceremony in the Great Hall attended by the President of the United States, MacLeish took the oath of office under the most commonplace circumstances. On July 10 during a routine call for mail at the Conway Post Office near his farm, he was sworn in by the local postmaster, a notary public. There were no witnesses or press coverage of the event.[18]

On Monday, October 2, MacLeish assumed his duties at the Library. He was 47 years of age, of medium height, slender, and robust. Frequently he dressed in tweeds. The staff, MacLeish's colleague David C. Mearns wrote, "sensed at once that the new chief possessed unusual personal qualities, a first-rate mind, which absorbed and penetrated and understood; energies that could be at once exhausting, graceful and yet dynamic; marked powers of concentration and a concern for rationalization; an insistence on definition; and a gift of expression beyond any similar gift they had ever known. . . . His drive was tremendous, and the fresh air that he brought with him was invigorating. Working with Archibald MacLeish was almost never easy, but it was almost always fun." [19]

The Library in 1939 had a collection of nearly 6 million books and pamphlets in addition to uncounted millions of manuscripts, maps, pieces of music, and prints. The staff numbered about 1,100 and the annual budget amounted to slightly more than $3 million. Space had doubled earlier that year with the opening of the new Annex Building.

But the Library also possessed some long-neglected problems. Putnam had ruled like a patriarch, and his tenure had extended over 40 years. The Library in 1939, MacLeish wrote, "was not so much an organization in its own right as the lengthened shadow of a man. . . . to succeed Mr. Putnam was a good deal like inheriting an enormous house at Stockbridge or Bar Harbor from a wise, well-loved, strong-minded, charming and particular uncle who knew where everything was and how everything worked and what everyone could do but had left no indications in his will." [20]

Less than three weeks after taking office, Mac-Leish began a thorough review of the Library, acting upon complaints he had received from librarians inside and outside the Library. On October 19, in his first general order, he asked division chiefs for a report on their book selection procedures. In November he launched a study of the personnel situation, appointed staff committees to examine the processing and acquisitions operations, and called in investigators from the General Accounting Office and the Bureau of the Budget to survey fiscal procedures.

At the same time MacLeish realized that changes in the administrative organization were needed. As Librarian, he was required to sign virtually every personnel action, voucher, book order, and piece of correspondence. "Since I have a constitutional disinclination to signing documents I do not know to be right," he wrote, ". . . the situation was difficult—not to say downright impossible." [21] Moreover, he was directly responsible for supervising over 35

separate administrative units.

The reports, submitted in December, showed the alarming extent of the problems. The Processing Committee found that 1.5 million of the Library's 5.8 million books and pamphlets had not been fully processed and were not represented in the main catalog. The backlog, moreover, was increasing at the rate of 30,000 a year. The Acquisitions Committee discovered that serious deficiencies in the collections existed in fields for which there was no regular review by subject specialists. Of 40 major subject fields in the collections, 15 received no attention, 13 inadequate attention, and only 12 relatively adequate attention. The Bureau of the Budget reported that separate accounting records were maintained by no less than eight administrative units and that receipts and disbursements were handled by five units. The survey of staff salaries revealed that the Library's average, entering, and professional salaries were substantially below their counterparts in other government agencies and in research libraries. Furthermore, Congress had not appropriated funds for within-grade increases for eight years.

Early in 1940 MacLeish prepared a request, based on the initial studies, for supplemental appropriations for fiscal year 1941. [22] He asked for $4.2 million, a substantial increase of more than $1 million over the previous year, and 287 new positions to reorganize the Library and to meet needs which had been deferred until the Annex was completed. In his first appearance before the House Subcommittee on Legislative Branch Appropriations on February 20, he explained that the large request was "the first in many years in which the long-existent and long-maturing needs of the various Divisions of the Library, and of the Library as a whole, have been fully presented to the Congress."

On March 13 the Committee on Appropriations issued a detailed report in which it stated "its pleasure at the industrious and intelligent manner in which Mr. MacLeish has entered upon his duties." In recommending an increase of $340,000, barely a third of MacLeish's request, it emphasized that it had not attempted to meet all the Library's problems. "First and foremost," the committee reported, ". . . is the necessity of preventing any further arrearage in the matter of processing material . . . and attacking accumulated arrearage; and second, the preservation and putting into condition of material already in the Library." [23] To meet these pressing problems, MacLeish was given a coordinator and 50 new positions for the processing divisions. The committee denied MacLeish's requests for a reference service coordinator, area specialists, and book fund increases; for additional research staffs for the Legislative Reference Service; and for salary increases, recommending that Library jobs be reviewed in a complete reclassification survey.

In an editorial on March 30, the *New York Times* commented that although the new Librarian did not get enough to keep the Library in "apple pie order" or to pay living wages to his staff, he did get a "testimonial from the committee that it had faith in Mr. MacLeish as an administrator and as a cultured and scholarly man."

To comply with the Congressional mandate, MacLeish on April 10 appointed a committee of three outside technical experts to study the processing operations in depth. Known as the Librarian's Committee, the group consisted of chairman Carlton B. Joeckel from the University of Chicago, Paul North Rice from the New York Public Library, and Andrew D. Osborn from Harvard. Their 303-page confidential report, submitted after six weeks of searching investigation, strongly recommended changes not only in the processing divisions but in the Library's administration as a whole. The report placed heavy blame for difficulties on the profusion of independent administrative units. The situation was "in all probability the largest and most diffused span of control to be found in any American library . . . . Small wonder that the Library of Congress is often described as a group of libraries within a library. It is in effect a loose federation of principalities, each with strongly developed traditions and with administrative and technical idiosyncrasies." [24]

At the end of June, nine months after he took office, MacLeish began to reorganize the Library, basing the changes solidly on the findings of committees and experts. They were hindered to some extent by Congress' denial of requests for new administrative positions. In a series of general orders, MacLeish divided the Library into three broad departments. Only the Copyright Office and Law Library, created by statute, remained intact.

MacLeish consolidated all housekeeping activities, including personnel, accounts, disbursing, buildings and grounds, the secretariat, and publications, into an Administrative Department. Verner W. Clapp, a staff member for 17 years, was named budget officer and administrative assistant in charge of the department. All subject and reading room divisions were combined into a Reference Department. Luther H. Evans, whom MacLeish had brought to the Library a few months earlier as Legislative Reference Service chief, was given charge of the department in addition to his other duties. The new Librarian also consolidated all processing activities, including acquisitions, cataloging, preparation of cards for catalogs and materials for the shelves, and the sale and distribution of printed cards, into a single department. L. Quincy Mumford came in September on a one-year loan from the New York Public Library to head the Processing Department.

The departmental structure remained in force for three years. In July 1943, MacLeish centralized all acquisitions activities, previously divided between the Reference and Processing departments, into an Acquisitions Department. Still short of administrators, he appointed Clapp as department director. Abolishing the Administrative Department, MacLeish placed Evans, Chief Assistant Librarian, in charge of all administrative functions. He appointed David C. Mearns, previously reference librarian under Evans, head of the Reference Department. Not only did the rotation give the Library a practical administrative interchangeability, but it prevented what MacLeish called an "academic isolationism which has had such harmful effects in American universities. . . ." [25]

The reorganization which occurred within each department has been described in detail in the Librarian's annual reports for the years 1940 through 1944. A retrospective account of the reorganization prepared by MacLeish and his staff appeared in the October 1944 issue of the *Library Quarterly.*

After the reorganization had been under way only a short period, library observers called it "a nearly incredible metamorphosis." [26] At the end of MacLeish's tenure, Harvard librarian Keyes D. Metcalf commented that "Mr. MacLeish's greatest triumph is that he 'got away' with the reorganization. It seems very doubtful whether anyone else in his position would have done so much in five years. This is the considered judgment of librarians who know him best and have seen him in action." [27]

While the reorganization was getting under way, MacLeish and his principal officers held a series of meetings during the summer of 1940 to define the

Library's objectives. These explicit statements of Library policy, the first in the institution's history, generally followed the declarations and practices of previous Librarians. The idea for a set of clearly defined objectives, MacLeish said, came from Civil Service Commissioner Arthur Flemming, who suggested it in connection with the reclassification of Library personnel. The Librarian's Committee also strongly recommended the formulation of a set of objectives to ease some of the institution's organizational problems. The meetings at which the policies were hammered out were not, MacLeish wrote, immediately successful: "One or two of the more articulate of my elder colleagues approached the discussion in the spirit of the senior benches at a faculty meeting: change was undesirable and any discussion which might lead to change was in doubtful taste. The Library of Congress was too big and too old—above all, too old—to ask itself what it was doing and why and for what purpose." [28]

The Statement of Objectives, which first appeared in MacLeish's annual report for 1940, defined the Library's objectives with regard to three categories of users: first, Members of Congress; second, officers of the federal government; and third, the general public. A book selection policy to meet the anticipated needs of these categories of users was outlined in the Canons of Selection:

1. The Library of Congress should possess in some useful form all bibliothecal materials necessary to the Congress and to the officers of government of the United States in the performance of their duties. . . .
2. The Library of Congress should possess all books and other materials (whether in original or copy) which express and record the life and achievements of the people of the United States. . . .
3. The Library of Congress should possess, in some useful form, the material parts of the records of other societies, past and present, and should accumulate, in original or in copy, full and representative collections of the written records of these societies and peoples whose experience is of most immediate concern to the people of the United States.[29]

MacLeish realized that the Library staff would need outside assistance to meet the lofty goals of the book selection policy. On September 1, with a grant from the Carnegie Corporation, he established a group of fellowships to be filled by young scholars from the faculties of universities and colleges. The fellows, who would spend a year on leave from their institutions, would survey the Library's holdings and make recommendations for purchases in their specialized fields. MacLeish also hoped that they would provide "the increasing liaison between the Library of Congress and American scholarship that the Library so pointedly needs." [30] The first five fellows surveyed the collections in modern European history, population, Romance languages, geology, and library science. In November the program was expanded to include members of the Library staff and other government agencies as associate fellows. In 1943 MacLeish recruited for the program a number of area specialists from the Office of Strategic Services to prepare lists of needed contemporary material on Africa, China, the Near East, Japan, the Balkans, and other war-related areas of the world. By 1944 nearly 40 fellows were participating in the program. That year, the Carnegie Corporation discontinued its grant. The withdrawal of funds, MacLeish wrote, "at a time when the Library's fellowships had clearly demonstrated their usefulness, not only to the Library of Congress but to national scholarship, was a tragic loss to both." [31] The fellowship program continued through the mid-1950's, but its impact was greatly reduced.

MacLeish substantially improved the format and content of the annual reports to Congress, making them readable and meaningful accounts of the Library's progress. During Putnam's administration they had consisted of a collection of divisional reports which related the Library's activities in a fragmentary, piecemeal manner. Announcing the changes in the 1941 report, MacLeish explained that his goal was to "arrive in time at a form of report which will exhibit the Library . . . in living form. We propose . . . to exhibit the Library in action—not what it possesses only, but what it *does* with what it possesses." [32] He expressed the hope that the reports eventually would be read by writers, scholars, teachers, and other professionals who might find the Library's resources useful. Reflecting the changing structure of the Library, the 1941 report related the year's activities by department. Subsequent reports dealt with the various functions of the Library, with chapters devoted to acquisitions, preparation of material for the shelves, and services to readers. In a year-by-year analysis of MacLeish's annual reports, Jerrold Orne, who served as a fellow in library science at the Library, commented: "It is a tribute to . . . Mr. Archibald MacLeish that the annual reports of the Librarian of Congress, having become really significant documents in the field of librarianship, have been recognized as proper subjects for careful review." [33]

A sense of urgency and strain caused by World War II ran throughout the MacLeish era at the Library. One month before he took office, German armies had marched into Poland. Two years later with the Japanese attack on Pearl Harbor, America plunged into war.

In October 1941, President Roosevelt appointed MacLeish director of a new war agency, the Office of Facts and Figures, in addition to his duties as Librarian. During the following 16 months his double duties demanded that he frequently be away from the Library. In his absence, the Chief Assistant Librarian, Luther Evans, served as Acting Librarian. MacLeish's job as director of the Office of Facts and Figures was controversial from the start. Created to act as a clearinghouse for information released by government agencies on the national defense effort, the agency was given insufficient power to control or coordinate the issuance of releases. Its publication early in 1942 of a pamphlet describing Nazi propaganda tactics drew criticism from Congress and the news media.

MacLeish's connection with the office had an almost disastrous effect on the Library's appropriations for book purchases for fiscal year 1943. At the House Committee on Appropriations subcommittee hearings on February 19, 1942, he was questioned about the agency's relationship to the Library. It is, MacLeish replied, "that I am related to both, and that for the moment the Office . . . is in the Library of Congress because we have not been able to get space anywhere else in town." As for time to do both jobs, MacLeish wryly remarked, "Like a lot of other people in town I have stopped sleeping and given up Sundays. . . ." [34] When the appropriations bill came up for a vote on March 18, during an ill-attended session of the House, Representative Everett Dirksen offered an amendment to cut the book budget from $173,000 to $55,000 "to save money," and, in effect, to prevent the Library from buying books beyond its regular continuations. Rising in Dirksen's support, Representative John Taber charged that he was "very leery of the operations of the gentleman who is Librarian. . . . He is the head of the Office of Facts and Figures and he has been putting out press releases which will not hold water. . . ." The amendment passed on a teller vote 64 to 42. In June, a House-Senate conference committee managed to restore the fund to its original amount.

But the incident left its mark on MacLeish. He was particularly incensed by the fact that only two newspapers had taken any notice of the near disaster. In a speech before the American Library Association, on June 26, 1942, the Librarian condemned what he called the prevailing mood of antiintellectualism in America: "It was not news that an attack had been made upon an institution of learning. . . . It was not news that the leader of the attack had unconsciously revealed a fear of books. . . . Fifty years ago an attack upon a great library, an attempt to deprive the people of this country of their books, would have brought down upon the politician who attempted it a storm of criticism in the public press. Today it passes almost without comment." [35]

In late March the Office of Facts and Figures moved from the Annex Building to quarters in Foggy Bottom. In July it merged with other agencies to form the Office of War Information, for which MacLeish was appointed assistant director in charge of policy matters. He served in this capacity until February 1943, when he resigned to return full-time to the Library.

As Librarian and as a war agency official, MacLeish became a leading American spokesman for the cause of democracy. The personal convictions and beliefs that he had conveyed in poetry during the 1930's found their expression in public speech during the next decade. His colleague and successor Luther Evans described his popularity: ". . . because he could so eloquently address himself to a militant, informed and free people he was repeatedly called upon by those in authority to give expression to the national interest." [36]

Between 1939 and 1944, MacLeish delivered more than two dozen major speeches to audiences of librarians, journalists, booksellers, students, writers, and others across the country. His addresses were collected and published in three volumes: *A Time To Speak* (1941), *A Time To Act* (1943), and *Champion of a Cause* (1971).

In the Founder's Day address at the Carnegie Institute in Pittsburgh, given a few weeks after he became Librarian, MacLeish eloquently stated a theme which was to dominate his wartime messages—the necessity of education for the preservation of democracy:

Our age, as many men have noticed, is an age characterized by the tyranny of time. Never more than at this moment was that tyranny evident. Those of us who are concerned, for whatever reason, with the preservation of the civilization, and the inherited culture of this nation find ourselves in a situation in which time is running out, not like sand in a glass, but like the blood in an opened artery. . . .

We face a situation which has an "either" and which has an "or" and we will choose or fail to choose between them. . . . For the failure to choose in the world we live in is in itself a choice. The "either" as I see it is the education of the people of this country. The "or" is fascism. We will either educate the people of this republic to know and therefore to value and therefore to preserve their own democratic culture or we will watch the people of this republic trade their democratic culture for the non-culture, the obscurantism, the superstition, the brutality, the tyranny which is overrunning eastern and central and southern Europe.[37]

MacLeish had very definite ideas about the role of librarians in wartime. They have a responsibility, he said, far beyond simply delivering books to readers. "They must themselves become active and not passive agents of the democratic process,"[38] he told members of the American Library Association on May 31, 1940. His speech before the group which a year earlier had denounced his appointment, was greeted with applause. He pursued the idea that a librarian is more than a "check boy in the parcel room of culture" in a 1940 article for the *Atlantic Monthly*. "Librarians," he wrote, "are keepers also of the records of the human spirit—the records of men's watch upon the world and on themselves. In such a time as ours, when wars are made against the spirit and its works, the keeping of these records is itself a kind of warfare. The keepers, whether they so wish or not, cannot be neutral."[39]

MacLeish frequently was called upon to draft speeches and letters for President Roosevelt and other government officials. Included in MacLeish's papers in the Library of Congress are drafts he prepared for Roosevelt's 1941 and 1945 inaugural addresses, the 1943 Jefferson Memorial dedication ceremony, the 1944 State of the Union message, and a number of other occasions. Robert Sherwood, then a presidential adviser, described MacLeish's work in the midnight speechwriting sessions at the White House: ". . . we would spend most of the night in the Cabinet Room, producing another draft which would go to the President with his breakfast in the morning. Sometimes we would send a call for help to Archibald MacLeish, Librarian of Congress, who would come in late at night to help bring a diffuse speech into focus."[40]

In December 1940, at the height of the bombing raids in England, officials at the Library of Congress decided to develop contingency plans for the evacuation of their most valuable possessions. The plans were made, MacLeish wrote in the 1941 annual report, "not on the ground of present danger, but on the only less persuasive ground that the collections of the Library were of such great value that they should not be subjected to *any* foreseeable and forfendable danger, however remote."[41]

The enormous task of surveying the collections for items which would be removed in case of danger was accomplished during January and February 1941 under the supervision of Jerrold Orne, a Library fellow. Irreplaceable manuscripts, maps, music, prints, and rare books were selected for immediate evacuation. Books and pamphlets relating to American history and literature, a collection upon which a new Library could be built, were chosen for secondary removal. Valuable materials which were essential to the conduct of a government in wartime were marked for removal to a safe location in the Library. That spring, hundreds of staff volunteers listed and tagged every item that was to be moved, a task which consumed 10,000 hours in overtime work. Several thousand specially made plywood packing cases were purchased. After dropping plans to build bombproof storage shelters because of a nationwide shortage of steel, concrete, and manpower, Library officials, on the advice of military authorities, selected storage sites on certain college campuses. Congress appropriated a total of $130,000 for the precautionary measures.

Three weeks after Japan attacked Pearl Harbor, the Library began the evacuation under the supervision of Verner Clapp. The Declaration of Independence, the Constitution, the Bill of Rights, the Gutenberg Bible, the Stradivarius violins, and a copy of the Magna Carta, which the British government had placed in the Library's care for the war's duration, were placed in hermetically sealed, waterproof containers and transported under military escort to the U.S. Bullion Depository at Fort Knox, Ky. During the next five months the Library sent 5,000 cases of material in 29 truckloads to fireproof buildings at the University of Virginia in Charlottesville, Washington and Lee University and the Virginia Military Institute in Lexington, Va.,

Librarian MacLeish (left center) examined the Constitution of the United States when it was returned from its wartime storage place on October 1, 1944. To MacLeish's left are Verner Clapp and David Mearns. George Skadding, Time-Life Picture Agency, Copyright Time, Inc.

and Denison University in Granville, Ohio. In addition, the Library took action to safeguard its catalogs, built up at large expense over many years. The Union Catalog and its staff were moved to Virginia. More than 8 million cards from the main catalog and shelflists were microfilmed, and the film stored safely outside of Washington.

Of the most valuable documents only the engrossed copy of the Declaration of Independence made a public appearance during the next two and

a half years. It was brought from Fort Knox under strict security and displayed at the Jefferson Memorial at its dedication in April 1943 during the Jefferson Bicentennial celebration. All the documents were returned to public view at the Library on October 1, 1944, several months after the Normandy invasion. MacLeish declared that their return had "the same spiritual and intellectual symbolization for the people of this country that the return of the lights to London had for the people of London." [42]

Immediately after Pearl Harbor the Library expanded its services to meet the demands of government war agencies. On December 8, it set up a 24-hour telephone reference service for defense agencies. Over the following months it circulated thousands of books, prepared special bibliographies, and provided study rooms for government researchers in the Annex Building. At one point the Division of Special Information, which eventually became the Research and Analysis Branch of the Office of Strategic Services, occupied an entire floor in the Annex.

The Library's Division for the Study of Wartime Communications prepared reports on public opinion and propaganda, and the defense section of the Legislative Reference Service provided special translations, abstracts, and bibliographical documentation. The Map Division staff maintained exhibits of military campaign maps in the Capitol, updating them daily. A restricted collection of 20,000 items of enemy propaganda and other war material was organized in the Thomas Jefferson Room. The Music Division produced foreign language training records and basic music courses for the army. Books on democracy were collected in a "Democracy Alcove" in the Main Reading Room.

The onset of war aggravated the Library's already serious personnel situation. The number of staff members leaving for better paying jobs elsewhere in the government swelled, while others enlisted or were drafted into military service. By 1942 staff changes were four times as numerous as they had been two years earlier. In 1943 the turnover reached a peak of 150 percent, dropping the following year to 115 percent. Though the workweek was increased from 39 to 44 hours and then to 48, the loss in experience and the need for constant training took a heavy toll. From the beginning of his administration MacLeish had fought for higher wages for his staff. It was his first priority in the appropriations request for fiscal year 1941; however, Congress recommended instead that a reclassification survey of all jobs be conducted. Started early in 1941 by the Civil Service Commission, the survey proceeded slowly because of other wartime burdens on the commission. In his annual reports, MacLeish repeated again and again his dismay over the Library's low wages. In one of the most eloquent passages, written at the height of staff turnovers, he said: "The Library . . . lost hundreds of men and women, as it should have lost them, to the armed services and to the war agencies. But it lost other hundreds of men and women whom it should not have lost, for it lost them, not because of the war, but because the Library . . . is at a permanent disadvantage in competing with other employers. It is unable to offer equal salaries for equal work." [43]

The results of the reclassification survey, completed in the fall of 1944, vindicated MacLeish's convictions. Of 1,224 positions surveyed, 600 were upgraded, 8 were lowered, and 616 largely custodial jobs remained unchanged. MacLeish wrote in his final annual report, undoubtedly with a deep sense of relief, "It is gratifying to realize that individual members of the staff, long undercompensated for their services to the Government, are now receiving adequate financial recognition. It is equally gratifying to realize that the Library of Congress pay scales will now enable the Library to recruit and hold professional personnel of the high qualifications and ability which the Library's work requires." [44]

While the job survey eventually improved staff salaries, MacLeish's personal belief in "government by discussion" encouraged staff participation in Library activities. "Men of certain temperaments," he wrote, "find talk annoying—particularly talk in public enterprise. Talk, they say, wastes time. . . . But talk, kept within proper limits, can save time also and can gain what time alone might lose." [45] At Evans' suggestion, MacLeish in 1942 set up the Librarian's Conference, a daily meeting in the Librarian's office at which department heads and other chief administrative officers debated policy questions and received special assignments.

A channel for employee suggestions and criticisms was also created in 1942 with the appointment of a Staff Advisory Committee, composed of union and nonunion representatives. The committee, along with other staff members, actively participated in the drafting of a landmark policy which gave employees the right to appeal grievances to a board of reviewers. The new policy drew praise from other federal agencies and MacLeish was asked to prepare an article about its development for the government publication *Personnel Administration*. Professional employees who met informally to discuss technical processing questions were organized officially in 1944 as the Professional Forum. Under MacLeish's leadership, the forum conducted monthly discussions on methods of controlling library materials.

Recognition of the Library as a major cultural institution, established under Putnam by the founding of endowments for music, art, and poetry, was heightened during the MacLeish years, not only because of his own standing as a significant American poet but because of the eminence of the artists and writers he brought to the Library. Among them were European war refugees, including the French poet and diplomat Alexis Saint-Léger Léger, who became a Library fellow in French literature, and German writer Thomas Mann, who joined the staff as a consultant in Germanic literature. Arthur A. Houghton, Jr., well-known American collector of rare books, was appointed curator of the rare book collections.

In the spring of 1941, MacLeish launched a program in which he must have taken special pleasure—the Library's first series of poetry readings. Financed by a grant from Mr. and Mrs. Eugene Meyers of the *Washington Post,* the "Poet in a Democracy" series brought to the Library a remarkable group of poets. Robinson Jeffers read in February, Robert Frost read to thunderous applause in March, Carl Sandburg lectured and sang ballads in April, and Stephen Vincent Benét read in May. Hundreds of Washingtonians packed the Coolidge Auditorium and hundreds more were turned away at the door. Plans were made for another series but, because of inadequate funds and MacLeish's attention to affairs outside the Library, the poetry readings were not continued.

MacLeish envisioned the chair of poetry, established in 1936 by Archer M. Huntington, as potentially a position of prestige and distinction for American poets. In a letter dated September 13, 1940, MacLeish told the benefactor what he had in mind:

. . . the Chair of Poetry . . . could be made a source of great strength to American poetry by making it available to a succession of poets who would use it not as a Library position for Library purposes, but as a means of carrying on their own work for a period. Over the course of many years, the Library would be enriched by the presence from time to time of such men. The occupants of the Chair would be enriched by the experiences of the Library and the world which immediately surrounds it and the award would become, I should suppose, one of the greatest distinctions in American letters.[46]

In 1941 MacLeish removed Joseph Auslander from the poetry chair by appointing him to a newly created job as gift officer. Consultant since the chair was established, Auslander had devoted himself principally to soliciting gifts for the collections and to speaking tours of the country. The post re-

mained vacant for two years, apparently because of MacLeish's frequent absences from the Library. Finally in the summer of 1943, he announced the appointment of Allen Tate, a distinguished poet and literary critic, to a one-year consultantship beginning in July of that year. Tate was responsible for the development of the literary collections as well as the editorship of the new quarterly which MacLeish was launching. Tate was also instrumental in organizing the fellows in American letters, a group of eight prominent American writers including Katherine Anne Porter, Carl Sandburg, and Mark Van Doren. The fellows, who gathered for their first meeting in May 1944, were to advise the Library on policies governing its literary collections and services. Under Robert Penn Warren, MacLeish's second poetry consultant, they inaugurated the Library's program of recording poets and novelists reading selections from their works.

The idea for a separate publication to announce new acquisitions was kindled when MacLeish observed his friend Justice Frankfurter struggling with catalog card proofs of Library acquisitions. "I was convinced," he wrote, ". . . that a library created to serve the people of a great democratic nation through their representatives and their officers of government owed its principal clients a more appetizing account of its newest holdings than a pile of catalog cards in printer's proof could give even to those who had the patience to consult them." [47]

The method of reporting acquisitions in the annual report was also unsatisfactory, MacLeish felt. The accounts were scattered throughout the report, new holdings were reported months after their arrival, and only exceptional additions to the general collections were mentioned. MacLeish in August announced the publication of a journal "to report upon the Library's acquisitions in an informative and useful manner. . . ." The journal would have, he said, a "humanistic approach" directed toward cultivated people of general interests. With Tate as editor and with articles contributed by the Library's staff, consultants, and fellows, it would be an effort of "cooperative scholarship." The first issue, appearing in November of 1943, was well received. Among the letters of praise was one from Frankfurter:

And now I can tell you with warmth my delight over the Libary of Congress Quarterly Journal. . . . once more you make me wonder where else you could have put your unusual combination of gifts to such germinating purposes, and at the same time not stifle your ultimate ache for creative expression.

Anyhow the Journal . . . is one more of those strands which you are weaving to give our society the pattern and the purpose of a gracious civilization.[48]

Although MacLeish continued to serve President Roosevelt at the Library until the end of 1944, he apparently had expressed a wish to leave as early as the summer of 1943. Responding to a letter from MacLeish, Roosevelt wrote on June 9: ". . . I do appreciate what you have written for though I wish you could keep on as the head of the Library of Congress. I will occasionally bear it in mind to keep a weather eye open. It is going to be difficult and I honestly believe impossible to find anybody to occupy your chair."[49]

By fall, MacLeish had in mind a possible successor. In a confidential letter to Roosevelt on November 12, he suggested Julian Boyd, librarian at Princeton University. (Boyd eventually declined Roosevelt's offer of the librarianship.) "As for myself," MacLeish wrote in that letter, "I should like my resignation to take effect as soon after January 1, 1944, as possible, but, in any case, before March. I can be considerably more useful in back of my own typewriter than back of a Library desk, and I want to get into the fight again as soon as I possibly can. The time seems to me to be getting shorter."[50]

But MacLeish was not to return to his typewriter for some time. During the winter 1943–44, MacLeish worked on a series of radio broadcasts for NBC's Inter-American University of the Air. In March he went to London as a delegate to the Conference of Allied Ministers of Education, a forerunner of the United Nations organization. And, in December he was nominated for a new post at the State Department as assistant secretary of state in charge of public and cultural relations.

The battle over MacLeish's confirmation to this new position was even more acrimonious than that over his nomination to the Library five years earlier. The attack against MacLeish was led by Senator Bennett Champ Clark, who, at the Senate Foreign Relations Committee hearings on December 12 and 13, interrogated the poet on his writings, particularly his early verse. "I was never so conscious of the effort to remove the word *poet* from the common vocabulary . . ." MacLeish recalled years later. "The word *poet* was pronounced with a particular intonation by a certain Senator from Missouri. . . . The

implication . . . being that this man regards himself as a poet and this obviously disqualifies him not only for public life, but for those sensible conversations . . . by which ordinary men communicate."[51] On December 19, the Senate confirmed MacLeish's appointment.

With his confirmation as assistant secretary of state, MacLeish resigned from the librarianship. The news that MacLeish was staying in government service compelled President Roosevelt to write him this note: "I think it is thrilling that you are not leaving us. The only trouble is that you jump from one mausoleum into the other. This is not meant to be derogatory on my part, for both the Library of Congress and the Department of State have long and honorable histories. This ought to hold you."[52]

In the State Department, MacLeish participated in the drafting of the United Nations charter at the San Francisco conference in April 1945. He followed through the charter's ratification by the U.S. Senate that summer before resigning from his government post on August 17. He had submitted his resignation to President Truman on April 13, the day after Roosevelt's death. In his tribute "April Elegy," MacLeish expressed his feelings and those of other Americans: "We did not know we would weep so for him. . . . There were many who loved him, but even those who loved him did not know."[53]

Before retiring to his New England farm to begin writing again, MacLeish completed his work with the United Nations. In 1945 he served as chairman of the U.S. delegation to the London conference which established the United Nations Educational, Scientific, and Cultural Organization (Unesco) and composed the introduction to its constitution. The following year he headed the American delegation to Unesco's first general conference in Paris.

In 1949 MacLeish returned to Harvard, teaching until 1962 as Boylston Professor of Rhetoric and Poetry. The following year he was appointed Simpson Lecturer at Amherst College, a post from which he retired in 1967. In the 30 years since he left government service, he has published numerous articles, plays, and collections of verse. His book *Collected Poems 1917–52* received the 1953 Pulitzer Prize in Poetry and his play *J.B.* received the Pulitzer Prize in Drama in 1959.

MacLeish did not sever his connections with the Library of Congress after leaving in 1944. He continued his interest as a fellow in American letters,

The ninth and eleventh Librarians of Congress, MacLeish (right) and L. Quincy Mumford, on December 4, 1956. LC–USP6–3149C

serving from 1949 to 1956. When Librarian L. Quincy Mumford proposed discontinuing the fellows program, MacLeish urged that the Library "ought in some way to hold the gains made in the brief years in which the Fellows flourished. It would be tragic if the country's national library and the country's writers drifted back into the condition of mutual disinterest which obtained fifteen years ago." [54] The fellows program was disbanded in 1957, to be replaced by consultants representing a broader field of literature. In addition to recording his poetry for the Library's poetry archives, MacLeish has presented readings from his works in the Coolidge Auditorium, most recently in March 1976.

MacLeish's few but fruitful years at the Library were perhaps best summarized by the 10th Librarian of Congress, Luther Evans. After recounting MacLeish's achievements in the 1945 annual report, Evans concludes: "In these, and in a myriad other ways, the brush of the comet gave a new dimension to the Library. But the outstanding characteristic of that brilliant episode is not the fact that so much was consummated in so short a time, but rather that there is now so little to repent." [55]

NOTES

[1] Martha Hillard MacLeish, *Martha Hillard MacLeish (1856–1947)* (Conway ? Mass.: Privately printed, 1949). This journal kept by MacLeish's mother provides an intimate view of their family life. In a foreword, Archibald MacLeish traces the history of his Hillard seafaring ancestors.

[2] [Stanley J. Kunitz], ed., *Living Authors; a Book of Biographies,* edited by Dilly Tante [pseud.] (New York: H.W. Wilson Company, 1931), p. 246.

[3] W.A. Swanberg, *Luce and His Empire* (New York: Charles Scribner's Sons, 1972), p. 106.

[4] David C. Mearns, "The Brush of a Comet," *Atlantic Monthly* 215 (May 1965) : 92.

[5] Dennis Thomison, "F.D.R., the ALA, and Mr. MacLeish: The Selection of the Librarian of Congress, 1939," *Library Quarterly* 42 (October 1972): 390–98.

[6] Roosevelt to Frankfurter, May 3, 1939, Frankfurter Papers, Library of Congress.

[7] Frankfurter to Roosevelt, May 11, 1939, Frankfurter Papers.

[8] MacLeish to Frankfurter, May 15, 1939, Frankfurter Papers.

[9] MacLeish to Roosevelt, May 28, 1939, Franklin D. Roosevelt Library, Hyde Park, N.Y.

[10] MacLeish to Roosevelt, June 1, 1939, Franklin D. Roosevelt Library.

[11] Roosevelt to MacLeish, June 6, 1939, Franklin D. Roosevelt Library.

[12] U.S., White House, Executive Office, Press conference transcript no. 551, June 6, 1939, microfilm copy in the Manuscript Division, LC.

[13] "M'Leish Assailed in Debate in House," *New York Times,* June 8, 1939, p. 2.

[14] "San Francisco Conference," *Library Journal* 64 (October 1, 1939): 750.

[15] M. Llewellyn Raney, "The MacLeish Case," *Library Journal* 64 (July 1939): 522.

[16] Ralph Munn, "Correspondence With Mr. MacLeish," *A.L.A. Bulletin* 33 (October 1, 1939): 708.

[17] Ibid.

[18] "The Swearing in of Librarians of Congress, 1899–1945," Memorandum from the Office of the Librarian, August 16, 1954, LC Archives.

[19] David C. Mearns, *The Story up to Now; the Library of Congress, 1800–1946* (Washington: Library of Congress, 1947), p. 209.

[20] Archibald MacLeish, "The Reorganization of the Library of Congress, 1939–44," *Library Quarterly* 14 (October 1944): 279.

[21] Ibid., p. 280.

[22] As required by law, MacLeish submitted in October his estimates for fiscal year 1941, based on the amounts actually appropriated for fiscal year 1940. With congressional approval, he filed a supplementary letter of estimates after making his personal examination of Library needs.

[23] U.S., Congress, House, Committee on Appropriations, *Legislative Branch Appropriation Bill, 1941,* 76th Cong., 2d sess., H. Rept. 1764, March 13, 1940, p. 10.

[24] Paul North Rice, Andrew D. Osborn, and Carleton B. Joeckel, "Report of the Librarian's Committee to the Librarian of Congress on the Processing Operations in the Library of Congress," June 15, 1940, p. 16, LC Archives.

[25] MacLeish, "Reorganization of the Library," p. 315.

[26] Harry C. Shriver and Cedric Larson, "Archibald MacLeish's Two Years as Librarian," *Saturday Review of Literature* 24 (October 18, 1941): 10.

[27] Keyes D. Metcalf, "Merits Respect and Gratitude," *Library Journal* 70 (March 1, 1945): 213.

[28] MacLeish, "Reorganization of the Library," p. 295.

[29] U.S., Library of Congress, *Annual Report of the Librarian of Congress* (hereafter cited as *ARLC*), 1940, pp. 24–26.

[30] *ARLC,* 1941, p. 17.

[31] MacLeish, "Reorganization of the Library," p. 297.

[32] *ARLC,* 1941, p. 11.

[33] Jerrold Orne, "The Annual Reports of the Librarian of Congress," *Library Quarterly* 14 (July 1944): 239.

[34] U.S., Congress, House, Subcommittee of the Committee on Appropriations, *Legislative Branch Appropriation Bill, 1943,* 77th Cong., 2d sess., February 19, 1942, p. 7.

[35] Archibald MacLeish, *Champion of a Cause; Essays and Addresses on Librarianship,* comp. Eva M. Goldschmidt (Chicago: American Library Association, 1971), p. 89.

[36] *ARLC,* 1945, p. 12.

[37] MacLeish, *Champion of a Cause,* pp. 21–22.

[38] Ibid., p. 60.

[39] Archibald MacLeish, "Of the Librarian's Profession," *Atlantic Monthly* 165 (June 1940): 790.

[40] Robert Emmet Sherwood, *Roosevelt and Hopkins, an Intimate History* (New York: Harper and Brothers, 1950), p. 215.

[41] *ARLC,* 1941, p. 12.

[42] "America's Priceless Documents Reappear," *Life* 17 (October 16, 1944): 43.

[43] *ARLC,* 1943, p. 73.

[44] *ARLC,* 1944, p. 28.

[45] MacLeish, "Reorganization of the Library," p. 314.

[46] MacLeish to Huntington, September 13, 1940, LC Archives.

[47] Archibald MacLeish, "Coöperative Scholarship," *Library of Congress Quarterly Journal of Current Acquisitions* 1 (July, August, September 1943): 1.

[48] Frankfurter to MacLeish, December 6, 1943, Frankfurter Papers.

[49] Roosevelt to MacLeish, June 9, 1943, MacLeish Papers, LC.

[50] MacLeish to Roosevelt, November 12, 1943, MacLeish Papers.

[51] Archibald MacLeish, *The Dialogues of Archibald MacLeish and Mark Van Doren,* ed. Warren V. Bush (New York: E. P. Dutton & Company, 1964), p. 34.

[52] Roosevelt to MacLeish, December 1, 1944, MacLeish Papers.

[53] Archibald MacLeish, "April Elegy, April 15–April 12," *Atlantic Monthly* 175 (June 1945): 1.

[54] MacLeish to Mumford, September 2, 1955, LC Archives.

[55] *ARLC,* 1945, p. 13.

Luther Evans

Man for a New Age

by William J. Sittig

When the United States emerged from World War II as perhaps the most powerful nation on earth and the undisputed leader of the democratic world, it soon became clear to most thoughtful Americans that their newly acquired position of strength required the assumption of new responsibilities both at home and abroad. The American people and their institutions struggled at first with varying degrees of success to define these responsibilities in terms of their own internal democratic traditions and practices and their role in the international arena. This struggle, indeed, continues to the present day.

The Library of Congress was no exception in this period of self-examination. It is likely that there were few people in America in the immediate postwar years who were as qualified to lead this great cultural institution as was Luther Harris Evans. A man of wide vision, committed to democratic ideals and international harmony, Evans was to play an influential role in the nation's and the world's affairs during the mid-20th century.

When President Truman nominated Evans to be Librarian of Congress on June 18, 1945, he chose a man whose entire career and activities up to that point seemed to have eminently qualified him for the position. Evans' early years had not been easy, however. He was born on October 13, 1902, the son of Lillie Johnson and George Washington Evans, at his grandmother's farm near Sayersville, Bastrop County, Texas. His father, a railroad section foreman for the Missouri, Kansas and Texas Railway, soon bought some acreage in the vicinity, where the young Luther assisted in the farm chores and in caring for eight younger brothers and sisters. He began his education in a one-room, one-teacher schoolhouse near his home and graduated from nearby Bastrop High School, first in a class of seven.

Evans entered the University of Texas, from which he received a bachelor's degree in 1924 and his M.A. a year later. His major subjects were political science and economics, and he participated in the activities of the debating society and the student

Luther Harris Evans, 10th Librarian of Congress, 1945–53. Drawing by Lila Oliver Asher, dated February 15, 1949. LC–USZ62–58936

William J. Sittig is technical officer, Research Department.

newspaper. Evans had helped finance his education at the University of Texas by hard work in the local cotton fields and later as a part-time instructor.

Before commencing his doctoral studies, Evans worked his way by ship to Europe in the summer of 1924 to study the governments of England, France, and Switzerland, and the activities of the League of Nations. The new international organization had so intrigued him that it provided the subject matter for his high school valedictory address as well as his doctoral dissertation. On returning from Europe, he became an instructor at Stanford University, where he oriented freshmen to the problems of citizenship and studied for a doctorate, which he was awarded in political science in 1927. His dissertation, "The Mandates System and the Administration of Territories under C Mandate," showed early evidence of his careful attention to facts and details and an optimistic faith in the work of international organizations—characteristics that would mark his future endeavors.

During the Stanford years, Evans married Helen Murphy, who had been a fellow student of his at the University of Texas. Mrs. Evans, dignified and energetic, was to effectively assist her husband as a hostess and an active participant in his professional concerns throughout his career. They have one son, Gill Coffer, who, like his father, became a political scientist.

In 1927, after receiving his Ph.D., Evans taught government at New York University for a year and then political science at Dartmouth College from 1928 to 1929. He next received an appointment to an assistant professorship of politics at Princeton University, where he served until 1935. Besides teaching, Evans wrote numerous articles and book reviews for professional journals on politics, colonial administration, and international relations. He began work on his book *The Virgin Islands, From*

One of the aims of the Historical Records Survey was to locate and organize documentary and archival materials often housed in the most deleterious conditions. Masked HRS workers, upper left, inventorying records in a subcellar below river level in New York City. A survey worker, upper right, culling old materials in the Utah County Courthouse, Ogden, Utah. Luther Evans, HRS director, helping a worker identify a glass negative from the C. M. Bell photographic collection in an old barn in Lanham, Md., below. Work Projects Administration, photos no. 69–N–14841–C, no. 69–N–22192–C, and no. 69–N–2975 in the National Archives.

Naval Base to New Deal, a detailed study of the United States' administration of the islands from 1917 to 1935.[1]

Evans' career was then to take a new course, involving him in an activity for which he seemed to have had little preparatory background or relevant experience. When his teaching contract at Princeton was not renewed, perhaps because of his involvement in politics,[2] Evans journeyed to Washington to draft plans for a nationwide archival survey, an undertaking that was to evolve into the Historical Records Survey sponsored by the Works Projects Administration. Evans' name had been suggested to Harry Hopkins, chief administrator of the WPA, by Raymond Moley, professor of public law at Columbia University and a member of Roosevelt's "brain trust." Moley had become acquainted with Evans through one of the latter's students at Princeton and believed that he would be just the person for this new enterprise.

Evans attacked his new assignment with gusto. After consulting with representatives of the National Archives, the American Council of Learned Societies, the National Park Service, and others familiar with earlier plans and projects, he submitted outlines of the purpose of the survey and the method of administration, a proposed budget, and a recommendation for the appointment of an advisory committee on surveys of state and local archives to assist the administrator.[3] On October 1, 1935, Evans was appointed to the technical staff of the Washington office of the WPA as "supervisor of historic projects" and an initial funding of just over $1 million was made available the next month. The Historical Records Survey was soon placed under the aegis of the Federal Writers' Project and, when this relationship proved unsatisfactory, Evans convinced the WPA directors that the survey should be an independent unit of Federal Project One, that unit of the WPA which administered the programs on art, writing, music, and theater. This arrangement lasted until the Emergency Relief Administration Act of 1939 abolished Washington-based operations, permitting only state and local projects. Later that same year Evans resigned as national director of the survey to assume new responsibilities at the Library of Congress.

The faith that Moley and Hopkins had had in Evans' abilities was not misplaced. In his four years as supervisor of the survey, Evans gave ample evidence of the administrative and professional competence he was to bring to his later positions. In many ways this was unexpected. For, as one chronicler of the Federal Project One recognized, "his professional career before 1935 gave him no special claim to consideration in the field of archives and archival administration, and he was untried as an administrator."[4] He not only secured the independence of his office, assembled an energetic and dedicated young staff, and maintained good working relations with professional associations and other interested groups but also established effective liaison and control over the state units and was able to keep the man-year costs of the program at an acceptably low level. For all of these reasons, the Historical Records Survey was never subjected to the sometimes violent public and congressional criticism directed against the other Federal Project One programs.

Under Evans' stewardship, the survey made significant contributions toward the nationwide inventorying of public and church records, manuscripts, and imprints. All the programs were sponsored on the local level, utilizing unemployed white-collar workers, and operated under archival procedures established in Washington. The organization, recording, and preserving of documents was done for the purpose of making these materials more widely accessible for research purposes. Some of the significant projects undertaken by the survey were inventories of county archives, the Early American Imprints Inventory—later edited by the Library of Congress and incorporated into the National Union Catalog—an annotated bibliography of American history, and a manuscripts program. The last was of special interest to Evans, who helped devise the cataloging rules that became the basis for the preparation of the National Union Catalog of Manuscript Collections by the Library of Congress. Speaking before the Pennsylvania Federation of Historical Societies in 1938, Evans explained why he attached so much importance to the manuscript program:

Historians must come more and more to a recognition of the fact that the vital approach to history is not through general movements, but through the lives of individuals, the lives of small communities, and the lives of business and other groups. It is the development of individual and group endeavor over a period of years with which we must concern ourselves rather than arbitrarily delineated subjects and topics which are in reality fabrications of the human imagination.[5]

Perhaps sensing the intent of Congress to abolish the Washington-based leadership structure of the WPA programs under Federal Project One, Evans had by mid-1939 strengthened the direction of the survey's projects at the state and local levels. In effect, he had worked himself out of a job. But the success of his administration of the Historical Records Survey and his outgoing, pleasant manner were not to go unnoticed.

In September 1939, he met for the first time the newly appointed Librarian of Congress, Archibald MacLeish, who soon asked him to serve as his director of the Legislative Reference Service. He had served in that capacity for less than a year when he was named Chief Assistant Librarian and for awhile was simultaneously director of the newly formed Reference Department. Evans also served as Acting Librarian during MacLeish's absences for governmental wartime assignments and after the Librarian's resignation on December 19, 1944, to become assistant secretary of state in charge of public and cultural relations. So Evans was no stranger to the Library when he ascended to the librarianship and, indeed, had been an active participant in the institution's development during MacLeish's comprehensive reorganization of the Library into functional departments.

Evans was sworn in as 10th Librarian of Congress on June 30, 1945—nearly two months after the surrender of Germany and three months before Japan's capitulation. He realized early in his administration that the end of the war had catapulted the United States into a new and different world, and its institutions, including the Library of Congress, would have to assume new leadership responsibilities. Writing in the Washington *Sunday Star* in late 1945, Evans explained:

For the Library of Congress, as a part of the state, an era has ended; a new era begins. It is necessary to bear in mind the fact that our civilization has been threatened with destruction, and to remember that destruction has been avoided only through an unprecedented mobilization of man's knowledge of himself and his environment. . . . No spot on the earth's surface is any longer alien to the interest of the American people. No particle of knowledge should remain unavailable to them.[6]

To revitalize and augment the Library's collections and to expand its services in light of the new situation were the immediate aims of the new Librarian. He and his staff went to work analyzing the actual work situation and the arrearages which

had accumulated during the war years and projecting the necessary budget increases for acquisitions, higher salaries, and expanded services. The result of these studies was a lengthy report, "Justification of the Estimates, Library of Congress, Fiscal Year 1947," which Evans considered "the most important state paper to issue from the Library since the Report of the Committee on Library Organization in 1802." [7] The careful work that had gone into the preparation of the justification notwithstanding, Congress was in no mood to accept the request for $9,756,852, an amount almost twice that appropriated to the Library for fiscal 1946. The Congress did grant $6,069,967 in fiscal 1947, including substantial increases for the Copyright Office, the Legislative Reference Service, and a motion picture project, but allowed no additional sums for the purchase of library materials and the expansion of other basic activities. Part of the reason for the extensive cut from the requested sum was the desire of Congress to reduce all federal expenditures following the war. More importantly for the Library, in its report on the 1947 budget proposals the House Committee on Appropriations suggested "the need for a determination as to what the policy of the Library of Congress is going to be in the way of expansion and service to the public and the Congress."

This need for a determination of policy occupied Evans for a substantial part of his administration. As a start he assigned David C. Mearns, director of the Reference Department, the task of preparing a historical statement on the Library and its activities. The result, *The Story up to Now,* was published as part of the Librarian's annual report for 1946 and is still the most comprehensive recent

history of the Library of Congress. Next he appointed a Planning Committee, chaired by Keyes D. Metcalf, the director of Harvard University Library, and composed of distinguished librarians, government officials, and private scholars, to consider the functions of the Library and especially its

Librarian Evans looks on while Chief Justice Fred M. Vinson and President Truman examine a leaf of the Constitution on display in the Library of Congress. The President and the Chief Justice had participated in the ceremonies on Constitution Day, September 17, 1951, marking the completion of special measures taken to preserve the Declaration of Independence and the Constitution. Evans observed in his annual report for 1952: "The story of the preservation of these documents appealed to the country's imagination. But only the most deluded could attach more importance to their physical well-being than to the preservation of the principles for which they stand. The Library will be no less devoted to those principles when the documents symbolizing them are no longer in our custody." In December 1952 the Declaration and Constitution were transferred to the National Archives. LC–USZ62–58942

role for the future. The committee submitted its report in March 1947 to Evans, who transmitted it to appropriate Congressmen and committees. The report outlined a future program for the Library in terms of service to the Congress, other federal agencies, local libraries, learned institutions and organizations, the business community, and individuals and described the kinds of collections which the Library ought to maintain.[8] It is unclear what Congress thought about this effort and its conclusions about the Library's role—it was never fully considered or even discussed with the Librarian.

Despite Evans' attempts to explain his plans for the Library, Congress never came to share his broad view. It is true that appropriations regularly rose each year—with the exception of 1948—but these increases were largely absorbed by mandatory pay hikes and higher prices for books and other materials over which the Library had no control. Nevertheless, the Library did not stop growing during the Evans years and he was able to initiate, albeit on a smaller scale than he would have wished, many of the projects he felt were necessary. Evans, it must be remembered, was no stranger to austerity measures. The Historical Records Survey was one of the most cost-effective and efficient programs of the WPA and always had to operate within a tight budget.

When President Truman told Evans of his intention to appoint him to the librarianship he gave him several specific directives. The day after his interview at the White House, Evans interpreted the President's instructions in a letter to a friend: "He [the President] wants the Library to give service to Congress, but he wants it also to be 'the Library of the United States' and give increased service to the little libraries all over the country." [9]

The first of these objectives had been of special concern to Evans from the time he had been appointed director of the Legislative Reference Service. Although separate funds had been appropriated for service to Congress since 1915 and a separate staff had been created for dealing exclusively with legislative matters, it was not until 1946 that the existence of the Legislative Reference Service as a separate unit within the Library and its functions and relations to Congress were definitively recognized by legislation. The Legislative Reorganization Act of 1946, specifically section 203, established "in the Library of Congress a separate department to be known as the Legislative Reference Service" and outlined its activities. The act authorized the appointment of senior specialists in agriculture, economics, housing, and other broad fields of interest to Congress. These specialists were to prepare analytical reports on important policy matters and be available to the committees of Congress for consultation and special assignments. Evans insisted that all work for Congress should be of the highest quality and completely objective and nonpolitical. It was mainly due to the high standards which he set that Congress came to rely more and more heavily on the Library's services and favored the Legislative Reference Service with increased appropriations, proportionately higher than were provided for other Library activities.

Although he had a difficult time in convincing Congress, Evans strongly believed, as did President Truman, that the Library of Congress was the "Library of the United States." He was certain that his conception of the Library's role was simply a continuation of the policies firmly established by his predecessors from at least the time of Ainsworth Rand Spofford. If anything, Evans' conception of the Library's role was in worldwide terms. In no other area was the enlarged scope of his concerns to be as evident as in the development of the collections.

During the MacLeish years, the Library of Congress had been obliged to direct a large proportion of

Luther Evans draped in a tribal blanket presented to him at a ceremony on the Oklahoma reservation of the Otoe Indians in November 1946. Evans had accompanied Julian Boyd, Princeton University librarian and editor of the Thomas Jefferson Papers, to receive a photostat copy of a letter written in French by Jefferson to Chief Standing Buffalo in 1806 as a friendly gesture following the Louisiana Purchase. Cornell Capa, Time-Life Picture Agency, Copyright Time, Inc. LC–USZ62–58939

its resources and energies toward assisting the national war effort. Special research projects, extended services to federal agencies, and even the enormous task of evacuating sizeable parts of the collections to remote storage areas throughout the country had diverted the Library's attention from its more traditional activities and curtailed the amounts of monies available for the growth of the collections. More importantly, the demands placed on the Library during these years had revealed large gaps and deficiencies in the collections. Evans illustrated the problems in an article in the Washington *Sunday Star*.

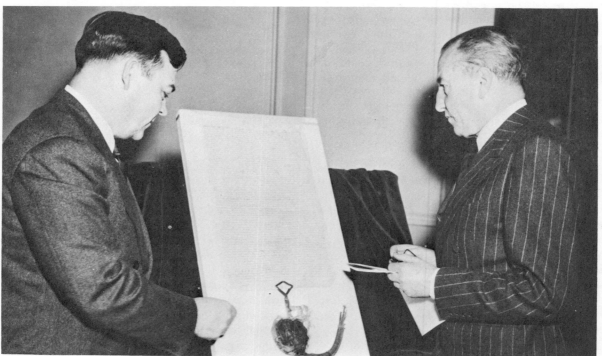

Its [the Library's] weather data on the Himalayas had assisted the air force to cross the "hump" but the want of early issues of the Voelkische Beobachter prevented the transmission of the first auguries of Naziism, and the failure of satisfactory coverage of the plans of European cities resulted in the destruction of a few great intellectual monuments.

In other words, the lesson which the war has taught us is the lesson that, however large our collections may now be, they are pitifully and tragically small in comparison with the demands of the Nation.[10]

Evans personally believed that the Library of Congress was only half the size it should be to adequately perform its national obligatons. Indeed, this was perhaps the principal reason for his hefty budget requests for fiscal 1947.

Evans' assessment of the situation was based on his experiences during the war years as well as his own investigations. At the request of the American Council of Learned Societies, he prepared a study of the Library of Congress and other large American research libraries from 1939 to 1945.[11] He reviewed the activities of these institutions, emphasizing collaborative efforts and the great increase in the use of the newer technologies such as microfilm and motion pictures. He further noted: "The war has emphasized how interdependent is the world of scholarship and how greatly we had been relying upon acquisitions from other countries to support advanced research in America."[12] The Library of Congress, with the help of military and other government agents, had been able to maintain a some-

what steady flow of acquisitions from abroad, but it was not nearly enough.

Evans placed much emphasis on securing materials while they were current and obtainable. Blanket order arrangements with foreign dealers were initiated. Priced exchange agreements for the international exchange of official publications, and participation in various cooperative arrangements, such as the Farmington Plan, all helped fill the Library's shelves with foreign research materials. Another significant activity in this direction was the organization of special projects to microfilm manuscripts and other valuable cultural resources in foreign repositories. Copies of the manuscript collections in St. Catherine's Monastery on Mt. Sinai, selected archives of the Japanese Foreign Office, and the official gazettes of the Mexican states were added to the Library's collections and made available to the American research community.

Evans' efforts were unstinting in making the basic documents of foreign cultures available to American scholars. But he strongly believed that the original source materials belonged in the countries of their creation. In 1949 Evans announced a policy later described in his annual report for 1953 (p. 12): "the Library would not buy or accept as a gift, except under terms that permitted its restitution, any document that appeared to have been removed from another country in violation of its laws governing the protection of cultural resources." As a consequence, Evans initiated the restitution of several important manuscripts to their countries of origin. On Columbus Day 1952 the Library returned a letter of Christopher Columbus, written in Seville in 1504, to the Library of the Real Academia de la Historia in Madrid, from which it had disappeared during the Spanish Civil War.

Cultural reparation was a principle Evans followed in private as well as public actions. He took great satisfaction in delivering to the Archbishop of Canterbury and the director of the British Museum "Alice's Adventures Under Ground," Lewis Carroll's handwritten book which was the forerunner of his great classic. As a personal gesture, Evans had been able to arrange for the purchase of the manuscript "Alice's Adventures" at a public sale with the assistance of Lessing J. Rosenwald and A. S. W. Rosenbach and other donors of private funds.[13]

Although the war period had exposed the weakness of the foreign materials collections of the Li-

The Librarian and Mrs. Evans greeting João Neves da Fontoura, minister of foreign affairs of Brazil, at a reception held in the Hispanic Room of the Library of Congress for the foreign ministers of the American republics, who were meeting in Washington in the spring of 1951. At the right is Mauricio Nabuco, Brazilian ambassador to the United States. During the Evans administration, numerous distinguished foreign visitors were invited to the Library of Congress. LC–USP6–1742C

Luther Evans with a facsimile of Queen Victoria's April 29, 1865, letter of condolence to Mrs. Abraham Lincoln, written on the occasion of the death of the President. When Princess Elizabeth visited the Library of Congress in 1951 she was especially interested in the letter from her great-great-grandmother. As a gesture of international goodwill, the Library had a facsimile of the letter made for Queen Elizabeth II, which Dr. Evans presented at Buckingham Palace on November 4, 1952. LC–USP6–6659A

brary, Evans put no less emphasis on the acquisition of Americana. Besides relying on the operation of the copyright laws and expanding domestic exchange programs, he actively sought and encouraged the receipt of gifts. Among the distinguished American collections acquired between 1945 and 1953 were the papers of Orville and Wilbur Wright, Cordell Hull, Frederick Law Olmsted, Gen. John J. Pershing, and Owen Wister; musical manuscripts of John Philip Sousa and George Gershwin; Alfred Whital Stern's collection of Lincolniana; an early motion picture collection presented by Mary Pickford; and the personal library of President Woodrow Wilson. Other gifts received during the Evans years which have helped place the Library of Congress among the most important repositories of our cultural heritage were the Giant Bible of Mainz, presented by Lessing J. Rosenwald; Leonard Kebler's Cervantes collection; the manuscript of W. Somerset Maugham's novel *Of Human Bondage;* the collection of original manuscripts, letters, and autographed first editions of Hans Christian Andersen, presented by Mr. and Mrs. Jean Hersholt; and autograph manuscripts and other materials included in the Rachmaninoff Archives, given to the Library by the great Russian composer's widow.

During the Evans administration, the Library's collections increased an amazing 28 percent, from about 24.9 million items on June 30, 1945, to 31.6 million in mid-1953. This despite congressional restraints on the appropriations available for the purchase of Library materials. But the truly outstanding feature of the period was the quality of the materials acquired. It would be difficult to identify any comparable stage of the Library's history in which the resources available to serve the nation's research needs were so dramatically and richly augmented.

Evans realized, of course, that increased acquisitions alone were useless without a concomitant effort to process the materials and then make them available to users. Not only were the control problems intensified by the huge influx of materials during his tenure, but there was a massive backlog of unprocessed materials which had accumulated during the war years. Early in his administration, addressing a group of midwestern librarians on the problems of the Library of Congress, Evans acknowledged the situation: "I think the controls we have had in the past are quite inadequate, not nec-

essarily as to quality, but rather as to a combination of quality, coverage and timeliness. The cataloging and bibliographic work now done in libraries is not to be relied upon to give the complete and current control of published material which our objective requires." [14]

In order to effect this control, Evans proposed a 10-year project to eliminate backlogs and provide access to the staggering amount of current receipts. He was never able to obtain sufficient funds to hire the staff to fulfill these objectives and, as a result, new methods of simplified cataloging were implemented. Rules for limited cataloging were adopted and many older, lesser used materials were given a form of temporary control termed "Priority 4" treatment. The adoption of new cataloging arrangements and changing imbedded habits was not an easy task. Addressing a librarians' conference in 1946, Evans explained some of the difficulties of the catalogers and how he attempted to overcome them:

> The catalogers have been in a tough psychological spot, and have responded sometimes with irritability and poor spirit. But the fault was primarily the fault of the administrators who failed to give the catalogers a clear idea of what their job was—what values they were to relinquish to achieve larger production, etc. I am convinced that firm and democratically-arrived-at answers to the cataloging problems can be found, and that there need be no special psychological problems in the cataloging area.[15]

Evans was also concerned with developing a rationalized set of standards for the description of library materials—standards which would be effective, simple, and useful to the national library community as well as the Library of Congress. With the assistance of an advisory committee representing varied library interests, the Library issued in 1949 the *Rules for Descriptive Cataloging in the Library of Congress,* a milestone in the codification of library processing standards. Aware of the increasing importance of special materials, Evans encouraged the development of cataloging rules for sound recordings, motion pictures, filmstrips, books for the blind, manuscripts, prints, and photographs.

American libraries had come to rely heavily on the Library's schedules for the classification of library materials. Consequently, much effort was devoted during Evans' administration to the revision and updating of many of them, most notably in the fields of medicine and military science. A new schedule, Class K, for law materials was proposed and, with the aid of the American Association of Law Libraries, a start was made in 1952 toward the development of a law classification scheme.

As a means of providing greater access to the cataloging records maintained in card trays at the Library of Congress—a need strongly felt by librarians and researchers—a program to publish the Library's catalog cards in book form was adopted. The *Cumulative Catalog of Library of Congress Printed Cards* appeared in 1947, followed by other similar catalogs of books and special materials such as films, maps, and music.

Increased attention was also paid to other means of bibliographical control. Control of serials received first priority. A Serial Record Division was established in 1953 to handle the annual receipt of more than two million serial pieces. During the war period these publications had assumed added importance for defense-related research and as primary sources for keeping abreast of the latest developments in the fields of science and technology. The Library published *New Serial Titles,* the first supplement to the *Union List of Serials,* and, in cooperation with other institutions, union lists of newspapers of Latin America and the Soviet Union.

To improve the service of the Library's expanding collections to its users was a prime objective which Evans had hoped to attain with increased appropriations. Although funds were never sufficient for this purpose, several modest but significant steps were taken to expand reference services. In the eight years of Evans' administration the number of readers using the Library's collections nearly doubled, with much of the increased demand coming for materials dealing with science and technology and those areas of the world—such as the Soviet Union, East Asia, and Africa—of increasing importance to the United States.

Evans took a personal interest in the establishment of a science division. The Library already had a strong science collection but lacked the specialist staff to fully interpret it to users. Thomas Jefferson's personal library, purchased by the Library in 1815, contained nearly 500 scientific items. To this modest beginning were added the Smithsonian deposit, initiated in 1866, the publications of numerous U.S. federal agencies, and the materials received by international exchange. The Library's science collections were acknowledged as the most diversified, if not the largest, in the United States. In 1948, Evans remarked that ". . . the Library feels that it is justified in considering itself as the National Library of Science as well as the National Library generally." [16] A small Science Division was finally created in June 1949 and three years later a Technical Information Division was organized to provide research and documentation services on contract for the Defense Department. During this period, Evans also worked out an arrangement with the Department of Agriculture Library and the Army Medical Library, recognizing these institutions as the national libraries in the fields of technical agriculture and clinical medicine, respectively.

Creation of two small divisions, one dealing with European affairs and the other with the Slavic countries, and the addition of a Korean specialist to the staff of the Orientalia Division strengthened the Library's area studies programs. Evans expanded the cultural role of the Library by the creation of a Folklore Section in the Music Division, the initiation of a series of recordings of distinguished poets and authors reading their works, arranging for the public broadcast of the Library's concerts, and encouraging a broader and more imaginative exhibits program. Of special note in the last category was the series of exhibits honoring important anniversaries in the history of the states. Other reference services encouraged by Evans were various cooperative bibliographic projects, primarily in support of scientific research, and the publication of numerous guides on specific subjects and collections. The *Catalogue of the Library of Thomas Jefferson,* edited by E. Millicent Sowerby, was prepared during this period.

A listing of all the activities and achievements of the Library of Congress during the Evans years would be a lengthy task. Even a cursory perusal of the annual reports of the Librarian of Congress from 1945 to 1953 reveals that this was a period, perhaps unparalleled in the Library's history, of enormous vitality and accomplishment. Verner Clapp, Evans' Chief Assistant Librarian, noted, "There is no doubt that it was the personality of the Librarian that set the pace of this pressure for accomplishment. His own long hours and merciless schedule were known to all." [17] Evans was untiring in his efforts to make the Library of Congress an exciting place at which to work as well as to exploit its full potential in serving its various constituencies. He expected the staff to be equally enthusiastic.

Evans took special pride in his efforts to encourage the staff and include them as much as possible in the management process. He was a firm believer in "democratic participation." Writing as guest columnist in a local newspaper, Evans stressed the importance of good morale in achieving high productivity and enunciated the three principles on which he operated:

First, the various members of the staff of an organization . . . must be made to feel that there is within the group an equality of treatment on the basis of merit for all the members of the group.

There must be no discrimination unrelated to the merits of a person's performance and his attitude based upon differences of sex, or of race, or of religion.

The second great principle is that all members of the group, with variations of degree in terms of differences of ability and assignment, should be invited to participate in some appropriate way in the process of deciding . . . upon the goals of the staff activities, upon the major policies of organization and procedure, and upon the major policies to be followed in attempting to reach the established goals. . . .

In my opinion there is also a third, most important, basis of staff morale. This is an adequate system of communication of information to the staff members.[18]

As MacLeish's chief assistant he originated the practice of regular meetings with department directors and other officers. Later, as Librarian, he expanded this concept by including staff members at all levels in the consultation process. The staff had never before been so involved in advisory groups, luncheons, and professional associations as they were in the Evans years. The Librarian himself kept the staff constantly informed of his official activities by detailed accounts in the weekly *Information Bulletin*. The Library was cited by the Federal Personnel Council in 1952 as a paradigm for government agencies in the application of democratic principles to administrative practices.

Evans approached with equal energy President Truman's second directive, to increase the Library's service to the "little libraries all over the country." Not only by expanding the Library's cooperative efforts and consulting on a regular basis with library representatives but also by touring the country explaining the Library's activities and services did Evans seek to meet this objective. In 1949 he told the Texas Friends of Libraries, "One of my chief goals since I came to the Library of Congress has been to strengthen and increase the services it jointly performs with libraries throughout the country. . . . I conceive the relationship of the Library of Congress to the public libraries of America as a relationship of partners."[19]

Evans, of course, was sincere in his commitment to the strengthening of libraries throughout the nation but he also realized that the Library of Congress, because of its limited resources, could not provide all the services on a nationwide basis that perhaps it should. He strengthened those services of the Library of Congress on which the American library community had come to rely, such as the card distribution program and the National Union Catalog. But he also encouraged the growth of specialized collections in individual libraries and the expansion of regional programs, and he urged local libraries not to rely on the government to build federal branch libraries or establish interagency loan centers supported by federal funds. He believed the federal government should do much more for the nation's libraries, but his own experiences with Congress had chastened him to the realization that it might be wiser to rely on local initiative.[20]

Although not a librarian by education, Evans was assiduous in his attention to national library activities. The American Library Association, which had staunchly and unsuccessfully opposed the appointment of his predecessor, was reluctant to stand against Evans. The fact that he had been appointed from the ranks of the staff—Spofford had been the only other Librarian with prior experience in the institution—might have helped assuage their fears. In any case, Evans was in frequent demand as a speaker before various library groups and he was always a useful ally in the fight for common goals.

Librarianship and libraries were not the only topics of concern to Evans. He toured the country tirelessly and wrote numerous articles forcefully stating his views on education, censorship, McCarthyism, and international cooperation. If one common theme or guiding philosophy can be found throughout Evans' expressions it was his belief in the free flow of ideas, a concept seriously threatened in the mid-20th century. Typical of his concerns were the words Evans wrote in 1949:

We have lived in an age when, in the mouths of vicious, perverse and cunning men, false words corrupted and degraded and destroyed. It is a duty, perhaps, indeed, the principal duty of this generation to restore the dignity, the confidence, the influence, the benignity of words. Unless we can, we shall be confronted with intellectual and moral famine. Starved minds and starved spirits breed totalitarianism and madness just as bitterly and suddenly and inexorably as do hungry stomachs. Minds can atrophy.[21]

Luther Evans, chairman of the U.S. National Commission for Unesco, goes over the annual meeting agenda with Eleanor Roosevelt at the second session, October 3, 1952, in Washington. Congress created the commission to advise government officials on United Nations activities. United Press photograph. LC–USZ62–58937

And, in 1951, speaking to librarians in California on the American situation:

> The most serious threat to free libraries at home is the threat of censorship. . . . [The censors] are willing to deny the whole concept of freedom in order to strike a blow against ideas which they find unwholesome. Such people are generally rather emotional and not very well led and it is possible, usually, to thwart them with a clear and firm statement and the courageous maintenance of principle. This we must do if we are serious about the relation of free libraries to a free world.[22]

It was the achievement of international understanding, however, that was to significantly attract his attention. From his early interest in the League of Nations to his support as Librarian of Congress of international cooperative effort, he never lost interest in international affairs. In November 1945 MacLeish, as assistant secretary of state, asked Evans to be a member of the United States delegation to the London conference which established the United Nations Educational, Scientific and Cultural Organization as an important component of the fledgling United Nations structure. After this organization was officially created, Evans served in various capacities as delegate to the General Conference, member of the Executive Board, and member and chairman of the United States National Commission for Unesco. As head of the Library of

Congress, Evans involved the staff in the new organization's activities, particularly in relation to the problems of standardization of bibliographical controls and the development of the Universal Copyright Convention. In addition, he devoted more and more of his time to addressing American audiences encouraging them to support Unesco and its programs for peace.

In the early 1950's, Evans was devoting almost as much attention to Unesco matters as he was to those of the Library of Congress. He believed that the programs and purposes of the two institutions paralleled each other in so many mutually beneficial ways that there was no serious conflict of interest. But there was a conflict in the amount of time he could spend on the two activities. This problem came out into the open during the House Appropriations Committee's budget hearings in March of 1952 when Evans was attending a Unesco executive board meeting in Paris. Two members of the committee, Christopher C. McGrath of New York and Walt Horan of Washington, suggested that Evans "get another job some place." Horan bluntly stated, "He is not running the Library. Perhaps he should be associated with the State Department." Although Clapp, who was representing the Library at the hearings, strongly defended Evans as a man who worked 18 hours a day and weekends and kept in constant touch with the Library during his absences, some Congressmen were never completely convinced that Evans was effectively fulfilling his responsibilities on Capitol Hill.[23]

It did not come as a total surprise 15 months after the McGrath-Horan attacks when Evans decided to devote his full energies to the cause of Unesco. On July 1, 1953, at an extraordinary session of the General Conference, he was elected as the third director-general of Unesco and tendered his resignation to President Eisenhower to be effective July 5.

Evans' term as director-general from 1953 to 1958 came at a critical point in Unesco's development. He had been preceded by two eminent personalities, Julian Huxley, British scientist and intellectual, and Jaime Torres Bodet, Mexican diplomat, educator, and writer. Although both these men lent their great personal prestige to the development of the organization and significantly laid its ideological foundation, neither of them was particularly effective at management and coordination. So, Evans' experience of nearly 20 years as a professional administrator weighed heavily in favor of his appointment even though there was strong opposition to him as an American citizen. At that time Americans headed four of the other specialized United Nations agencies and many member states feared the direction of United States policies during the McCarthy period.

Evans' years as director-general were marked by efficient administration, close personal liaison with the member states, and the launching of several major programs. Although no less committed to the ideals of Unesco than his predecessors, he was less ambitious in his proposals and stressed long-range needs rather than dramatic crash programs. In his presentation speech before the UN General Assembly he expressed his approach, emphasizing a new focus on indirect action:

> It is fair to say that . . . Unesco's budget does not allow it to abolish illiteracy everywhere or to make the benefits of science or of culture available to all people by direct means. Some direct action we can take as, for example, when we train groups of selected fundamental education workers to train larger groups in their own countries . . . but our main line of action consists in facilitating and stimulating government action by our member States. . . .[24]

Evans applied many of the same techniques of administration which had proved successful at the Library of Congress. He encouraged democratic participation at both the headquarters level and through the use of an elaborate structure of outside advisory committees and professional consultants. But working with an international staff presented new kinds of difficulties.

Throughout his administration he was confronted with the need to balance the rights of the American members of the Unesco staff with the loyalty procedures and orders issued from Washington. He had to decide which qualities were most important in the organization's personnel. Reviewing in 1963 some of the management problems of Unesco, he stated:

> It is my view that Westerners have grossly exaggerated the priorities deserved by efficiency, good organization, clear procedures, clear definitions of authority, limited span of control, and similar criteria. More emphasis should be given to the important target; namely, achieving a situation as to personnel that permits the right attitudes and ideas to govern the operations. At the stage it had reached ten years ago, what Unesco really needed was a good representation in its work of the different ideas, attitudes, and cultural approaches existent in the member states.

. . . a wide representation of the inefficient and under-developed peoples in the secretariat is absolutely essential to the good of the Organization.[25]

A significant innovation in Unesco's programs under Evans was agreement to the concept of major projects. Involving a number of countries and various disciplines and extending over many years, these projects differed significantly from the more traditional programs of the agency. In 1957 work began on three major projects—arid zone scientific research, Latin American rural education, and East-West cultural exchange.

Other achievements of Unesco from 1953 to 1958 were the 1956 agreement on the protection of cultural property in the event of war; the addition of a new area of concern—the peaceful uses of atomic energy; closer cooperation with other UN agency projects, such as the Expanded Program of Technical Assistance; the integration of the Soviet Union into the organization's activities; and the establishment of the Universal Copyright Convention.[26] Evans took special pride in the last accomplishment, for he had long worked for its creation as a member of the United States National Commission for Unesco.

In his post-Unesco years, Evans has continued to lend his expertise and exuberance to numerous projects and organizations concerned with international peace, libraries, and education. Immediately after returning from Paris he attempted to spend a few years of relaxation in Texas, but he was soon called upon to serve as a consultant for the international studies program at his alma mater in Austin. In 1959 he became director of a study of federal department libraries for the Brookings Institution. The final report of the study[27] recommended among other things the transfer of the Library of Congress, except for the Legislative Reference Service, to the executive branch and the establishment of a Federal Library Council. Only the latter has become a reality, in the form of the Federal Library Committee, which works toward

Luther Evans, director-general of Unesco from 1953 to 1958, presents a gift of $24,000 to John B. Coulter, agent-general of the UN Korean Reconstruction Agency, at a ceremony on October 12, 1954, at the UN Headquarters in New York. Unesco and the UN Women's Guild collected these funds to establish a children's ward in Korea for war casualties. Also present at the ceremony were, back row, left to right: Benjamin Cohen, assistant secretary-general of the United Nations, in charge of public information, Mrs. Honorio Roight, president of the UN Women's Guild, and Ben C. Limb, permanent observer of Korea to the United Nations. Courtesy of the United Nations.

improved coordination and planning among the libraries of the federal government.

After directing another project—this one concerning the educational implications of automation for the National Education Association—Evans returned to academia in 1962 as the director of the international and legal collections at Columbia University. He devoted much of his attention there to the development of a new library serving the School of International Affairs and retired in 1971

from his position as director of the international collections. Retirement is hardly the correct word for Luther Evans' current status. As president of World Federalists U.S.A. and an active participant in such groups as U.S. People for the United Nations and the U.S. Committee for Refugees, he is still striving to promote peace and international goodwill. He will not be content until he is assured that the United States has found its proper place in "the new world."

NOTES

1 Luther H. Evans, *The Virgin Islands, From Naval Base to New Deal* (Ann Arbor: J. W. Edwards, 1945).

2 Verner Clapp, "Luther H. Evans," *Library Journal* 90 (September 1, 1965): 3386. This article, which is a slightly revised version of one which appeared in *Bulletin of Bibliography* 24 (September-December 1964): 97–103, is a concise, sympathetic account of Evans' career.

3 William F. McDonald, *Federal Relief Administration and the Arts* (Columbus: Ohio State University Press, 1969), p. 759. Much of the account of the Historical Records Survey and Evans' directorship is taken from this work, pp. 751–828.

4 Ibid., p. 765.

5 Luther H. Evans, "The Historical Records Survey," *Pennsylvania Federation of Historical Societies Year Book,* 1938, p. 30.

6 *Sunday Star* (Washington, D.C.), December 2, 1945.

7 U.S., Library of Congress, *Annual Report of the Librarian of Congress* (hereafter cited as *ARLC*), 1946, p. 233. The full text of the justification is reproduced as Appendix I, pp. 307–447.

8 The full text of the Planning Committee report appears as Appendix I, *ARLC,* 1947, pp. 101–8.

9 Evans to John C. L. Andreassen, June 17, 1945, Library of Congress Archives. Andreassen worked under Evans for the Historical Records Survey, later served in the United Nations Relief and Rehabilitation Administration (UNRRA), and came to the Library in 1946. In 1947 he was appointed director of the Department of Administrative Services.

10 *Sunday Star* (Washington, D.C.), December 2, 1945.

11 Luther H. Evans, "Research Libraries in the War Period, 1939–45," *Library Quarterly* 17 (October 1947): 241–62.

12 Ibid., p. 247.

13 For a delightful account of the Alice episode, see Luther H. Evans, "Return of Alice's Adventures Under Ground," *Columbia Library Columns* 15 (November 1965): 29–35.

14 Luther H. Evans, "Problems Facing the Library of Congress," *Special Libraries* 36 (December 1945): 469.

15 Luther H. Evans, "Suggestions for a Program of Library Cooperation" (based on an address given before the Inter-American Library Conference, Pan American Union, Washington, D.C., March 30, 1946), p. 23.

16 Luther H. Evans, "The Library of Congress as the National Library of Science," *Scientific Monthly* 66 (May 1948): 411.

17 Clapp, "Luther H. Evans," p. 3388.

18 *Times-Herald* (Washington, D.C.), September 3, 1952.

19 Luther H. Evans, "The Case for Libraries in the Southwest," in Texas Library Association, *News Notes,* 25 (July 1949): 101.

20 A good exposition of Evans' thoughts on the relationship between libraries and the federal government can be found in University of Pennsylvania Library, *Changing Patterns of Scholarship and the Future of Research Libraries* (Philadelphia: University of Pennsylvania Press, 1951), pp. 36–40.

21 Luther H. Evans, "Words and Works," *Association of American Colleges Bulletin* 35 (October 1949): 434.

22 Luther H. Evans, "Free Libraries and a Free World," in *A Symposium in Public Librarianship* (Berkeley: University of California School of Librarianship, 1952), p. 44.

23 For an account of the McGrath-Horan criticism, see *Times-Herald* (Washington, D.C.), March 31, 1952.

24 United Nations, General Assembly, *Official Records,* 8th Session, Plenary Meetings, 451st Meeting, October 5, 1953, p. 224.

25 Luther H. Evans, "Some Management Problems of Unesco," *International Organization* 17 (winter 1963): 87–88.

26 For discussions of Evans' years as director-general of Unesco, see Walter H. C. Laves and Charles A. Thomson, *Unesco; Purposes, Progress, Prospects* (Bloomington: Indiana University Press, 1957), pp. 301–11; and T. V. Sathyamurthy, *The Politics of International Cooperation; Contrasting Concepts of U.N.E.S.C.O.* (Geneva: Librairie Droz, 1964), pp. 122–32.

27 Luther H. Evans et al., *Federal Department Libraries* (Washington: Brookings Institution, 1963).

Lawrence Quincy Mumford

Twenty Years of Progress

by Benjamin E. Powell

Monday, September 12, 1921, dawned clear and bright in Pitt County, N.C., as Lawrence Quincy Mumford prepared to leave the village of Hanrahan and his father's farm for Durham and Trinity College. Most of the tobacco was in, but the cotton and corn remained to be harvested. Normally, Quincy picked cotton and pulled corn in afternoons after school and on Saturdays, so the farm would be short one hand for the fall harvest, and Grifton High School would be without its most gifted orator and debater. As Mumford climbed aboard the Norfolk and Southern passenger train in Greenville, the county seat, with a tuition scholarship to Trinity in one pocket and his latest high school medals in the other, his thoughts and hopes for the future did not include having his name engraved in stone in Washington as the eleventh Librarian of Congress. He was following his brother Grover, who was graduated the previous year, to the small Methodist College which would shortly become Duke University.[1] His immediate goal was receiving a college education in preparation for a teaching position; a career in law might come later.

Changing to the Southern Railroad in Raleigh, the state capital, Mumford arrived in Durham late that afternoon. Durham, then a town of about 20,000 inhabitants, was a major tobacco manufacturing center. The streetcar, crowded with freshmen and returning upperclassmen, took Mumford along Main Street from the station to the college and passed the manufacturing plant and storage warehouses of the Liggett & Myers Tobacco Company. From the open windows of the plant drifted the odor of tobacco being processed, a sweet redolence not unlike the aroma from a barn of curing Pitt County tobacco. In the 1920's tobacco curing required constant attention day and night, and Quincy took his turn staying all night at the barn to ensure that the proper temperature was maintained. Since the duties never completely occupied the attendant's time, frequently in the evenings friends would drop by for a game of cards, banjo strumming and singing, or a neighborly visit. As the car rocked along between the complex of buildings made famous by Chesterfield cigarettes, Quincy must have

L. Quincy Mumford in his tenth year as Librarian of Congress. Photograph courtesy of Harris and Ewing.

Benjamin E. Powell is university librarian emeritus of Duke University.

The Phi Beta Kappa group in Mumford's senior year at Duke University, from The Chanticleer *of 1925. Julian P. Boyd, professor of history at Princeton University and editor of the* Papers of Thomas Jefferson, *appears on the left, the third from the top. He is currently serving on the Library of Congress American Revolution Bicentennial Program Advisory Committee.*

remembered the old tobacco barn with a touch of homesickness.

Born in Hanrahan in Pitt County, N.C., on December 11, 1903, Lawrence Quincy Mumford was one of 10 children of Jacob Edward and Emma Luvenia Stocks Mumford.[2] In the coastal plain region of North Carolina, Pitt County has long been a prosperous farming area where cotton, corn, and tobacco are the principal crops. Jacob Mumford was a successful tobacco farmer who depended heavily upon his family to help cultivate and harvest the crops. Although each son's departure for college reduced his work force, he shared his wife's determination that every child in the family who wished a college education should be allowed to have it. Quincy worked regularly on the farm when school was not in session, but during slack periods—rainy days and after the crops were "laid by"—he assisted

at the Hanrahan post office, which was run by his sister and brother-in-law in one of the two stores in the crossroads village.

Until Mumford went to high school in Grifton, three miles away, he attended a one-room—later two-room—school in Hanrahan. Neither the elementary school nor the high school had a library, and the nearest public library was 75 miles away in Raleigh. The reading material available to him, therefore, was generally limited to school texts. Not until he enrolled in Trinity College did he have access to many books. However, material for debates and orations was available in the high school or through the extension division of the University of North Carolina. Quincy exploited these sources and became an outstanding debater and orator in Grifton High School, where he won school and district honors as well as the praise of his teachers and peers. He played baseball in high school and later developed a passable game of tennis. A left-hander all the way, he could have capitalized more upon his port-side delivery but chose instead to participate in other extracurricular activities as he maintained a brilliant academic record.[3]

At Trinity, where literary societies still played large roles in the academic and social life of the campus, new male students were expected to visit each of the two societies on the first two Saturday nights of the school term. Those wishing to join a society then indicated a choice between Columbia and Hesperia. Mumford joined the Hesperian Society to which his older brother had belonged and immediately entered into its activities. He participated in three debates his freshman year, winning the coveted Freshman Debater's Medal, three his sophomore year, and two during his junior year. He began to appear more frequently as an extemporaneous speaker his last two years, speaking nine times on topics ranging from "How I Profit From My Swimming Lessons" to "Reaction and Peace." The frequency and quality of his activity in the society's programs persuaded the Hesperians to award him the Hugh Lyon Carr Medal for excellence in public speaking and debating in his senior year. Mumford's leadership in the society was not confined to debating and public speaking. During his four undergraduate years he served as secretary, historian, vice president, and president and represented Hesperia on the board of the *Chronicle,* the student newspaper, which in those days was directed by the two societies.[4] His proclivity for entertaining, which enlivened social gatherings at conferences of librarians through the years, was commented upon in the *Chronicle* of April 4, 1925, after he spoke on the solemn topic of "Honesty," as one of several extemporaneous speakers to perform at a meeting of the Hesperian Society. Only his use of "scandalous illustrations," the reporter wrote, prevented the session from putting the members to sleep.

Mumford's activities and honors outside the society, except for his participation in dramatics, were associated mainly with scholarship. Before graduating magna cum laude in 1925, he won freshman and sophomore honors, sophomore and junior scholarships, and membership in the Physics Club and 9019, an honorary scholastic society open to rising juniors in the university. He was among 10 members of his class elected to Phi Beta Kappa at the end of three years. In his senior year he became a member of the Bachelors Club, a local social fraternity whose roster included several undergraduates distinguished for leadership in student activities, scholarship, and athletics. The college lacked a highly developed drama department, but a talented volunteer director enabled a few plays to be presented each year. The opportunity for student participation, therefore, was limited. Quincy tried out occasionally and in his senior year was selected to play the roles of the marquis de Mirepoix in *Monsieur Beaucaire* and Bellerese in a widely acclaimed production of *Cyrano de Bergerac*.[5]

Creation of the Duke Endowment by James Buchanan Duke in December 1924 with a gift of $80 million led to the establishment of Duke University around the 86-year-old college. New schools of theology, medicine, forestry, and engineering and the formal organization of a graduate school demanded that the college library of 75,000 volumes be strengthened as expeditiously as possible. Library development envisioned growth of staff as well as teaching and research materials. Mumford, who had worked in the library for three years as a student assistant, was encouraged to accept a full-time position in the library while studying for a master's degree. He had not yet considered librarianship as a possible career, but during the next year he learned much about the opportunities for bright young men in university librarianship from Louis T. Ibbotson, assistant librarian, who recently had received a degree from Columbia University's School of Library Service. He could scarcely refuse the appointment, since it would enable him to earn a master's degree, thus improving his opportunity for a teaching position—his goal when he entered college—while allowing him to decide whether he wished to enter librarianship. For his master's study, which could have been pursued in education, English, or physics, he chose English. In the spring of 1928 Mumford presented his completed thesis entitled "Recognition and Discovery in the Comedies of Shakespeare."[6]

In the fall of the same year, Mumford had completed arrangements to enter the School of Library Service at Columbia University. While he made no commitment to return to Duke upon completion of his studies, he was assured a position, and his colleagues hoped he would return. Actually, Mumford

This illustration of the Bachelors' Club appeared in 1926 in The Chanticleer, *during Mumford's first year in graduate school.*

debated with himself throughout the summer whether to choose librarianship as a career. Even the thought of teaching had been discarded for the moment. Only a few days before leaving for Columbia he conferred with tobacco officials about a position in one of the local plants or perhaps in a plant abroad. College acquaintances employed in the industry were then in Turkey, where much of the tobacco indispensable for the blends was grown. The requirement that employees agree to remain overseas for a stipulated period probably discouraged him from pursuing a career in tobacco. So, in September 1928 he joined a group of young men and women—several of whom were to achieve distinction in librarianship—in East Hall, the small red brick building which then served as the administrative center for the School of Library Service. He worked part-time in the school library, mostly nights and weekends, minding the desk, charging out books, shelving books, and the like. Some of his own assignments could be completed while on duty.

Years at the New York Public Library, 1929–45

Mumford was strongly attracted by New York City and the New York Public Library. In the spring of 1929 he accepted an offer from Keyes Metcalf to join the staff at Fifth Avenue and 42d Street. He began, as have so many distinguished librarians through the years, as a reference assistant in the General Information Division on the third floor. For two years he answered questions across the desk and by phone, assisted with use of the card catalog, and directed patrons to information elsewhere in the library. No other library post in this country provides the beginning professional librarian wider knowledge of the kinds of information scholars, research workers, and students seek or greater familiarity with a broad range of sources of information. Mumford's decision to work for the New York Public Library remained a happy one for him and the library, and increasingly he shared responsibility for the administration of that great institution during his 16-year tenure.[7]

Shortly after he joined the staff, Quincy met Permelia Catherine Stevens, a children's librarian in the NYPL system. They were married on October 4, 1930. Pam, who is remembered fondly by many librarians and acquaintances of the Mumfords as a friendly and gracious hostess, died in 1961. Their only child, Kathryn, attended the University of Michigan and Mt. Holyoke College; she is now Mrs. Lawrence Deane. Later, on November 28, 1969, Quincy married Mrs. Betsy Perrin Fox.

At Mumford's confirmation hearing in the Senate, Metcalf said that he had met Mumford more than 25 years before when Mumford was studying at Columbia and Metcalf was in charge of the central building of the New York Public Library.

> I offered him his first position after he completed his training, and he started out by doing general reference work at the library's information desk. The quality of his work was such that, 4 years later when a general administrative assistant was needed in the office, Mumford was selected. Three years later when the largest and most complex division of the library, the catalog division, needed a new chief, he was chosen. . . . In both positions, Mr. Mumford's success was outstanding. . . . in 1940, I was a member of a group that was called in to advise the Librarian of Congress on the Library's reorganization. We arranged to have Mumford lent for a year . . . to the Library of Congress to reorganize the processing department, the largest, and again the most complex, single department in this Library. He did this difficult and intricate job with the most conspicuous success and then went back to New York where, in 1943, he became coordinator of the general public services in the big building at 42d Street and Fifth Avenue.
>
> In a quiet way he is a man of forcefulness who gets things done. I do not hesitate to recommend him wholeheartedly for the position for which he has been nominated by the President.[8]

Metcalf also said he considered Mumford the best judge of people he had ever known. His admiration and respect for Mumford's ability were shared by his distinguished colleagues Harry M. Lydenberg and Paul North Rice, both of whom had served as head of the Reference Division of the New York Public Library and president of the American Library Association.

In the quiet, effective manner that characterized Mumford throughout his professional career, he assumed successively the positions noted by Metcalf. His experience in the nerve center of the library, the Main Information Desk, equipped him admirably for participating in formulation of policy for administering the library and directing the activities of such departments as Cataloging and Preparations, both closely associated with user access to materials. It was his aim, he said, "to see that readers obtained the assistance and information which they desire, and to emphasize constantly the importance of courteous service."[9]

As chief of Preparations, Mumford organized procedures and devised methods of expediting the hundreds of thousands of publications in all languages that flowed into the library. The director of such a program must understand how much information the user needs for each title in the public catalog and the maximum the library can afford to provide, while making materials available expeditiously and at low cost. Some scholarly and experienced catalogers want the users' finding list to be a complete bibliographical record, and a supervisor who can direct changes requiring abandonment of a long-standing philosophy must have the respect and confidence of his staff. Mumford's sound knowledge of all aspects of acquisitions and cataloging and his demonstrated concern about staff problems enabled him to convince his colleagues of the practicality and necessity of the changes he proposed. As a consequence, processing procedures were simplified and improved, resulting in substantially increased production and economies in time and money.

During 1943 and 1944 Mumford served the New York Public Library as coordinator of the general services divisions, with responsibility for seeing that services were maintained at a high level notwithstanding wartime inroads upon the staff. The library was giving extensive assistance to the armed forces and other governmental agencies, and it was imperative that, despite the shortage of manpower, there be no breakdown in assistance to the public. During this period Mumford also assisted in the planning of an extension to the main building to provide more space for users and books.

Mumford's varied experience in New York was considerably strengthened and extended from September 1940 to August 1941, when he took a leave of absence to reorganize and coordinate the processing divisions of the Library of Congress shortly after the end of Herbert Putnam's 40-year term as Librarian. Despite Putnam's distinguished leadership, the organization and procedures of the Library needed overhauling. Not only was the span of control excessive, with 34 division officers reporting directly to the Librarian, but about 1.5 million of the estimated collection of 5.8 million volumes and pamphlets in the Library had not been fully processed and were not represented in the Main Catalog.[10] Archibald MacLeish's advisers singled out Quincy Mumford as librarianship's ablest man in the area of cataloging and processing.

During this period, Mumford, with the cooperation and support of the administration and the entire staff of the Library of Congress, succeeded in revising the processing methods and procedures and streamlining the flow of work, In effecting the recommended reorganization, the capabilities of hundreds of staff members had to be reevaluated to fit them into positions where they could be most effective. Among the results were 300 appointments and promotions and a substantial increase in the number of volumes processed.[11] In the Librarian's 1941 annual report, Archibald MacLeish said of these recommended changes: "Mr. Mumford . . . has effected a minor—perhaps a major—miracle in the Processing Department, where he has not only administered the reorganization of the divisions involved, but directed as well the renovation and improvement of many of the basic technical procedures." [12]

Mumford reported that the Processing Department was reorganized to bring into it all divisions of the Library that previously had been engaged in processing books, pamphlets, and other materials and distributing printed cards. To move toward the objective of processing adequately and expeditiously as much as possible, new procedures for invoices and vouchers were adopted, a central serials file was created for recording at one point all incoming serials, and a central process file containing a record of all books on order or in the catalog process was established. Administration of cataloging was reorganized to abandon the two divisions of cataloging and classification in favor of three: Descriptive Cataloging, Subject Cataloging, and Catalog Preparation and Maintenance. The functions of cataloging that previously had rested in the Card Division were transferred to Cataloging.[13]

Service at the Cleveland Public Library, 1945–54

As the trustees of the Cleveland Public Library began to search for an assistant director who might succeed Director Clarence Metcalf upon his retirement a few years hence, they found Mumford to be a logical candidate. There were few men of his stature whose experience encompassed all aspects of administration in a major research library: information and reference, acquisition and cataloging, work with personnel, planning, and participation in high-level decisions.

During Mumford's nine years in Cleveland, the budget of the library was increased 92 percent. As assistant director, one of his first responsibilities was to study the processing activities which were dispersed among four departments. He was at home with such problems, since he had wrestled successfully with similar challenges not only at New York Public and the Library of Congress but also at Columbia University and the Army Medical Library. From the beginning he assisted in preparing the overall budget and generally was responsible for presenting it to the County Budget Commission.

Upon Mumford's appointment as director of the Cleveland Public Library, his thoughts and philosophy concerning the function of a great public research library were expressed in the November 7, 1950, issue of the *Cleveland News:* "The first function should be as a reliable center of information and an educational agency. It must supplement schools . . . [and] provide a means of learning from the cradle to the grave." The library's responsibility is "to acquaint people with the library and to take the library to them. We must find more and more ways to do the latter. If we find television can be used to help sell the library, I am for it." While promoting the kind of service the library had given over the years, Mumford hoped to publicize the library and its facilities on some kind of television program which would describe books as important to satisfactory living.[14]

Describing the new director as dapper and neatly groomed, the *News* reported on November 8: "The Cleveland Public Library seems assured of continuing good performance and progress with [the] appointment of L. Quincy Mumford. The assistant director, who came here five years ago, is intimately acquainted with the administrative problems of this nationally-known institution, and is a man with a positive concept of the library system's importance."

Although the library's budget was increased during Mumford's administration, funds did not permit expansion of the main library or construction of an annex for housing little-used books and some non-public services for which plans had been prepared by the director and his staff. Available funds were used, however, for improving salary schedules to meet changing conditions. Since these adjustments were not sufficient to satisfy all of the director's recommendations, Mumford compensated for this to some degree by improving vacation and sick leave benefits and by allowing the staff more input in policy at the advisory level. Meanwhile, services were ex-

tensively publicized through television, and the lending of materials was increased by the establishment of a new branch and the institution of two large bookmobiles. The television programs initiated in 1951, estimated to reach an audience of 60,000 persons, were successful in their purpose, which was "to acquaint the community more fully with the resources of the library and to carry educational content to viewers on a variety of subjects within the framework of books." [15] Mumford regarded the improvement of the financial status of the library, in which his ability to deal with appropriating bodies played a large part, his rapport with the board of trustees, the increases in staff salaries, his relationship with the union, the extension of services through branches and bookmobiles, the inauguration of a film circuit and a new charging system, and the general growth in public awareness of the library as some of his major accomplishments at Cleveland.

Despite the impact of the early years of inflation which followed World War II, Mumford was administering the Cleveland Public Library with the kind of leadership provided by two of his predecessors, William Howard Brett and Linda Eastman, when he was nominated for the post of Librarian of Congress in 1954. His professional interests and participation in the life of the city were evidence of the rapport he shared with professional colleagues and his acceptance by the community at large. He was elected president of the Cleveland Library Club, 1946–47, the Ohio Library Association, 1947–48, the Library Committee of the Ohio Post-war Planning Commission, 1947–48, and the Executive Committee of the Cleveland Occupational Planning Commission, 1950–51. Other memberships which brought him in close association with the business and social leadership of the city included the Chamber of Commerce, the Cheshire Cheese Club, the Mid-Day Club, the Cleveland City Club, and the Torch Club.[16]

During his years in Cleveland, Mumford's activities and responsibilities in the American Library Association, which he joined in 1932, were increased as he assumed the chairmanship of such committees as Photographic Reproduction of Library Materials (1944–46) and Federal Relations (1950–52) and the Audiovisual Board (1952–53). When ALA held its annual conference in Cleveland in 1950, Mumford acted as the local chairman. Meanwhile he had been a director of the Film Council of America and the Great Books Foundation. These activities, together with his articles in professional journals and his participation in national and regional conferences, brought him to the attention of the nominating committee of ALA and to the presidency of the association in 1954–55.

Mumford's election to the presidency of the association over Francis St. John, the director of the Brooklyn Public Library, who appeared to be favored in the race, indicated the respect for him that existed at all levels in the profession. St. John had been more frequently in the limelight and had created a favorable image, but Quincy's name was familiar to the multitude of members engaged in cataloging and acquisition and to reference librarians and public library administrators, all of whom knew of his solid contributions in New York, Washington, and Cleveland. As president of the association, Mumford emphasized the role of the library in education and the stimulus ALA should give libraries and librarians in promoting reading and learning.

Library of Congress, 1954–74

Quincy Mumford was the first professionally trained librarian to become Librarian of Congress. Nominated by President Eisenhower on April 22, 1954, and confirmed by the Senate on July 29, he was sworn in and assumed his duties on September 1, two months after accepting the gavel as president of the American Library Association. Mumford followed Librarians Luther H. Evans, 1945–53, Archibald MacLeish, 1939–44, and Herbert Putnam, who directed the Library with a tight rein from 1899 to 1939.

Congress was proud of the Library and thought of it as its own. Those appointed to administer the Library were expected to be mindful of that special relationship and to be willing to give the highest priority to the needs of Congress. Putnam enjoyed an easy rapport with Congress until his last decade in office, but neither MacLeish nor Evans made special efforts to cultivate friendly relationships. Moreover, their outside activities diverted much of their time from Library of Congress business. MacLeish, who had been opposed by professional librarians but quickly accepted by them after assuming office, was delegated increasingly by President Roosevelt to represent him in affairs of state: first

as director of the Office of Facts and Figures, then as assistant director of the Office of War Information, and later as representative to the early meetings of Unesco. When finally he was named assistant secretary of state, he resigned the librarianship. Evans, who had been Chief Assistant Librarian under MacLeish, likewise was increasingly absent from his office and Washington on matters having no immediate relationship to the Library. He resigned in 1953 to become director-general of Unesco. As a consequence, relations between the Library and Congress deteriorated until finally support for the Library suffered.

Congress wanted Evans' successor to be more responsive to its needs and to devote his full time to his duties. That was apparent in the questions asked Mumford in his appearance before the Senate Rules and Administration Committee for confirmation hearings. One of the questions was, ". . . if you found that the Library of Congress was neglecting its primary duty—that for which it was established—that of service to the Congress, and was going into other fields to the detriment of Congress, you would be willing to correct that situation?" [17]

Mumford understood from the beginning that one immediate aspect of his responsibility as Librarian of Congress was to restore the confidence of Congress in the Library and its administrators. His responses satisfied the committee, and published expressions concerning his appointment were favorable. He was approved by librarians and spokesmen for the world of books and publishing. The Ohio delegation to Congress recommended him strongly. Representative Frances P. Bolton of Ohio said of him:

L. Quincy Mumford [is] a man of great capacity and experience. We in Cleveland are regretting our loss. But we rejoice that in this larger service he will go from strength to strength.

There is no doubt but there is need of a very real housecleaning in the Library of Congress . . . the Library has fallen into patterns of inefficient and unwise operations. Good organization and economic use of staff will be welcomed by all who use its facilities.[18]

Representative Bolton made the above remarks while presenting for inclusion in the *Congressional Record* an editorial from *Publishers' Weekly* praising the selection of Mumford for the post:

The functions and influence of the library have been steadily broadened in this century. . . . This broadened conception of the functions of the library which are so firmly imbedded in the L.C. practice came under question when Congress recently opposed the requested appropriations for the library. The review of the facts and functions of the library which this aroused gave opportunity for vigorous restatements of what the country has come to expect of its national library.

Quincy Mumford is well versed in the best traditions of the American library and can be relied on to maintain and extend further the broad usefulness of the institution he is to direct. . . . The thousands of librarians who sustain the standards of professional American librarianship have put their stamp of approval on his competence and vision by electing him president of the American Library Association.[19]

Librarians generally favored Mumford. Nevertheless, among the leadership of the Association of Research Libraries, consisting predominantly of directors of university libraries, there was a wait-and-see attitude. Mumford was not a university librarian, and the Cleveland Public Library was not a member of their association, so he was not well known to the university group. The Library of Congress assumed a leadership role under MacLeish and Evans in attempting to resolve problems of concern to research libraries. They were able to make commitments which seemed to be natural responsibilities of the national library but which would have been beyond the capabilities of a university library. Leaders of ARL were apprehensive that Mumford might be cautious about offering the facilities and the influence of the Library of Congress in national and international librarianship to head up new bibliographical and acquisition projects of interest to all the nation's libraries.

It appeared to participants that there was indeed less Library of Congress leadership in the discussions at ARL meetings after Mumford's confirmation. He seldom took the floor to commit the Library or to encourage creating projects that could not develop effectively without its active involvement. Nevertheless, a backward look at the period 1954–74 reveals that the Library of Congress did continue to provide much of the kind of leadership and support that had characterized earlier years. The principal differences, apparently, were that Mumford seldom made commitments without discussing their implications with his associates, and this generally was done back in Washington with the pertinent facts before them.

The attitude of Congress toward the Library was apparent in the very first budget hearing after Mumford's appointment was announced. Representative Walter Horan, chairman of the House Subcommittee on Appropriations, interrupted the hearings on May 10, 1954, at which the Library of Congress was ably represented by Acting Librarian Verner W. Clapp and several of his colleagues, to express dissatisfaction with the budget presentation. He requested that Mumford, not yet confirmed, appear before the subcommittee on May 12. He also requested that the Library staff present, on the same day, a detailed picture of appropriations and expenditures by division for the last five years, together with a stronger justification for the desired increases.[20]

Mumford attended the continued session on the 12th and was warmly welcomed. He confined his remarks, however, to a declaration that during the coming year he would study the operations and obligations of the Library. Since Chairman Horan had requested that the numerous laws relating to the Library of Congress be codified to disclose more clearly what Congress and the nation should expect of it, Mumford assured him that he would give the matter his attention. Among the questions from members of the subcommittee which were to recur year after year were: Why are so many new people needed? Why is obsolete material of benefit to no one acquired and retained? When can arrearages in cataloging be eliminated? And how are study rooms in the library assigned? [21] But the atmosphere, generally, was friendly at this and at subsequent hearings. In the first 10 years of Mumford's administration, appropriations increased from $9,399,736 to $24,081,800, and the staff, including those on salaries transferred from other agencies, increased from 2,459 to 3,390. Representative Frank T. Bow of Ohio asked in 1957 when the Library of Congress could be expected to reduce some of its requests. Mumford replied that he would be remiss if he did not present the needs as seen. He emphasized that everything requested was needed.[22] The Library of Congress must grow, he said, "to meet its responsibilities for service to the Congress, to Government agencies, and to the public." The issues with which Congress deals change constantly, and Mumford believed that the Library of Congress should have research materials covering these issues, and, once acquired, they should be preserved.[23]

The subcommittee queried Mumford often in the early 1960's about automation and electronics and how the Library of Congress expected to utilize the

new technology. In the 1963 hearings, Senator Mike Monroney was concerned about job discrimination and fair employment practices in the Library.[24] The next year he reminded Mumford that the current request more than doubled that of 1957. He could understand why this would be true in a space or missile program, but why in a library?[25] Moreover, he and his colleagues were annoyed by a recent article in *Saturday Review* which suggested that the Library of Congress was being neglected by Congress. The writer declared that Congress' apparent lack of interest in and neglect of the Library, as indicated in its reduction of requested appropriations and in its indecision about the third building, should not be charged specifically against Congress, the Joint Committee on the Library, or the subcommittee on Appropriations, but rather against the organization in Congress on which the Library is based. Policy guidance, he said, comes from one committee, appropriations from another, and the new building decision from yet another. He gave special praise to Senators B. Everett Jordan of North Carolina and Claiborne Pell of Rhode Island but thought that the

Librarian L. Quincy Mumford watches as former President Truman signs the visitor's register in the Manuscript Division on June 21, 1957. LC–USP6–3215–C

committee as a whole gave the Library too little time and attention.[26] Mumford declared that he disagreed with the point of view of the article; on the contrary, he said, "Congress . . . has been quite understanding to our needs and has been responsive to the requests that have been presented."[27]

Monroney also wanted to know how many books were consulted each year and by how many people, and how many inquiries were handled during a year. On the basis of information available to him in the Library's reports and in the staff presentation, he concluded that each inquiry handled by the Legislative Reference Service cost $21 and required one-half of a day of a staff member's time.[28]

The presentation must have been convincing because an increase in appropriations of almost $4 million for 1965 was approved. And so went the requests and appropriations through 1974: Congress was often reluctant but always interested in the solid and persuasive presentations by Mumford and

As part of the Public Law 480 program, books are loaded on a betjak in Djakarta for delivery to the bindery. LC–USP6–5168A

his colleagues, who sometimes were assisted by the library associations, especially by ARL. In 1972, when Mumford presented a requested increase in appropriations of more than $9 million for 1973, Senator Ernest F. Hollings commended him for a fine presentation.[29]

The demands upon the Library of Congress during the two decades of Mumford's administration were greater than those of any previous 20-year period. New aspects of growth and development in the third quarter of the century, which had to be dealt with wisely and expeditiously, included the increase of knowledge and publication, the need for quick access to new knowledge, technological prog-

ress and its potential for storage, retrieval, and transmission of information, and equalization of job opportunity. History will reveal whether the Library of Congress under Mumford's direction met successfully the challenge of the times, but a summary review of some of its major accomplishments will permit a less than objective evaluation to be made only a year after Mumford's retirement.

The need for more cataloging assistance from Washington continued to be discussed regularly and vigorously at professional association meetings. The Library of Congress, which contributed materially to alleviating the problem when it began the distribution of printed catalog cards in 1901, was encouraged to assume leadership in further reducing cataloging costs and accelerating cataloging for U.S. libraries. Two acute problems dominated decisions at the Library of Congress: lack of catalogers and lack of funds for the comprehensive acquisition of books published abroad. Actually, the Library's appropriation for books in 1954–55, exclusive of those for the Law and Supreme Court libraries and for the Division for the Blind, was only $260,000, less than what was being spent in a dozen or more university libraries. The principal sources of the Library's growth traditionally had been exchanges and books deposited for copyright.

The flow of books was to be accelerated and cataloging relief provided in the National Program for Acquisition and Cataloging (NPAC) and the Public Law 480 program, but before they became effective, the Library of Congress, assisted by a Council on Library Resources, Inc. (CLR), grant, took the lead in an experiment with cataloging a book before it was published. The basic idea, which goes back to the 1870's, was explored with publishers and librarians, who responded favorably. In cataloging in source, the Library would catalog each publication on a rush basis, supply the publishers with the cataloging entry, and they in turn would print it in the book.[30] At the conclusion of the experiment in 1960, the Library reported sadly that cataloging in source failed to indicate that it would resolve the chronic cataloging problem because of "the very high cost . . . to both publishers and the Library of Congress, disruptions of publishing schedules, the high degree of unreliability of catalog entries based on texts not in their final form, and the low degree of utility which would result from the copying of these entries."[31] There was conviction, however, that the general idea had merit and should not be abandoned. Eleven years later, in 1971, the Library of Congress and the Association of American Publishers, working closely with Verner Clapp, who was by then president of CLR, initiated a full-scale feasibility study of Cataloging in Publication. With matching grants of $200,000 each from CLR and the National Endowment for the Humanities to the Library of Congress for the two-year study and with the full cooperation of publishers and librarians, feasibility was established. In 1974 the program, with funds appropriated by Congress and with support given by 655 publishers, facilitated the cataloging of 18,565 titles.[32]

Distribution of catalog cards and printing of the Library of Congress author catalog four decades later were milestones to be remembered. During the early years of Mumford's administration a con-

tract was completed for publication, in 610 volumes, of the *National Union Catalog, Pre-1956 Imprints,* which would include imprints recorded by other North American libraries. The first volumes of this highly significant bibliography—an important finding list and cataloging aid to research libraries the world over—appeared in 1969.[33]

Cataloging in Publication is beginning to satisfy this country's nagging need for prompt cataloging information for domestic imprints. But in the early 1960's this cooperative publisher-library service still was in the future, and technology was yet to be tapped. In response to questions from Senator Leverett Saltonstall of the Senate Subcommittee on Appropriations in 1960 and 1962 about the Library's plans to utilize electronics, Mumford assured him that the matter was being studied and that the Library expected to assume its proper role but wished to develop its program on a solid foundation.[34]

A 1961 grant of $100,000 from CLR "enabled the Library to engage a team of leading experts in computer technology, data processing, systems analysis, and information storage and retrieval . . . to examine the organization, storage, and retrieval of information in the Library of Congress not only from the point of view of the functioning of a single institution but also from that of a research library whose activities are interrelated with those of other research libraries."[35] The results of the survey, directed by Gilbert W. King, were published in January 1964 as *Automation and the Library of Congress.* They led to the appointment in June 1964 of Sam S. Snyder as information systems specialist, a post which had been vacant since 1962. His first responsibility was to develop a system for producing "machine-readable catalog data in a standardized format not only for use in producing book catalogs but also for distribution to other libraries." A natural sequel would be "a production process for printing catalog cards with computer-controlled photocomposition equipment.[36] The King report concluded, among other things, that automation was technically and economically feasible in large research libraries in areas of bibliographic processing, catalog searching, and document retrieval, but that retrieving the intellectual content of large collections of books by automation was not yet practicable. Not possible at the moment, but only because of lack of equipment and funds, was a computer store of the catalog cards of the Library of

Congress and other research libraries which would permit them to be brought together in a single system under effective bibliographic control. Such a system was estimated to cost $50 to $70 million, but the report recommended that the Library of Congress, because of its central role in the nation's library system, take the lead and make this a long-range objective.[37]

Development of the standard format for processing catalog cards, authorized in 1964, was sufficiently advanced in 1966 for distribution of MARC (MAchine-Readable Cataloging) tapes containing complete cataloging data to a selected list of libraries. Service was inaugurated on March 27, 1969, and at the year's end "nearly 60 subscribers were receiving cataloging data on tape for all monographs published in the United States in English and cataloged by the Library of Congress."[38] By the time of Mumford's retirement in 1974, French and German were added to the English-language books. These MARC tapes now carrying all current cataloging in most roman alphabet languages and all Cataloging in Publication records for monographs, plus current cataloging in all roman and romanized nonroman alphabet languages for serials, demonstrate that automation can play an important role in the storage and retrieval of information.

The Library of Congress, however, could not be expected to supply cataloging assistance promptly for books it did not possess, nor could it, without substantially increased book funds, satisfy the demands of scholars needing current foreign publications. The Higher Education Act of 1965 initially contained little support for staffing or collection building in the major university libraries upon which the nation depended heavily for research support. The world of scholarship, ALA committees concerned with cataloging, and ARL agreed that the act was a logical vehicle through which to strengthen the book resources of the national library while enabling it to provide centralized cataloging assistance to the other libraries of the country. Librarian Mumford and his staff concurred and joined forces with ARL and ALA in presenting a request to Congress to amend existing legislation "to enable the Commissioner of Education to transfer to the Librarian of Congress for acquiring as far as possible all library materials of value to scholarship that are currently published throughout the world and providing catalog information for these materials

promptly." The compelling reasons for the request were: college and university libraries cannot gain cataloging control over the larger output of publishing; materials are of little value until cataloged; few libraries have enough language competence to catalog the books received; and centralized cataloging in the Library of Congress utilizes that Library's competence while avoiding duplication of cataloging effort in other libraries.[39]

With strong support from the library and publishing worlds, the act was amended, giving the Library of Congress a clear mandate "to provide new and unparalleled services for the benefit of other libraries."[40] William Dix, librarian of Princeton University, reported to ARL that the Library, "with real vigor and imagination, had pushed right ahead in developing the program."[41] Congress' approval to create the National Program for Acquisitions and Cataloging, initially with modest funding for three years, has been a remarkable success story. Arrangements were made in 1966 for cooperation with England, France, West Germany, Norway, and Austria; in 1974, 40 countries were participating. Not only is much foreign scholarly material which otherwise could be missed brought into the country, but millions of dollars in cataloging costs are being saved for libraries everywhere.[42]

Impetus for NPAC may have been sparked by the amendment to the Agriculture Trade Development and Assistance Act of 1954 permitting use of counterpart funds for buying and cataloging for U.S. libraries current books and serials in certain countries. In 1958 the Library of Congress initiated implementation of the Public Law 480 program to procure Indian official publications for the Midwest Interlibrary Center, the University of California at Berkeley, and the University of Pennsylvania. Mumford sought to extend the program in 1960 to purchase current imprints in other countries where a surplus of U.S.-owned foreign currencies existed. However, even with strong support from ARL, he was not able to overcome the mild objections of the Subcommittee on Appropriations. Permission was received to inaugurate programs in India, Pakistan, and the United Arab Republic with extension to other countries to come later.[43] This program, likewise, has resulted in a sound expenditure of federal funds; moreover, teaching and research programs, especially Asian programs, have been greatly strengthened and cataloging problems have been reduced for the participating libraries.

In his continuing efforts to strengthen the resources of the Library, Mumford emphasized the importance of a research capability adequate to enable it to cover the broad range of requests from Congress. Additional books, an increase in staff, and more sophisticated facilities were needed. Accordingly, under the Legislative Reorganization Act of 1970, the Legislative Reference Service—that part of the Library which works exclusively for Congress—was expanded into the Congressional Research Service, which at that time had a staff of 438 specialists, including 50 librarians. The act provides that the Librarian of Congress encourage and promote CRS in rendering to Congress expeditious and effective service, and that he accord the Service complete independence and the maximum administrative independence consistent with its objectives.[44] Though the Library of Congress may be considered the national library, a library for scholars, or an international repository, the Congress is assured by this act of a library to serve its needs.

Only in the last quarter century has careful study been given preservation of books and serials published on wood pulp and other inferior paper. Newspapers received early attention because back files were bulky and deterioration was clearly apparent. Efforts to convert them to microtext were initiated in the 1930's and accelerated in the years immediately following World War II. The Library of Congress was one of the first libraries to preserve all of its newspapers on microfilm. A national program for the preservation of books was urged by ARL committees and individual librarians, and all turned to the Library of Congress for leadership. The program should be based, they agreed, in a major research library where a large percentage of the books requiring treatment would be found and where federal funding could be made available for this national problem. The Library of Congress responded in 1967 by creating a Preservation Office and appointing a preservation officer. A CLR grant to ARL and the Library of Congress enabled a project to be launched to explore the problems of identifying and preserving the thousands of books deteriorating in the nation's libraries and assessing the management problems involved.[45] The project disclosed that books that

were brittle in the Library of Congress generally were deteriorating in other libraries. However, one copy usually could be found to be satisfactory for filming and preservation.

Another CLR grant permitted establishment of a Preservation Research Laboratory in the Library of Congress in 1970.[46] By 1973 progress had been made in deacidifying and restoring lost strength to brittle sheets, salvaging materials damaged by floods, fires, and other catastrophes, and preserving and restoring records on nitrate film. The Library of Congress has been making a notable contribution to repositories of information in that it is discovering how materials are deteriorating, determining how to combat and correct these problems, and making this information generally available. The studies conducted at the Library constitute a major step in advancing curatorship the world over.

Mumford was the third Librarian of Congress to obtain an appropriation for a new building: Ainsworth Rand Spofford spent 26 years securing funds for and constructing the present Main Building, which was occupied in 1897, and Herbert Putnam worked for 12 years to get the Annex, which was completed in 1939. In response to Mumford's critical need for additional space, the James Madison Memorial Building was authorized by Congress in 1965 after long study by the Library staff and is now nearing completion.[47] Work on the building, for which $123 million has been appropriated, was started on May 1, 1971. Much credit for securing approval of the plans and the appropriation belongs to the late North Carolina Senator B. Everett Jordan, chairman of the Joint Committee on the Library during the period when the matter was being discussed actively in Congress. Completion of the third building will eliminate inconvenience to users while saving the Library millions of dollars in annual rental fees and staff time wasted by wide dispersal of activities.

The Madison Building should, in addition, ease the staff morale problems of recent years which to some extent have been fueled by poor working conditions. Until the 1960's the problems related to staffing the Library were restricted to securing adequate funds and finding candidates with the requisite training and experience. Recently, however, employing and providing equal opportunity for minorities and women have added new dimensions to the problems of administration. When Senator

Bronze medallions of James Madison by Robert A. Wein-man, 1975. Photographs courtesy of the sculptor.

Monroney questioned Mumford about job discrimination in 1963, Mumford reported to him that the percentage of blacks employed in all grades exceeded the percentages in other federal agencies. Although the Library of Congress employed twice as many blacks in GS grades 1–4 as other federal agencies—36.6 percent against 18.2 percent—Monroney hoped that training for advancement from these lower grades was being provided. Because of inadequate basic education, many who joined the staff as janitors and charwomen would have difficulty securing enough training in languages and other areas for much advancement; however, Mumford explained that the Library's fair employment practices officer, appointed the previous year, was regularly counseling interested staff members about training opportunities open to them.[48] Staff counseling, recruitment, employee training, and equalization of job opportunity were to receive increased attention in the late 1960's. Nevertheless, a member of the staff presented to the ALA council at the 1971 meeting in Dallas a set of grievances concerning racial discrimination in recruitment, training, and promo-

tion practices in the Library of Congress. The ALA council unwisely passed a resolution authorizing an inquiry into the Library's practices, thus drawing the association into a matter with which the Library of Congress was already dealing more successfully than other government agencies and research libraries.

Upon direction of the Joint Committee on the Library, the Library of Congress presented no testimony before the ALA inquiry committee when it met in Washington. But Mumford and his staff had already begun to improve communications between staff and management and to provide more productive and satisfactory working conditions. Ad hoc Human Relations Committees were formed in the Office of the Librarian and in each of the six departments of the Library, and a Human Relations Council was created where matters of concern to the staff might be discussed.[49] Development of the Affirma-

tive Action Plan in 1973, with the requisite program officers for recruiting, training, counseling, and communicating, together with supplemental appropriations for implementation of the new programs, enabled the Library to make notable progress during Mumford's administration. Mumford's final year saw the development of the Affirmative Action Plan for fiscal 1974, which included some significant advances in the area of equal opportunity. The plan established a Coordinating Committee to assure program effectiveness in each department; the Training, Appraisal and Promotion (TAP) program was initiated with what was then 50 opportunities for employees to be trained at Library expense and to receive promotions after demonstrating competence in the higher position; and research on the Library's employment tests was completed, eliminating or correcting those tests found to be defective.[50]

Mumford's philosophy of caution in placing the Library of Congress in a position of leadership on many issues and programs has been alluded to above. Leadership, he said, "in the absence of line authority, must strike a delicate balance between domina-

tion and encouragement. Those who urge the Library of Congress to greater leadership would be the first to cry out against attempted government dictation. . . . In hewing the fine line between the two positions, perhaps the Library of Congress has of late been too careful to remain in the background rather than pushing to the vanguard."[51] Perhaps his policy of caution encouraged preparation of a memorandum by Douglas Bryant, associate director of the Harvard University Library, on what the Library of Congress does and what it should do for the government and the nation. The paper was prepared by a leader among university librarians, at the direction of Senator Claiborne Pell of Rhode Island, and was placed in the *Congressional Record* for May 24, 1962.[52] Although performing more national library functions than any other national library in the world, the Library of Congress appeared to some of the directors of research libraries and others in the world of scholarship not to be responding to needs as promptly and as imaginatively as it should. President Kennedy viewed the Library as a great cultural center and is reputed to have wished a return to the kind of leadership MacLeish gave the Library in the early 1940's. Although no new statement of what the Library of Congress should be had been recorded, ARL was concerned that it did not appear diligent enough in seeking funds to support the programs of interest to research libraries. Bryant recommended (1) that the Library of Congress be made the national library, transferred to the executive branch, and directed by a great leader and administrator who would be advised by a Library board of 10 to 12 members; (2) that American research libraries should be collecting more material, exercising better bibliographical control, and preserving and replacing deteriorating materials, all of which require the active participation of the federal government; and (3) that new federal programs were needed in such areas as research and experimentation in the application of modern technology to library purposes, assistance to underdeveloped countries in strengthening their libraries and in creating bibliographies listing their current publications, preservation of research materials, federal grants-in-aid to research libraries, and programs of scholarships and fellowships to recruit and train librarians.

Mumford obviously was disturbed by the paper. In his reply, which was inserted in the *Congressional Record* of October 2, 1962, by Senator B. Everett Jordan, he characterized the Library as the de facto national library, many of whose programs had been seriously hampered by lack of space. He did not agree that the Library should be in the executive branch and thought some of Bryant's recommended programs were inappropriate for the Library. Although Bryant repeated several of the recommendations of the Library of Congress Planning Committee of 1947, which Librarian Luther Evans appointed, and although he apparently was not informed about all of the Library's current programs, Mumford thought the memorandum served a useful purpose by calling attention to the problems of research libraries and possibly bringing more understanding and rallying more support "not only in the Congress, but in the Executive Branch, within the library profession, and among the clientele of research libraries." [53]

The discussion about the Library, which Senator Pell hoped the memorandum would stimulate, was realized, and much of the talk was constructive. Mumford agreed that an advisory board was desirable but advocated a high-level, permanent com-

mission, perhaps similar to the present National Commission on Libraries and Information Science. He had been aware of the need to improve communications with the library and scholarly communities, he said, and early in 1962 he had created three liaison committees to serve as channels of information and advice: one was composed of representatives of the major national library associations, another consisted of distinguished men in the humanities and social sciences, and a third represented the scientific community. Mumford hoped these committees would be of value to the Library while also being useful to the professional and scholarly fields represented by them. [54]

In his report for the temporary National Advisory Commission on Libraries, Mumford defended the Library's deliberate pace in undertaking all the programs expected of it and in fully utilizing the potentialities of electronics, explaining that the Library was moving as fast as available resources and advances in technology permitted. While he and his staff favored having the Library of Congress designated the national library, they cautioned that such status would require, in addition to new legislation, an acceptance by Congress of the need for substantially larger funds on a continuing basis. [55] Furthermore, they thought that obtaining a new building and funds for national library functions were more important than a change of name.

As Mumford approached retirement, the mounting problems of the Library allowed little time for complacency or for reflection upon its progress during his 20-year administration. Despite reports that services and materials were deteriorating for lack of space, that staff morale was being impaired by discrimination in hiring and promotion, and that the confidence of a segment of the library profession was being eroded by what was termed a lack of vigorous leadership in the Library of Congress, the Librarian could look back upon two decades during which the collections were increased from 33 million to 74 million items, the staff from 1,564 to 4,250, and annual expenditures from $9,400,000 to $96,696,000. [56] In addition to the major achievements already described, other innovations realized during Mumford's administration included: indexing and filming of the papers of 23 Presidents; preservation on safety film of the large deposit of early motion picture film; extension of books for the blind to all the physically handicapped who are unable to use conventionally printed material; establishment of the Near Eastern and North African Law Division, the African Section, the Children's Book Section, and the National Referral Center for Science and Technology; founding of the National Union Catalog of Manuscript Collections; initiation of *New Serial Titles;* and inception of probably the most rigorous American Revolution Bicentennial program in the government, established for the use of both scholars and the general public.[57]

As Senator Jordan reviewed the first decade of Mumford's administration of the Library, he recalled that when the new Librarian assumed office in September 1954, Herbert Putnam sent him this message: "Welcome, and may good will, good fortune, and good cheer attend you ever." Jordan continued: "The past decade . . . has indeed been attended by good will, good fortune, and good cheer. . . . our National Library has emerged as a major force in this Nation's quest for peace and prosperity." The chairman of the Joint Committee on the Library, after enumerating the accomplishments of the Library, added that "Dr. Mumford, a modest man, would not want to take credit for these major achievements," but Congress would be remiss "not to take note of the anniversary and to congratulate him on his effective service as Librarian of Congress." [58] Mumford's close friend and associate Rutherford D. Rogers believes that Mumford's administration will rank among those of Spofford and Putnam in accomplishments. Assuming the post of Librarian when relations between the Library and Congress were not harmonious, Mumford soon won the confidence of that body. Gradually he developed the budget support that enabled the Library to approach its most pressing problems—some of which required attention before he took office—and to develop a vigorous and effective overall program.[59] He achieved this while directing the Library in his normal low-key manner. His able and loyal administrative assistants were given maximum independence and encouragement to make recommendations and to participate regularly in decision making. As gregarious as his natural shyness permitted, Quincy displayed an enthusiasm for life and an unswerving trust in his colleagues and friends.

It may appear incongruous in the light of his image, but up to 1975 Mumford undoubtedly was the most traveled Librarian of Congress. That distinction should not be associated with his eagerness for the spotlight, but rather with the Library's worldwide interests, extended by NPAC, Public Law 480 and shared cataloging, and, of course, the speed today at which one can move across continents and oceans. Though traveling was squeezed into Mumford's schedule at home and obviously at some sacrifice, goodwill was generated in Austria, Belgium, Egypt, England, France, Holland, Hungary, India, Italy, Japan, New Zealand, Pakistan, Poland, Romania, Russia, West Germany, and Yugoslavia, where he attended meetings, and even in Antarctica, where he went as a guest of the U.S. Navy.

Mumford's health obviously had an impact upon the direction he could give the Library during his last two years in office; nevertheless, the President extended his tenure a year beyond the mandatory retirement age, allowing him to continue in office until December 31, 1974.[60]

Although he did not return to the library staff of his alma mater, Quincy has maintained close ties with the institution. In the 1950's he was invited back to the campus to be initiated into Omicron Delta Kappa, an honorary undergraduate fraternity, and to receive an honorary degree. When a board of visitors for the university library was created he became its first chairman. Back in familiar surroundings he could be persuaded occasionally to entertain his friends with his flawless imitation of the tobacco auctioneer's chant. And reminded of the long-ago afternoons when the dormitory echoed with his baritone rendition of "Carolina Moon" and "Blue Skies" as he showered in preparation for a social evening, he could pick up the lyrics of these and other popular songs of 50 years ago and sing them through without missing a syllable.

Two decades is a long time for one administrator to grapple with problems in this fast-moving world. But Mumford could look back upon 20 years of substantial achievement for the Library of Congress and research libraries in general. The Madison Building, though late in coming, will stand as a monument to his persistence and persuasion and to his rapport with key Members of Congress. The national library as it stands today bears testimony that it was wisely directed by Lawrence Quincy Mumford and that the eleventh Librarian of Congress will be remembered as having achieved more for the Library than any one of his predecessors.

NOTES

[1] Quincy's younger brother, Bruton, a dentist in Norcross, Ga., was graduated in 1930. Grover entered business after a few years of teaching in high school and college; he is now retired and lives in Greensboro, N.C.

[2] Printed biographies of L. Quincy Mumford list Ayden as his birthplace because the village of Hanrahan no longer has a post office of its own.

[3] Conversation with James E. Coltrane, a Greensboro attorney who was a class behind Mumford and whose father was superintendent of Grifton High School during Quincy's years there.

[4] Minutes of the Hesperian Literary Society, 1921–25, Duke University Archives, Durham, N.C.

[5] Duke University catalogs and *The Chanticleer*, 1921–25.

[6] A copy of Mumford's thesis may be found in the Duke University Archives.

[7] Personal communication from Keyes D. Metcalf, November 21, 1975.

[8] U.S., Congress, Senate, Committee on Rules and Administration, *Nomination of Lawrence Quincy Mumford To Be Librarian of Congress*, 83d Cong., 2d sess., July 26, 1954, pp. 25–27.

[9] Mumford to Ralph A. Ulveling, May 11, 1954, Cleveland Public Library.

[10] U.S., Library of Congress, *Annual Report of the Librarian of Congress* (hereafter cited as *ARLC*), 1940, p. 11.

[11] Mumford to Ulveling, May 11, 1954.

[12] *ARLC*, 1941, p. 11.

[13] L. Quincy Mumford, "Account of the Reorganization of the Processing Department at the Library of Congress," in American Library Association, Division of Cataloging and Classification, *Catalogers' and Classifiers' Yearbook*, 10, pp. 45–56.

[14] *Cleveland Press*, November 8, 1950.

[15] Mumford to Ulveling, May 11, 1954.

[16] Alumni Office files, Duke University.

[17] *Nomination of Lawrence Quincy Mumford To Be Librarian of Congress*, p. 9.

[18] *Congressional Record*, 83d Cong., 2d sess., August 12, 1954, vol. 100, Appendix, p. A5987.

[19] Frederic G. Melcher, "Mumford Will Carry On the Great L.C. Tradition," *Publishers' Weekly*, August 7, 1954, p. 534.

[20] U.S., Congress, House, Subcommittee of the Committee on Appropriations, *Legislative Branch Appropriations, 1955*, 83d Cong., 2d sess., May 10, 1954, p. 241.

[21] Ibid., May 12, 1954, pp. 296–97, 337.

[22] U.S., Congress, House, Subcommittee of the Committee on Appropriations, *Legislative Branch Appropriations, 1958*, 85th Cong., 1st sess., May 8, 1957, p. 203.

[23] Ibid., p. 129.

[24] U.S., Congress, Senate, Subcommittee of the Committee on Appropriations, *Legislative Branch Appropriations, 1964*, 88th Cong., 1st sess., H. Rept. 6868, June 6, 1963, pp. 201–4.

[25] U.S., Congress, Senate, Subcommittee of the Committee on Appropriations, *Legislative Branch Appropriations, 1965*, 88th Cong., 2d sess., H. Rept. 10723, April 17, 1964, p. 9.

[26] A.L. Todd, "The Luckless Library of Congress," *Saturday Review*, April 11, 1964, pp. 44–45.

[27] *Legislative Branch Appropriations, 1965*, p. 23.

[28] Ibid., pp. 33–35.

[29] U.S., Congress, Senate, Subcommittee of the Committee on Appropriations, *Legislative Branch Appropriations, 1973*, 92d Cong., 2d sess., H. Rept. 13955, February 29, 1972, p. 298.

[30] *ARLC*, 1958, p. 13.

[31] Ibid., 1960, p. 8.

[32] Ibid., 1974, p. 4.

[33] U.S., Library of Congress, "L. Quincy Mumford; Twenty Years As Librarian of Congress, September 1, 1954–September 1, 1974; a Record of Progress," presented by the Librarian's Conference, pp. 3, 17.

[34] U.S., Congress, Senate, Subcommittee of the Committee on Appropriations, *Legislative Branch Appropriations, 1961*, 86th Cong., 2d sess., H. Rept. 12232, May 20, 1960, pp. 14–20; idem., *Legislative Branch Appropriations, 1963*, 87th Cong., 2d sess., H. Rept. 11151, April 25, 1962, pp. 23–24.

[35] *ARLC*, 1961, p. xv.

[36] Ibid., 1964, pp. xxx–xxxi.

[37] Ibid., 1963, pp. xiii–xiv.

[38] Ibid., 1969, p. 3.

[39] Ibid., 1965, pp. 10–11.

[40] Ibid., 1966, pp. 25–27.

[41] U.S., Library of Congress, *Information Bulletin*, February 10, 1966, p. 84.

[42] *ARLC*, 1974, pp. 2, 13–14.

[43] *Legislative Branch Appropriations, 1961*, pp. 11–13; U.S., Congress, Senate, Subcommittee of the Committee on Appropriations, *Legislative Branch Appropriations, 1962*, 87th Cong., 1st sess., H. Rept. 7208, June 13, 1961, pp. 12–37.

[44] Charles A. Goodrum, *The Library of Congress* (New York and Washington: Praeger Publishers, 1974), pp. 133, 270.

[45] *ARLC*, 1967, pp. 92–93.

[46] Ibid., 1970, p. 75.

[47] Ibid., 1965, p. 11.

[48] *Legislative Branch Appropriations, 1964*, pp. 201–6.

[49] *ARLC*, 1972, pp. 8–9.

[50] Ibid., 1973, pp. 8–9.

[51] Ibid., 1962, p. 110.

[52] *Congressional Record—Senate,* 87th Cong., 2d sess., May 24, 1962, vol. 108, pt. 7, pp. 9158–60.

[53] *ARLC,* 1962, pp. 94–95, 109.

[54] Ibid., pp. xii–xiii.

[55] Douglas M. Knight and E. Shepley Nourse, eds., *Libraries at Large; Tradition, Innovation, and the National Interest* (New York: R.R. Bowker, 1969), pp. 446, 464–65.

[56] U.S., Library of Congress, *Information Bulletin,* January 3, 1975, pp. 1–5.

[57] Ibid.

[58] *Congressional Record—Senate,* 88th Cong., 2d sess., September 1, 1964, vol. 110, pt. 16, pp. 21217–18.

[59] Rutherford D. Rogers, "LQM of LC," *Bulletin of Bibliography* 25, no. 7 (September–December 1968): 161–65.

[60] *American Libraries* 5, no. 3 (March 1974): 118.

Index

☆ U.S. GOVERNMENT PRINTING OFFICE : 1977—O–237–909